SOUTHERN SNOW _____

The Winter Guide To Dixie

RANDY JOHNSON

D0877909

Appalachian Mountain Club
BOSTON, MASSACHUSETTS

SOUTHERN SNOW
The Winter Guide to Dixie
by Randy Johnson
Copyright © 1987

Editorial direction: Aubrey Botsford, Jan Fitter
Production: Renée M. Le Verrier
Book and cover design: Joyce C. Weston
Maps: David Cooper
Composition: Shepard Poorman Communications Corp.
Cover photograph: Randy Johnson

PHOTOGRAPHS: by G. Forest (p. *xii*), by Randy Johnson (pp. *xvi*, 2, 78, 88, 124, 126, 162, 166, 204, 208, 216, 245, 254, 289, 292, 348), courtesy of Sepp Kober (p. 28, 66, 116), courtesy of Rich Hopkins (p. 72) from *Did It Snow in '77* (Pioneer Press), by Hugh Morton (p. 102, 206), by Craig Phillips (p. 118), courtesy of Virginia State Travel Service (p. 150), courtesy of Gatlinburg Chamber of Commerce (p. 198).

ISBN: 910146-62-4

5 4 3 2 1   86 87 88 89

SOUTHERN SNOW

To my dad, who took me to my first
snowy southern summit.

Contents

Preface

JUST for a moment, consider the logic behind choosing a ski area. Since skiers always seem to head north, it must be safe to assume that the farther north you go, the more snow falls.

In most places, that may be true. But in the Southern Appalachians, elevation overcomes location. Southerners are discovering that eastern America's highest mountains offer a wide variety of downhill ski resorts and snowy trails for hikers and Nordic skiers. This book is the first guide to the region's increasingly sophisticated winter recreation resources.

Unlike past and present magazines dedicated to southern skiing, *Southern Snow* brings an information-packed overview together in one volume. The type and breadth of information included here would fill many issues of any magazine and would still be less than systematic. Beginning with chapters on weather, southern skiing's history, winter driving, and current background on winter sports in the South, *Southern Snow* prepares the reader to appreciate guide entries for resorts in seven Appalachian states.

Again, unlike some periodicals, *Southern Snow* describes the areas covered from an independent ski writer's perspective, unaffected by the presence or absence of advertising. Instead of offering brief capsules, the descriptions in this book go into depth and enable well-informed comparisons among resorts. You won't find endless, inaccurate charts of statistics and prices in *Southern Snow*.

Pertinent data about resort sizes are included, and basic price ranges in Chapters 4–6 enable readers to narrow down their choices. But more usefully, at the end of each entry in Parts 2 and 3, Southern Snow offers addresses and phone numbers, many toll free, to obtain each area's latest, most accurate prices. Even the most recent ski resort round-ups in newspapers contain price inaccuracies. Major prices for lifts and other services can change suddenly.

This book chooses to offer insight and analysis rather than reams of statistics. With a handful of up-to-the-minute brochures and *Southern Snow*'s guide entries, the reader has a resource on southern winter sports unmatched by any magazine or newspaper article.

Where trekking trails are covered, *Southern Snow* often suggests specific loop trips for Nordic skiers and winter hikers.

This book grew from the unexpectedly wintry climate of the Southern Appalachians and obviously owes much to the people who explored snowy summits and built ski resorts in Dixie. In that sense, *Southern Snow* is a tribute to all those who've made winter sports a lifestyle for southerners. I hope this book helps expand that lifestyle.

Photographs

Part One

INTRODUCTION TO THE SOUTHERN SNOWBELT

Climate

IN THE Southern Appalachians, a cool arm of New England reaches into the baking heart of the South. From the Atlantic Ocean, Chesapeake Bay, and the urban centers of Washington, D.C., and Richmond, the Virginia piedmont stretches west across hot pine forests. Foothills rise, and then a hazy blue rill marks the horizon. This mass is the 4,000-foot spine of the Blue Ridge, the Appalachian Front Range. Atop these peaks is Shenandoah National Park and the Skyline Drive. Beyond, to the west, the Blue Ridge drops into the flat patchwork of the Shenandoah Valley, part of Virginia's Great Valley. From Shenandoah National Park south, the Blue Ridge and the Blue Ridge Parkway meander through the George Washington National Forest, drop to Roanoke, and rise again, heading south to the North Carolina border.

Heading west again, from the Shenandoah Valley, the Alleghenies of the George Washington National Forest rise to meet the Virginia/West Virginia state line. In West Virginia, the Alleghenies continue in a seemingly endless series of ridges higher than 4,000 feet, running southwest to northeast and separated by steep, narrow valleys. This washboard terrain covers fully two-thirds of West Virginia, aptly called the Mountain State. Here, in the Monongahela National Forest, the Potomac River starts on summits just under 5,000 feet high.

From southeastern West Virginia, the rippling Alleghenies spread south into Virginia as the Jefferson National Forest. At the North Carolina/Tennessee line, they become the Unakas, draw closer to the Blue Ridge, and rise more massively than any peaks north to the Arctic Ocean. Virginia's highest peak—Mount Rogers, at 5,729 feet—is the first major summit of this North Carolina bulge in the Appalachians. High plateaus and ranges link the Cherokee National Forest in Tennessee to Pisgah in North Carolina.

South toward Asheville, the Blue Ridge again pulls east, spinning off the Black and then the Craggy mountains. The Blacks rise to the East's highest summit at Mount Mitchell (6,684 feet). From the Craggies, the Blue Ridge Parkway, plummets from its ridge down into Asheville.

Further west, across the widening gulf between the Blue Ridge and the Unakas, the Smokies heave to heights only feet lower than that of Mount Mitchell and stay nearly as massive for 70 trail miles. Beyond Asheville, the Blue Ridge again bulks up as Pisgah National Forest. Then it heads south, turns west along the Balsams, and intersects the Smokies. South of this great turn in the Blue Ridge Parkway lies Nantahala National Forest and high plateaus and ranges like the Snowbird, Cowee, and Nantahala. From this region, the great ranges diminish into northern Georgia and Alabama.

To this day, Dixie's steamy image shrouds these mountains in misconception as shadowy as the mists that swirl around the Blue Ridge and the Great Smokies. When explorer-anthropologist Horace Kephart ventured into the Smokies in the early 1900s, his trip was sparked by the region's anonymity:

When I prepared, in 1904, for my first sojourn into the Great Smoky Mountains . . . I could find in no library a guide to that region . . . Had I been going to Teneriffe or Timbuctu, the libraries would have furnished information aplenty; but about this housetop of eastern America they were strangely silent; it was terra incognita . . . I could see that the Southern Appalachians . . . are nearer the center of our population than any other mountains that deserve the name. Why, then, so little known?

In that dustiest room of a great library where "pub.docs." are stored . . . at last a clear idea of the lay of the land. And here was news. We are wont to think of the South as a low country with sultry climate: yet its mountain chains stretch . . . from Virginia to Alabama . . . an area somewhat larger than England and Scotland, or about the same as that of the Alps . . . the greatest mountain system in eastern America is massed in our Southland. In its upper zone one sleeps under blankets the year round.

In North Carolina alone the mountains cover 6,000 square miles, with an average elevation of 2,700 feet, and with twenty-one peaks that overtop Mount Washington [in New Hampshire, 6,288 feet]. (Excerpt taken from Kephart's *Our Southern Highlanders*)

These uplands are islands of the North deep in the American South. In West Virginia's Canaan Valley and Cranberry Backcountry, cranberry bogs mimic the tundra of Canada's James Bay area. The black and red spruce of New England form shadowed stands, and the paper birch and snowshoe hare reach their southernmost limits. In Virginia, North Carolina, and Tennessee, red spruce and dense fir forests cover the highest peaks.

Unexplained, natural meadows make some mountains appear to reach above the treeline. Although no southern summit reaches high enough to be truly alpine, many don't miss by much. Were North Carolina's Mount Mitchell only 1,500 feet higher than its nearly 7,000 feet, scientists say it might reach above the trees.

The Canadian and New England plant species in the South were pushed down from the North during the last ice age. When the ice receded and the air warmed, the cold-climate plant communities retreated to the summits, where today's mountaintop weather sharply contradicts the South's sunny stereotype. The history of these ancient highlands has revolved around this not so subtle contrast.

In the 1500s, the Spanish explorer Desoto crossed the Appalachians. He complained that it was cold in June near Asheville.

Native American Indian tribes made their permanent villages at low elevations, away from the awesome weather on the high peaks. They did relatively little hunting at the highest elevations, except in the warmest months, because game was scarce there. Speculation is that some high caves where artifacts have been found were ritual sites, perhaps related to encounters with the ferocity of the weather. Kephart thought the Cherokee seemed afraid of the high mountains.

When early white settlers began venturing westward from the eastern seaboard, the Appalachians formed a physical and climatological barrier that would have political significance. Little settlement occurred in the mountains, especially at the high elevations. Daniel Boone's goal was to cross the peaks, not live in them.

By the Revolution, settlements west of the mountains, in what is now eastern Tennessee, were motivated in part by the unwanted control the British were exerting in the east. Major Patrick Ferguson directed the British war effort toward the westerners, pledging to "lay waste" their settlements "with fire and sword" unless he gained their support for the king. Ferguson didn't have time to carry out his threat. In 1781, the mountaineers climbed over the Appalachians, defeating Ferguson at his Carolina foothill encampment. On their march, these "Over Mountain Men" encountered ankle deep September snow in Yellow Mountain Gap.

During the next half-century, mountain populations grew slowly. Scots-Irish settlers from New England moved down the Great Valley of Virginia, fanning out to the high, isolated hollows of the West Virginia,

Tennessee, and North Carolina mountains, where the climate seemed most like home.

When the Civil War came, most of the mountain folk sided with the Union. Kephart said the mountaineers remained unheard of "until they startled the nation on the scene of our Civil War, by sending 180,000 of their riflemen into the Union Army." One commentator wrote that the South finally realized "what a long, lean, powerful arm of the Union it was that the Southern mountaineer stretched through its very vitals . . . The North has never realized, perhaps, what it owes for its victory to this . . . southern mountaineer." A Civil War song recalled the highlanders' homes: "I'd rather be on the Grandfather Mountain,/A' takin' the snow and rain/ Than to be in Castle Thunder,/A wearin' the ball and chain."

After the war, the southern state capitals ignored their "Yankee" western counties. In North Carolina, state maintenance didn't come to mountain roads until the 1920s. When construction of the Blue Ridge Parkway began along the crest of the mountains in 1935, the larger public discovered an isolated mountaineer society, still pioneering almost 100 years after the Civil War. Drafty log cabins characterized this "land of do without." But so too did a culture rich in handicrafts, music, and Elizabethan speech patterns. Long after the era of the Wild West, the vast rippled realm of the Appalachians harbored a remnant of America's colonial past, hidden from the modern eyes of "outlanders" and their "outlandish" ways. Even today, pockets of this culture and pride in the past help keep the Southern Appalachians one of America's most colorful regions.

Until this century, the southern mountains' physical barriers, from their impenetrable rhododendron to their enigmatic climate, rendered them largely inaccessible. In 1856, the Trotter Brothers, of the Shenandoah Valley, Va., town of Staunton, were responsible for delivering the U.S. Mail across the high parallel ridges that make up West Virginia's border with Virginia. It seems that during the winter of 1856, West Virginia postmasters became annoyed with the Trotters' delays and wrote the Postmaster General, who sent the Trotters a reprimand. In response, one Trotter pointed out to the Federal official that "If you knock the gable end of Hell out and back it up against Cheat Mountain and rain fire and brimstone for forty days and forty nights, it won't melt the snow enough to get your damned mail through on time."

The mountain climate itself has helped end the isolation. From Mississippi to Virginia, summer is as hot and humid as its reputation suggests.

In the 1880s, southern aristocracy began a mountain travel trend that continues today. Like Bostonians making their summer migrations to the White Mountains of New Hampshire, southerners began retreating to the cool, high Appalachian regions, where resort hotels—The Homestead in Virginia, The Greenbrier in West Virginia, The Green Park Inn, Grove Park Inn, Esseeola Lodge, High Hampton Inn, and Cloudland Hotel in North Carolina—all invited the wealthy up to "The Land of the Sky." What the visitors found were delightful summer days in the seventies during months when their lowland hometowns were near 100 degrees. Even on those few days when the mercury topped 80 by a degree or two, evenings offered sweater weather and slumber under the blankets that Kephart found so noteworthy.

By October, the "summer colonies" dispersed. Mountaineers holed up for the winter, often amid snowy spindrift rising from drifts around their cabins.

The Blue Ridge Parkway has built its reputation on this cool-weather identity, as have modern mountain travel attractions and resort developments. Today, ski slopes have become the wintertime attraction, and since the sixties, the southern mountain recreation picture has become as diverse as that of any mountain region in America. Climatological surprises can abound. A West Virginia whitewater paddling event might take place in an April snow storm. An Easter hike on Grandfather Mountain can end in eight inches of snow. Hiking that same trail in June can reveal that on the peaks, the leaves haven't even budded out. Summer throughout the region can mean occasional lows in the forties and the smell of wood smoke. July visitors to the highest southern mountain towns will realize that most people living in New England are experiencing hotter days. By August, temperatures are getting cooler again. A golden, high-altitude light illuminates the upper peaks, and in September the first leaves turn on birches, beeches, and maples—the same trees that lend their picture-perfect foliage to autumn in the northern states.

By October, backpackers waking up on Old Rag or Mount Rogers, in Virginia, can find a dusting of snow and hoarfrost on the autumn foliage. Cross-country skiers in North Carolina have skied on more than a foot of snow before the end of October. And downhill skiing has started as early as November 2.

Elevation may be the most important cooling factor in the year-round climate of the Southern Highlands. The earth's sun-warmed surface is the atmosphere's primary source of heat, so elevation cools air by about 3.5

degrees per thousand feet. This means that on a 90-degree day in Charlotte, North Carolina's Mount Mitchell is likely to be 69 degrees. If clouds block the sun, if the wind is blowing, or if it's raining, all of which are likely, then the temperature could be 59: 31 degrees difference! In winter, the contrast can be even more striking.

Elevation is critical, but there are other factors at work. Clouds help determine how much sun reaches the earth and how warm or cool it is for people on the ground. Clouds can make a warm summer day cooler and a winter day colder. Cloud cover also helps determine how much rain or snow falls and how fast snow melts.

Rising air produces clouds, and cloud cover caused as air rises over high elevations is an important contributor to the snowy winters and cool summers of the Southern Appalachians. In the continental United States, only the Pacific Northwest receives more annual precipitation than the high peaks of the South.

According to the National Climatic Data Center, these factors give North Carolina the most diverse climate in eastern America. Average coastal temperatures in the state roughly parallel those of interior northern Florida, whereas mountain averages are lower than those of Buffalo, New York.

Some of the severity of the southern mountains' climate arises from their western location. Nearly 500 miles from the coast, the North Carolina/Tennessee Appalachians are far from the moderating effect of the Gulf Stream and are more likely to feel the effects of cooler air masses moving through the northern and central states. In summer, these air masses often lack sufficient force to displace Bermuda high-pressure systems stalled off the eastern seaboard. These highs, rotating clockwise, often bring hot, humid tropical air into the Southeast, blocking cooler air from the north and west. The cooler air masses then move northeast as they confront the air above the humid lowlands, often bringing showers and cooler air to the mountains.

Latitude, too, plays a role. West Virginia's greater distance from the equator means that the sun is lower in the sky at any given time, shines for fewer hours, and transmits less heat to the earth's surface than in the mountains of North Carolina. At comparable elevations, summertime average high and low temperatures are cooler in West Virginia, although not by much.

The following chart illustrates the average daily high and low temperatures at selected locations for June, July, August, and September.

Average daily high and low temperatures at selected locations for June, July, August, and September.

		JUN	JUL	AUG	SEP
Canaan Valley, W.Va.,	High	75.1	77.7	76.9	71.4
3,200 ft.	Low	48.9	52.4	50.5	44.6
Boone, N.C.,	High	76.5	78.2	78.0	72.3
3,300 ft.	Low	55.1	58.6	57.5	50.8
Banner Elk, N.C.,	High	73.6	76.4	76.3	71.4
3,700 ft.	Low	51.4	55.1	54.5	49.3
Big Meadows, Va.,	High	70.5	74.3	73.8	67.9
3,500 ft.	Low	52.5	56.4	56.0	50.0
Grandfather Mt., N.C.,	High	66.1	68.8	68.4	63.2
5,200 ft.	Low	52.1	55.7	55.6	50.5
Mt. Mitchell, N.C.,	High	65.0	67.0	66.0	62.0
6,684 ft.	Low	49.0	52.0	51.0	46.0
Columbia, S.C.,	High	90.3	92.0	91.0	85.4
300 ft.	Low	67.2	70.3	69.4	63.5

The North Carolina valley town of Boone, at virtually the same elevation as Canaan Valley, is less than 3 degrees warmer on an average summer day. But at night, the more northerly Canaan Valley is significantly cooler than Boone. Even though both benefit from the settling effect of cooler air, Canaan, unlike Boone, has recorded below-freezing temperatures every month of the year.

During the day, however, Canaan Valley, at 3,200 feet, warms up more than North Carolina peaks like Grandfather Mountain or Mount Mitchell. Canaan Valley's unique shape and encircling 4,000-foot ridges create the possibility for warm summer days—an average of three days a year when the temperature exceeds 90 degrees. Although not as cold at night, Boone does not reach 90 degrees in an average year. The reason lies in the substantially higher summits that surround Boone and neighboring Banner Elk.

Unlike Canaan Valley, Banner Elk, at 3,700 feet, is surrounded by peaks up to 6,000 feet. These high peaks and the clouds they create make Banner Elk's summer temperature average very similar to Canaan's. At night, Banner Elk's and Canaan's temperatures dip with the sinking of cool air. West Virginia's higher latitude takes temperatures at Canaan slightly lower than in Banner Elk, yet the summertime similarity in temperature is remarkable when one considers that Banner Elk lies more than 200 air miles south of Canaan Valley.

Big Meadows, a ridge-top recreation area in Shenandoah National Park, illustrates another effect of elevation.

Although lower than Banner Elk, Big Meadows enjoys cooler summer days. Like Canaan, Big Meadows is much farther north, but as a mountaintop, it doesn't experience the buildup of heat that takes place in an enclosed valley like Canaan Valley or Banner Elk. At night, though, their valley locations make Canaan Valley and Banner Elk cooler.

The highest ridges of eastern Tennessee are the coolest in the state, especially where they abut the higher landmasses of the Blue Ridge. In the northwestern North Carolina high country, Tennessee touches a multicounty plateaulike area of 3,000- to 4,000-foot valleys and higher peaks—such as Grandfather Mountain and Mount Mitchell—where summertime high temperatures are 10 degrees cooler than even Canaan's. The Highlands-Cashiers area of southwestern North Carolina is similarly lofty. These high landmasses are more prevalent in North Carolina than in West Virginia or Virginia.

Virginia's coolest mountain climes lie astride the western border, where peaks rise to meet the 4,000-foot-plus ridges of West Virginia's Potomac Highlands. A good example is Mountain Lake, at 3,800 feet, near Blacksburg. Another cool spot is near Mount Rogers, Virginia's highest peak, on the state's southernmost border. Mount Rogers is the first peak in the North Carolina massif of the Blue Ridge, where surrounding counties mimic the cool summers of the nearby North Carolina highlands.

At Grandfather Mountain, the Blue Ridge rises directly to 6,000 feet from the less-than-1,000-foot elevations of the baking North Carolina foothills and piedmont. This escarpment of more than a vertical mile is one of the east's major elevation changes. North and south of Grandfather, indeed all the way into southwestern North Carolina, this Front Range of the Appalachians raises a formidable defense against the heat of the flatlands.

The north central mountains of Virginia are a different story. East of the Alleghenies at the West Virginia state line, the Shenandoah Valley of Virginia drops to less than 1,000 feet. Summertime temperatures here may be cooler than in the piedmont part of Virginia, but they are hot nonetheless: temperatures in the nineties are not uncommon. East of the Great Valley, ridge-top sites on the Blue Ridge, like Big Meadows in Shenandoah National Park and Wintergreen Resort beside the Parkway, both at 3,500 feet, are cool Blue Ridge refuges from the heat.

Due west of the Shenandoah, the major ridges of the West Virginia Alleghenies bottle up the heat in the Shenandoah Valley. The higher, cooler air over this large area of mountains creates cloud cover and rainfall. The West Virginia Alleghenies and the Smokies and Blue Ridge of North Carolina create rain and snowfall that don't reach areas at lower elevation. Just east of the high North Carolina mountains, hemmed in by them in fact, is Asheville, at 2,000 feet. Although high enough for some summer cooling effect, the city often is less than 5 degrees cooler than the hottest piedmont cities and is frequently 15 degrees warmer than high mountain towns. Despite its proximity to the mountains, Asheville is the driest place in North Carolina.

In both winter and summer, the higher western mountains wring the moisture from the prevailing western storms. For that reason, Asheville, the Shenandoah Valley, and indeed the Virginia Blue Ridge of Shenandoah National Park and Wintergreen all lie in the "precipitation shadow" of the higher ranges to the west.

The drier climate of areas just east of the high mountains is caused by the warming of descending air masses once they clear the high peaks. This phenomenon makes precipitation less likely even a few miles away. Although the west receives more precipitation over the year-long cycle, the effect takes place whichever direction a storm is moving and even within mountain ranges, creating many small microclimates. Even during high-country snow storms, some valleys may receive rain or no precipitation at all.

In summer, eastern locations receive their significant rainfall from thunderstorms, hurricanes, and low-pressure systems from the Gulf of Mexico, all striking the mountains from the southeast. These storms are usually directed into the mountains by high-pressure systems off the coast, whose clockwise wind pumps wet air into the peaks. In winter, all of these factors come into play with the addition of a major new variable: cyclonic winter storms that batter the Appalachians from the west.

Only unusual winter weather interrupts the winter storm systems that continually pummel the Southern Appalachians. The usual pattern is repeated major infusions of low pressure with trailing bitter blasts of cold air every three days or so. This constant midwinter pattern gives the Southern Appalachians their high average snowfall.

Midwinter finds these storms at their most consistent, yet they can begin in autumn, sometimes September, usually October. Spectacular scenes of rime-ice-blasted peaks above autumn-carpeted valleys result from these early "winter" storms. Often, late storms of this kind create a parallel situation in April and May. Snow-covered daffodils are not uncommon in an Appalachian Spring.

The direction from which these storms come and whether they bring rain or snow are functions of the northern jet stream. This upper-level steering current of air is most volatile in winter as it seeks equilibrium between the extreme cold at the North Pole and the warmth at the equator. Each hemisphere has a jet stream that affects the path of major storms. Winter jet-stream patterns often originate over Alaska and Canada and drive arctic air masses south and east. The jet stream determines if and where these storms strike the Southern Appalachians.

Patterns do exist. At times, the jet stream dives down into the West, often through the Rocky Mountain states, then swings up west of the Appalachians along the Mississippi River and into eastern Canada. This route can mean a snow drought on the entire East Coast. An accompanying high-pressure system frequently stalls along the coast, pumping warm air up along the eastern mountain chain. This scenario is relatively unusual and often spells disappointment for ski enthusiasts and resort operators.

More often with this pattern, the jet stream bisects the southern mountains and more northern ranges receive cold and snow. Atlantic high pressure brings warm Gulf air to the southernmost summits.

Only Old Man Winter knows where the dividing line will be. Sometimes northwestern North Carolina summits are the southernmost cold and snowy peaks. At other times, the line lies north of North Carolina, yet snow falls as far south as Mount Rogers. With this pattern, the line between snow and rain, cool and cold, is often in southern West Virginia —one reason why the Mountain State nets 30 to 50 percent more snowfall than higher North Carolina summits. All of these bisecting patterns usually mean snow for New England: West Virginia is just the snow storm's first stop.

For the southern skier, a better pattern occurs when the jet stream dips into the Midwest and swings up, bringing cold to the whole of the Appalachians. Whether or not it snows, the downhill ski resorts can create fine skiing with machine-made snow.

Another pattern good for snow making is the jet stream's swing down through the Ohio River Valley across the Southern Appalachians and then up, out over the Atlantic. This route also can cause a New England snow drought if the winter storms go out to sea far enough south. Frequently, though, this pattern yields good snow-making weather and skiing for the entire East Coast. A stalled high-pressure system over the Rockies can also result from this pattern, a situation that produced memorable western snow droughts between the midseventies and mideighties.

Natural snow obviously requires more than dry arctic air, however. When the jet stream swings down with cold air and carries snow storms up the East Coast, Gulf of Mexico moisture is the source of the snow. Atlantic high pressure, rotating clockwise, forces warm moist air up to meet the arctic air masses. When the jet stream and accompanying cold moves far enough south, the Appalachians can be white from Alabama on up. More often, the snow line bisects the southern ranges, dropping a white cover from the Smokies north.

Below this line of cold, the southernmost ranges get rain. Luckily for southern winter enthusiasts, even when all of North Carolina's peaks are getting a winter shower, snow is often falling in West Virginia. Frequently, when a winter rain occurs, the storm ends as snow, and cold returns. Downhill ski conditions can recover quickly with snow making, and even cross-country ski conditions can stabilize.

When the jet stream enters the South and swings back north over the ocean, moisture from the Gulf of Mexico can benefit the extreme Southern Appalachians more than the West Virginia mountains or New England. Deep snows occur, especially when a wet air mass driven up from the south by high pressure collides at the mountains with arctic cold. These Sou'easters dump large amounts of snow, sometimes even east of the mountains. Virginia's and North Carolina's mountains are particularly susceptible to them, and North Carolina's deepest recorded snow occurred this way. In 1927, 31 inches fell in two days in Nashville, N.C., only 125 miles from the Atlantic. These southeastern storms are the ones that occasionally inundate snowless cities like Atlanta and make the evening news.

Most of the East's winter storms thus originate as "Panhandle lows" from the area of northern Texas, or as "Gulf lows" from the Gulf of

Mexico. Either way, they travel major, identified storm tracks that can envelop the southern mountains. Since the early sixties, these extratropical cyclones, as they are technically known, have accounted for the massive news-making snow storms that periodically bury East Coast cities from Washington, D.C., to Boston.

The macro jet stream patterns are subject to exceptions. Individual storms can defy the patterns or break them as new patterns emerge. Even when the southern mountains are bisected by the jet stream, with West Virginia receiving the most snow, the more southerly peaks are snowy for a time. Besides the jet stream, another West Virginia snowfall advantage is the "Lake Effect," the phenomenon that brings blizzards to Chicago and Buffalo.

The Lake Effect arises from the temperature difference between arctic air masses and the Great Lakes. That disparity creates evaporation: so much water rises into the air that at times the lakes appear to be steaming. Snow first falls on neighboring states, but as the wet, cold air mass makes its major rise over West Virginia's mountains, substantial snow blankets both the slopes oriented to the west and north and the high peaks. Even when the accumulation is light, the Lake Effect can create sunny days of snow flurries that add up, often to inches per day. Add the likelihood of cooler temperatures at West Virginia's more northern latitude and the result is the South's best powder snow.

Of all the factors affecting southern snow, elevation may be most significant. When midwinter rain is in the offing, elevation won't always stem the flood in North Carolina or New England. Both regions have their winter bouts of drenching downpours. But under average and even marginal conditions, high elevation often makes the difference between rain or snow, and between a dusting or a heavy blanket.

The impact of elevation varies in different places at different times. Roan Mountain, a 6,300-foot rise on the Tennessee/North Carolina state line near Boone, aptly illustrates the importance of altitude. Roan is only 400 feet lower than Mount Mitchell, but unlike Mitchell, where other mountains lie to the west, Roan bulges dramatically 4,000 feet above the foothills of upper East Tennessee, the first major mass to confront snow storms coming from the west. Roan also occasionally receives snow from both the southern and more northern storm tracks, giving it on average more snow than the Smokies but less than West Virginia.

Frequently, the lowland ridges of East Tennessee will be brown and snowless, while Roan and the adjacent high-country ski resort region will have general snow cover. At times, only Roan will receive snow from a storm that falls as rain elsewhere, even at the ski resorts. In this region, many cross-country skiers have driven through rain into a winter wonderland of frosted trees and quickly deepening snow drifts. When snow falls on Roan, it generally arrives earlier, accumulates deeper, and stops later than at the lower elevations.

Besides colder temperatures at higher elevations, more moisture actually leaves the clouds as they get higher: precipitation is a function of elevation. So a given amount of snow at a low elevation usually means more at higher altitudes. A foot of new snow at 4,000 feet can leave 2-plus feet on the highest peaks.

By early February 1985, Roan had had only three weeks of cross-country skiing owing to an unusually warm December that had also affected New England. From February 11 through 13 that situation changed, and skiers had weeks of deep snow and the best powder skiing in memory. The storm started as a massive low-pressure system just above the Gulf of Mexico. Moving northeast, it intensified over the mountains of Tennessee and North Carolina. During the afternoon of Monday, February 11, snow began falling across the high peaks and plateaus of western North Carolina and grew heavy.

Heavy snow and blizzard conditions prevailed into the late evening, when warmer air forced a change to mixed rain and snow, even at altitudes of 4,000 feet. By midnight, lightning and thunder attended downpours at low elevations and punctuated renewed snowfall higher up. Soaking of the snow created a heavily consolidated snowpack. Then temperatures fell dramatically.

During the next day, February 12, Asheville began receiving snow. On the high peaks, curtains of showering snow continued that night and all the next day. The main storm had passed, but it didn't pull away bringing in clear, cold weather in the usual way. Instead, the storm's track drew "cloud streets" of Great Lakes moisture down into collision with the same mountains that had just received the main brunt of the storm. Such Lake Effect snow normally strikes West Virginia as a more northerly storm tracks into New England. This time, the strength of the storm brought the lake-born snowfall to southwestern Virginia and western North Carolina.

On February 13, Asheville had cleared with 6 inches of snow. Roan Mountain, Mount Mitchell, and the Smokies all received more than 20 inches. For the next two days, Lake Effect snow continued to deposit dry powder on top of drifts more than 10 feet deep. Highways across lofty gaps were closed for more than a week.

Storms like this, although outside the norm, are common enough to make the southern mountains around Roan a viable cross-country skiing venue, even when sparse early snows and warm or rainy interludes delay the start of the ski season. It is not unusual for the snow to melt completely. But big storms often bring good skiing back for another multiweek stint, and the cloudy, sun-blocking weather on the heights produces relatively long periods of skiing.

Even without big storms, deep accumulations occur. After an early February thaw in 1986, most cross-country skiers thought Roan Mountain's ski season was over. When a cold pattern returned in midmonth, a series of 2-inch snowfalls in mountain towns like Boone weren't enough to convince even locals that skiing had returned. Each of Boone's 2-inch snows left 6 and more inches on Roan. Depths up to 20 inches brought almost another month of skiing. Only a cross-country ski report publicized the unexpected accumulation.

All of the factors just described give the South's snowbelt startling yearly averages that equal or exceed the snowfall in many of America's snowy northern cities. According to the Climatic Atlas of The United States, West Virginia's zone of 100 inches of annual snowfall boasts the East's greatest accumulation south of New England. It is not uncommon for peaks in this zone to measure more snow than all but the highest and snowiest New England ski areas. West Virginia's greatest snowfall accumulates in the mountain counties of Preston, Pocahontas, Tucker, Randolph, Pendleton, and Grant.

Canaan Valley's twenty-year weather records show an average of 100 inches at 3,250 feet. At more than 4,000 feet, surrounding peaks and the Dolly Sods Wilderness average between 120 and 150 inches. Early ski area operator Bob Barton says Canaan received 450 inches of snow in the winter of 1959–60!

Pickens, south of Canaan at 2,750 feet, is called the snowiest weather station in the state. Data from 1952 to 1964 average 160 inches a year. Records for sixty years reduce that annual average to 127 inches. Although figures are difficult to estimate with accuracy, adjacent higher-elevation areas can be expected to yield substantially more snowfall. Twenty air miles from Pickens, Snowshoe and Silver Creek ski resorts claim, and may receive, 180 inches of snow annually at 4,800 feet on Cheat Mountain. Those averages are double the yearly snow total of

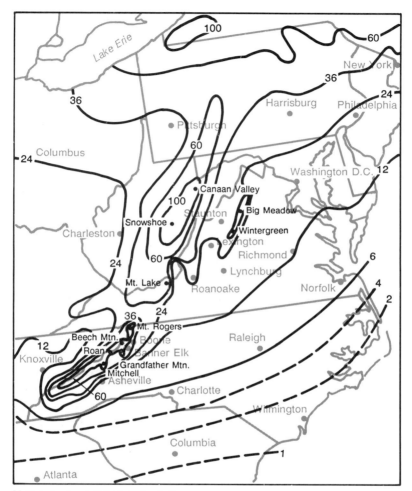

Mean annual total snowfall.

Buffalo, New York. Statistics for the town of Richwood and the Cranberry Wilderness, west of Snowshoe, show 80 inches of annual snow, but more is likely.

Obviously, lower snowfall can be expected east of West Virginia's high mountains. Still, the rest of the Southern Highlands measure up to snowfall standards worthy of regions far to the north.

At the South's upper reaches, western Maryland's Garrett County averages 80 inches of snow annually. Moving down into Virginia, along the state's western border, Allegheny Mountain sites generally receive between 30 and 60 inches. Mountain Lake resort, near Blacksburg, has recorded a ten-year average of 54 inches at 3,870 feet.

Farther east, Shenandoah Valley sites, including Roanoke, average around 24 inches of annual snow. But, at 3,500 feet in Shenandoah National Park, Big Meadows has recorded a ten-year average of 41 inches. Wintergreen ski resort, south of Shenandoah, receives under 40 inches of annual snow.

Because Mount Rogers lacks a weather station, its claim to Virginia's greatest snowfall is the best guess of those experienced with the 5,700-foot mountain. The other likely site of the state's deepest snow is Mountain Lake, with 54 inches. Supporting the case for Mount Rogers are its altitude and the fact that Grandfather Mountain, 50 miles south of Rogers, receives 58 inches of annual snow at 5,300 feet. Rogers, unlike Grandfather, isn't blocked by nearby peaks, so it's plausible that Mount Rogers receives 80 inches of annual snowfall. Even Grandfather Mountain's annual average is greater than Denver's, Chicago's, or Boston's.

West of Grandfather, 5,505-foot Beech Mountain towers over eastern Tennessee. The ski resort claims 90 inches of yearly snow. A conservative guess is 80 inches.

Like Beech, Roan Mountain is on the western edge of the mountains. Looming on the horizon southeast from Roan, at 6,684 feet, is Mount Mitchell. Both deserve their own circles on the climate map. According to state park statistics, Mount Mitchell measures an average of 104 inches a year, joining West Virginia and bringing that "nowhere south of New England" distinction to North Carolina. Although the latest five-year data show 92 inches of accumulation on Mitchell, more is likely.

Using a temperature model to estimate summit weather data, Leffler and Foster, in a study titled "A Guide to Temperatures on 150 Appalachian Mountain Summits," concluded in 1979 that Roan and Mitchell, although different in height, are virtually identical in winter temperature. Accepting that, both very likely receive 100 inches of snow a year.

At Clingman's Dome, Great Smoky Mountain National Park's highest peak, average snowfall is probably 80 inches. Cataloochee ski area, east of the Smokies in Maggie Valley, receives 45 inches at its 5,400-foot peak. The very highest parts of the Parkway and the Shining Rock Wilderness probably get about the same amounts.

As noted earlier, accumulation of these averages begins in October. Winter's more sizable accumulations start in November. The average first inch of snow is on the ground before November 30 in West Virginia's central highlands, a date comparable to that for eastern Maine, mid-New Hampshire, western Vermont, western New York, Michigan, central Wisconsin, and southern Minnesota. Mountainous western Virginia and northwestern North Carolina receive their annual first inch of snow, on average, by December 10, an achievement equaled by Chicago and Boston.

By November, the southern mountains may receive their first significant accumulations, usually from 3 to 8 inches, often around Thanksgiving.

December monthly totals are highest by far in West Virginia: nearly 2 feet at Canaan Valley and likely more higher up. Totals drop to about 8 inches at Mountain Lake and Big Meadows in Virginia, 10 inches at Grandfather, and an estimated 10 to 12 inches at Beech, Roan, and Mount Mitchell. The best bet for sports on natural snow in December is a trip to West Virginia, although a large snow storm might hit late in the month further south (a white Christmas in the southern mountains is not unusual). But out of the four winter months, December averages the least snow.

No one skis with the entire average annual snowfall underfoot, so *when* the snow falls may be more important than how much falls annually. In the South, *when* means January and February. By then, periods of deep snow are common, with February's monthly totals averaging the greatest of the year. January is a close second.

Even areas with rather low annual figures for natural accumulation can offer snowy trails, since most of the South's yearly dose falls in two months. The farther south one goes, the more true this prediction seems to be.

The key winter months of January and February offer an average of over 53 inches of snow, more than 4 feet, at West Virginia's Canaan Valley. Surprisingly, the highest North Carolina summits equal Canaan's January and February total. In fact, Mount Mitchell, and likely Roan, exceed Canaan's February snowfall averages. But Canaan receives more snow in January, bringing the more northerly valley into a dead heat for the two months with the two substantially higher North Carolina summits.

From West Virginia and Mount Mitchell, January and February's combined totals drop to 22 inches at Shenandoah National Park's Big Meadows, 35 at Mountain Lake, and 30 at Grandfather Mountain. During the height of winter, the 1,000 to 1,500 feet that Roan and Mitchell rise above Grandfather give the higher peaks 40 percent more snowfall!

March registers a surprising third in snowfall among the four winter months, often on the basis of heavy snows in the first two weeks. Poor winters rebound then with deep snow. In fact, most record daily snowfalls in the southern mountains have occurred in March.

As in December, snowfall in the West Virginia mountains surges ahead in March, extending the region's lead over North Carolina in annual snowfall. Canaan Valley's 25.5-inch average is 6 inches more than usually falls on Roan and Mount Mitchell in March.

But the more southerly mountains can receive amazing amounts of snow at that time of year. Ski resort developer Tom Brigham says, "In the spring there's a lot of moisture coming up from the Gulf. With the right temperatures, especially at the altitude of Mount Mitchell, there can be some really big, freak snowstorms. West Virginia may average more but that state doesn't get the massive March snows of further south."

Unfortunately, the same snows that create such fine skiing can also strand mountain residents. In March 1960, 56 inches of snow blanketed Boone, requiring food drops from National Guard helicopters. Similar emergencies occurred in West Virginia in 1960, in 1976–77, and again in 1985. Coal company excavation equipment has been called in to help National Guardsmen deliver food and keep roads open. In such situations, the plight of isolated Appalachian towns often goes unreported while television news footage shows spinning motorists in Atlanta frustrated by a few inches of snow.

For Nordic skiers and hikers relying on natural snow, however, average days of snow cover may be a more meaningful statistic than average annual snowfall. The U.S. Department of Agriculture estimates an annual twenty to forty days with snow cover greater than 1 inch for southwestern North Carolina. Forty to sixty days is the estimate for southwestern Virginia, northwestern North Carolina, and middle West Virginia. The Mountain State's Potomac Highlands and extreme western Virginia net between sixty and eighty days of snow cover. In each of the snow bands, actual snow cover, sometimes an inch or less, probably exceeds these averages. See the chart below for the average number of days with snow cover of one inch or more for each of these areas.

To translate these data into an average number of weeks when snow

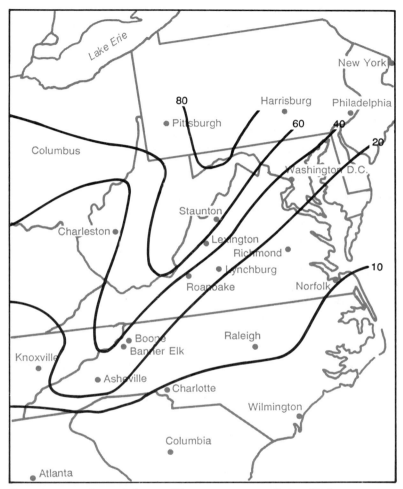

Average number of days with snow cover of one inch or more.

conditions are suitable for cross-country skiing, Roan Mountain, Mount Mitchell, and Mount Rogers usually offer from four to six weeks of skiing, with four weeks being very low and with an estimated average of five weeks. In recent years, though, eight to ten weeks of skiing has been the maximum.

West Virginia's heavy snow zone usually offers between six and ten weeks of skiable conditions, with six weeks being very low and with an estimated average of eight or nine weeks. In recent years, the longest ski seasons have lasted twelve weeks.

For Dixie's downhill skiers, asking when to ski is not the same as asking when natural snow falls. Fickle fluctuations in snowfall have made snow-making machinery a fixture at downhill and some cross-country ski resorts all over America. Southeastern ski areas have led the world in accepting snow making.

The surprisingly cold climate of the Southern Appalachians is the key. Dixie resorts have become some of the nation's best-equipped and most aggressive producers of machine-made snow. For the machine-made blizzards to begin, all that's needed is a temperature below freezing and low humidity.

The average date of first frost in the Dixie Appalachians ranges from mid-September in West Virginia to early October in northwestern North Carolina. Virtually the entire mountain range from western Maryland to just south of the Smokies experiences from 120 to 150 days when the low temperatures are below freezing. At some high-altitude sites, the number of subfreezing days could fill six months.

With this type of climate and a growing demand for skiing in the South, some resorts start up their snow guns and open in November. In 1984, four of the six resorts in northwestern North Carolina opened at Thanksgiving, three featuring snow cover over the entire length of all their trails. Although unusually warm weather plagued the entire East that December, these resorts had a fine Thanksgiving ski week.

Under good, even average conditions, then, a handful of the biggest Dixie slopes will be open for Thanksgiving. If the weather doesn't cooperate, the first blast of cold in early December will launch snow making. Although all of the slopes at a southern resort may not be open in early December, conditions can be excellent. Since the Christmas vacation is a key factor in winter profitability, the southern resorts do everything they can to have as many slopes as possible open for the holidays.

December and March are cold months in the mountains, but January and February are the coldest. These months usually bring the best downhill skiing and the most energetic snow making. Now March too, especially the first two weeks, is being recognized as a good time to ski. Early March has traditionally been the closing date for Dixie's ski areas, most often because skiers mistakenly think warm weather in Atlanta

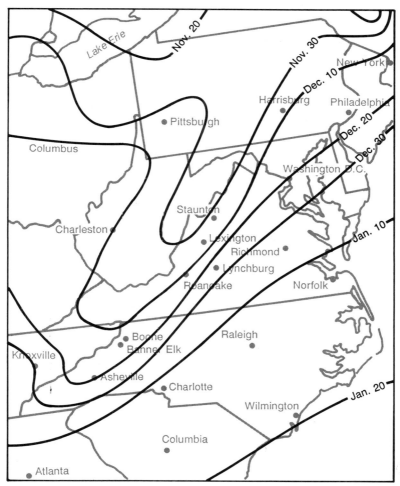

Mean first day of 1″ snowfall.

means no skiing in the mountains. Word is getting out, though, that the resorts have the winter's biggest base of snow in March and want to stay open. Many resorts have a real commitment to the spring skiing market. Firm policies are to stay open to designated dates, if the weather or natural snow allow, or to close "as late as possible." Some resorts, like Snowshoe in West Virginia, routinely go into April.

Snow totals at the highest Dixie downhill and cross-country ski sites range from 80 to 180 inches and parallel many northern accumulations. Beech Mountain in North Carolina and Mount Rogers in Virginia, for instance, receive an average snowfall similar to that of Burlington, Vermont (79.1 inches). Mount Mitchell and Roan Mountain in North Carolina and Canaan Valley in West Virginia receive snow totals comparable to those of downhill and cross-country ski areas in the lower Mount Washington Valley near North Conway, New Hampshire (100 inches). The highest West Virginia resorts and cross-country parks, like Snowshoe and Blackwater Falls State Park, above Canaan Valley, receive yearly accumulations similar to those of Mad River Glen Ski Resort in Vermont and Hunter Mountain in New York (120 inches) and Wildcat Mountain in New Hampshire (174 inches).

There are differences between the South and the North, of course. Perhaps the most significant is temperature. The lower latitude of the Sunbelt creates just that: a belt of greater solar warming effect. Again, though, elevation, orientation of the slope, and the cooling of the wind on exposed locations can greatly reduce the snow melt that takes place in the southern mountains when the temperature rises above freezing.

Of course, an average high temperature above freezing does not mean that every day is above freezing at the site. In fact, stretches of colder weather, often after snow storms, can preserve good snow conditions for long periods. The important fact for winter sports enthusiasts is that the mountain sites discussed here have mean temperatures, the average of the maximum and minimum, near or below freezing for three of the four months between December and March. At the highest elevations, average temperatures below freezing can be expected for all four winter months.

But averages are not extremes. From West Virginia to the Smokies, it is not unusual for the coldest nighttime temperatures to dip to between 5 and 15 below zero. At 5,200 feet on Grandfather Mountain, this happens about seven times a winter. Cold nights throughout the Southern Appalachians regularly dip to near zero on the highest peaks. At their coldest, Dixie's summits have experienced temperatures down to 35 degrees below zero.

At the higher and more exposed locations in the South, strong winds blow often. The wind's cooling effect on warm-blooded creatures, called the wind-chill factor, can make a moderate temperature life threatening for the unprepared skier or winter mountaineer. For instance, a 50-mph wind can make a 25-degree day feel like 25 below zero.

Average high, low, and mean winter temperatures at selected locations for December, January, February, and March

		DEC.	JAN.	FEB.	MAR.
Canaan Valley, W.Va.,	High	38.4	37.3	39.1	46.4
3,200 ft.	Low	19.4	18.4	18.9	24.8
	Mean	28.9	28.1	29.0	35.6
Big Meadows, Va.,	High	38.1	33.0	35.3	46.0
3,510 ft.	Low	31.4	15.3	17.4	27.0
	Mean	34.7	24.2	26.3	36.5
Banner Elk, N.C.,	High	44.7	41.8	43.5	50.8
3,700 ft.	Low	23.7	21.0	22.3	29.2
	Mean	34.2	31.4	32.9	40.0
Grandfather Mt., N.C.,	High	38.7	35.5	37.0	45.0
5,300 ft.	Low	22.7	18.6	20.3	27.9
	Mean	30.8	27.4	28.2	35.2
Mount Mitchell, N.C.,	High	40.8	34.2	38.0	41.5
6,684 ft.	Low	24.8	18.3	20.8	25.4
	Mean	32.8	26.3	29.4	33.4
Columbia, S.C.,	High	57.9	56.9	59.7	66.5
300 ft.	Low	34.1	33.9	35.5	41.9
	Mean	46.0	45.4	47.6	54.2

When high winds and severe cold arrive together, as they frequently do, the southern mountains can be arctic. Few places illustrate that more effectively than Grandfather Mountain. At Grandfather, only August and September escape the possibility of winds over 120 mph. The highest recorded wind on the peak is 161 mph, with winds over 140 mph measured ten times in twenty-two years. Winds over 50 mph are regular occurrences in winter. Although more severe than most, Grandfather suggests just how cold an exposed southern summit can be.

Nowhere do the southern mountains routinely serve up as much cold or snow as do the highest, coldest, windiest peaks in New England. But those northern summits, many above the tree line, don't harbor ski resorts and touring sites. At any given time in winter, the southern

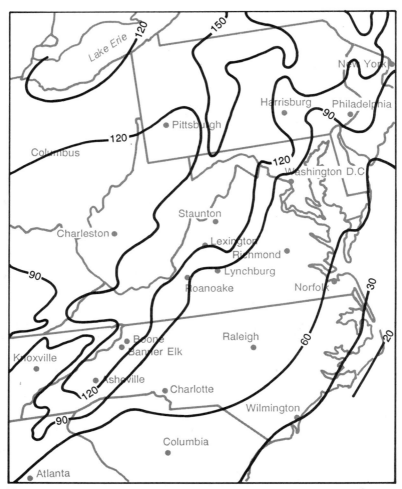

Mean annual number of days where the temperature is 32° and below.

mountains can have as much snow and skiing or winter hiking as the region to our north—sometimes more.

The trick to enjoying southern snow sports is knowing when and where the snow is best. This book is an introduction to that knowledge. Specific information for any given trail or ski area, in any one winter, requires personal contacts in snow country and attention to ski reports.

The chapters on specific winter sports and the guide entries suggest ways to gain up-to-the-minute knowledge of snow conditions. Cable television's Weather Channel has proved a reliable reflector of Southern Appalachian snow. An ear to your own favorite weather forecast on TV or a call to your mountain weather informant can get you the news you need. With it, you'll gain an understanding of one of Nature's surprises: the Southern Snowbelt.

History

THE HISTORY of skiing in the southeastern United States is unique and colorful. Skiing in other American venues evolved based on widespread public awareness of common heavy snows in those regions. For Sunbelt skiing to be practical, the public had to learn of the surprisingly snowy climate of the southern mountains. And eventually, to be economically feasible, southern resorts had to become the world's first to rely almost solely on snow making.

But the commitment to snow making came second. Skiers searching for natural snow, not entrepreneurs, first brought skiing south of Pennsylvania. Between the efforts of the first "civilian" snow seekers and the later investment of entrepreneurs, skiing has blossomed in a region known more for sun than snow.

Before 1930, skiing in the South consisted mostly of stranded northerners, rarely seen, climbing up and skiing down hills in the southern mountains and, more often, in large cities after freak snow storms. One of those cities was Washington, D.C.

Since the earliest, obscure phase in the history of southern skiing, no other single factor has had more impact than the Ski Club of Washington, D.C., (SCWDC). In 1986, the club was fifty years old. In practically every one of those years it has taken major steps to improve skiing in the South. The club's efforts literally bridged the gap between wanting to ski and being able to ski.

When it was founded in 1936, the club's first task was to find snow. Harold "Hal" Leich, a club founder, and others scouted the Washington environs for snowy hills. In Glencoe, Pa., they found the slope and hospitality they were looking for.

A special excursion car was added to the Sunday Baltimore and Ohio Railroad train, and local farmers would pick up skiers at the Glencoe train station. This southern "ski train" was running at the same time that ski trains were becoming a new way for skiers in Boston and New

York to get to New England ski areas. Later, in the 1950s, similar trains would run from Washington and Baltimore to Maryland's Marsh Mountain, and still later, to Wisp ski area.

At Glencoe in 1936, local farmers would take skiers in, housing and feeding them. A miller opened his mill for square dancing, and church women sold sandwiches. The enthusiasts skied in farmer's fields after horse-drawn harrows "groomed" the slopes. Some skiers returned in the off-season to help wrest rocks from the Glencoe fields. One autumn, Leich remembers, eighteen wagon loads of rock were removed from one slope. That winter, though, snow was so sparse that the hill was never skiable.

As early as 1939, North Carolinian Tom Alexander was said to have ski slopes planned for his property in Maggie Valley, N.C. But the ski area he had jotted on an early planning map would not materialize until 1961. By the early 1930s, the first interest in skiing was being recorded in Banner Elk, N.C., now the hub of the six North Carolina high country slopes. In the mid 1930s, a Lees-McRae College industrial education instructor discussed skiing with his students, and soon the shop was turning out skis. The students even formed a ski club. A Depression-era guide to North Carolina shows skiers on Beech Mountain's snow-covered meadows before 1939.

Late in the 1930s, SCWDC members and Potomac Appalachian Trail Clubbers from D.C. found a number of good ski sites in Shenandoah National Park. One of those was Pinnacle Knoll slope, an old pasture from turn-of-the-century mountaineer days that was accessible from Skyline Drive. At the clubs' request, the National Park Service kept it clear to enhance skiing. Three years of removing rocks and weeds made the slope "like a golf course" and skiable on 3 inches of snow, according to Hal Leich.

Another favorite Shenandoah ski site was the 2½-mile drop from Skyland Resort to the Shenandoah Valley on the Old Skyland Road. This run drops 2,000 vertical feet, and Leich says, recalls the Carriage Road from the summit of Mount Moosilauke in New Hampshire. Under sufficient snow, the Appalachian Trail was popular then, as it is now, among cross-country enthusiasts.

The Potomac Appalachian Trail Club and the SCWDC formed an interclub committee in 1939 to scout another site, a Savage River State Forest location in Maryland, now New Germany State Park. A glowing report from the committee secured the cooperation of the Maryland

Department of Forestry. Slopes along the eastern side of Meadow Mountain were mowed, and Civilian Conservation Corps (CCC) workers cut the Whiskey Hollow Trail. This run was "the only expert trail south of the Mason-Dixon line" with an 800-foot vertical drop. The winter of 1939–40 brought substantial snow and crowds. Skiers were ferried from the base to the top by pick-up truck, according to old-timers still working at New Germany Park.

At about the same time as slopes were being cut in New Germany, the first rope tow south of the Mason-Dixon line was established just outside the park on the Garrett County, Md., farm of Mr. Samuel Otto, with the involvement of the Western Maryland Ski Club, from Cumberland. A CCC truck was used at one time to power the 600-foot tow, which ran through the 1940s.

Weekend trips to these informal ski sites required coordination, and a ski club grapevine grew up. The person receiving the snow report would call six assistants, who would each call another six, and so on. Car pools were set up for weekend trips.

By the end of the 1930s, city skiers, once seldom glimpsed, were becoming more visible at grassy hills and parks throughout Washington when snow fell. The SCWDC offered a dry-land ski school in the fall, using folded-newspaper skis on a hardwood floor. Appalachian Mountain Club member Doug Burckett is credited with introducing the SCWDC to the practice method in 1936.

By the early 1940s, while the SCWDC was spending weekends in Pennsylvania, Maryland, and Shenandoah National Park, the Great Smokies Ski Club had been formed and was skiing at Newfound Gap and Indian Gap in the Smokies. In 1940, a good snow year, a former freshman ski coach at Dartmouth College, with friends, began frequenting Indian Gap on the road to Clingman's Dome. There too, the National Park Service helped maintain ski slopes. Today, only cross-country skiing is popular in the national park; ironically, the favorite area is on the Clingman's Dome Road near Indian Gap.

After World War II, another ski site was started near New Germany, Md. Called Gunterstown, this area had the second ski tow below the Mason-Dixon line, operated by Dave Gunter. Also during the late 1940s, Hoopole Mountain, near Oakland, Md., was the site of the Deep Creek Ski Trails, which included night skiing.

By this time, a number of fairly sophisticated ski areas had appeared in south-central Pennsylvania. The most popular was probably Laurel Mountain near Ligonier. The more formalized facilities of the Pennsylvania slopes attracted regular visits by SCWDC members, who in February of 1947 began weekend ski trips by bus. These trips were the start of a travel trend that today is popular among southern ski clubs, church groups, and other groups.

With the war over, Hal Leich returned to Shenandoah to try to revive skiing at Pinnacle Knoll. The once clear slope was overgrown, though, and the National Park Service refused to let the club clear the area.

In 1948, machine-assisted skiing came to Washington with the ski club's installation of a portable, gas-powered rope tow in Rock Creek Park, on Linnean Hill near the National Zoo.

The $400 tow was purchased with a $2 fee from club members. The National Capital Parks Department responded enthusiastically, clearing brush for the tow and installing flood lights for night skiing. The hill was even designated for skiing only to avoid conflict with sledders. The tow pulled its first ski clubbers up Linnean Hill a week before Christmas 1948, after a 5-inch snowfall.

The following snowless winter launched a new phase in the history of the SCWDC and the modest beginning of big-time skiing's dip into the South. The winter of 1949–50 started snowless and stayed so through February at all nearby ski sites. Writings of the time claim that only Canada had snow. Then SCWDC council member Art Kurle (pronounced "Curly") says that club members "could stand it no longer. Hal Leich and Gorman Young headed for West Virginia to look for snow."

They found it, a huge drift on a cleared pasture in Canaan Valley, south of Davis, W. Va. Kurle says this true story somehow got turned around by "a now forgotten newspaper writer" who said the drift was spotted on a spring flight by two airline pilots and that their conversation was overheard by an SCWDC member. "Not so!" Art Kurle says. "It was Hal and Gorman, just exercising good common sense and pioneering skills." By the end of the season, club members had tried the drift and landowners Irene and Hobart (Hobe) Mauzy had their first run in with "them crazy skiers," a relationship that would last a decade.

In 1950, all that marked the site that would become the South's first major ski area was a huge, irregular snowdrift in an apple orchard under Cabin Mountain. In West Virginia, skiing would consolidate its foothold in what most would call the Southern Appalachians, and with the invention of snow making, the sport was destined to spread down to Alabama and Georgia.

Ironically, in the winter of 1949–50, as ski club members were skiing the Mauzy's drift for the first time and planning a ski area, snow making for skiing was being invented.

Who invented snow making and when is a topic of debate. John Mathewson, as an early representative of Larchmont Engineering, a Massachusetts manufacturer of farm irrigation systems, installed many of the South's first snow-making systems. He says the idea for snow making originated with a skier named Wayne Pierce.

At Mohawk Mountain, Conn., Pierce had skied on tons of crushed ice spread on the slope by owner Walt Schoenknecht when the resort started its second season with no snow. Pierce and two friends formed Tey Manufacturing and experimented with primitive snow making in 1949. Mathewson says the system was granted a patent in 1950 and was tried for the first time at Mohawk Mountain in December 1949.

During that early experimentation, Mathewson says, Joseph C. Tropeano, owner of Larchmont, contacted Tey, visited Mohawk Mountain, and began experimenting with snow making based on the already patented idea of mixing pressurized air and water inside a snow gun. By the mid-1950s, Larchmont's efforts had helped snow making become a practical technology. At that time, Mathewson represented Larchmont and was taking that technology to the South. In 1959, Larchmont purchased Tey's original patent.

Larchmont Engineering offers a different version of snow making's invention. In 1950, the story goes, Joseph C. Tropeano had been engaged by the Minute Maid Orange Juice Co. to devise a way to protect orange groves from subfreezing temperatures. Tropeano knew that under very humid conditions oranges could be safe from freezing at temperatures down to 26 degrees. It was his intention to create a cloud of vapor to simulate high humidity. Using compressed air and water propelled from a "gun" that resembled a sprinkler system, Tropeano made a foglike mist during warm weather tests. However, the cold weather test, held in Lexington, Ma., was a suprise. "To everyone's amazement," says Tropeano's son Joseph T. Tropeano, the machine made snow.

Tropeano was depressed. He went home, says his son, and flopped dejectedly down in front of the television. That evening the TV news described the snowless plight of New England's ski areas. The only nearby skiing, the announcer said, was in Canada's Laurentians. Something of a "wise guy," Tropeano called the station and said, "whad'dya mean no snow? There's snow right here in Lexington!" That brought the news crew to Tropeano, and the day after the "Snow in Lexington!" spot aired, Mount Sunapee Ski Area in New Hampshire had a truck in Lexington wanting the snow machine. In 1951, Larchmont Engineering began small-scale marketing of the primitive machines. That continued until the 1960s, when southern ski areas began pursuing snow making on a grand scale.

In West Virginia, the winter of 1950–51 brought changes to the Mauzy's pasture. The ski club's drift was created by a rill in the meadow that ran down the slope and against the prevailing wind. Two drifts actually formed. The upper one was about 700 feet long and 50 to 200 feet wide, depending on snowfall. Drifted snow depths varied between 10 and 25 feet. The lower drift was smaller, but after good natural snow, both drifts joined and general snow cover created a fairly large slope. Even prolonged rain didn't melt the drift.

The site had immediately attracted a small cadre of true believers who spoke affectionately of "the hill" and "the glacier" and led the way in upgrading the slope into Cabin Mountain ski area, as it became known. A poem and even a film about the area sprang from the romantic dedication of these SCWDC members to their sport. The club movie called the slope "Driftland."

With the discovery of Driftland, some club members perceived a home ski area that the club could develop and call its own. Others perceived a nearly 200-mile drive from D.C., a limited club treasury, and the need for a lot of labor. The club formed a study committee of discoverers Hal Leich and Gorman Young, with Ed Couch, Art Kurle, and Paul Tarver.

The mayor of Davis, Jim Meyer, offered building materials for a "summit" tow house and warming hut, Ed Filler, co-owner of the local telephone company, volunteered workers and rope-tow poles; and Oscar Heitz, Irene Mauzy's brother, volunteered slope grading. And the Mauzys approved a lease of the land. Lumber was secured for the hut, as was a rope for the tow. The committee recommended the club support the project at a cost of $550.

Politics then came into play. An unfavorable reaction from some members postponed a disposition on the project until the first, well-attended meeting in the fall, when the club gave the go-ahead. Four weekends later, the rope tow was running—in a 9-inch November snow storm.

The next winter, even Pennsylvania skiing was wiped out by rain, but Driftland came through. The standard run on the side-sloping drift was a series of long left turns to avoid dropping off the right side of the cornice onto the grass. A skier familiar with the ski area says, "One thing you can say about Cabin Mountain skiers, they sure know how to turn left."

While the Cabin Mountain ski area was getting underway in West Virginia, skiing was again becoming a topic in North Carolina. In 1951, a group calling itself the Roan Mountain Advisory Committee was proposing a ski tow and slope on Roan Mountain, a nearly 6,300-foot peak bisected by the North Carolina/Tennesee state line near Spruce Pine, N.C. Noting interest in skiing at mountain locations like Banner Elk and Gatlinburg, *Tri-County News* Editor S. T. Henry, of Spruce Pine, said the tow would likely be in by winter 1952 and would probably be the first south of the Mason-Dixon line.

Even had the tow been installed, Maryland had already gained that honor. It never was, and like other aborted downhill ski areas in the Great Smoky Mountains and Shenandoah National Park, Roan today draws flocks of cross-country skiers who relish the absence of mechanized lifts.

Back in Canaan Valley, the winter of 1953–54 brought plentiful snow and close to 100 skiers on a good weekend day. Driftland drew from as far away as Charleston, W.Va., Pittsburgh, Baltimore, and Richmond. The portable rope tow on the lower drift was overloaded, and the warming hut held only twelve people (the thirteenth meant burns for those crammed against the wood stove). A ten-year lease was negotiated, a new lower-drift tow was built, and a warming-hut addition was added to the Mauzy's house.

SCWDC members would set the grapevine abuzz with snow reports, and calls went out to Worden's Hotel in Davis for reservations. On winter Saturday nights, dancing and partying were the norm. By the winter of 1954–55, Davis had its first independent ski rental shop, and at Cabin Mountain the South's first regularly scheduled instruction at a ski resort began. On Washington's Birthday, the South's first Winter Carnival came to Davis, with ski races at Cabin Mountain and the premier of the region's first ski film—"Driftland," photographed by Joe Gray and Ed Couch, with original music by George Gray. Cabin Mountain now needed a full-time administrator, and Ed Couch was chosen.

By 1954, another North Carolina ski effort was underway, this time on Mount Mitchell, eastern America's highest peak at 6,684 feet. E. M. "Bob" Carr of Asheville's Educational Lumber Co. had gone to Yale, friend Robert G. Beard had gone to Princeton, and both liked skiing. "A group of us realized how much snow these high mountains got and decided we didn't need to go to Vermont." Carr and cohorts formed the

Mount Mitchell Ski Club, received permission from then Governor Luther Hodges to ski in Mount Mitchell State Park, and spent $1,000 in dues to have a 100-by-500-foot slope cleared in 1957. To reach the state park access road, though, skiers had to drive on the Blue Ridge Parkway. The National Park Service refused to say they'd keep the Parkway open to the state park road. Without the commitment from the National Park Service, Governor Hodges declined to operate the ski slope as a state ski area, in part to keep North Carolina from competing with a private ski area expected to open soon. The slope was never skied by downhillers. As at other snowy sites, cross-country skiers have moved in to fill the void, but even today, National Park Service gates and road-plowing policies often keep the Deep South's snowiest Nordic ski site off limits to the public.

The year 1955 brought competition for Cabin Mountain. That year, Robert Barton, III, left law school at the University of Virginia in Charlottesville. "I was getting fat in law school," Barton says. "I'd been skiing in New England and the West and when I got back East, I didn't think any skiing at all was going on near me. Then I heard the D.C. Ski Club had a ski area in West Virginia, and I joined immediately. I didn't even think the club existed when I first heard about it." In 1954, Barton visited Cabin Mountain for the first time.

That same year, he resolved to open another area nearby and chose a slope on Weiss Knob, pronounced "weese" by the locals and "vice" by Barton, who pronounced the word in the standard German way, meaning white. Today, Canaan Valley ski resort is located on the same site.

Barton's commercial ski area was the first in West Virginia and the farthest South. Like the SCWDC's Cabin Mountain, Weiss Knob relied on natural snow.

The area operated into 1959, despite its problems with high winds that blew snow off the slope, its poor beginner area, and a long, bumpy access road that many people tried to avoid. Barton at times had to haul skiers in by horse-drawn sled. The easiest grades on the hill were at the top of the slope, and the runs became very steep at the bottom, roughly the reverse of most ski slopes.

In the late 1950s, Barton wanted ski instructors for Weiss Knob and contacted the Austrian Information Bureau in New York. "It was a big thing back then to have Austrian instructors," Barton remembers. He was referred to Sepp Kober, a fully certified Austrian instructor and former national coach who had spent a year at Stowe. When Kober showed up in 1958, says Barton, "I could see immediately that there was nothing in Canaan Valley appropriate to a man of his background. Sepp was destined for greater things."

During the winter of 1958–59, Kober was ski school director at Weiss Knob, with weekend teaching duties, and a part-time instructor for Helmuth "Ace" Heise at Marsh Mountain in Garrett County, Md., later called Wisp.

Heise had started the ski area during the winter of 1956–57, the year after Barton opened Weiss Knob. Newspaper clips indicate that Marsh Mountain installed snow making and lights for night skiing in 1957. Although it wasn't intended to cover the entire ski area with snow, Heise's snow-making system was the first below the Mason-Dixon line.

Marsh Mountain is the earliest southern slope that still exists. Interest in winter sports blossomed in Garrett County in 1951, when the Deep Creek Lake–Garrett County Promotion Council was formed. The council funded initial development of the ski area and engaged the B&O Railroad to run ski trains to the slopes from Baltimore and Washington. The council still oversees the marketing of Garrett County's extensive winter offerings.

Heise and associates eventually purchased the slope as Recreational Industries, Inc. In the late sixties, a major base lodge, a chairlift, and added snow making were installed. Today, Wisp ranks as one of the region's largest resorts.

Always family run, Wisp maintained conservative management that emphasized slope improvements over real estate development. The resort prospered while others went bankrupt in an early seventies real estate slump. Today, Wisp claims the South's longest run. A new hotel/condominium project is modernizing the resort's base facility and adding sophisticated lodging opportunites.

Back in Canaan Valley, Barton says, Kober's aerial ski maneuvers really wowed the crowds: "Trick skiing like Sepp's just wasn't heard of."

In 1959, Barton decided to move Weiss Knob. With prodding and help from Kober and John Mathewson, the Larchmont snow-maker salesman, Barton located a site on another summit of Cabin Mountain, Bald Knob. Here the slopes were steep at the top and gentle at the bottom. The wind blew snow onto the slopes, and access was much easier. And like those running The Homestead in Hot Springs, Va., where Kober was simultaneously designing slopes, Barton was installing snow making at Weiss Knob. Both systems began operation the same winter, 1959–60.

Bob Barton's fondest memories of those Weiss Knob #2 years in the late fifties and early sixties revolve around Anita Louise Love. It seems Sepp Kober had met Anita Love at Stowe after arriving in America. Barton doesn't know whether Love came to Canaan Valley to see Kober or just to investigate the skiing, but he remembers her phone call and visit. The autumn before Weiss Knob #2 opened, Barton and Love were married. Later, when a ski school director for Weiss Knob didn't arrive as promised, the Louise Love Ski School was christened.

Beyond that, Barton has characterized the years that followed Weiss Knob #2's opening as "bitter" ones. Too much snow that first winter ruined business since severe weather conditions kept people away, and the Bartons moved to Richmond, Va., to work toward paying off their debts. Barton ran the slope by commuting, then leased and finally closed it. Barton attributes some of the difficulties to the state of West Virginia. Seeing the popularity of winter sports activity, the state was buying up land in the valley to develop its own ski areas. Nearby Blackwater Falls State Park, now a popular cross-country ski area, had opened a lodge expansion in 1957, and Canaan Valley State Park was the next step. Land condemnations by the state spooked investors and doomed Weiss Knob, Barton says.

The Bartons moved around a lot in the years that followed, mostly in Vermont and Pennsylvania, where Barton managed snow-making operations and ski rental shops for a variety of ski areas. The Louise Love Ski School debuted at many of those slopes. In 1972, Barton managed the opening operations of Alpine Lake ski area near Terra Alta, W.Va. The persistent entrepreneur, whose "dream was to be part of the ski areas I knew would open here," still lives in Canaan Valley and has operated the Weiss Knob Ski Shop since 1981.

Outside the Canaan Valley area, the years 1958 and 1959 were important ones. Two ski areas opened with the South's second and third snow-making systems. Neither exists now.

Shawneeland ski area opened in January 1958 west of Winchester, Va., becoming that state's first commercial ski area. Maryland contractor Don Lamborne had purchased 9,000 acres of land near Winchester in 1955 and opened Shawneeland for housing in 1956, a development that today has 500 homes. Realizing the growing interest in skiing sparked in the nation's capital by the opening of early slopes, Lamborne wanted to add skiing to Shawneeland. He approached a D.C. ski shop owner, and his resolve to open the slopes was stiffened by the fellow's rudeness. "He really made me mad," Lamborne says. "I said a ski slope didn't really seem all that difficult to build and the guy told me if I knew what I was talking about, I wouldn't be asking so many dumb questions. A month later, I had the slopes cut.

"When we opened in 1958, a year before The Homestead," Lamborne says, "we had snow making too. We hired a fellow, I forget his name now, from Manchester, N.H., and he came down for three months while we built a snow-making system." The area operated from 1958 to 1975, with rope tows and night skiing.

Lamborne attributes the ski area's demise to the greater drawing power of the newer, more sophisticated southern ski areas. He says the resort might have survived had it been built at Shawneeland's 3,000-foot elevation instead of at 1,000 feet, the bottom of the property.

The other new snow-making slope was Bald Knob, a resort started near Beckley, W.Va., by John McKay in 1958–59. Although Bob Barton's Weiss Knob #2 was located on Bald Knob in Canaan Valley, he couldn't call it that because McKay's slope, located on Flat Top Mountain, had nevertheless been named Bald Knob one year earlier.

McKay was convinced he could build a ski resort in the South. He had learned to ski in North Conway, N.H., while a student at Bowdoin College in Maine. "We would go on weekend ski trips, meet our dates from colleges in Boston, and ride the 'Toonerville Trolley' ski mobile lift at Mount Cranmore."

McKay developed Bald Knob with gusto—perhaps too much. He confesses that the area's "quite a few trails," two rope tows, quonset hut snack bar, and rental shop were too much too soon. The $250,000 investment, raised through the sale of stock, couldn't compensate for "the fact that there just weren't enough people then who knew how to ski." Even the snow-making system, which occasionally made yellow snow owing to cows in the high pasture, couldn't assure profitability. "Everybody lost a lot of money," McKay says. "We were just 15 to 20 years premature."

McKay's fondest memories are "teaching a lot of people to ski," and introducing one of the region's important ski personalities to the sport. "After we opened, little Bobby Ash would often hang around the area. His father was a school principal in Beckley so he'd often come out and help around the slopes. He never took a ski lesson, just watched others, put the skis on and taught himself to parallel ski. I'd never seen anyone do that." Ash had actually started skiing, untutored and without lessons, on powerline rights-of-way just after World War II. He later received patents for snow-making machines and helped design and manage some of the South's biggest slopes.

McKay's Bald Knob slope closed in the early sixties after three seasons. Today, McKay takes his grandchildren to the new WinterPlace ski resort, just a few miles from the old Bald Knob. Occasionally, someone reminds him that they still hold stock in Bald Knob.

By the late fifties, the SCWDC's Cabin Mountain ski area was feeling competition from a growing number of slopes. Attendance began to decline. Frank Louckes took over as manager after 1957 and improvements continued, including the last major construction at the area, an administration building and ski shop. But, Art Kurle says,

> "the hardy band of believers that had built and developed the area . . . was getting smaller. Skiing experienced explosive growth in the late fifties. . . . People who embraced the sport in those years were able to . . . enjoy unprecedented luxuries in lodging and uphill transportation. They tended to look down on rope tows, box lunches, outdoor privies, and sleeping in station wagons; they had completely bypassed the pioneer phase of skiing. Their preference was luxury."

The resort was a memory by the early sixties.

"Today," pioneer Kurle says, "there is no visual clue from Route 32 that the area even existed; all that really remains is our marvelous drift and a few scraggly apple trees."

Contributing to Driftland's demise was the early sixties opening of Skyline ski area, later Rappahanock, on the eastern flank of the northern section of Shenandoah National Park near Washington, Va. Ironically, former Cabin Mountain ski area administrator, and later Skyline manager, Frank Louckes discovered the site while looking closer to home on behalf of the SCWDC, whose members had been skiing the Davis, W.Va., slopes. Skyline soon became the SCWDC's "official skiing spot." Today, the slopes are overgrown.

After one year as ski school director at Weiss Knob, Sepp Kober had left for The Homestead, the first ski area in the South to combine total snow-making coverage, exceptional ski facilities, and accommodations. In short, The Homestead was the region's first ski area that could rightly be called a ski resort.

The Homestead added another variable: survival. Except for Heise's

Marsh Mountain, all the ski areas that predated The Homestead, even those that had snow making, do not now exist. When Wisp substantially boosted its snow making in the sixties, The Homestead's system was already covering the entire ski area and setting an example for the region, the nation, and the world. And Kober, in designing and helping build new slopes at The Homestead and the new Weiss Knob in 1959, had embarked on an involvement in southern skiing that lasts to this day.

After opening its ski slope in 1959, The Homestead, overnight, became the region's premier ski area, not only for the quality of its skiing and its unmatched accommodations, but also for expert ski instruction and area managment under the direction of Kober. Kober's expertise, his wide ranging publicity activities, and his involvement as a representative for lifts, ski equipment, and snow making made his influence felt, in one way or another, from Weiss Knob to all the southern slopes that followed. Kober's slope design, management, and consultation directly shaped at least ten southern resorts. His young associates went on to create other ski areas. One has said that "in the early years, there wasn't a new chairlift, rental ski, or ski school director that didn't go through Sepp."

The Homestead has been known since the mid-1700s, first as a mountain inn, then as the massive, five-star hotel and resort of recent times. In the mid-1950s, Daniel Ingalls, Homestead chairman of the board, and Thomas Lennon, corporate president, were noticing the resort's winter decline in business. Hearing of the increasing effectiveness of snow making, The Homestead's principals checked weather records and decided to add skiing. That decision, along with the investment of $1 million, was destined to make the resort a four-season draw. Larchmont was contacted to provide snow making, and Kober was recommended to the resort as a ski professional capable of running the ski area.

Now, as then, Kober's winter garb typically includes an elastic ear-warmer headband that seems to have swept his now gray hair permanently back like that of a ski racer underway. Born in Igls, Austria, Kober was the son of an Austrian hotelier. He followed his father into that profession, but Kober's true love was skiing. In 1938, he made the Austrian national ski team at age sixteen. Then came war, and Kober spent perhaps his most formative skiing years as a ski trooper in the German army.

After the war, Kober was certified as an instructor and coached the Spanish national team in 1951 and 1952 and the Norwegian team between

1954 and 1957. Then he went to Stowe, and following the lure of new horizons, came South to Canaan Valley in 1958.

At Homestead, Kober supervised the construction of slopes located in part on the Old Goat golf course, an early training ground for Sam Snead, later Homestead's golf pro.

Kober also led the way in what may be his profession's most important acheivement: the creation of the southern ski market. Homestead's "Come South to Ski" promotional campaign signaled the start of mass public awareness of skiing in the South. Traveling extensively, Kober met skiers at department and sporting goods stores that were just starting to stock ski equipment. He addressed fledgling ski clubs and interested groups of all kinds. There were television and radio appearances. Coupled with the appeal of The Homestead itself, Kober's reputation attracted scores of print media writers, netting wide publicity for the resort and the sport. At The Homestead, Kober helped establish the newspaper and wire service practice, now common, of running ski resort photos when slopes open or when major winter storms strike. Homestead became *the* place to ski, and Kober became known as the Father of Southern Skiing.

The first lift to the top of The Homestead's 550-foot vertical drop was a skimobile, a trestle with sledlike cars like the one then and still in use at Mount Cranmore in North Conway, N.H. Although the lift was picturesque, skiers tired of having to remove their skis to ride it, and in 1979, The Homestead expanded its slopes, installed a double chairlift, and increased its vertical drop to nearly 700 feet.

During this time, Tom Alexander brought skiing to North Carolina at Cataloochee, a cattle and guest ranch in Maggie Valley that is popular today as a warm weather equestrian center.

Twenty years after first considering a ski slope, with snow making being perfected, Alexander made his move. Like others before and after, Alexander saw skiing as a way to provide summer employees with year-round work.

The resort opened the weekend before Christmas 1961 with a 1,000-foot slope, a 300-foot beginner area and 3 inches of natural snow. For some reason, Alexander really didn't believe snow making would work at Cataloochee until he actually saw the guns spewing snow. In a major 1968 relocation, the resort was moved to a nearby site and a chairlift was built to serve slopes with a 740-foot vertical drop. Alexander died in 1972, and his son-in-law Rick Coker is now Cataloochee president and ski area manager.

A telling anecdote that Alexander left behind is worth repeating. By the early sixties, southern skiing was attracting attention elsewhere in the nation. Much of the national publicity was coming from northern writers taking the "backward South" story angle to an extreme. Derisive articles about the "Banana Belt of Skiing" and grits on the slope were common. One day, Alexander caught a photographer in the act of creating the ultimate unflattering photo of Cataloochee.

Alexander hadn't been paying much attention to the photographer until "someone noticed he had gone over in the pasture with my cattle and was trying to drive them over onto the slopes. When I got within hollering distance I asked him what he was trying to do. He said he wanted me to let down the fence and drive my cattle onto the slopes, saying it would make a real good photo for his magazine." Alexander evicted the fellow.

Prior to Cataloochee's opening, Tom Alexander consulted with Larchmont's John Mathewson, with Sepp Kober, and with Birmingham, Ala., dentist Dr. Tom Brigham. "Doc" Brigham, as he's known today in the ski industry, was a New Englander who came South. He brought along a passion for skiing that he never relinquished, and after reading an article in *Reader's Digest* about snow making and hearing about the opening of The Homestead, he decided that skiing was feasible in Dixie.

While maintaining his Birmingham dental practice and a professorship at the University of Alabama School of Dentistry, Brigham launched weather research and exploratory forays into the snowiest southern mountains. His name and vision were to become important forces in the development of the region's biggest ski resorts. Some say Brigham brought "big resort" skiing to the South.

When Cataloochee opened, Doc struck out for the northwestern North Carolina high country. He fondly describes memories of "sitting around a big fireplace, sipping brandy, planning the slopes, looking into the future. Tom would wax philosophical at times. In those days, Cataloochee was a romantic ranch in the high mountains. They raised their own beef and grew their own vegetables," Brigham remembers. "That was a wonderful time."

The year 1961 also saw Gatlinburg ski area open in Gatlinburg, Tenn. Gatlinburg started with a new wrinkle: the city purchased the land for the resort and entered into a long-term lease with the Gatlinburg Ski Corporation, an organization made up of local stockholders interested in bringing skiing to Tennessee. Plans were announced in January 1961, after a consultation visit by John Mathewson of Larchmont. The ski area opened in the winter of 1961–62.

After Gatlinburg's first few years of operation, another noteworthy European arrived on the southern ski scene, but via a different route than Kober and others from the Continent. During World War II, Rolf Lanz, a Swiss native, became intensely interested in the ski business. The war had interrupted the flow of tourists to Switzerland, though, so he contented himself working in his family's beauty shop and skiing in amateur races. In 1955, Lanz moved to Atlanta, where he continued in the hairdressing business. When Gatlinburg opened, he became a regular skier there, and eventually, staffing changes elevated Lanz to the position of director of skiing and the ski school.

Lanz attributes his entrance into southern skiing to being "in the right place at the right time." He built on his early familiarity with and love of skiing and learned about snow making "on the job."

In view of the impact of European ski professionals in shaping the ski industry in America, it is ironic that in Lanz's case, southern skiing shaped the professional, creating an offbeat opportunity to "realize a childhood dream." That strange turn of events created a new career for Lanz, who has now been at Gatlinburg for nearly twenty years. "That's why I'm so dedicated to Southern skiing," Lanz says.

A steep and icy access road created problems for Gatlinburg in the early years, so in 1972 developer Claude Anders built a 2.2-mile, 120-passenger aerial tramway. In 1975, Anders acquired the ski resort itself, which was by then dependent on the tram. The resort became Ober Gatlinburg, and the arrival of the Rode family, a German circus group, brought the Bavarian motif and "Oom pah pah" entertainment of the area's Old Heidelberg Restaurant. That same year, 1975, Anders added a 5-acre artificial "snow," Astro-Turf ski slope for summer skiing.

In 1981, Gatlinburg undertook a major $3.5-million expansion that added a huge, 62,000-square-foot crafts and shopping mall with an ice skating rink, and an open-air black bear display. In January 1982, two four-person chairlifts opened, along with three new slopes, among them the resort's longest run.

In 1962–63, the Blowing Rock Ski Lodge opened in Blowing Rock, N.C., becoming the first of the present six North Carolina ski resorts near Boone. Actually, the resort was under construction in 1961, and for a while the goal, unrealized, was to tie Cataloochee as North Carolina's first ski slope.

Interest in winter recreation near Boone was formalized in March 1960 when members of the Boone Chamber of Commerce announced that the following winter, commercial winter sports opportunities would be available. That same month, the snowiest winter on record in northwestern North Carolina was coming to an end, and National Guard teams were going home after ferrying food to snowed-in mountain residents. The chamber appointed a committee manned by Alfred Adams, W. H. Gragg, and Wade Brown to study winter tourism opportunities. The following year, Blowing Rock Ski Lodge was under way.

M. E. Thalheimer initiated the ski resort project with a letter requesting snowfall data from the Blowing Rock Chamber of Commerce. Thalheimer purchased land from Grover Robbins, and he engaged the L. A. Reynolds Construction Co., of Winston Salem, N.C., to grade the resort's slopes and parking lots and the V. L. Moretz & Son Lumber Co. for building materials. Thalheimer was president and manager of the resort.

The project succeeded in selling stock, but because the resort was required to hold all funds in escrow until $200,000 had been collected, major suppliers were "encouraged" to take payment in stock. Thus Herb Reynolds and D. Grady Moretz, Jr., became members of the board of directors and received stock in the ski lodge.

The slopes opened to huge crowds. "The rich and famous came in droves," Grady Moretz recalls. Kober associate Tony Krasovic initiated the mountain's ski rental and instruction programs. He was followed by Peter Reinecke, a German referred to Thalheimer by Kober.

In 1965, Blowing Rock Ski Lodge added night skiing, but funds remained scarce, and pressure for changes resulted in Thalheimer turning over management during the winter of 1965–66 to Jack Seibert. The slope lost more money, Moretz says, and the following year, Fred Allen became manager. In 1967–68, the slope was leased to International Speedway. There still wasn't enough money to pay the loans, though, so the bank called the note. Moretz, Reynolds, and Earl B. Searcy, all original directors, brought in Lloyd C. Caudle and W. Harold Mitchell and bought the Blowing Rock Ski Lodge by paying the bank. With the exception of Searcy, who died in 1971, and Herb Reynolds, who was replaced by his son Jon, the same group owns the resort today.

Under the revised ownership, the resort reopened in the winter of 1968–69 with "old wooden skis," a rope tow, and a new name—Appalachian Ski Mountain—suggested by the new director of skiing and former ski patroller, Eric DeGroat. Appalachian got its first double chairlift in 1969 and its second, along with a lodge expansion, in 1972. North Carolina's first quad chairlift was installed there in 1984, and another lodge expansion more than doubled the size of the first facility at Blowing Rock Ski Lodge. Unlike other high-country slopes, Appalachian relied on skiing rather than real estate, and so was able to avoid financial problems during the surge of resort bankruptcies in the early seventies.

Since 1968, Appalachian has experienced steady improvement, with conservative management under the guidance of Grady Moretz. The area has also been a backdrop for other distinguished careers in southern skiing. Ab Hayes has been day supervisor at Appalachian since the first days of Blowing Rock Ski Lodge. Chief engineer Frank Coffey of Tweetsie Railroad, a steam train theme park in Blowing Rock, N.C., installed the snow making at Appalachian, then went on to Hound Ears and Beech Mountain. Snow maker Hardin Greene has worked at many high-country ski slopes. When cold weather hit at Appalachian, he used to anticipate heavy snow making with the utterance, "I'm going to tilt the mountain tonight."

A significant event in the history of southern skiing occurred in 1968 when a long-haired accountant, Boone resident, and former ski patrol director at Blowing Rock Ski Lodge named Jim Cottrell met up with Grady Moretz. Cottrell, a Charlotte college instructor, was organizing a physical education course in downhill skiing. He aimed to bring students up to Appalachian on five weekends to be instructed for college credit. Moretz agreed, and that winter Jim Cottrell, his brother Jones, and a few other novice ski instructors initiated an independent ski school at Appalachian. In all, 114 students answered the call.

The following summer, Cottrell was living in Charlotte next door to a man named Jack Lester. The aging Lester sported a shaved head; an intense, charismatic, and driven personality; a flair for the dramatic; and a very interesting past. Newspaper and magazine articles a few years later would say that Atlanta native Lester was the first American to graduate from Australia's West Point, the first American commisioned in the Australian Army, the youngest stage director ever at the Grauman-Chinese Theater in Hollywood, a Vaudeville dancer, and a former manager for both Marilyn Monroe and the singing group The Ink Spots.

Lester, Cottrell says, had had a mild heart attack in Charlotte while managing show business tours, "and that's where he stopped." At some mall ski show, he'd met Clif Taylor, originator of the Graduated Length Method (GLM) of ski instruction, whereby skiers start on small skis and progress to longer ones. Lester was sold on the GLM idea, and that winter, at Beech Mountain, he was introducing former North Carolina Governor Terry Sanford to the sport using the short skis when the Austrian ski school director ordered him off the slopes over the public address system.

Lester was embarassed and mortified. His associates of the time today point to that one experience as motivating the frenetic, some say brilliant promotional efforts that characterized the years before his death in 1975.

When Lester met Jim Cottrell, the French-Swiss Ski College was born. Appalachian Ski Moutain was where Lester would build his ski school. He would show the arrogant Austrians that Americans would have American ski instructors. At the time, perhaps no one imagined how successful he would be.

The next winter, 1969–70, Lester and Cottrell launched their business from a card table in the Appalachian Lodge. They employed the group-booking concept that Cottrell had used the winter before, bringing in hundreds of college and school groups, church groups, even thousands of military personnel from the U.S. Army Special Forces, diverting Green Beret skiing students from Europe to North Carolina.

The army wanted to cut an injury rate of up to 65 percent among servicemen learning to ski in Europe. French-Swiss proved itself. "Out of a group 5,000 Green Berets," Lester said, "there was one fracture . . . In fact . . . if you'd been here last year, you could have seen a group of Green Berets drop from helicopters with 60-pound packs, put on skis and ski down the slope. This after one week of instruction for a group who had never been on skis before." Navy Seals, cadets from the U.S. Naval Academy and West Point, the Harvard racing team, Yale physical education classes, and thousands of others followed.

One year, over 100 separate institutions were giving academic credit for French-Swiss instruction. In one 48-hour period, French-Swiss gave over 3,000 ski lessons. And no wonder—Lester said his rates were "bringing skiing to the working man." For $8.50, a daily skier received ski rental, lift ticket, unlimited instruction, and a boot and binding clinic. For lengthier packages, three meals a day cost $5. In 1974, French-Swiss affiliated with the new Sports Award Program of the President's Council on Physical Fitness and Sports. The school awarded more of the patches for alpine skiing than any resort in the country. Lester was named the program's national director for skiing, and he and Cottrell were named program developers for the council.

Technically, French-Swiss is credited with bringing the GLM into the South. The same winter that French-Swiss started, Austrian instructor Eric Bindlechner brought GLM to Sugar Mountain, near Banner Elk, N.C., using the new Headway system from his previous post as assistant ski school director at Killington in Vermont, where GLM originator Clif Taylor had perfected it in the late fifties. Bindlechner's key role at Sugar in the mid-1970s included running one of the South's first ski schools affiliated with the Professional Ski Instructors of America (PSIA).

Meanwhile, Lester was doing the promoting. While some newspaper articles called him a huckster, others claimed he was a promotional genius. Without doubt, Lester put southern skiing and the French-Swiss Ski College on the map. Locally, though, his braggadocio rubbed some people the wrong way. Eventually, says an associate, "people who thought his claims were just hot air realized he was accomplishing what he said he would." Immodest, to say the least, Lester reveled when local newspaper and Chamber of Commerce representatives reversed their skepticism and praised him as the "magic promoter."

Whatever their feelings, no one could deny that when Lester brought Jean Claude Killy to Boone a week before the 1972 Winter Olympics in Japan, he accomplished a pivotal public relations coup in the life of southern skiing and the French-Swiss Ski College. Killy's first feature film, *Snow Job*, premiered in Boone during that three-day visit. Lester, resplendent in his silk ski pants, fur boots, and American eagle-embroidered sweater, was, with Killy, the center of a major media event. Killy returned in 1973, during his comeback, to race in North Carolina and elsewhere in America on the pro circuit.

In early 1974, Lester brought Lunar Astronaut Charles Duke to Boone to celebrate the fifth anniversary of French-Swiss. Later that year, Killy returned again to launch the ski season on the new "Magic Carpet" snowless ski slope that French-Swiss had purchased from Sky High ski area near Pinehurst. On that trip, Killy and Lester went to West Virginia to meet with representatives of Snowshoe ski area and Rossignol ski equipment. Killy was at the time a product representative for Rossignol and was about to become a promoter for Snowshoe. The resort's new Cup Run would be named one of his favorite slopes in the world.

Lester's eventual goal was to franchise the French-Swiss ski school nationally and internationally, starting with the ski school at Snowshoe.

However, he never realized his long-term plans. The following summer he underwent open heart surgery, and less than a year later, a massive heart attack killed him. Cottrell carried on, assisted by Mike Lamb, a Colorado instructor who arrived at Appalachian in the midseventies and later moved to Sugar Mountain after Eric Bindlechner left.

In 1976, Cottrell hosted the first North Carolina Winter Special Olympics. The next year, and every year since, the Southeastern Winter Special Olympics brings up to 200 physically challenged athletes from nine southern states to Appalachian for competition in downhill and, starting in 1981, cross-country skiing. The program has allowed representatives from the South to participate in three International Winter Special Olympics. In 1982, Special Olympics founder Eunice Kennedy Shriver attended the southeastern games. Cottrell in particular and French-Swiss in general have taken a prominent place in the field of ski instruction for the physically challenged.

When Jack Lester died, his style of promotion ceased at French-Swiss. The focus shifted from major media events to Cottrell's group marketing approach. Cottrell has expanded his advanced lesson program, a benefit of Appalachian Ski Mountain's new slope expansion. New too are group ski rentals at a French-Swiss shop south of Boone and complete group package planning. Why the extra service? "Some people take only one lesson, and that may determine whether they ever get on skis again." This attitude, sifted between Lester's promotions and Cottrell's year-round marketing to diverse groups, turned French-Swiss into one of the major creators of the southern ski market.

In 1964, several years before French-Swiss was formed, Grover and Harry Robbins developed Hound Ears Lodge and Club and opened a ski slope. That year, Hound Ears had North Carolina's first chairlift. The resort was for members and guests originally. Hound Ears Lodge is one of only two Mobil-rated, four-star ski resort accommodations in the South. After Hound Ears, Beech and Sugar mountain opened in Banner Elk and became the two largest ski resorts in northwestern North Carolina.

Surprisingly, neither Beech nor Sugar mountain was responsible for the first lift-served skiing in Banner Elk. In 1965, some enterprising hobbyists installed the first rope tow in this town that now calls itself the "Ski Capital of the South." Auburn and Nelta Andrews owned a shaded bowl that was becoming popular with sledders. Auburn had been a Lees-McRae College student during the first surge of North Carolina ski interest at Lees-McRae in the 1930s. Dr. Charles Wiley had the idea to buy a tow, sold stock to physicians, and used his Jeep to power the lift.

Later, the tow was powered by an Opel engine. Lights were installed, and skiing became popular. Local families and Lees-McRae College students "had a big time," Nelta Andrews says. One night while sledding, Dr. Wiley involuntarily became airborne then crashed, rolling onto the field with a sharp pain in his chest. He later told Auburn he'd have to remove that big rock out in the meadow. Andrews laughed, knowing there were no rocks. Wiley had slammed into a frozen "meadow muffin."

Later, the big ski areas opened. "The squirrels ate the tow rope; we just sorta faded out," Nelta Andrews now says. The old engine and pulleys still sit in the field.

In 1965, the building of Bryce Resort in Basye (rhymes with racy), Va., became another example of how European ski expertise fused with local interest to bring skiing to America, including the South. Around 1965, it's said, Paul "Pete" Bryce took a hard look at his family's mountain property, including a white frame summer hotel started in 1904 by his grandfather, and decided to make it pay. His goal became to create Virginia's third ski area.

Sepp Kober was called in to design slopes with names that recall the locally prominent illegal liquor business so common to Appalachia. The base lodge was itself originally called Moonshine Lodge when it opened in 1966. The resort had Virginia's first chairlift.

Kober's crew of former Homestead instructors handled the building and then initial running of the resort. The director was Othmar Mair, and Dieter Baer, another Austrian who also taught at The Homestead, ran the ski school. Baer now runs the ski school at the Maryland ski resort Wisp.

Bob Ash, the young Beckley, W.Va., skier who had frequented Bald Knob, ran the snow-making operation. Early on, Ash had started venturing to The Homestead. "We amazed the Austrians," he says. "We were red necks from Beckley." Later, Ash became a Homestead instructor before moving on to Bryce.

Just after Christmas during the resort's first winter, temperatures soared. To keep the slopes open for guests, Bryce bought truckloads of crushed ice and spread it on the slopes. The *WASHINGTON POST* ran the story.

In 1966, brothers Horst and Manfred Locher arrived at Bryce to comanage the ski school. Their journey brought them from New Zealand via a round-the-world boat cruise and a bus ride to the Virginia resort from Mexico. How did Horst Locher, now ski area and school manager, and Manfred Locher, now general manager, come to arrive at Bryce? "Sepp Kober helped us get here," Manfred says.

The brothers admit they came to America for employment and economic opportunities that didn't seem available in the crowded European skiing industry. Like the first 1930s wave of European ski immigrants in the West and New England and like Sepp Kober in the South in the 1950s, the Lochers were filling a void created when ski resorts blossomed and professional instructors and managers weren't available locally. "In the fifties," says Manfred Locher," skiing in the United States was young and American resorts had to bring in Europeans to staff ski schools. Some came to market lift equipment, but eventually, American ski instructors filled ski schools."

But the immigration didn't end with the Lochers, who themselves "brought in Gunther Jochl as a ski instructor." Jochl, who arrived in America in 1971, is now manager at Sugar Mountain in Banner Elk.

In 1969, Pete Bryce sold the resort to Joe Luter, and in 1975, Luter sold it to a group of Bryce property owners. Also in 1975, Horst Locher brought grass skiing from Europe to Bryce and America for the first time. In 1979, the World Grass Skiing Championships were held at the resort.

As Pete Bryce was planning his resort in 1965, Tennesseean C. P. "Bud" Edwards, III, was assembling a large tract of land near Mars Hill, N.C., and initiating the Big Bald development, now called Wolf Laurel. The resort was one of the earliest major western North Carolina recreational residential areas. Sheep have grazed on the high meadows in the area since the Civil War, and the last wolf packs in the state were located in the vicinity. The ski slopes opened in 1970–71. A double chairlift leading to an upper poma tow serviced the 700-foot vertical drop, and initial snow making was installed the in winter of 1972–73.

The tasteful intent of the developers showed initially in the hand-hewn log cabins that were constructed as accommodations by a crew of local craftsmen headed by Clay Jenkins, the resort's first employee. After economic woes in the early seventies, Georgian Fondren Mitchell took over as president of Bald Knob Development Corporation. The ski area has benefited, too, from the long-term commitment of Varden Cody, outside manager; Paul Bailey, lift manager; and John Goin, ski lodge manager. Colonel Tom Barr managed the ski area from 1974 to 1982, and Tim Walker, currently directing Wolf Laurel's ski school and ski patrol, has been with the resort off and on since the early 1970s.

Big increases in snow making since 1980 and the construction of a 1-mile intermediate slope, Wolf's Crossing, in 1983, have greatly expanded Wolf Laurel. In 1986, changes at Wolf Laurel are expected to yield further major expansion for the ski resort.

In 1966, High Meadows opened on a golf course near Roaring Gap, N.C. Developed with an inn/motel and restaurant by a group of investors, the small two-slope ski area is currently owned by three of the original developers, Clyde Reavis, Charles Swift, and C. B. Hughes.

Slopes were also cleared at Seven Devils in 1966, and the resort opened in the winter of 1966–67 as the high-country's third. Herb Reynolds developed the resort with early planning help from Gardner Gidley, a Winston-Salem designer affiliated with that city's Tanglewood development. For years low attendance and inadequate snow making plagued Seven Devils, keeping the resort closed or operating on weekends only. Reynolds' son Jon and Gardner Gidley managed the area in 1979–80, improving slope grooming and expanding the lodge.

Jon Reynolds now owns the resort and has taken his father's place on the board of directors at Appalachian Ski Mountain. Gardner Gidley's son Tom is marketing director. In 1983–84, the slope's name was changed to Ski Hawksnest, and in 1984–85, the ski area added a new rope tow and beginner area and the lodge was completely remodeled. Also that year, Ski Hawksnest became the site of the Nordic segment of the Southeastern Winter Special Olympics. The residential area around the slopes became the North Carolina town of Seven Devils in 1981, and townspeople passed a beer and wine referendum in 1985.

Also in 1966, Sapphire Valley ski resort, near Highlands, N.C., opened, as did Coonskin Park, a natural snow, municipal ski slope in Charleston, W.Va. Sepp Kober designed Sapphire, and Dieter Baer ran the area the first few years. In 1980, a new slope opened, boosting Sapphire's vertical drop to 425 feet. In the early 1980s, Sapphire Valley joined the chain of Fairfield resort communities, becoming Fairfield/Sapphire Valley.

Beech Mountain, then the largest of the South's ski resorts, opened in the winter of 1967–68. But by then, "the Beech" had been in preparation for seven years. In July of 1960, two Alabamans had taken a hike in Banner Elk that launched the dream. Ten years later, Beech and Sugar mountains would be the reality that both hikers barely glimpsed that drizzly, foggy summer day. Tom "Doc" Brigham and Serena "Chessie" MacRae met at 5:00 that morning in Linville at the Eseeola Lodge. Neither had ever been to the Pinnacles of Sugar, and after a drive to Norwood Hollow, the two set out on the climb. Some hours later, after struggling over irregular boulders, they reached a crag "and there unfolded a view," MacRae remembers.

At the time, Brigham didn't like all the boulders at Sugar. In March of 1960, Brigham, John Grenier, and two Boone residents, purchased an option on the "rockless" upper slopes of Beech Mountain from Bill Elder, and they formed a group to acquire the more than mile-high land. Ted Randolph, John Grenier, Joe Simpson, Chessie MacRae, and Doc Brigham together created a corporation and bought the summit that today claims the East's highest ski area.

By 1963, difficulties had arisen in financing the land. The Robbins brothers were at the time developing Hound Ears, and Brigham convinced Grover Robbins that the land at Beech would be a good next step. The brothers' firm, Appalachian Development, purchased the land in 1964. In 1966, Brigham was hired by the Robbins' Beech Mountain development group, the Carolina Caribbean Corporation. The idea was to develop Beech and a condominium resort on St. Croix and to attract clients who would purchase access to both.

Land sales went very well for a while. Prospective buyers were housed at Hound Ears and shown the site. By December 1967, the slopes were ready to open. Real estate sales were excellent in those early years, and through the early seventies, Beech maintained a position of leadership in the emerging southern ski industry.

When Brigham, along with Chessie MacRae and her husband George, left Beech in December 1968, they were able to join another group of interested ski developers that had already been put together. Property was being assembled on Sugar, and the second resort was already being planned. Brigham, who would later develop two more ski areas, overcame his earlier worries about Sugar's rocky character. "I've since learned to be content with rocks," he now says.

Retired Air Force General Alexander Andrews and Nashville, Tenn., banker and financier Albert Johnson purchased nearly 2,000 acres on Sugar's summit. George MacRae owned 900 acres, and together with land owned by Julian Morton and two Norwood Hollow farms, the parcels would become the next of North Carolina's "big two" ski resorts. The land was being assembled while Tom Brigham designed the slopes. Sel Hannah and Ted Hunter of Sno-Engineering, a New Hampshire ski area consulting firm widely used and respected in the South, approved the slope design, and construction began in early 1969.

The Sugar Mountain landowners incorporated on December 1, 1969, and the slopes opened for skiing on December 29. A young, former ski instructor at Homestead and snow maker at Bryce named Bob Ash came on as mountain manager in 1971. In 1974, Ash earned Sugar a prominent feature article in *Ski Area Management* magazine describing innovations he had instituted in creating Sugar's sophisticated snow-making managment system. Ash also hired Danny Seme as the South's first professional ski patroller.

Real estate sold relatively well, MacRae says. But financing became a problem in 1972, and just as it got worse in 1974, Sugar started a pedestrian village condominium complex, Skyleaf, that was supposed to be linked to the mountain's base by an aerial tram. That summer, Doc Brigham left his post as Sugar Mountain company president, in a conflict over goals and financing, and headed for his next project, wresting Snowshoe out of West Virginia's mountains. Brigham was replaced by E. Davison Potter, the developer of the tram plan. By 1974, says MacRae, Sugar was in financial straits.

The year 1974 was a low point for southern ski resorts. The St. Croix condominium development paired with Beech Mountain had bankrupted, "bleeding Beech Mountain white" and losing between $8 and $10 million for the parent company, Carolina Caribbean. Beech, Sugar, and many others, were experiencing unprecedented financial problems. The reasons were many. America's economy was reeling from the oil crisis, recession, and high interest rates, all factors that kept second-home buyers out of the resort real estate market. Without their bread and butter income from real estate, only skiing was left to fill the void for winter resorts. The slopes continued to make money, but it wasn't enough.

And as bad luck would have it, the winters of 1972–73 and 1973–74 were among the warmest and most snowless in more than twenty years, even in New England. The crisis in eastern America's ski industry made national news. At that time, Doc Brigham says, "you couldn't borrow money with a borrowing machine."

During those years, Beech Mountain's preeminent position began to erode. Bob Ash was mounting the superior snow-making program at the new and easily accessible Sugar Mountain. In 1972, Beech limited public access to its slopes, and Sugar's appeal increased. Something had to be done, and in fall 1974, Beech operations manager Fred Pfohl hired Bob Ash away from Sugar. In the winter of 1974–75, Eric Bindlechner was acting general manager at Sugar, and from Beech, the word went out that the resort would again focus on skiing. A 2-foot Thanksgiving snow storm launched the season.

In February 1975, Carolina Caribbean Corporation went bankrupt after nearly a year of successful skirmishing with creditors by its new president, Roger A. Hard, who had just overseen Beech's first acceptable ski season in three years. After the bankruptcy at Beech, Hard resigned to become president of Sugar Mountain Company, which had itself been without a company president since the fall of 1974.

Sugar's ill-fated Skyleaf project had required the resort to ask its creditors to suspend payment of interest and principal on loans. Despite Hard's presence, land sales still plummeted. The real estate market, according to then executive vice president Bob Quinlan, was in "a drought."

Quinlan, former vice president of finance at Beech, had made the move to Sugar with Hard. There, he was joined by his friend and University of Florida fraternity brother Hiram Lewis, Sugar Mountain's director of marketing. Both had worked together previously in Atlanta, and in 1975, Quinlan and Lewis left Sugar to start Alpine Ski Center, a now massive ski shop at the entrance to Sugar Mountain. The business rode the postbankruptcy rise of southern skiing then just beginning. Alpine expanded to include shops in Raleigh and Charlotte. In 1985, at the start of its tenth year, Alpine won the Southern Ski Retailer of the Year Award from Ski Industries America (SIA).

Alpine's success reflects the role of ski retailers in the rise of southern skiing. From the first few ski shop offerings of sporting goods and department stores in the 1950s, ski retailers have spread across Dixie. Some, like Princeton Ski Shop in Baltimore and Ski Haus in Rockville, Md., have won SIA retailer awards. Others, like the Sportin' Life, Tennis & Ski, Edelweiss Ski Haus, CMT Sporting Goods, Bair's, Ski Chalet, and Par 3 shops, are multistore chains in major cities. There are dozens of single independent shops, many at or near ski resorts. All help keep skiing visible across the Sunbelt.

An interesting slice of après-ski history preceded Alpine Ski Center's occupancy of the original building at Banner Elk. In the building, Bill Shephard, Joe Seme, now a Boone artist, and father Dan Seme, Sr., ran a "notorious" night spot called the Hub Pub Club. Dan Seme's son and Joe's brother, Dan Jr., later an associate of Doc Brigham, worked at the club as a bartender. His daytime work on the slopes at Sugar allowed him "to invite all the girls down to the club, and all the guys followed." A "happening place" resulted. Entertainment included a prefame Jimmy Buffet, poker-faced comedian Jackie Vernon, and the Kingston Trio. Avery County at the time was very dry. "We spent one Halloween on the roof just guarding the place," Dan Seme remembers with a laugh.

In 1976, Sugar Mountain changed hands. Atlanta developer Earl Worsham bought controlling interest in the resort in March 1976. In May, financial problems forced the resort to close, and by July, Sugar was open under the new management of Diversified Equities Limited, a Mississippi corporation. But creditors were still pressuring the company, and the following winter the slopes were leased to new operators, Blue Knob Recreation, Inc.

At both Beech and Sugar, resurgent ski operations, although profitable, could not offset the drain created by the still slumping real estate market. Bankruptcy resulted.

When Hard left Beech in 1975, the fate of the resort was uncertain. Luckily, sparked by the involvement of Hunter Furches, the Beech Property Owners Association secured a lease with the bankruptcy trustee to operate the ski area through the winter of 1975–76. Many property owners were instrumental in the arrangement, among them Robert Yelton, George Handley, Alan Holcombe, and French Moore, an Abingdon, Va., dentist who was active in the National Ski Patrol and later became Mayor of Abingdon. Fred Pfohl remained as operations manager, and Ash was again a consultant. For the winter of 1976–77, Ash stayed on, replacing Pfohl, and a five-year management contract for Beech was signed with Resort Management, Inc., under the direction of Colonel Norman G. Smith.

In the winters of 1976–77 and 1977–78, the cold and snow returned in record proportions. Under Blue Knob Recreation, Inc., Sugar Mountain's attendance was up dramatically in 1976–77. Ironically, the infusion of money to Blue Knob couldn't forestall bankruptcy for Sugar in 1977. In 1978, for $2.6 million, partners Dale Stancil and Ray Costin bought the resort, which became Sugar Mountain, Inc.

Conservative management followed. When Stancil and Costin took over, Gunther Jochl became general manager and is still running the ski resort today. Mike Lamb arrived from French-Swiss to head the marketing effort and continue Sugar's Professional Ski Instructors of America-member ski school. In his years at Sugar, Lamb became an oft-heard spokesman for PSIA—one reason why the organization's ski schools and clinics prevail in the South. Jochl took advantage of two back-to-back snowy winters to break the 100,000-skier mark. Under Jochl, the resort has become known for aggressive snow making, careful grooming, and November openings, including the South's earliest-ever starting date in the month of November: the second day. Attendance has since broken the 200,000 mark.

The resort was large when it opened and experienced few changes up until the late 1970s. Since Sugar was leased by Blue Knob, though, snow making has been expanded dramatically, the lodge has been substantially enlarged, the entire 1,200 feet of vertical drop—the greatest south of West Virginia—is lit for night skiing, and a new slope and lift take the skiing to an adjoining gap.

At the top of the new slope, Sugar's now diverse real estate and lodging development includes Sugar Top, a ten-story, 320-unit summit condominium started in 1981, then expanded, and finished in 1985. The massive structure created intense controversy, gained national news coverage, and in 1984, prompted the state of North Carolina to pass a ridge law regulating the size of buildings constructed on mountain crests. Also in 1981, Gunther Jochl purchased Volkl of America, the distributorship for the well-known West German ski manufacturer.

Adjacent to Sugar Top, the Sugar Ski and Country Club surrounds the lift on the new slope, offering slope-side outdoor hot tubs, other amenities similar to those at Sugar Top, and spectacular views. Together, the condominiums and country club represent the South's most controversial slope-side accommodations. In 1985–86, Sugar greatly expanded access to the top of the mountain by installing a second double chairlift to the summit.

In 1968, Renegade Ski Resort opened near Crossville, Tenn. That same year, a Boone Area Chamber of Commerce Committee was formed to plan a North Carolina Snow Carnival. The success of the January 1969 carnival prompted a change in its name in 1970 to Snow Carnival of the South, held that year in the second week of February because weather records showed greater average snowfall at that time. For at least two years, races at the event were sanctioned by the International Ski Racing Association. They were claimed to be the first professional races ever held in the South and in 1972 drew racers like "Spider" Sabich and Billy Kidd.

The carnival folded in the midseventies, primarily another victim of recession and hard times in the ski industry. Robert Bingham, developer of Adams Apple Racquet Club near Banner Elk, was president and prime mover behind the carnival.

The 1970–71 Ski Carnival of the South was dedicated to Grover Robbins, Jr., who died in March 1970. With his brother Harry, Grover Robbins had developed Hound Ears Lodge and Club and ski area, as well as Beech Mountain.

In the early seventies, a number of new ski resorts were born, in one case accompanied by one of the more tragic incidents in the history of southern skiing. The Jones family, residents of Mentone, Ala., since the 1940s, decided to open the East's southernmost ski area in 1970. Cloudmont was built on Lookout Mountain. The second night of snow making, the night before the resort was to open, a snow-making pressure pipe exploded, killing owner Jack Jones, Jr. His son Gary Jones has operated the resort ever since.

Georgia's only ski area was the dream of Larry McClure. Sky Valley opened in 1970 with a distinctive gabled base lodge on nearly 2,500 acres near Dillard, Ga. Dieter Baer directed the ski operation with his father Ludwig "Luggi" Baer, an Austrian instructor certified under Hannes Schneider, father of the "Arlberg method," which was the first widely practiced ski instruction technique using stem and parallel turns. Dieter Baer brought over his partner at Wisp, Ludwig Grimm, as well as other Austrians, in part to provide music at the lodge. The group helped inaugurate Oktoberfest at the Georgia town of Helen, which was remodeled into Alpine Helen to spark tourism. In 1978, Sky Valley incorporated.

The winter of 1970–71 also brought the opening of Mill Ridge, the sixth of the North Carolina high country's resorts. Begun by Buck Smith and Mill Ridge Developers, the resort floundered in 1973. It was then purchased by Ridge Community Developers, a corporation formed by Mill Ridge property owners, among them attorney L. T. Dark and Clyde Burke. The corporation sold resort amenities to the Property Owners Association, and the ski area was sold in 1979, and then again in the early 1980s to Lou Pitts. With expansions and good management by Pitts, Mill Ridge has grown to include a wide variety of slopes and a large ski resort atmosphere in a small, family setting.

Canaan Valley ski resort opened in the winter of 1971–72, but its origins went back to the early sixties when the state of West Virginia began acquiring land for Canaan Valley State Park on the site of Bob Barton's first Weiss Knob. That first year of 1971–72, New Hampshire native Uel Gardner was manager, the first of his many jobs in the South. His New England ski work had started in the 1950s and included ski patrolling, coaching, instruction, operation of ski schools, and stints as ski area manager at the Balsams Wilderness and Tyrol, both in New Hampshire.

The summer after the ski area opened, the golf course and cabins began operations. A massive guest lodge was completed in 1977. The state-owned facility is leased to Murray Dearborn, whose son Andrew became ski area manager at the tender age of eighteen in 1975. A year later, Canaan ski instructor and later ski school director John Lutz brought the Blind Outdoor Leisure Development (BOLD) program from Colorado and initiated the South's first and now largest ski program for the blind. Canaan's physically-challenged-skiing specialty extends to hosting the West Virginia Winter Special Olympics.

Ground breaking took place for Massanutten ski area near McGaheys-ville, Va., in 1970. John Hopkins started the resort and was joined by Del Webb Corporation, developers of Arizona's Sun City. The ski area was partially designed, constructed, and then finalized by Uel Gardner. After a brief dry run in early 1972, the resort became popular as Virginia's biggest ski area. Del Webb purchased the resort in 1974, then sold it to two local businessmen and North Carolinians B. Dale Stancil and Ray Costin, both still owners of major southern slopes.

Massanutten initiated a timesharing resort, Massanutten Village, in the late 1970s and was purchased by John Swaim in 1980. Under Swaim, Massanutten went bankrupt in 1983, was operated by a trustee during the winter of 1983–84, and was purchased by Eastern Resort Management in 1984.

By the time Sugar Mountain was operating in the early seventies, Doc Brigham had determined that West Virginia's Potomac Highlands held the South's best hope for a premier ski resort. With Danny Seme, B. J. Hungate, John Grenier, and others, Brigham acquired land near Slatyfork on evergreen-covered Cheat Mountain and set about creating Snowshoe, a resort that later advertisements would call "A Mountain Among Mole-hills." The peak is one of the southernmost limits of the snowshoe hare: thus the name. "We couldn't very well call the ski resort Cheat Moun-tain," Brigham says with a laugh.

The first year, 1974–75, lodging was nonexistent and the resort didn't open until January. Cup Run, then and now the slope with the region's greatest vertical drop, opened to rave reviews. But Snowshoe's repeated financial woes started that year with the realization that the resort quickly needed extensive on-mountain lodging. Added financing came from the state of West Virginia through Governor Arch Moore, and Snowshoe continued to develop, but it went bankrupt in 1976. With coal mining magnate Frank Burford, Brigham reorganized the resort and greatly expanded lodging on the slopes. Burford bought the resort shortly thereafter. Cold winters brought huge crowds, but cash flow problems still prevailed, requiring frequent new financing.

Snowshoe became a town in 1979 and in the early 1980s emerged as the region's number-one resort. Frenetic construction brought new lodging, restaurants, a conference center, and other amenities. New expert runs carried the slope total over thirty, including the Hawthorne slope equaling Cup Run's vertical drop. In 1981, Brigham left Snowshoe management to build Whistlepunk Village and Inn at the resort.

By the mid-1980s, Snowshoe's available lodging had exceeded slope capacity, causing crowding, and attendance had dropped. Massive investment in a valley golf development drained funds, and by 1985, the resort was again bankrupt.

For the winter of 1985–86, Danny Seme and B. J. Hungate returned. The Hawthorne slope was abandoned, its lift scavenged to refurbish Cup Run. The court has directed that Snowshoe be sold. Seme says the ski area's slopes could be substantially expanded and hopes the resort will be bought by experienced ski area managers with money to invest.

While Snowshoe was planning its winter debut in 1974, development started in Virginia on one of the region's most flawlessly created resorts, Wintergreen. The 11,000-acre mountain-top resort on the Blue Ridge came into being when BLM Associates introduced the property to Cabot, Cabot, and Forbes, a Boston developer of high-rise office parks. The group worked with Sea Pines to market the resort, and during the 1975 recession, Wintergreen became the property, through a southeastern subsidiary, of Bankers Trust Co. of New York City. In 1984, the bank sold the resort to Wintergreen Partners, Inc., a property owners corporation.

The initial slope system, then the latest contribution to the South by ski pioneer Sel Hannah, opened in the winter of 1975–76 with Clif Taylor, originator of the graduated length method of ski instruction (GLM), as ski school director. The resort made a major slope expansion in 1982. Its artfully designed highland slopes feature Virginia's only 1,000-foot vertical drop, designed and built by Uel Gardner, ski area manager since 1977.

By the time Wintergreen added its beautiful Wintergarden spa complex in 1985, the resort had become known as one of the region's major, perhaps best, ski resorts. An absence of financial woes, elegant facilities, and scrupulous slope maintenance have made Wintergreen a premier four-season destination.

Cascade Mountain, Virginia's newest ski area, opened in 1977 near Fancy Gap, a Blue Ridge Parkway access point easily reached on Interstate 77. Dewey Belton purchased the Cascade land in the early 1970s and started Scenic Developers, Inc. The resort opened for skiing in January 1977, a year after the ShoreMount Corporation had acquired Cascade through foreclosure. In 1984, Cascade Mountain Corporation purchased the ski area from ShoreMount.

In 1980, North Carolina skiing took on an agricultural angle when cabbage farmers Gene Head and Ricky James opened Ski Scaly in Scaly Mountain, N.C. The area, almost on the Georgia line, was intended to provide winter work for summer farmhands. Ski Scaly, its slopes entirely on a farm, is one of only a few ski areas in the nation funded partially with loan's from the Farmer's Home Administration. In 1983, the Heads became sole owners of the four-slope ski area.

The 1980–81 season was pivotal for southern skiing. Snow droughts in the North and West and a cold, average snow year in Dixie created wide visibility for the sport. Network morning news programs were saying the South had the best skiing in the country. That same year, the infant High Country Host organization in northwestern North Carolina launched its innovative skiing promotion program. Among its efforts was a toll-free ski report.

Certainly southern ski resorts would have financial woes after 1980, but that winter showed the strength of skiing in Dixie and the preeminent position of North Carolina's high-country cluster of slopes. Doc Brigham's first two big ski resorts, coupled with four others and supplemented by strong warm weather tourism, were indeed making good.

By the early 1980s, Brigham's attention was again turning to new possibilities. Danny Seme recalls Doug Keith suggesting that they get together and build another ski area after leaving Snowshoe in 1981. Seme turned to Doc and asked, "Do you think you have another one in you?" Doc replied, "Yeah, I guess I have one more."

"That carpetbagging dentist" as one West Virginia mountain newspaper called him, then purchased land on Job Knob, near Harmon, and with Danny and Carol Seme, Doug Keith, and B. J. Hungate opened a road and slopes for Tory Mountain in 1982. The name derived from a group of British loyalists who supposedly found refuge there during the Revolutionary War.

As yet unrealized plans for Tory include a vertical drop of 1,500 feet and an eighteenth-century European-style pedestrian village. Brigham continues his efforts to finance Tory. Seme says the wait has only helped. "We don't want a plan that won't work. We're not going to do Tory Mountain the wrong way."

A second major ski area on Cheat Mountain debuted beside Snowshoe in December 1983. Silver Creek's eleven north-facing, wide-open slopes and the futuristic lodge that began partial operation in the second year were an attractive alternative to Snowshoe. In 1985, bankruptcy forced developers John Kruse, Leonard Jackson, and Edward Davis, all of American Resort Services, to yield ownership to the Federal Savings and Loan Insurance Corporation (FSLIC) as receiver. Kahler Corporation subsidiary Ski Resort Management Corporation was hired to manage the resort for 1985-86. Bill Bozack, who oversaw ski resort construction for Sno-Engineering, the New Hampshire consulting firm, remained in his three-year position as ski area manager.

When the decade-old Canaan Valley, W.Va., resort community of Timberline opened ski slopes in 1982, a rope tow served the lower third of runs that reached to Cabin Mountain's evergreen summit. Sno-cat skiing was offered for higher slopes, and then the ski area closed, never having installed the first chairlift to the top. The Allegheny Properties development of David Downs, owners of Timberline, with slopes designed by Fred Soltow, is stirring investor interest and may complete its trail and chairlift plans in the next few years.

West Virginia gained its most recent major ski area in 1982, complete with an unheard-of Mountain State feature: interstate highway access. WinterPlace, at Flat Top, W.Va., had been the dream of a number of ski enthusiasts for some time. The early Bald Knob ski area is close by, and the eyes of locals Bob Ash and Jerry and Sam Laufer had often wandered to the mountain's slopes. Ash and the Laufers purchased land for the resort, Ash designed the slopes, and in 1982 Highland Properties acquired the land and WinterPlace took shape under the management of Greg Confer, Mike Cline, and Don Everhart. Improved by increments, Winter-Place promises to be a successful and exciting ski area.

In 1982, Tri-South brought Sepp Gmuender and Paul Bousquet to Beech Mountain. Gmuender, a native of Switzerland, was former manager of Ski Windham in New York. Bousquet, a former general manager at Killington, came south from Bousquet ski area in Massachusetts, which had been started by his parents in 1932 as one of the nation's earliest ski resorts and was the first destination for early ski trains from New Haven, Conn., to the Berkshires.

Together, Gmuender, as ski area manager, and Bousquet, as public relations director, revitalized Beech. Slopes were regraded, massive snowmaking improvements were made, and a new lift was added and old ones overhauled. The new management also started the mountain's popular Winterfest.

Bousquet moved to New Hampshire's Loon Mountain in 1985, the same year liquor by the drink passed a referendum on Beech, then the highest town east of the Rockies. The newly wet resort attracted a number of nightspots, becoming the ski resort nightlife draw in the high country. Gmuender stayed when the resort was sold to North Carolinian Ray Costin in early 1986. The new owner plans growth for Beech, now known as a strong competitor to Sugar Mountain.

Without good ski instruction, ski areas might never have become economically feasible. The certified Austrians and other Europeans were first. Then Americans, like Dick Heckman at Cataloochee, began teaching and affiliating with national organizations like the Professional Ski Instructors of America (PSIA), the recognized leaders in American ski teaching. Weathering long drives to New England for instructor training, southern teachers became intensely professional. Today, PSIA Region 4, which includes the South, is the organization's largest and most active unit. Now PSIA training and tests are regularly held throughout the region. Independent schools such as the French-Swiss Ski College and Sepp Kober's staff of Europeans add to the high quality of ski teaching in the Southeast.

While new resorts were sprouting and old ones evolving, the ski industry in the region was getting organized. In 1961, a southeastern ski area organization started with Doc DeRoches of Pennsylvania's Laurel Mountain as president and Sepp Kober as vice president. Pennsylvania left the group, and in 1964, the Southeastern Ski Areas Association (SESAA) was finalized, with Cataloochee's Rick Coker as president. Sepp Kober, Murray Dearborn of Canaan, and Uel Gardner have since served as presidents.

In 1977, SESAA launched the southeastern ski reporting service. The program was an offshoot of the first ski reporting service, founded by Frank and Girtrud Ellis in the early 1950s in Connecticut. The telephone ski report service grew out of a radio program Frank Ellis did for WTOR in Torrington, Conn., in the late 1940s. By the midseventies, the service had grown nationwide. When Ellis died in 1977, his service ended, and the SESAA replaced it that December. In the years that followed, Tom Lanier has become the voice of southern skiing on dozens of radio stations. The service also reports to newspapers and has been standardized by SESAA to remedy early ski report abuses that the organization felt harmed the ski industry.

States began ski area associations. North Carolina was first, in 1977, with Rick Coker as president. Later presidents were Grady Moretz and Gunther Jochl. The group worked effectively with the North Carolina state legislature to pass the South's first Skier Safety Act in 1981. Local legislators Pinky Hayden, David Diamont, and Donald Kincaid worked with ski association members Bob Ash, Jim Cottrell, Gunther Jochl, Grady Moretz, Tom Barr, and North Carolina Attorney General Rufus Edmisten, among others, to pass the bill.

The West Virginia Ski Areas Association was formed in 1983, with WinterPlace general manager Greg Confer, formerly of Beech and Mount Tom, Mass., as its first president. The West Virginia state legislature passed a Skiing Responsibility Act during the winter of 1983–84.

From these regional organizations, Rick Coker and Grady Moretz have gone on to serve on the board of directors of the National Ski Areas Association. That organization was formed in the early sixties with Sepp Kober and Tony Krasovic of Blowing Rock Ski Lodge on the first organizing committee.

Few organizations have promoted ski safety in the South as effectively as the National Ski Patrol. From the start, skiers familiar with first aid patrolled the areas, but the SCWDC was the region's first formal connection with the National Ski Patrol System (NSPS), now the world's largest winter rescue organization.

The National Ski Patrol was the first national ski organization to spread into the South. Much of that early history can be traced in the travels of Keith Argow and, as he puts it, the "twenty other people who really made the difference."

In the early sixties, Argow was an SCWDC ski instructor at Skyline, a now defunct ski area in northern Virginia that was popular with the club. At the time, the SCWDC's patrol efforts were part of the Potomac Section of the Southern Appalachian Region of the NSPS. Gatlinburg requested patrol assistance and when no one responded, Argow became a Patrol Examiner from his new base with the U.S. Forest Service in Atlanta. He set in motion the training the South previously lacked. Patrol activity focused on Cataloochee, Hound Ears, and Blowing Rock Ski Lodge with contributions by pioneering patrollers like Dave and Lynn Dillard, Carl Lathrop, Eric DeGroat, Roger Bollinger, and Jack Britt. In 1964, the Ski Patrol formed the Southern States Section of the Southern Appalachian Region of the Eastern Division of NSPS. Argow, transferred from the Potomac Section, was the new section chief.

By 1967, so many new resorts and patrols had emerged that the Deep South Region of the Eastern Division was formed. The region's two sections were Carolina Highlands and Western Carolina. By 1970, Harry Pollard, Jr., soon to be national director of the NSPS, had visited the region and knew of its phenomenal growth. In 1971, the South acheived division status. Argow was its first director and the Southern Division was the first in the nation to join a ski area operator's association.

In the beginning, Argow says he was pleased that the South was in the hinterlands and there were no national figures "looking over my shoulder. Things were informal and we had a 'testing as teaching' perspective. Most early patrollers were uninspired by the beauracracy and wanted to be insulated from it."

Today the Southern Division is hardly insulated. In 1980, Sugar Mountain patrol leader Sherry Perry became the nation's first woman to be named Outstanding Professional Patroller of the Year. Dr. Harwell Dabbs, a former Southern Division director, is the designer of a splint that uses skis. The Dabbs splint is a Ski Patrol catalog item.

Southern patrollers point with pride to the Benbow family as the best example of regional commitment to the Ski Patrol. Charles and Doris Benbow's entire family are senior ski patrollers, a few are patrol directors and winners of numerous awards. Charles is a former division director. "They're legendary," says Argow.

The first Nordic Patrol was organized in 1972 in Gatlinburg for the Great Smoky Mountains by Lynn Pace, Tom Moss, and others. In 1984, Pace was the first southerner to be named National Outstanding Nordic Patroller of the Year. A patrol was started at Shining Rock in 1979 by Tom Thomas, Carl Mimms, and others, and the High Country Nordic Patrol was formed in 1983. With a developing Nordic contingent, the

Southern Division initiated its own winter mountaineering course at Mount Rogers. Each February, dozens of downhill patrollers switch to skinny skis.

Like the Nordic Ski Patrol, cross-country skiing in the South developed only recently. Before the midseventies, Nordic skiing in the South was virtually invisible. The late seventies' snowy winters gave the sport a spark of popularity. Then the snowiest southern summits became the focus, and "skinny skiers" realized that high elevations offer good skiing.

Rental cross-country skis were available at some metropolitan outfitters as early as the midseventies, but mountain rentals didn't become plentiful near ski sites until the late seventies. Among the first to offer them were New River Outfitters and Footsloggers in Boone, N.C., and Trans-Montane Outfitters in Davis, W.Va. In North Carolina in 1978, John Elder created the South's first on-site cross-country ski center when he marked trails, rented skis, and offered lessons on the Elder's mile-high meadows atop Beech Mountain.

By 1980–81, Footsloggers and their affiliates, High South Nordic Guides, and New River were both offering tours and lessons, some by trained Eastern Professional Ski Touring Instructor (EPSTI) teachers. Canaan Valley State Park had its first cross-country center. In the winter of 1981–82, White Grass Ski Touring Center opened in Canaan Valley and Elk River Ski Touring Center debuted near Snowshoe. That year, White Grass and New River Outfitters sponsored the region's first instructor training courses by the Nordic PSIA and Cataloochee staged its first telemark race.

Some of the growing appeal of telemark, or cross-country downhill skiing at southern slopes can be traced to Cataloochee. Richard Coker, Jr., one of the resort's second generation of Cokers, was among the first southerners to become proficient at the old telemark turn, a graceful cross-country move popular before Hannes Schneider revolutionized the sport after World War I. Cataloochee's 1981 telemark race was the region's first and the start of a yearly series of races held across the South. Another Cataloochee telemarker, Keith Calhoun, won the 1982 North American Telemark Championships in Crested Butte, Colorado.

In the winter of 1982–83, High South Nordic Guides received the Tennessee cross-country concession at Roan Mountain State Park. Besides owners Steve Owen, Ken Johnson, Jeep Barrett, and Betsy Johnson, instructors included Hart Hodges—grandson of Governor Luther Hodges, who had supported early skiing on Mount Mitchell—and James

Randolph—son of Alabaman Ted Randolph, who had been involved in the development of Sugar Mountain.

That same year, the Richwood, W.Va., Chamber of Commerce, the U.S. Forest Service, and interested skiers launched Richwood Winter Adventure. The enterprise marked and maintained extensive Nordic trails in the Cranberry Backcountry, published a map, and installed a 24-hour telephone snow report.

Promotion of the fine cross-country skiing around Richwood has become a priority of local enthusiasts like Dr. Clemente Diaz, who practices in Richwood and is a U.S. Nordic Ski Team physician. With the founding of the Richwood Ski Club in 1981, visibility for cross-country soared. Skiers like Kitra Burnham, Tim Coffman, Mike Marshall, Jorge Hershel, and others have offered educational and economic benefits to their town and have offered Nordic skiers the South's best-marked National Forest trail system.

Richwood, like Garrett County, Md., is among the South's best examples of community involvement in both downhill and cross-country skiing. Some Richwood residents, like Bronson McClung and Mayor Hyer Sutton, have been voicing support for a downhill ski area near the town for years. Declining mining and timber industries are prompting the focus on tourism. In 1985, the town voted to hire a consulting firm to study nearby sites, and future development of a downhill or cross-country ski resort seems possible.

By the mid-1980s, a new North Carolina ski resort was underway in Banner Elk. While helping create Beech and Sugar mountains, General Andrews was acquiring land under the spectacular conical summit of Hanging Rock, the prominent peak seen from Sugar Mountain. The resort hasn't been named but is being called Diamond Ridge for planning purposes. The ski area is expected to use the new, high-speed detachable chairlifts. Development will proceed slowly, with an opening possible in the late 1980s. With close to 200 acres of skiing and a 1,700-foot vertical drop planned, the resort could be the largest in the region if fully developed.

Andrews' associate Bob Ash, who designed the resort, is now head of his own snow-making company, Snow Storms, Inc. Ash's snow guns are in wide use in North America and have been chosen for the 1988 Winter Olympic Alpine events in Alberta.

Southern skiing's future looks bright. With continuing improvements in snow making and grooming, resorts are better able to weather periods when Mother Nature doesn't cooperate. Even a few cross-country ski areas may soon have snow making.

West Virginia in particular is boosting Nordic skiing with fine state park ski centers. They seem likely to improve as spas and amenities are added. Further south, cooperation between the U.S. Forest Service, the National Park Service, state parks, and skiers needs to grow to realize the potential of places like Roan Mountain, Mount Rogers, Mount Mitchell, and sites along the the Blue Ridge Parkway.

Elsewhere in the nation, large downhill and Nordic ski resorts are located on public land. The snowiest southern summits are government owned, but overseers have resisted development for downhill skiing, perhaps wisely. For that reason, development of low-impact cross-country trails should be a priority in construction budgets. Nordic skiers' growing willingness to pay user fees may help in developing untapped southern sites beyond their limited budgets for recreational improvement. Maryland's state parks in Garrett County are an example of skier trail fees at work.

Meanwhile, conservative management is improving the stability of southern downhill resorts. Dietar Baer of Wisp speaks for many when he says, "resort and real estate mismanagement account for more southern ski resort bankruptcies than the weather or climate." Danny Seme has a similar and wry perspective: "Southern skiing's past problems haven't been with climate or equipment, they've been with management. When you're dealing with Mother Nature, you better be prepared. Experience is the key. Beech, Sugar, Snowshoe. These resorts were southern pioneers. In the Old West, not all the pioneers made it."

Al Traver, a New Englander and early 1970s administrative director of Sugar Mountain Co., points out that "the need to develop lodging and services in isolated places required massive investment in southern resorts that wasn't needed in New England, where summer lodging already existed."

"Even during the gas crisis and the bankruptcies," says Bob Ash, "the ski operations at Beech and Sugar and the others were making money. It was real estate that was losing the money. Without skiing, the slopes that got into trouble would have floundered a lot sooner."

The insurance crunch, too, is threatening ski and recreation areas everywhere, not just in the South. Skier safety laws notwithstanding, lawsuits and large settlements are making liability insurance prohibitively expensive. (Hound Ears decided to remain closed one recent season, rather than pay for insurance.) And lift ticket prices rise with insurance rates.

Some ski area associations are exploring self-insurance, but the solution may lie in legislation and in skiers taking responsibility for their own actions. "Be aware, ski with care" should be the motto of every skier.

One trend that is improving the health of Dixie slopes is incorporation by ski resort communities. Although it has at times been controversial, many ski resort villages are becoming towns. The trend is to help create an enforceable tax base for better roads and services, control development, and allow alcohol sales where surrounding populations do not share the lifestyle of many winter and summer visitors. A lot of the new year-round residents of the mountains are attracted to the resort towns by the communities' urban perspective on issues like alcohol and entertainment. Incorporation illustrates another impact of ski resorts on the mountains: besides salaries for local workers, the resorts have brought a strong tax base to many mountain counties.

Change is coming to the southern Appalachians, and sophisticated ski resorts and strong warm weather tourism are making the biggest southern slopes increasingly similar to the nation's more heralded ski areas. For too long, the many skiers of America's other ski regions have thought that southern skiing lies outside the mainstream. "You mean you can ski down there?" is still the reaction of many. Today, southern skiing has come of age, with a particular set of problems and a colorful history of involvement in the larger story of skiing in America. That past even includes Howard Head's creation of the first metal/synthetic skis in Baltimore in the late forties and early fifties.

America's greatest number of potential skiers reside in the South, and resort operators in the North and West are realizing that the region's potential is maturing at southern slopes. Dixie cities like Miami, Atlanta, and Washington, D.C., claim the biggest ski clubs in the nation. "The South has the strongest growth market for skiing in the country," says Jim Branch of Sno-Engineering, Inc., the New Hampshire ski area design and consulting firm.

The rest of the country is also realizing the value of snow making. Even the northern snowbelt has winters of poor snowfall. Snow making is the answer, and resorts nationwide can thank the South for today's technology. "If it hadn't been for early interest and support by southern resorts, snow making and skiing would not be where they are today," says Joe T. Tropeano, of the early snow-making company, Larchmont. "For that, the South deserves national credit."

Skiing in Dixie is an impressive achievement of will. The ranks of those who made the sport happen run into the many thousands, from devoted 1930s ski clubbers searching for snow and sleeping in station wagons, to intrepid Austrian and American professionals struggling to live their sport in Appalachia's often unstable economy, to ski area managers weighing the decision to start the snow guns.

The existence of major ski areas in the South represents unprecedented vision and economic risk. Skiing came South on the dreams of true believers.

Getting There

WINTER recreation can be best just after a natural snow storm. Often, the best trips occur when a storm strikes while you're at your destination. Whatever the particulars, travelers in the highest Appalachian mountains face active snowfall, winding roads, and high elevations. The combination requires preparedness, especially for Sunbelt motorists who rarely drive in the snow. Where skiing and winter hiking are concerned, safety may be most important before you arrive at the trailhead or ski resort.

Preparation should start before you leave home. No doubt countless skiers have ventured into the mountains ready for snow only to find dry pavement. That situation is not nearly as frustrating or dangerous as being unprepared and facing a blizzard. Granted, you may encounter very average temperatures. Then again, weather conditions may be extreme. In the latter case, there is no substitute for the right pretrip auto maintenance, which should include a tune-up and an oil change. When the temperature drops, warm weather oil turns to glue in your engine. Replace it with multiweight oil such as 10w/30. The oil change will also rid your engine of moisture that can freeze in a colder climate. Moisture can also build up in your gas tank, causing stalling or a frozen fuel line. Use a can of dry gas to carry this moisture through your engine, and keep your tank more than half full to help prevent condensation. Be careful, too, not to introduce new moisture into your tank. During a snow storm, choose the gas nozzle on the sheltered side of the pump. Snow caked in the nozzle on the windward side may fall into your tank. Moisture can also freeze inside your door handles, locking you out of your car. Use a lock deicer or lubricant before you reach the high elevations.

Make sure your antifreeze is rated to −50 degrees, and have a reliable battery. When the mercury dips to 10 below zero, an old battery that provides a good charge at sea-level temperatures may cease to function. Some skiers in this situation stay two or three days longer than planned.

Traction is the next concern. Luckily, front-wheel drive is fast replacing rear-wheel drive on most foreign and domestic cars. Even going uphill, a correctly equipped and driven front wheeler easily outmaneuvers all but four-wheel drive vehicles, and many ski enthusiasts are buying the down-sized American four-wheelers or the popular Japanese and other foreign makes.

Whatever your drive train, snow tires give better traction than standard radials, but in very snowy weather, chains are the ultimate accessory. Most southerners won't often need snow tires, so consider a pair of the new radial tire chains for the blizzard that inevitably arrives when you least expect it. Compared to heavy link chains, the aircraft-cable units are much easier to install and adjust and are less likely to damage your car, less expensive, and very effective. Practice installing your chains at home. A snowy roadside is no place to learn. Chains cost decidedly less when purchased before you reach ski country. Mountain retail and rental outlets get top dollar.

For safety, there is simply no alternative to snow tires or chains. In bad weather, state patrols or mountain police departments routinely require this equipment. Emergency agencies must ensure that the single road to an isolated ski resort community is not blocked by ill-equipped cars.

Suggestions for winter driving techniques all seem ambiguous, in part because experience is the key. But don't be discouraged. Understanding the dynamics of snow driving, even in theory, will help.

Proper speed depends on the condition of the road's surface and on your traction. Generally, cars with good tires on plowed but snow-covered roads will have sufficient traction to drive at reasonable speeds. Straight, uncongested roads in this condition can be safely driven at 20 to 40 mph. Curves should be taken cautiously; brake well before turning the wheel, and use only gentle pressure on the brake pedal or, preferably, brake by gearing down.

The smoothest, safest braking is accomplished with the engine. Manual transmission vehicles slow down better using this method, and because the clutch and gas can be feathered, they also are easier to get moving in snow. If you are driving with an automatic transmission, downshift manually so the transmission won't shift unexpectedly, slowing you down so abruptly that it causes a skid.

The oft-heard driving rule "If you skid, steer in the direction of the slide" is trite but true. And be prepared to react the same way when the car slides back in the other direction. In winter driving, one good skid deserves another.

That rule, though, is the only the beginning of a good theory of winter driving. Accidents and bottlenecks on banked snowy curves almost always happen because slow-moving high-side cars break traction and slide down into climbing cars. To avoid sliding into oncoming cars, vehicles on the high side should straddle the high edge of the road. This levels the car out and prevents a slide by gripping deeper snow. If low-side cars slide off to the edge of the plow line and into snow, they too frequently get better traction and keep going.

Sensitivity to the angle of the road is as important as awareness of the attitude of your car. A vehicle traveling straight on a flat road covered with solid ice, even down a hill, will not slide as long as the wheels keep turning. All too often, the driver who sees ice tries to slow down or change direction on the slick surface, causing a spin. If the car had been allowed to travel unimpeded over the ice, nothing would have happened.

On a curve, of course, a car's inertia can cause a skid, even without braking. When you come to a curve in the snow, slow down before you reach it, then straddle the edge of the road through it with only the engine slowing you down. Trouble usually occurs when the road is clear and a driver encounters a snow-covered stretch in a shaded curve. If this happens, brake hard on the dry pavement before the curve, then keep the car stable, changing direction smoothly and as little as possible, until you're again on dry road. Most of all, anticipate ice in shaded areas, and be especially alert for such areas in mountainous terrain where cliffs may keep sunlight from reaching the road.

Motorists can lose control on even gentle curves when surprised by ice. If a curve is gradual enough, it is possible to "pretend" that a bend in the road doesn't exist. With proper positioning before the turn, and compensation after, you can often steer straight through the apex of the turn, quickly altering your direction when you emerge on the dry pavement.

A common mistake for inexperienced snow drivers is driving too slowly. Trying to climb a hill without momentum can break traction, causing spinning wheels and a precarious journey back down. Likewise, going down too slowly can exceed the grip of your tread and cause a sliding, accelerating loss of grip. Remember, if you start to skid going up or down, never lock your brakes: an uncontrollable slide will result. Pump your brakes, but keep your tires rolling. That movement creates steering control. If you must, steer into a snow bank or other buffer before gaining too much speed.

Going up a hill, calculate the speed you need and if you need to accelerate, do so on the flat before you reach the upgrade. Using a higher gear on the way up may also prevent spinning wheels.

Once you're on a snowy hill, you are committed. Whatever happens, do not simply stop and block traffic while your passengers mill around wondering what to do or trying to push you slowly uphill. At best you'll tie up traffic; at worst another car could hit you. Have enough consideration to pull over and let more capable vehicles and drivers get by. One poorly equipped or inexperienced person can turn a snowy hill into a multihour, life-threatening traffic jam.

This courtesy also applies to vehicles wanting to pass. Don't presume to set the pace for five cars behind you, especially if you rarely drive in snow. Mountain locals often travel great distances to work, and many have the cars and experience needed to go 45 when you're driving 10. Don't be a belligerent, crawling roadblock. Pull over at a safe place. In general, in fact, if you aren't confident that you can handle conditions, get off the road. If you aren't keeping up with traffic, take a break and let others proceed while you wait for better conditions.

Driving in deep, untracked snow, more than any other case, requires speed to keep up momentum. A slow driver will go nowhere in unbroken snow, where the main problem is getting started. Often, a vehicle can negotiate deep snow, especially downhill, once it gets going. This situation is one of many where a shovel is handy. Even a short runway cleared in front of the tires can be enough to get the wheels rolling. Many times, you'll also have to dig compacted snow out from under the vehicle's chassis.

Once you've gotten moving, stay in a lower gear at higher rpms to maintain momentum. A high gear will have less torque available if you hit a drift and begin to bog down. If that happens, having to shift to a lower gear will further slow you down. Only sufficient speed can carry you over the deep snow that will build up under your car. If you bog down, you may have to dig out again.

If you begin to slide in deep snow, keep your speed up as you steer toward the skid. Simply keep going and regain road position further on. Of course, if other traffic is approaching, you may just have to slow down and risk getting stuck again.

Winter driving, like skiing, is dynamic, so expect that you're going to skid and weave. The successful blizzard motorist, like the good skier, is one who works with, not against, the physics of ice and snow.

Perhaps the most important winter driving suggestions come into play after you've arrived at the resort or trail. If you really fear driving in snow and are heading for a downhill ski vacation, consider slope-side lodging or a resort that offers shuttle bus service. The availability of such amenities is covered in Part 2 of this book.

When you park your car, especially at an isolated trailhead, remember that snow accumulation or wind-blown drifts can make it harder to leave than it was to arrive. Some back roads and trailhead parking areas are plowed last, and ski resort developments could have the same problem. For these reasons, park facing downhill, toward the way out, and where drifting snow won't block your exit. Don't, though, back into a wall of plowed snow. You may plug your exhaust pipe. If at all possible, park facing away from the prevailing wind. Your engine will retain some of its heat for quite a while if sheltered this way. The cold may also freeze your parking brake, so don't use it.

It may sound like a cliché, but don't forget a bag of sand and a shovel. Even if the condo or trailhead parking lot does get plowed, your vehicle is likely to be surrounded by a ridge of icy, compacted snow. The bigger the snow storm, the higher this ridge can get. In such conditions, thousands of ski trips have been ruined because the driver forgot the shovel. While you're clearing the snow from around your car, clear your windows and lights completely. More than one collision has resulted from snow-covered brake lights, and obstructed vision is a common cause of accidents. Lastly, when you get ready to head up to your lodge room, make sure you have your car key before you lock the vehicle. If you're starting a ski tour or winter hike, zip or safety pin both car keys in separate packs or pockets. And don't forget to turn out your lights!

Downhill Skiing

IN THE NORTH and West, the nation's most reknowned ski resorts beckon. But America's ski industry isn't the giant it is today because of a handful of megaresorts. The popularity of skiing is the result more of friendly neighborhood slopes than of the monster ski areas that vie for the world's ski travelers.

Northern and western snowbelt residents were trying local ski areas in the 1930s. Southerners didn't have that same opportunity on any scale until the early sixties. But residents of Dixie are making up for lost time. Every winter, hundreds of thousands ski the region's twenty-plus resorts. As noted earlier, most of the nation's potential skiers live in the South.

Even the smaller ski resorts below the Mason-Dixon line are catching up to those in the rest of America in quality. The biggest southern slopes are major resorts as measured by national attendance figures. Their skiing, ambience, and amenities increasingly resemble those of world class resorts.

There are differences. Southern slopes are small when compared to the biggest in North America. A size of 100 or so slope acres is big in the South. Large Colorado ski areas like Breckenridge boast more than 1,000 acres. Vertical drops of 800 to 1,500 feet top the list in the South. Most big ski areas in the country have 2,000 feet of vertical; Vermont's Killington has over 3,000, and Wyoming's Jackson Hole over 4,000. A run of 2 miles is long at a Dixie ski area. One Killington trail is 10 miles long!

These figures may sound like reasons to fly out West and up North, and more and more Southerners are doing just that. The region's residents, particularly skiers, are the nation's most consistent out-of-region travelers. But Dixie resorts are the perfect place to learn, and even experts have reasons to ski in the South.

The obvious drawbacks to long-distance travel make the South's ski areas attractive. When you don't compare southern ski areas with the very biggest, their vertical drops and slope acreage are respectable and comparable to ski resorts in all regions of America.

The South shines if you count on night skiing to expand your slope time. Few of the biggest national resorts offer skiing under the lights. Altitude is another factor. An Atlanta resident can ski hard all day at Sugar or Snowshoe. At Aspen, a flatlander can get out of breath just tying a shoe. The two days it takes to acclimatize to high altitude are an added expense that some westering skiers don't count on.

Size itself can have drawbacks. A big southern ski area will have fifteen to thirty trails, more than adequate for a varied and interesting ski week. Even an expert will only ski a fraction of Killington's 100 trails in a week. Big vertical drops sound nice, but 6 miles down 3,500 feet can seem a lot like work. And many big-mountain skiers have to spend hours studying trail maps, not to mention getting lost, missing lunch with their friends, and even ending up miles from the car when the lifts close.

In sum, southern slopes can offer interesting, enjoyable terrain without boggling the mind or overtaxing the body. In some cases, smaller can be better, especially when it's 1,500 miles closer to home.

Differences in sheer size aside, the skiing experience at southern slopes is increasingly similar to that found in other regions. Snow is a major reason.

No matter how much snow "usually" falls, snow droughts up North and out West have convinced the rest of the country that machine-made snow is important for a ski area that cares about its customers. Midwinter ski vacationers often find natural snow as part of the skiing surface in the South. But with its lower annual snowfall, the South has led the nation in the use of snow making. Southern ski areas are among the world's best at the art of making snow. The machine-made product is heavier than natural snow but much more resistant to skier traffic. During the cold winter nights in the Southern Appalachians, snow makers create fine dry snow and excellent skiing conditions. The slopes might not always offer "powder skiing," but even out West, the average ski condition is packed snow. And southern slopes, especially those in West Virginia, do in fact see powder snow conditions.

Even midwinter rain, an event you might associate with the South, can also occur at resorts in the North and West. In fact, a brochure for one of the biggest Northern ski areas shows people clad in plastic trash bags skiing in the rain! The experience may not be as much fun as skiing on fresh natural snow, but the pamphlet maintains correctly that slope conditions can be very enjoyable during and after rainfall. If it ever rains on your ski trip, use the trash bag idea to keep dry, and enjoy the soft snow and lack of icy spots. And be patient. Rain rarely has a severe impact on southern slope conditions. With their massive snow-making systems, southern resort managers pride themselves on a fast restoration of fine conditions when the cold returns. Chapter 1 covers when and where natural snow falls and when downhill slopes are open.

Southern resorts, while constantly upgrading their snow-making ability with increasingly sophisticated systems, are also known for their expertise at grooming the snow. Tanklike snow machines tow the latest attachments to manicure slope surfaces. In winter, the machines turn icy spots into granular surfaces, pack down deep heavy snow, or smooth and redistribute snow altered by skiing. In the spring, heavy, wet snow can become a velvet surface with the proper grooming.

Snow making can have its negative side, of course. At times, resorts make snow when skiers are on the slopes. It would be nicer to ski without negotiating the spray of snow guns, but the machines are a necessary evil, and goggles can limit the inconvenience. After all, if you were skiing through a natural snow blizzard in the Rockies, visibility could be even worse.

Generally, beginners are less intimidated when they learn to ski close to home, and accessible local slopes give needed practice even to experts who spend a week out West each year. Wherever you are on the skier spectrum, the South is a credible destination for a ski vacation. As elsewhere in America, southern slope developments have concentrated in clusters. These groups of ski areas combine attractive variety with accessibility. Canaan Valley and the Snowshoe/Silver Creek combo in West Virginia, the North Carolina high-country slopes near Boone, and Cataloochee and Wolf Laurel near Asheville each offer a number of ski areas to try during a weekend or week-long stay. In these multiresort settings, a ski vacation is similar to what skiers find at resort clusters in Mount Washington Valley in New Hampshire, Lake Tahoe in California, and Summit County in Colorado.

Services tell the story. Years ago, a southern ski trip meant sleeping in a mom and pop motel and watching TV for après-ski entertainment. That's still an option, but lodging and entertainment at southern slopes have come a long way in the sport's thirty years.

Accommodations range from country inns to ten-story summit condos, slope-side lodges and roundhouses, chain motels, Victorian hotels, secluded chalets, quaint bed and breakfast establishments, and log cabins. Overnight lodging prices can range from $15 for a bunk and breakfast to hundreds of dollars for a huge slope-side home. The ski areas and individual lodging establishments rent their own facilities, but often a number of real estate and lodging agencies represent a variety of accommodations. Many facilities have on-premises pools, pubs, Jacuzzis, saunas, and health clubs. Even fancy slope-side lodging can be reasonably priced if two or more couples or families share the rent for a condominium and cook some meals, perhaps with food brought from home.

Dining is diverse, much of it memorable. Fast food is available at slope cafeterias and burger chains, but distinctive dining includes traditional mountain fare served family style and everything else from Continental to Swiss, Chinese, Italian, German, and almost any other cuisine you might imagine.

Après-ski life doesn't stop with a soak in a hot tub. Major Dixie slopes cater to conferences, so a wide variety of options exist. It used to be that nightlife, including dancing and alcohol, were more available in Colorado and New England than in the South. Today, though, beverage options increasingly include spirits, and after-dinner entertainment runs the gamut from live music to comedy. Winter festivals, special events, and concerts add even more variety. And like nationally known ski areas, many southern resorts have on-slope photo services to help you take the excitement home. Where resort towns flank ski areas, even more diversity exists. Many warm weather travel attractions have established winter hours, and everything from movies to college drama, touring dance companies, and lectures are nearby.

Don't stay home if you don't ski downhill. Active alternatives at southern slopes include hiking trails, cross-country skiing, ice skating, sledding, snowmobiling, horse-drawn sleigh rides, and even ice fishing. Of course, facilities exist for tennis and other racquet sports, and many resorts run recreation programs with organized activities from interior decorating to craft classes and swimnastics. More than ever, a southern ski vacation is a complete winter vacation too. There is more to do than just ski, and the resort write-ups in Part 2 and the index furnish specifics.

People can and do fly to southern ski areas, but most skiers drive. Although some slopes are isolated, many are close to four-lane and interstate highways. For those who don't want to drive, more and more buses are carrying skiers to the slopes. Ski clubs, church groups, even radio stations offer inexpensive group transportation to the slopes, so check your group affiliations before using your car.

If you drive, you can put away your car keys for the duration of your stay at many southern slopes. Like some major resorts nationwide, Dixie ski areas and some lodging establishments offer free or inexpensive shuttle bus systems that take the hassle out of snowy roads. Slope-side lodging can provide the same convenience, especially where everything you want is available a short walk away. Few things are more enjoyable than strolling through a snowy resort village or starting the day with a warm-up run down the slope to the lift. Take your earplugs though: snow making may be music to your ears, but it can become simple noise after midnight.

Access involves more than how you get to the slopes. Information is the key to proper planning, and many ski areas, chambers of commerce, and promotional organizations are effectively packaging their offerings. Some feature toll free numbers for snow reports, reservations, and requesting information packets with the latest details on resorts, including winter calendars with dates for festivals and events.

Whether you base your vacation plans on *Southern Snow,* a newspaper article, or another ski publication, always get the latest rates and write-ups directly from the businesses involved. Although major offerings change slowly enough to make the price ranges below relevant for years, rates and policies fluctuate, at times within weeks of publication of even the latest newspaper roundup or seasonal guide.

The ski package is one way for beginners and experts to make a ski trip easy to plan and inexpensive. Ski resorts nationwide offer one lower-than-usual price for a package of services that may include resort lodging, ski rentals, lessons, slope tickets, and sometimes meals. Other lodging agencies and ski businesses also have packages, and groups can get even bigger discounts. Again, the newest rates may reflect changes only days old.

Whether or not you book a package, consider the convenience and savings of a multiday lift ticket. These passes often permit unlimited skiing and allow you to ski when you want without feeling compelled to overdo it to get your money's worth.

If you opt for a daily ticket, when and where you ski influence the value you get for your skiing dollar. Lift tickets vary in price depending on the resort's size and the time of day. Full-day sessions usually start at nine o'clock and end at four. Adult weekday tickets at the small to medium-sized slopes usually cost between $10 and $14, with weekend prices rising to $20 or $22. The biggest resorts will charge anywhere from the high teens to low twenties on weekdays and in the $24 to $28 range on weekends.

Child, student, senior, and other categories for young and old vary greatly from resort to resort and from year to year, often fluctuating wildly. Such rates are usually $3 to $7 cheaper per session, depending on whether it is a weekday or weekend. A resort's latest price sheet is the only sure guide, especially when early and late season discounts or other special rates are in effect.

Separate, less expensive rates apply to half-day sessions, which usually run from 1:00 to 4:00 but are sometimes available in the morning, and to night sessions, which usually run from 6:00 to 10:00. Twilight sessions combine afternoon and evening, with skiing from 1:00 to 4:00 and then 6:00 to 10:00.

The half-day ticket at most resorts, small or large, is rarely offered on weekends and is usually 75 percent of the daily price. The twilight ticket is often very near the price of the daily ticket. Night skiing is the cheapest session. Rates at the small to medium slopes range from $8 to $12, and at the largest slopes from $12 to $16.

For beginners, the key word for savings is *rent*. Everything you need is available, even those colorful ski bibs and parkas that help you avoid soaking wet blue jeans. Midweek savings make renting even cheaper, and when you know what you like, a resort area or home-town ski shop can arrange your purchase. Daily rentals for skis, boots, and poles range between $8 and $14. Average night rates are under $10.

Wherever you ski in America, the slopes, bars, restaurants, roads, bathrooms, and everything else will be most crowded and most expensive on weekends. The most boring part of skiing, waiting in line for the chairlift, will take longest on weekends. This problem is notable in the South, where smaller slopes and sizable crowds can indeed create lines. Take advantage of midweek skiing. Whether you plan a week-long or a one-day ski trip, arrange for winter vacation days during the week in January or February, or cultivate the flexibility to take off on short notice during the week if natural snow strikes or temperatures have been cold enough to make plenty of snow. The biggest slopes have midweek nightlife, and uncrowded weekday slopes let you enjoy southern skiing at its best.

If you must ski on weekends be tolerant of the waits. Remember that southern resorts are constantly adding new slopes and chairlifts and trying to keep lift lines short while still turning a profit. Many have upper-mountain lifts that service less crowded, advanced terrain, or multiple summit lifts that lead to easy trails down from the top. Both offer a way to avoid base lifts crowded by beginners going halfway up the mountain. Resort write-ups describe the short cuts.

Use your head in dealing with lift lines. Don't just flock to the nearest one. Examine the trail map, study the slope traffic, or ask a friendly ski patroller, instructor, or member of a resort host/hostess program for alternatives. And don't storm into the front office complaining about half-hour lift lines when the wait is actually twelve minutes. Everyone overestimates: use your watch if you want to offer criticism.

Even on busy days, good timing can yield enjoyable skiing. Consider being the first person on the slope. Eat early and take the first chair to the top. Late nighters and families will usually arrive well after the lifts start. Eat lunch at 10:30 when they arrive, then hit the slopes again at 11:30, and ski while they eat lunch. Take a break when they come back out, then ski through the late afternoon when most people are tired and leave early.

For all the money skiers spend on transportation, lodging, and equipment, far too many draw the line at the cost of a lesson. If you've never skied, don't make that error. The situation is a familiar one at ski resorts. The nonskier is ready to learn from a friend who knows how to ski. The only problem is that knowing how to ski is not the same as knowing how to teach someone to ski. Most people can read, but few would consider themselves competent to become first grade reading teachers. Often, the "teacher" in the story above takes the student to a much-too-difficult slope and ends up yelling "Just do what I'm doing! What's wrong with you?" The frustrated nonskier, soaked and sore, eventually walks off the slope or ends up rocketing down an expert slope, frozen with fear, at 45 mph.

This scenario may sound funny, but such stories can have unfortunate endings. One is that twenty minutes of unpleasantness convinces the student that he or she simply isn't capable of skiing. It certainly hasn't been any fun, so why continue falling? Why not just go home and forget it? The most tragic ending is an accident. Whether the student skier is injured or runs into someone who is, the result is the same. A safe sport has become dangerous.

This danger is at its worst when uninstructed skiers, particularly athletic young males, learn enough to point the skis downhill and stand up under high speed, usually on intermediate or beginner slopes. They're not falling, so they consider themselves "under control." Nothing is further from the truth. These unguided missiles terrorize the slope until someone turns in front of them or they fall in the path of another skier.

Such behavior shows why southern states have passed skier safety laws that make skiers liable for injuries they cause. The National Ski Patrol and ski area operators constantly emphasize the Skier Responsibility Code, one rule of which says skiers should ski in such a way that they can stop or turn to avoid skiers below them, lift towers, and snow-making equipment. Some experts ski too fast. But most injuries, especially from collisions, result not only because people are exercising bad judgment, but also because they simply can't ski. After learning the sport, a skier can enjoy high speed on advanced trails with fewer skiers. Parents and group leaders should be sure their younger charges fully understand why racing against their friends is unacceptable on a crowded beginner slope.

Instruction is particularly important in a discussion of southern skiing, because the region's National Ski Patrol units and ski area operators are among the country's most active in supporting and teaching safety. The South's volunteer and professional Ski Patrollers are at all times ready to help skiers on the slopes, but they would prefer to see skiers learn safe habits and skills before getting into, or causing, trouble. Every new skier should take a lesson.

Unlike a friend, the professional instructor has been taught to teach, using simple but sophisticated techniques to help you learn how to ski or how to ski better. Southern ski schools are staffed by professionals, most trained by the Professional Ski Instructors of America (PSIA) and members of official PSIA ski schools at southern slopes. Many schools have special training programs for children, like *Ski Magazine*'s SKIWee Program. Others have their own "ski and play" and even nursery programs to teach children and free up parents. Some ski school lesson plans allow students to go to the front of lift lines.

Downhill skiing costs money, but not as much as many people think. Package plans and wise rental arrangements can make skiing relatively inexpensive—less costly per hour, in fact, than other facility-dependent sports like racquetball and golf. From quality rental skis and bibs to a lesson, the costs associated with downhill skiing are reasonable when they succeed in creating a fine skiing experience.

Few activities are as gratifying as a ski run amid the beauty of nature's most scenic season. Alone or with family and friends, a ski vacation can be among life's most pleasant memories. For millions, those memories are made in Dixie.

Cross-Country Skiing

WHETHER you call it cross-country skiing, Nordic skiing, or ski touring, this oldest form of the sport offers the satisfying sensations, quiet and strong, of gliding through spectacular winter scenery. That appeal is much the same whether you ski in New England, Norway, or North Carolina.

Unlike Nordic skiing in other parts of America and the world, cross-country is relatively new in the South, and to find consistent snow, enthusiasts in Dixie generally focus on the highest mountain tops. Although that situation creates a unique set of complications, the difficulties can be overcome. For more and more southern skiers, the joys, and in some places the amenities of cross-country skiing are the same at home as they might be in New England or the West.

A snow-covered trail is the Nordic skier's first requirement, and Part 3 of this book shows that good trails are surprisingly abundant in high-snowfall areas. But deep snow is often confined to the high summits in the South, so would-be skiers may not realize that snow conditions are excellent only a few hours away. Even serious, experienced Nordic skiers sometimes assume there is no snow when mountain trails are in fact skiable. Accurate snow reports are the answer, and an ever-increasing number are available, some even toll-free. The entries in Part 3 list suggested snow reports, and Chapter 1 can help you better understand snow-producing weather patterns so that you won't miss good skiing, even when your local TV weather forecast doesn't mention snow.

Being informed and creating the flexibility to ski when the snow strikes make it possible to regularly sample the joy of cross-country skiing in Dixie. From the snow-covered openness of a hardwood forest in Shenandoah National Park, to hushed, frozen groves of Spruce in West Virginia, to awe-inspiring vistas framed by evergreens in North Carolina, southern Nordic skiers enjoy the same scenic rewards that make the sport so popular in more northern climes. But panoramic scenery isn't the only, or even primary appeal of the sport. Cross-country skiers eventually come to crave the smooth feeling of striding and gliding through a winter wonderland. The rhythmic beauty of the cross-country ski technique, called the diagonal stride, creates a sensuous and satisfying impression of oneness with nature. And although ski touring can be as strenuous as Olympic racers make it look, the proper choice of trail and pace can make even a beginner's first trip a relaxing one. Proper technique and pace can even take most of the work out of skiing uphill. The accomplished Nordic skier finds a powerful feeling of freedom and self-sufficiency that downhill skiers rarely sense on the ride up the chairlift or the plunge down the slopes.

Luckily, in recent years southerners have found it easier than ever to reach the ranks of competent cross-country skiers. The growing availability of instruction is one reason.

No matter where you first try cross-country skiing, a lesson should be your first step. Like thousands of downhill skiers, countless first-time Nordic skiers have struck off on their own or with experienced and well-meaning friends, only to find that few Nordic moves come naturally. Nordic skiing is an easy sport to learn for people of all ages. But the sadly popular cliché that cross-country is "as easy as walking on skis" is misleading. The goal, after all, is to ski, not walk, and a professional instructor greatly accelerates the student's ability to master essential techniques. Besides inviting a greater risk of injury, an untutored skier is more likely to end the first day on skis wondering what the attraction is and pledging never to try it again. On the other hand, the instructed skier gains a solid understanding of the basic maneuvers and an appreciation of why cross-country is the safest form of skiing.

It is true that many proficient skiers have taught themselves. That process, though, can take years instead of days, especially if you're being tutored by a friend who not only doesn't know how to teach, but who may also be making fundamental errors in technique. If you do intend to learn on your own, read a few books on cross-country technique so you know the basic moves. Then practice the specific techniques; perhaps a friend who is skiing correctly can help. The point here, though, is that professional instruction is more time and cost effective than self-instruction. Now that it is available in the South, why not benefit?

Today, professional Nordic ski schools are located in key cross-country areas of the southern mountains. Developed cross-country ski centers and outfitters combine to make ski lessons and instructional tours easily available. Set tracks, machine-made ski grooves in the snow, are groomed in at West Virginia ski centers, and at least one North Carolina touring location may soon offer track skiing. Not only do these firmly formed tracks make it easier to learn to cross-country ski, but the most advanced and effective diagonal stride is possible "in track." Many northern ski centers offer this amenity that is only now becoming available in the South.

Besides offering instruction, these outfitters and ski centers rent skis, and renting is an inexpensive way to decide which of the different kinds of cross-country skis you should buy. This decision is particularly important to Nordic skiers who will be touring in the South.

All cross-country skis are light in comparison to downhill skis. Since turning on steep slopes is the goal of the alpine skier, downhill ski boots are rigid, are made of synthetic materials, and attach to the ski at the heel and toe. Mobility is the goal of the cross-country skier, so Nordic ski boots range from low cut and shoelike to ankle high and reminiscent of light hiking boots. Cross-country ski boots are usually made of leather, and the bindings attach the boot to the ski only at the toe to permit the heel-raising diagonal stride that takes skiers across level terrain and even uphill.

At cross-country ski centers with set track, beginners usually learn on the widest skis that will fit in the tracks, because width enhances stability. The sides of these skis are nearly parallel, with little difference in width between the ski tip, or shovel; the middle, called the waist; and the end of the ski, called the tail. Rental boots are often leather, with three holes in the flat, bill-shaped part of the sole that protrudes from the front of the boot. These holes accept three pins that stick up from the binding. When the front of the boot is placed in the binding, the three pins mesh with the holes; a bale then folds down and latches the ski and boot together. This binding system, usually metal, is known by the width of the front of the boot: usually 75 millimeters. Each binding has a diagram of a foot, an arrow, or some other symbol to distinguish the left ski from the right.

At the ski centers, advanced skiers often use the very lightest and skinniest cross-country skis, with the least difference in width between the tip, waist, and tail. For maximum speed, these high-performance skis offer the lowest possible resistance to the sides of the tracks. For these skis, the light, running-shoe-like boots are used. The bindings, too, are different: instead of being 75 millimeters wide, they are often 50 millimeters wide, and they may be made of synthetic materials and may attach with two pins. Lately, lightweight, brand-specific boot/binding "systems" have started displacing even the 50-millimeter equipment. With these systems, either ski can fit on either foot. Increasingly, these simpler, narrow, "high tech" bindings are turning up on the skis that beginners use at ski centers with set track. The better cross-country skiers are even taking this lightweight, speed-oriented gear out onto back-country trails with untracked snow or snow tracked not by machines but by other skiers.

The ski centers offer set track, lodging, ski and rental shops, dining, and even nightlife. In the South, cross-country has traditionally been a back-country activity. The recent growth of the ski centers is giving beginners a place to learn and experienced back-country skiers a new place to hone their form. Suddenly, more southerners are enjoying an attractive social and resort side of cross-country skiing.

The back country, in contrast, is enjoyed on its own terms. Even in regions where set track ski centers are prevalent, back-country Nordic skiing is increasingly popular. Southeastern back-country skiing is much the same now as it was in the 1940s when members of the Ski Club of Washington, D.C., would unhook the heels of their cable bindings and shuffle over the snow-covered hiking trails of Shenandoah National Park. Back-country parks more often mark their trails with ski symbols now, and units of the National Nordic Ski Patrol work on some back-country trail systems. Still, cross-country skiers generally face the same responsibilities as winter hikers. (Chapter 6 discusses proper preparation for a cross-country ski tour or a winter hike.)

The trailgoer's responsibility starts with equipment, and proper skis top the list. Skiing on back-country trails requires a wider ski than track skiing does. Skis in this category are generally called light touring or just touring skis, and the narrower versions can be used in track. Most touring skis, though, are not only wider but also shaped differently than skis suitable for machine-set tracks.

The greater width and different shape of touring skis give added flotation in deep, fresh snow. Unlike more parallel track skis, touring skis, when viewed from above, have a subtle hourglass shape called sidecut: wide in the shovel and tail, narrow in the waist. This shape not only increases flotation but also creates a ski that will turn quickly when set on its edge. Touring skis generally have 75-millimeter bindings, and boots are higher topped and a little heavier and stiffer for control in deep snow and when turning.

Carrying the touring ski concept further, boots and skis get heavier until they best fit the term back-country skis. Boots in this category have thick, stiff vibram soles and solid leather uppers, and back-country skis often have light metal edges. This combination enables the skier to cope with deeper snow or icy conditions, to carry a heavier pack, and to more easily accomplish an effective snowplow and advanced turns like the telemark or even the parallel turn used by downhill skiers.

The next step beyond the heaviest back-country Nordic gear resembles the downhill ski equipment of the 1930s and 1940s. The similarity is appropriate because most of this gear is used exclusively to get to an appropriate place and go downhill skiing in a cross-country setting. Skis are wide, with heavy metal edges, and some of these Nordic/Alpine, or "Norpine" skiers even wear double boots similar to winter mountaineering boots but with a Nordic sole. This "downhill/cross-country" trend is a national one that is particularly visible and appropriate in the South. The development of this heavier cross-country gear was initiated not by manufacturers but by aggressive cross-country skiers in the West bent on venturing deep into the back country. The lightweight boots and touring or set track skis that prevailed as cross-country became popular in the early 1970s weren't up to the task. So skiers began experimenting with old alpine skis and the leather downhill boots of the fifties and early sixties. Soon they had resurrected the telemark, the oldest turn in skiing. Suddenly, Nordic skiers were tackling the steepest terrain with graceful telemarks.

The power and finesse of the telemark easily captures the imagination of any skier who has struggled to turn on cross-country skis. Nationwide, whatever their level of expertise, Nordic skiers stymied by hills are realizing that if you can't turn, you aren't a complete skier, and that falling down during every attempted turn isn't much fun. Thus the telemark craze has taken firm root, especially in the South, where the snowiest trails are often remote and rugged.

One result of this trend has been a dramatic surge in the number of Nordic skiers at downhill ski resorts. Every winter, a southeastern telemark series of races pits hard-core "tele" skiers against each other. On back-country trails, even the easy ones, more and more skiers delight in the downhill. In essence, the resurgence of the telemark turn has made cross-country skiing the complete and exciting sport that it is in the late 1980s. No longer can alpine skiers claim a corner on downhill thrills. And even sedate Nordic skiers are benefiting from the revolution in equipment that helps them overcome the old difficulty of turning their "skinny skis."

The various options in cross-country skiing make choosing the right equipment a key factor. The serious back-country skier who focuses on steeper, more demanding terrain is likely to want a ski with a light metal edge and a good deal of side-cut, and moderately heavy, vibram-soled boots. This is the lightest type of equipment that can also be used for serious telemark or parallel skiing on downhill slopes. A strong skier can still stride effectively with this equipment, as well as tackle slopes at the downhill resorts. Some expert skiers go one step further and own a very heavy pair of telemark boots and metal-edged skis that are similar in weight and appearance to downhill skis. These systems use 75-millimeter bindings exclusively, and the newest boots for this purpose incorporate plastic uppers similar to those on downhill boots.

For the less aggressive skier who wants to make effective trail turns but will be skiing easier trails, including perhaps some set track, a sturdy high-top boot and a touring ski with moderate sidecut will be best. No metal edge will be needed.

Serious Nordic skiers frequently own at least two pairs of skis, a back-country/telemark outfit and a lighter set for set track or touring. Other skiers have two sets of skis for a different, very traditional reason. No matter where you cross-country ski, you will encounter natural snow conditions that are less than ideal, usually early or late in the season. In that regard, today's Nordic skiers are like the downhill, natural snow skiers of the thirties, forties, and fifties. The solution to fluctuating snow conditions is the same now as it was then: own a good pair of skis and a pair of "rock" skis. By the time you've skied for a few years, your "starter set" will be nicked and gouged with rock scars. Go ahead and retire them, but if you've chosen them correctly, they'll still be useful when conditions don't permit using your newer skis. Sometimes, ski fever dictates that any snow is skiable. At such times, make sure your rock skis ride in the rack beside your new boards.

Going beyond boots and skis, part of the exciting new appeal of cross-country in the South and elsewhere is the growing realization that technique can be as important as equipment. In fact, advanced technique enables expert skiers on light, track-type skis with some side-cut and binding systems with running-shoe-like boots to telemark on back-country trails one minute and stride effortlessly the next.

Instruction and practice are the key. In the last few years, southeastern cross-country ski teachers have started offering frequent telemark clinics at downhill slopes. Many of these southeastern ski centers and outfitters also rent telemark gear, but many will teach skiers on their own lightweight equipment. On an extremely easy downhill slope with good snow conditions, even lightly equipped Nordic skiers can realize how easy and fun it is to turn effectively.

Most beginning Nordic ski lessons will teach the student how to step turn: raise one ski, place it in a new direction, put weight on it, and then step the unweighted original ski in the new direction. This maneuver resembles an ice skating turn. In fact, forceful, repeated steps of this kind is called skating. This skating technique has recently become very popular among racers and advanced skiers as a means of forward mobility on level and uphill terrain, much like the diagonal stride. Special skating skis are available for those forsaking the diagonal stride altogether. Skating is most popular at set track ski centers on packed snow, but any cross-country skier can enjoy the technique.

Easy, more level trails, as rated in Part 3 of this book, require step turns. Intermediate trails require effective and often linked step and skating turns or a snowplow turn to negotiate a curve on a downhill trail. And advanced trails require fast step or skating turns, strong snowplow turns, or a telemark or parallel turn to tackle curves that are often sharp and at the bottom of steep hills.

Because back-country trails are remote and many are designed for hiking rather than skiing, an introductory ski lesson in the Southeast should focus on turning and slowing down as much as on striding and climbing. Beginners should be proficient at pole-drag techniques for slowing down, and when conditions are suitable, they should learn the snow plow. Even skiers who are just becoming intermediates can learn the telemark. Beginning skiers should not shy away from a separate ski lesson at a downhill resort that focuses on turning. During a particularly warm or snowless period, or just early or late in the season when the only snow is machine made at the slopes, consider a downhill-oriented cross-country lesson at your closest ski center or outfitter. There are few better ways to improve your skill and extend the season.

Obviously, few beginners are up to a telemark run down an expert slope. As Part 3 of this book shows, though, there are many very easy level trails to start on. For many beginners, "walking on skis" is a necessary foundation for the rhythm and glide of long-term forward mobility. This invigorating locomotion requires those sliding skis to grip when you thrust back, or kick, and again the nature of the equipment comes into play.

To be able to grip and still glide, skis have another important characteristic called camber. When placed on the ground and viewed from the side, the middle of the ski under the binding is elevated off the ground like the arch in your foot. Only the tip and tail of the ski touch the ground. That raised central section is the key to grip. When the skier strides out on one ski after kicking, or glides down a hill with both skis side by side, the tips and tails of the skis are sliding on the snow. Only when the skier bears down on one ski, kicking back for thrust, does the center of the kicked ski really come in contact with the snow. On this "kick" zone, skiers place a special kicker wax that grips the snow; on waxless skis, an embossed pattern of grooves or a chemically treated insert creates the instant grip that thrusts the skier forward to glide on the tips and tails.

In the Dixie Appalachians, the method of grip a skier chooses is as important to skiing enjoyment as the kind of ski used. The latest statistics show that nationwide, more skiers buy waxless skis than waxable ones. In the Southern Appalachians, the vast majority of skiers will want to own waxless skis. The reasons lie in the mechanics of waxable skis. The skier who waxes for grip applies one of a variety of waxes to the kick zone, either a soft wax from a tube or a harder wax in a crayon-like dispenser. After rubbing on the wax, the skier uses a cork block to smooth it. The waxes come in various colors that correspond to air temperatures and the moisture content of the snow. Even with the recent development of simplified "two-wax systems," choosing the right wax and applying it correctly are complex processes for the skier, who is most often interested in skiing, not waxing. With the South's warmer temperatures, the soft waxes, called klisters, are often necessary, and applying them can be extremely messy.

To some purists, waxing is Nordic skiing. No doubt, a properly waxed ski will perform better and give greater speed with less work than a waxless ski. But skiers who learn to wax in New England or the West have an advantage that southern skiers do not. Waxes perform best when they match snow and temperature conditions perfectly. In those colder, drier climates, the correct wax is easier to choose, and it remains appropriate longer and with greater consistency. Southern temperatures usually rise significantly when the sun comes out. There is marked variability between the snow on a sunny field and that on a shaded trail, and southern snow generally has greater moisture content to begin with. All these factors make waxing an often exasperating task.

On the other hand, there are snowy days with dry snow and cold temperatures when even beginners will find it easy to wax. Southerners should be aware of this side of cross-country and may want to try it sometime in the future, in the South or elsewhere. Although southern ski renters carry waxless skis almost exclusively, some do rent waxable skis. So when the snow is consistent or your instructor is well versed in waxing, give it a try.

In general, though, for most of us below the Mason-Dixon line, and in fact for most skiers in America, waxless is the best compromise for convenience and enjoyment. There are many waxless patterns and methods to choose from. In the South, waxless skis with mohair inserts seem to be the least effective because they often cake up with wet snow and slow the skier down. Again rental skis of various kinds and the advice of your local cross-country professional should offer the best routes to a wise purchase.

Remember, though, just because your skis are waxless doesn't mean you can't use wax or other base preparations to enhance performance. Too many skiers, in the South and elsewhere, buy waxless skis, step into the bindings, and go. Many huff and puff and conclude that "this effortless kick and glide" isn't so effortless. Don't make that error.

The skis you rent for a professional lesson will usually have professional preparation. Most good ski shops and outfitters also prepare their skis properly. But some don't, so don't mistake poor ski maintenance for your own lack of skill.

Besides the kicker wax under the binding of a waxable ski, all skis, waxless and waxable, should be waxed on the tips and tails for smooth glide. This preparation is especially important for new skis just off the rack. If your retailer can't "base prep" your new boards, have it done at your closest mountain ski center or outfitter before you ski, or read up on the topic and do it yourself. Some suggestions follow. Be aware that they are very basic and that racers or serious skiers often use far more complex procedures.

Basically, the first step is to clean then gently scrape your ski tips and tails, using long, smooth strokes, with the metal edge of a wax scraping tool; avoid scraping the waxless base too deeply. Hold the scraper flat against the base and move it from tip to tail, avoiding pressure on the waxless pattern. The goal is to flatten and smooth the base, so expect some of the base material to come off in thin, very small squiggles. This process also removes fibers that often protrude from the base.

For midwinter skiing, a hard wax intended for cold snow is best for the tips and tails. Avoiding the waxless pattern, hold a block or tube of cross-country "glider" wax against an old iron and let it drip on the ski. Then quickly smooth the wax on the ski with the "warm" iron. Let it harden. Then again scrape the ski, smoothing the wax with the metal edge of the scraper. If you ski frequently, rewax the tips and tails a few times a season. Once before the season will be enough for most skiers.

This process seals the pores on the base of the ski. Open pores allow water and ice to cake on the ski, slowing the skier down dramatically. This can also happen to the waxless pattern under the kick zone. In fact, even with a properly waxed "glider zone," countless skiers slog along with snow and ice frozen to the waxless kick zone of their skis. Ice frequently builds up after you ski through a puddle or icy spot or after you ski over an area of wet, melting snow in direct sunlight and then go back into the shade; avoid damp spots when possible. And to help prevent ice buildup, use a commercially available product like "Maxi-Glide" before you ski. This teflon liquid is rubbed on the waxless pattern, sealing the pores. The pattern still grips, but no ice forms. Besides the popular Maxi-Glide for the kick zone, Nordic wax companies, like Swix, market their own spray-on preparations for both the kick zone and the glide area of the tip and tail. Investigate these products, but don't fail to adequately wax your skis first.

To remove ice from the kicker area, always use the plastic side of the ski scraper. Doing so thoroughly, taking care not to damage the waxless pattern, you may control ice temporarily. However, Maxi-Glide or a similar product is the best remedy. Frequent skiers should purchase Maxi-Glide by the bottle, with the application cloth, or spray cans of other kick zone sealers. These products cost more than $5, and infrequent skiers can avoid the expense by purchasing Maxi-Glide in alcohol-swab-like foil packets that will service an entire party of skiers for at least one day of skiing. Nordic instructors and trip leaders should be sure to carry this product. The combination of Maxi-Glide and glider wax gives the best performance that a waxless ski can afford.

Remember, too, that this is the South, and be aware that on warm days, even at high elevations with deep snow, conditions can create what experienced skiers call "spring skiing." Light clothes, warm sun, and deep snow are a real joy—unless you are trying to ski on glider wax that is intended for cold weather and drier snow. Again, the skier will find the going slow. You can avoid this problem by using a "universal" glider wax intended for a range of temperatures and not just for cold snow. A specific wax that matches the snow conditions will always give the best performance, though, so for warm days, remove your hard glider wax with a commercially available wax remover, and then rewax with a wet-snow glider wax. These waxes, some of them new, are usually in the red and yellow range. In fact, since springlike conditions occur in midwinter wherever you may ski in America, definitely become acquainted with changing your glider wax so that you can be flexible. More than one slogging novice has watched a properly waxed expert glide by on wet snow.

Besides skis, waxes, and instruction, the Nordic skier in the South can benefit from an awareness of other factors that affect the enjoyment of a ski trip. When to go is an important consideration. Chapter 1 details where and when the snow falls. The best guide to when to go is an eye on the weather map and a good snow report from a commercial ski center, from a chamber of commerce or promotional organization, and even from a ski resort, if it mentions natural snow. Most such reports are reliable, and a few are even toll free. Problems of reliability do arise, however, when these reports are prerecorded or secondhand. The best alternative is to cultivate a friend, even one who runs a ski center, who will be honest and up to the minute about snow conditions. Although no one can know how long snow will last or if cold weather will stay, mountain snow informants at least hear local weather reports and can look out the window; they can offer invaluable insight before you begin a four-hour drive.

Remember, too, that as you use this book and explore on your own, your favorite cross-country ski area may turn out to be an undeveloped one. The closest farm down the mountain may be the source of the best snow report; so approach locals in a courteous way, and you may get a snow-report phone number that is yours alone. But don't abuse the privilege with constant calls. And consider a thank you note or a gift.

Courtesy is also especially important on the ski trail. Cross-country is new in the South, so skiers should use restraint in dealing with other skiers or hikers who are unaware of basic rules of consideration or safety.

Since many fine southern ski trails are summer hiking routes, it is not unusual, especially in popular areas, for a skier to find a hiker, group of backpackers, or even a family of sledders walking in the ski tracks. At ski centers and among cross-country skiers, it is a firm rule not to walk in ski tracks. Besides ruining a fine ski trail, a hiker or skier's post-hole foot print in the snow can catch a ski tip and do serious injury. Dogs, too, are unwelcome and are often prohibited on ski trails because their prints also destroy ski tracks and reduce snow cover. In addition, dogs cause collisions or falls by getting in the way.

Of course, if you are skiing alone on a trail that no one else is likely to ski on, then dog tracks, dog feces, or your own footprints aren't unacceptable if they don't bother you and your companions. But remember that the ski season can be relatively short in the South. When one serious skier, or dozens of skiers, have traveled a great distance and made tracks through deep snow, they will likely take a dim view of your footprints or your German shepherd's. The best policy at popular ski areas is to pursue conduct that doesn't violate the rights of others. Skiing courtesy isn't law, so act in a way that preserves the best snow conditions for everyone.

If you find yourself in trouble on a steep trail and want to walk to easier terrain, stay on the very edge of the trail. It is certainly more work to walk in deep snow than on tracks. But lead skiers do the work so that they and others can enjoy the tracks. The first hiker should expect to do the same work on a separate walker's route beside the ski trail. If you encounter hikers walking in ski tracks, be courteous if you decide to enlighten them. Both hikers and skiers have the right to use most trails. The best policy is to share the trail. After all, if the skier weren't there, the hiker would have to wade in deep snow anyway, so hikers shouldn't object to making their own trails. Unfortunately, even winter backpackers in deep snow areas of the South rarely use snowshoes.

Skiers and hikers alike can help park and land managers solve user conflicts by contacting them and requesting that activities at the site be clearly organized. Ski courtesy posters can be placed at trailheads to educate the uninformed. Some popular trails could be designated for skiers, others for hikers or recreational and off-road vehicles.

This book describes cross-country trails that are gradual or otherwise suitable for Nordic skiing. Hikers can enjoy steeper trails or routes that are for other reasons not suitable for skiing. Part 3 of this book points out such trails, which frequently are in the same areas as popular cross-country routes. Personal advice from a skier to a hiker or posted walking suggestions can do much to help both groups have the best time possible.

Besides serving convenience, many ski "rules" have a basis in safety. For instance, skiers should never stop and gather in the middle of a trail, especially on a hill or in a blind curve. Always step to the side of the trail. And when climbing up a hill and rounding a turn, ski to the inside of the curve. Any skier coming down the hill will be pulled to the outside of the turn by inertia, and a skier who can't make the turn and falls, will fall to the outside.

When skiing uphill, always yield to the downhill skier, who may not have as much control. Also, step aside if you're overtaken from behind by a skier wanting to pass. Any skier wanting the right of way, going either down a hill or up, should call "track." When you hear this request, yield the track by stepping aside.

Of course, skiers can only become better at the sport if they challenge themselves. But that obvious truth is no reason for a beginner to venture onto trails that are rated difficult. Beginners who fall often on steep trails ruin snow conditions with the craters they make, called sitzmarks. Even if you fill these in, and you should, too many of them can make an advanced skier's trip less enjoyable than it could be. Often, too, beginners have to walk down off hills that exceed their ability, an experience that is usually less enjoyable than gliding on an easy ski trail. Most trails described in this book are rated for difficulty.

Generally, the ultimate consideration before actually skiing a trail is getting to the trailhead safely and being able to get back home. Chapter 3 discusses precautions that cross-country skiers should take to ensure safety. The importance of having a well-equipped car is even greater at an isolated trailhead parking area than at a developed ski resort.

More than parking facilities separate cross-country skiing from downhill and even from winter hiking. Nordic skiing just may be the perfect combination of effort and ease for people wanting to fuse the joy of skiing with the subtle but spectacular winter beauty of the Southern Appalachians . . . or any mountains.

Winter Hiking and Mountaineering

WINTER foot travel in the southern mountains takes many forms. Winter hiking can mean anything from a short walk through last fall's leaves, to a multiday, deep-snow traverse of a barren mountain crest.

The hiker or backpacker can encounter snow in November, or a balmy day in February. On a high trail in winter, you might be walking through a few inches of snow, or breaking trail through a few feet. At times, on or off trail, crossing ice can require rope and ice cleats called crampons. At its most technical and challenging, winter hiking and backpacking in the South can be called mountaineering.

All of these experiences are available in the South, and each requires a different level of preparedness. This chapter explores general winter trail opportunities in Dixie and suggests equipment and cautions for trips of a few hours or a few days. Part 3 lists all kinds of trails, from those suitable for a week of mountaineering to those ideal for an easy, half-hour family hike in the snow near a ski resort.

In the South, as in the East generally, the word variability best describes winter weather. A good snow report is the key to finding the conditions you want, especially if deep-snow hiking or ice climbing is your goal. But conditions can change. Chapter 1 suggests information sources. There is no better watchword for the southern hiker or cross-country skier than the Boy Scout motto, "Be Prepared."

Luckily for skiers and hikers, both sports rely on much the same equipment. Generally, the well-equipped winter day hiker or backpacker could just as readily go cross-country skiing. Proper clothing is the beginning and end of safety and enjoyment in the cold and snow.

The first item of equipment that hikers and skiers have in common is gaiters, leggings that attach under the boot and cover the laces, boot collar, socks, and lower pants. Gaiters usually reach up to just above the ankle or just below the knee.

In more than an inch or two of snow, gaiters are worth their weight in gold. Few things are worse than wet, cold feet, and gaiters help keep snow away from ski and hiking boots. They are especially useful for deep snow. A cross-country skier on a trail compacted by a track-setting machine will rarely sink into fresh snow, so ankle height gaiters will be fine. But for back-country skiing, hiking, or backpacking, knee-high gaiters are best. Plowing through drifts can push snow up to your knees, often soaking your pants. For skiers, knee-high gaiters also make fashion sense. Most people new to Nordic skiing take their time buying knickers, rightly thinking that you don't need to be in style to ski well or have fun. But gaiters are simply practical, and besides keeping snow out of your boots, high-top gaiters make pants look like knickers. The right equipment is always in style.

For really deep snow and severe conditions, winter mountaineers and back-country hikers and skiers may want "super gaiters" made of heavy pack cloth and sometimes insulated with synthetic fill material. Even settrack Nordic skiers on light equipment can purchase low-cut insulated overboots. These are particularly useful in unusually cold weather when an active racer's feet might not stay warm in the new, lightweight cross-country boots.

Not all gaiters guarantee warm feet, especially if they let melting snow pass through or if they trap perspiration. Although expensive, Gore-Tex gaiters may be best for waterproof, breathable performance. Even gaiters of water-repellent fabric, nylon, or cloth are preferable to coated, waterproof fabrics that trap perspiration and soak your feet and lower legs.

Ultimately, even with gaiters, some moisture will probably reach your footwear, and the boot is the critical factor in whether a hiker or skier has dry or wet feet. Although many of today's lighter skiing and hiking boots use Gore-Tex inserts, the back-country enthusiast will prefer leather boots. Even if the winter trekker doesn't expect much snow, a leather boot able to withstand cold, wet conditions is far better than a warm weather one that usually will have a thinner sole and a less insulated upper. Properly waterproofed leather is simply superior for the skier or hiker facing more difficult terrain, colder temperatures, and deeper snow. Even the back-country skier who fancies the lightest possible gear would do well to choose a modern boot/binding system based on leather.

Proper waterproofing means treating the boot with a quality leather product like Sno-Seal. Serious hikers often heat Sno-Seal in a stove-top pan of water and paint the melted waterproofing on with a brush.

The preference for leather may be qualified by the new trend toward plastic boots with foam insulation. Even the telemark-style cross-country ski boot is beginning to acquire plastic components. Today, plastic boots would be most attractive to mountaineers who plan to use crampons for ice climbing. And the relatively few southern ice climbers often carry plastic boots for use "on the climb." Some of these boots also seem suitable for heavy winter backpacking. However, most southern winter enthusiasts would consider plastic boots only if they anticipate out-of-region mountaineering or ice climbing. In most back-country settings, a leather boot is probably still a better choice for use in Dixie or elsewhere.

Hikers and backpackers interested in winter adventure in the South should certainly consider a stiff leather boot with a lugged, Vibram-style sole. The heavier loads of the winter camper are more manageable with a stiffer, heavier-soled boot, but do not fail to adequately break in the boots before use. Cold feet and blisters are an unbearable combination.

Whether or not you'll ever need the ten- or twelve-point ice cleats called crampons, a stiff boot will permit their use. Many high southern summits call for some form of gripper on icy stretches. At times, solid ice underlies snow, and most serious winter hikers should carry one of the many varieties of "instep crampon" that strap over the boot and position a series of spikes just in front of the heel. This style of crampon is invaluable in the South, especially on particularly steep terrain. Remember, when temperatures are too warm for snow, southern summits are as likely to receive an ice storm as rain.

Crampons, skis, and the proper hiking or touring boots won't do their jobs without the right socks. As in the past, the winter enthusiast's choice for an outer sock is wool, usually the thicker and more tightly woven the better. The choice for an inner sock has changed in the last few years. Today, polypropylene and spin-off synthetic fabrics are becoming extremely popular, especially for wear next to the skin. Polypropylene does not absorb water, unlike cotton, and very effectively wicks moisture away from the skin. This fabric has drawn universal approval from hikers and skiers used to the clammy, cold feel of inferior nonwool fabrics. Even wool, although warm when wet, is less comfortable than "polypro." The new fabric dries more quickly than wool and doesn't irritate the skin as wool can.

Your entire body can benefit from polypropylene in the form of long underwear. The fabric forms the first step of a winter-clothing philosophy based on the importance of layering your garments. Each layer performs a certain role, and if you get too warm, one or more layers can be removed.

This is especially important in winter hiking or cross-country skiing where heavy perspiration caused by exercise can combine with periods of rest and inactivity in the cold to create rapid chilling.

Polypropylene or newer similar fabrics contribute to warmth by drawing sweat away from your body. They quickly dry with body heat and provide a thin but effective layer of insulation.

Some manufacturers are meshing an inner layer of polypro, or some other new "miracle" fabric, with a thin outer layer of wool to create a light but unbelievably effective undergarment. Polypropylene undershirts also make excellent sleeping bag wear, and the more fashionable ones double effectively as a T-shirt in warm weather. Even in summer, a thunderstorm can be unbearably cold in a cotton T-shirt.

The next layer beyond underwear is also undergoing the polypropylene revolution. Wool pants, knickers, and shirts are as acceptable as ever, but newer garments perform better both as fabrics and as parts of a layering scheme. Sweaters combining wool and polypro are popular now, as are thickly woven polypro pile jackets and pullovers. In pile form, the fabric still wicks moisture away faster than wool while its thick, air space-filled weave creates excellent insulation. Even pants are being made of pile, and more conventional knickers are being lined with polypro.

For the outer, heaviest insulating layers, winter enthusiasts are shifting away from down, a disaster when wet. Many expedition-quality insulated parkas are available now with synthetic fill such as DuPont's Hollofil and Quallofil. Wool and synthetic fill combination-weave sweaters are available for lighter intermediate layers, as are quilted polypropylene jackets. Outermost layers are similarly diverse. On breezy, cold days, or even when it's only cool, a windbreaker can be more useful during exercise than a heavy parka. Some skiers and hikers use a sweater or pile garment in this type of situation, but a light outer layer still seems attractive, especially if you want to ski or hike fast and choose to dress lightly under your shell garment. Wind shirts and even pants also serve these purposes.

When it's snowing or raining, an active hiker or skier can quickly become drenched. Water repellent gear won't keep the melt out, and waterproof, nonbreathable fabrics keep the perspiration in. If you can't wait out the storm in a tent, the new Gore-Tex waterproof yet breathable fabrics are best. Most people agree that these miracle fabrics don't work a complete miracle, but they do seem to be the best available alternative. Again, shell parka and pants suit the skier, hiker, backpacker, and mountaineer. This outermost layer can serve a variety of functions, including keeping snow off your pants in deep drifts.

Gloves follow the same trends. Gore-Tex outer fabric and synthetic fill characterize the latest options. Many backpackers and mountaineers prefer the greater warmth of mittens. Light undergloves are popular in extreme cold, especially with photographers, and are useful when setting up camp or cooking. Gore-Tex overmitts are a good choice for the mountaineer or skier coping with extreme weather. And thick wool mittens or gloves, like wool socks, are still popular and effective.

Headgear is another bastion of wool. The typical wool hat or fold down "balaclava helmet" is a popular mountaineering accessory. But polypropylene/wool combinations are gaining ground, especially among people who find wool irritating.

For skiers and hikers, the headband ear warmer is a great accessory that keeps exposed skin warm and still permits cool air to reach the head, and the head dissipates more heat than any other part of the body. With that in mind, if you get chilly, cover your head first, then try a jacket. And if you heat up, remove your hat or switch to a headband before stopping to pack your jacket away.

Having the right clothes and using them correctly is the most important step in treading the thin line between being too hot while exercising and too cold after. The right clothes wick away perspiration that would otherwise chill the hiker or skier when exercise stops. Overnight backpackers can further combat dampness by carrying a plastic bag of body powder for use in camp.

Far too many hikers and skiers stay overclothed when strenuously exercising. Even when wearing polypropylene underwear, you should adjust your layers to minimize your clothing's dampness and your body's loss of fluids. At the first sign of warming up, even if it's only 100 feet up the trail, stop, strip off the heavier layers, and put them in your pack.

Don't underdress either; you need your available calories for exercise, not just to heat your body. When you stop to rest or before you emerge into a windy location, add all the necessary clothes—never let yourself get cold first. You may need that wasted warmth. Conserving warmth is the main precaution that can help you avoid the winter killer, hypothermia (or exposure), and its helpmate, frostbite. (Whether or not you have the fancy, expensive new clothing, the principles of layering can be followed effectively with most serviceable garments.)

Most commonly, frostbite occurs when cold freezes exposed skin, most often on the hands and face. If your partners spot these white, waxy patches on your face, cover up with a scarf or mask.

Frostbite of the feet is more serious and usually isn't detected as early; few people regularly remove their shoes and socks in the back country. Proper footwear is thus essential. Wet feet or inadequate socks help the freezing process, as do overly tight boots that hinder circulation—one reason why winter boots should be fitted to accept heavy socks without constriction. Wiggling cold toes can help, but if your feet become numb or lose feeling, take a look. You may need to place your feet on a partner's stomach, a skin-to-skin process that you can also use for your hands by placing them inside your shirt under your own armpits. Doubling up in a sleeping bag is another way to get warm in an emergency. Severe frostbite requires making camp and administering first aid, a topic with which winter skiers and hikers should be familiar.

Regulating effective clothing is the key to avoiding hypothermia and frostbite. This maxim is especially true in the South, where a blizzard can turn to rain and back again in the same day and unusually warm weather can become record cold. Staying dry and warm are the two winter challenges that all skiers and hikers must meet. As in New England, of those who do not succeed, some die and others have close calls.

No matter what kind of clothing you have, your body will stay warm only if it has fuel that it can convert to heat. Far too many skiers and hikers forget this fact and take a long hike or ski tour with no intake of food or water. When your body depletes its energy supplies and becomes weak and dehydrated, you lose both your mobility and your ability to ward off cold. Hypothermia begins, undermining your coordination and your basic bodily functions. As your supply of energy and heat dwindles, your blood supply shifts away from the extremities to protect vital organs. Your brain loses its acuity, your coordination gets still worse, you stumble, slur your speech, and make errors in judgment. Finally, if unassisted, you may fall asleep in the snow—forever. Only the experienced and aware realize when they are facing the first phases of hypothermia, and after the first phases, even a seasoned mountaineer is in trouble.

Prevention is a must. While you hike or ski, nibble energy foods and force yourself to drink water. Perspiring isn't the only dehydrator at work; every cloud of breath you exhale illustrates that even breathing is robbing you of moisture. Avoid alcohol consumption; it can also be a dehydrator. Carry liquid to drink or melt snow on a stove. Don't eat snow. To melt it your body must expend valuable energy, and the process can actually contribute to dehydration. Gorp, a mixture of nuts, granola, dried fruit, m&m's, chocolate chips, and any other high-energy food you like, provides a variety of energy sources.

Take in plenty of nutrition and fluids, regulate your clothing correctly, and you may never experience hypothermia.

However, most experienced skiers and winter hikers do. Shivering, especially when it is severe and uncontrollable, is the first, most benign phase of hypothermia. Beyond that, lack of coordination and fuzzy thinking set in. If you spend much time out of doors in deep winter, especially on back-country trails, you may experience some of these symptoms. Heed the first warning. Immediately refuel, rehydrate, and add clothes, or make the decision to set up camp and prepare hot food to quickly get the upper hand.

Just because hypothermia lurks behind the spruce doesn't mean a winter tour or summit hike has to be a macho contest with Mother Nature. The idea is to have fun, and the simple rules of winter safety provide the buffer. Some of these rules intend to prohibit the more deadly things that a hypothermic mind seems to find reasonable. One such rule is never to leave your pack behind in an effort to make better time. If you are that tired, that cold, that desperate, you should have set up camp and gotten warm and well fed long, long ago. If, because of poor planning or unexpectedly severe weather or terrain, you do find yourself overextended, your pack and it's contents are the best alternative to tragedy you have. Don't leave it. And don't overexert yourself in these situations. Beyond a certain point, you may not be able to regain lost energy and judgment.

Don't break up your party. If someone must go ahead for help, be sure that an experienced individual remains to keep the party together and to make a camp or find or construct a shelter. Hypothermic individuals often wander off alone and lose the trail. Ski or hike alone rarely, if ever.

Just as you anticipate the wind and put on a jacket, anticipate the unexpected and be prepared, well fed, and hydrated if you have to make camp in an unplanned place or ski out in the dark. Preparation includes taking the tools needed to survive on a winter trail. In the back country, you only have what you carry with you. Many hikers perspire too heavily or drink too little water because they haven't brought a day pack to store clothes or carry water and food. Always take a pack.

Hike the trail in summer, or know from first-hand advice what to expect. Summer hiking times often double with snow on the ground, so be sure you set camp-site and hiking or skiing goals that your party can meet. Always register with the ski patrol, touring center, or rangers, and acquire all necessary permits. And leave your itinerary with a responsible person whom you can trust to sound the alarm if you are later than a prearranged time. (If you are late for benign reasons, always call this person.)

Basics for the day pack begin with a detailed map; a compass; a first aid kit that includes moleskin or some other padding for blisters; some matches, either waterproofed or in a waterproof container; portable light source; extra clothes and food; and a plastic tarp, a large space blanket, some big plastic trash bags, or some other emergency shelter. Only the shortest walks in the snow should be undertaken without some extra food and clothing, a canteen, and a flashlight.

Spare ski tips are indispensable items for skiers in the back country. If you or someone in your group breaks a ski, a spare tip will make the trip out easy. And wrap your ski poles with duct tape. Apply the tape in a few places on each pole just as it is stored on the roll, maybe one-third of an inch thick. If you break a pole, you can unroll the tape and repair it.

Skiers or hikers taking an ambitious day tour or climb in extreme conditions should be prepared to bivouac in an emergency. Carrying a sleeping bag, closed-cell foam pad, and bivouac cover for each person would not be too cautious under very cold, snowy conditions when great distances are being covered. Under less extreme circumstances, one such outfit per party is advisable, if only in case of injury.

Many winter day trippers carry a gas stove and dehydrated foods, soups, or drinks for lunch. If the unexpected happens, these amenities can become lifesaving items. If everything goes well, a hot lunch is a real luxury. On short tours and hikes, carry hot food or drink in a thermos.

Whether camping or day skiing, if you do take a stove, carry one that is pump-pressurized by hand. The typical pressurized propane or butane canister stoves will not work in cold weather. Serious backpackers often have a light propane stove for summer and another Coleman or Optimus-type stove for winter. A mountaineering party bound for several days of remote camping would do well to also carry an alcohol tab or other emergency stove. On a less ambitious winter hike or ski trip, an alcohol tab or sterno stove can be a very light way to warm up lunch and a good emergency item.

Few pieces of equipment better illustrate the need for gear appropriate to winter conditions than a stove. Never count on a camp fire. It is the inexperienced summer camper, lacking a proper gas stove, who ends up destroying trail signs and shelters for firewood at a winter camp. There is no substitute for the quick easy access to steaming hot food that a small stove provides.

All hikers, skiers, and especially backpackers must be prepared to cope with darkness. Long before you buy batteries for the flashlight that should always be in your pack, pledge yourself to an early start. Darkness arrives very early in winter, usually before five o'clock. An early start is far more pleasant than the overexertion of trying to make up lost time when dark is closing in. If you can't get to the trailhead early, spend the night in a motel rather than camp in zero-degree weather after a long drive from a warm climate.

The frozen forests of the South can harbor surprises, so even if you are just out for the day, carry a flashlight, preferably a headlamp. Cooking dinner in the dark, skiing, hiking on a snowy trail, or any other activity that could require use of your hands is infinitely easier with a headlamp. Extra batteries are a good idea, and reverse the ones in your headlamp or flashlight to avoid accidentally illuminating the inside of a pack.

Sleeping in the snowy wilds is a rigorous undertaking. At high elevations in midwinter in the South, the backpacker or mountaineer should have a sleeping bag rated to 20 below zero. The South's cold dampness makes a synthetic-filled sleeping bag a better choice than a down bag. A closed-cell foam pad is best for deflecting the cold of the snowy ground.

Only the inexperienced expect to huddle around a campfire to keep warm. With the right clothing and a hot meal, more than one experienced mountaineer has surprised beginners by sitting contentedly outside on a sleeping pad in subzero weather. Down- or synthetic-filled booties and pants are key garments for after-dinner comfort.

In heavy snow and high winds, a summer tent will not offer enough shelter. Serious winter backpackers should own a four-season tent sealed with a seam sealant. Today's popular winter dome tents are more livable shelters than A-frame tents, especially when a long snow storm strikes or severe cold keeps you inside. A cook hole on the floor is also helpful then, and wide snow stakes may offer the only way to firmly pitch your tent in deep snow.

Another tool that is effective for pitching a tent in blizzard conditions is an ice axe. But as with snowshoes, full-size crampons, ropes, and ice-climbing picks and hammers, relatively few southerners carry ice axes into the back country. These tools separate the mountaineer from the backpacker. The difference between the two lies in the destination and the conditions encountered. The mountaineer heads for locations where open meadows or rocky terrain can be covered with deep snow and ice. Camping or climbing in exposed locations, high winds, and active, heavy snowfall can make for a southern ski or backpacking trip that is remarkably similar to above-tree-line climbing and camping in the West or New England, without the greater danger of avalanche in those areas.

Backpackers or overnight skiers venturing into the highest areas will come closest to these conditions if they plan ahead and cultivate the freedom to go when the heavy weather arrives. But the danger always exists of being surprised by snow and cold on these rugged heights, so whenever you go to the highest, snowiest places, be prepared for true mountaineering situations, especially if the more remote locations are your goal.

In the middle of the Great Smokies, high on Mount Mitchell, Grandfather, or Hump in North Carolina, or in the middle of West Virginia's Dolly Sods, snow can quickly fall to depths of 30 inches or more; heavy ice can make the levelest trail treacherous; and in high winds at 20 degrees below, conditions can equal those in the Canadian arctic. However unlikely a combination like this may seem in the South, it occurs frequently, and the grossly unprepared can be severely challenged.

Despite such conditions, few winter backpackers in Dixie carry snowshoes, as most do in New England. Snowshoes would be a good accessory in the South, especially if you intend to climb the highest mountains after substantial snowfalls. If you expect to break a trail in more than 15 inches of snow, purchase snowshoes (they are generally unavailable for rent in the South). You won't need to encounter more than a few heavy-snow hikes to make the investment a good one. In fact, backpackers bound for West Virginia's unusually snowy summits should consider snowshoes as a mandatory safety measure.

Many southern backpackers and mountaineers consider purchasing snowshoes and other mountaineering gear because they expect to undertake winter hiking trips in the North or West. For these people, the South can provide a good training ground, and all the equipment mentioned earlier will be suitable for out-of-region trips.

Snowshoes can also be a simple courtesy when hikers and backpackers are bound for trails frequented by cross-country skiers. Every winter, the snow on Mount Rogers or Roan Mountain is deep enough for backpackers to be better off using snowshoes anyway, and at these times, backpackers and hikers invariably sink knee deep through the tracks of cross-country skiers, who usually outnumber the walkers. These post-hole foot prints make skiing impossible and constitute a classic user conflict, as discussed in Chapter 5. With snowshoes, the hiker would actually improve the skiing, or at worst, do little damage, while also walking more easily and having more fun.

Although instep crampons will frequently suffice for less ambitious backpackers, it doesn't take much snow to make the more specialized ice axe useful as a hiking aid. Many New England backpackers carry them, even when they expect milder conditions than steep snow above the tree line, where the ice axe is designed to arrest sliding falls. If you foresee mountaineering under such conditions elsewhere in America, you should of course purchase an ice axe, but in the South it is optional.

Ice-climbing picks and hammers are usually much shorter than an ice axe, and these tools, generally speaking, won't help the hiker. They are specifically designed to pull climbers up ice flows and to be used with front-point crampons, ropes, and safety anchors that screw into the ice. Using such equipment requires considerable study, instruction, and skill. In the South, a hiker could use the pick point of an ice axe for a similar purpose, but only to gain stability going across ice, and never to climb up ice! Even this practice might require a safety rope and the knowledge of how to use it.

Southern ice climbers stress that cold sufficient to create strong, reliable ice is fleeting in the South. Suitable ice, in some places many hundreds of feet in height, does occur and is climbed by southerners, many of whom climb or plan to in the North and West. But safe climbing requires skill, experience, and, especially in the South, reliable knowledge of recent weather.

Huge ice fingers reach down many southern cliffs. High waterfalls freeze solid, and slide gullies appear as white scars on major peaks. The dedicated ice climbers find these usually north-facing, shaded flows and always climb "top roped" at first, with a safety belay rope anchored from the top of the ice to prevent falls. Only the most experienced parties tackle big ice using the lead-climber method, which is most widely known as a rock climbing technique.

Would-be southern ice climbers should either seek instruction from locally known experts or take lessons, perhaps for a fee, at a clinic or school. The closest programs are run by the Appalachian Mountain Club in New England. Training in rock climbing, a fine prelude to safe ice climbing, is widely available at the many nationally known rock climbing sites in Georgia, North Carolina, and West Virginia.

For those who have some training, or who despite warnings intend to learn on their own, never practice on large flows. Experts recommend that beginners tackle the many small, often road-side flows created at road cuts or on small streams. The Blue Ridge Parkway prohibits such activity. But U.S. 221 beside Grandfather Mountain and the highest part of Tenn. 143 on the way to Roan Mountain are two spots where ice climbers often ply their craft. As in rock climbing, this small-scale practice is called bouldering. But remember, even this activity can be dangerous, not the least of hazards being nearby moving cars.

Most winter enthusiasts in the South, however, will gladly dispense with the technical details and focus on the less rigorous sights and sounds of winter. For them, the South offers snow and more.

In some parts of America, autumn colors careen down with the first snowfall, and then, until spring, the scene is white. In the South, hikers gain an almost separate season, from mid-October to mid-December, when substantial snowfall is rare and the usually light snows offer sensations of winter without its arduous effort.

Granted, snow usually will dust southern summits while autumn flames below, and occasionally an autumn camping trip can become a midwinter enterprise. Thanksgiving backpackers have awakened to more than 2 feet of snow as far south as North Carolina. But the norm is a two-month stretch of crisp breezes and footfalls on equally crisp fallen leaves. This season is a fine time for would-be winter mountaineers to learn colder weather camping while they appreciate a taste of early-winter beauty.

Colors pale in a stark prelude to deep winter. November is the clearest, most panoramic month in the southern mountains. With summer's haze departed, views reach a hundred miles and each rugged summit stands in relief, its rocky cliff lines shed of leaves. Pungent wisps of wood smoke settle in deep valleys under pearl gray skies. This is a time when mountain people hunker down, haul pick-up loads of firewood, and stiffen their shoulders against a growing gray. Nature's spirit seems to wane. There is a snowless majesty in this world awaiting winter. From the peaks, the overcast conjures the image of a cloud-faced old character on the corner of an antique map, blurring with his breath the thin line between fall and winter. A favorite time for winter hiking, this transitional season seems to suit the southern mountains. Here the philosophical can pause, like nature, and cast a clear eye on life's horizons.

This aesthetic rewards those who venture into the early-winter woods. Best of all, the woods have shed their crowds with their leaves. And after this interlude, the snow comes and the easier hiking trails attract skiers and vacationers taking a day off from the slopes to see a different world. Higher up, mountaineers camp in the fiercest weather the South offers.

In the spring, be ready for winter snow and cold. The loftiest summits will have none of the green of the lowland South. For summer, the trails in this guide reach the best scenery and coolest climates in the South. Hike them at will. But before the cold and snow arrive, prepare for what's to come. Read the other introductory chapters, set up a contact for snow reports, ready your car, brush up on first aid, and be ready to go when the snow flies.

Part Two

DOWNHILL RESORTS

Maryland

Garrett County: Complete Winter Sports Area

Garrett County, Maryland, is the most complete winter sports area within easy driving distance, about three and a half hours, of Washington, D.C. Garrett, Maryland's snowiest county and the location of 4,000-acre Deep Creek Lake, the state's largest, receives average annual snowfall of 82 inches.

Garrett County represents the northernmost tip of southern skiing. In this region the rugged ridges begin to flatten out into high farm country with a distinctly Yankee feel. The architecture recalls Pennsylvania and New England. The frozen, snowy lake would look as much at home in mid-New Hampshire's lake district as in this county bordering the Mason-Dixon line. Southerners will find Garrett County a unique and attractive alternative to venues further south.

In fact, skiers in the Canaan Valley (Part 2) or Cooper's Rock (Part 3) areas of West Virginia have easy access to Garrett County, and vice versa. Check those entries for other possible ski sites, accommodations, and dining that can complement those in Garrett County.

Travel within Garrett is easy. Well-maintained roads serve the thousands of acres of state park and state forest land. Access is easy from the east, north, and west using Interstates 40 and 70 and the four-lane U.S. 48 to U.S. 219. From the southeast the fastest access is U.S. 50 from Interstate 81 at Winchester. The county seat, Oakland, is the hub of the Deep Creek Lake recreation area.

Garrett's winter activities are more diverse than those at most southern destinations. Besides downhill and Nordic skiing at Wisp, there are fine cross-country ski areas at state parks, where Nordic races are held each winter. See the contact information at the end of the entry.

Snowmobiles can be rented, and there are 35 miles of trails, and sometimes snowmobile tours, on state forest land. Use of state trails requires 4 inches of snow, and users must obtain a $5 permit at park headquarters. Maps are available at state forest headquarters and the Promotion Council office in Oakland. Garrett County is the site for the state snowmobile racing championships and other events.

A central, recorded snow report for cross-country skiers and snowmobilers is available 24 hours a day at 301/768-0895. The Herrington Manor/Swallow Falls (Part 3) phone number is also a 24-hour snow report for those parks that applies to the county in general— 301/334-9180.

Horse-drawn sleigh rides are available, and even ice fishing is popular, particularly at Deep Creek Lake State Park, where demonstrations are sometimes held.

Both of these Nordic parks have rental cabins. The reservation procedure is by lottery in summer, for a one-week minimum stay, and on a first-come, first-served basis in winter, with a minimum stay of two nights. For details, request "Cabins in Maryland's State Parks" from the State Forest and Park Office listed below.

The Wisp ski area has both dining and accommodations. Another lodging place is the Panorama Motel in McHenry, just across the lake from the ski area and opposite the Circle G Ranch (sleigh rides) and near the Crystal Waters Snowmobile Rentals at Garrett County Fairgrounds.

The Point View Inn, beside the lake and minutes from Wisp, has motel rooms. For a variety of accommodations and amenities, the choice in Garrett County is Will O' the Wisp, a condominium/motel combination with a range of prices; meeting facilities; indoor pool, sauna, and Jacuzzi; racquetball, and exercise rooms. The Red Run Inn is a bed and breakfast lodge on Mayhew Road near Herrington Manor State Park. The Casselman Motor Inn, in Grantsville, is a favorite for New Germany State Park Nordic skiers. The area has other extensive accommodations, including many motels and rental cabins and houses.

Fast-food establishments don't seem as prevalent in Garrett County as in most places. Independent restaurants are the rule, and some of the above accommodations are also Garrett County destinations for fine dining. At Will O' the Wisp, the 4 Seasons provides professional service and a warm, wood-toned atmosphere for what is often called the area's best food. The meal price includes appetizer through dessert.

The Trellis Room at Point View Inn serves delicious German specialties, and The Casselman features homecooked meals in a 160-year-old house first opened as an inn on one of the earliest roads west. Nearby is Casselman Bridge, a National Historical Landmark. When built in 1813, it was the longest single-span bridge in the country. The Red Run Inn's dining rooms serve a wide variety of gourmet food, including a breakfast for overnight guests. Near the Panorama Motel and Wisp, the Topsider Restaurant and Lounge offers inexpensive, hearty meals and a great breakfast special.

Most nightlife centers on restaurant lounges. Live music is featured at Zump's and Pizza Pub, both on U.S. 219, and at the Red Run Inn.

Area alpine ski shops include one of the South's earliest, Rudy's at Wisp, and also Tips Up Ski Shop at the entrance to Wisp. Cross-country ski rentals are available from Deep Creek Outfitters, beside the lake in downtown McHenry; at Wisp Ski Touring Center, next door to Wisp; and Dubansky's, a Nordic ski shop near New Germany State Park.

Warm weather in Garrett County means water sports. The Savage River is one of the East's premier whitewater runs, and Deep Creek Lake is a major boating, water skiing, and fishing destination.

Savage River State Forest has a 17-mile backpacking trail along the crest of Savage Mountain, from Savage River Dam to U.S. 40. The trail skirts the 2,000-acre Big Savage Wildland (no camping) and the High Rock Firetower (2,991 feet). A camping permit is required for backpacking.

Garrett County's resources are covered in a variety of free publications from the Maryland State Park and Forest Services and the Deep Creek Lake-Garrett County Promotion Council.

For more information, contact

Deep Creek Lake–Garrett County Promotion Council, Oakland, MD 21550. 301/334-1948.

MD Forest and Park Service, Department of Natural Resources, Tawes State Office Building, 580 Taylor Ave., Annapolis, MD 21401. 301/269-3771.

Ice Fishing: Deep Creek Lake State Park, Rte. 2, Box 70, Swanton, MD 21561. 301/387-5563.

Snowmobiling/Backpacking/Hunting: Savage River State Forest, Rte. 2, Box A-63, Grantsville, MD 21536. 301/895-5453.

Potomac-Garrett State Forests, Rte. 3, Box 256, Deer Park, MD 21550. 301/334-2038.

Allegheny Mountain Cross-Country Ski Citizen Race Series: Laurel Highlands Ski Touring Association, PO Box 3075, Greensburg, PA 15601.

Wisp: A Bright Future

Maryland's Wisp may be the one southern ski area best described not for what it is, but for what it will be. Since the slope's midfifties debut, its development has been consistent, conservative, and slope oriented. But the ski area's rejection of real estate has kept its base facilities simple—some might say too simple—and its slope-side amenities to a minimum. That's changing, however. Wisp is currently the site of a phased, condominium/hotel construction project that promises to transform it into one of the region's most attractive ski areas. Lodging and amenities are expected to be second to none in the South.

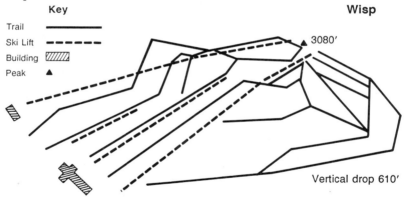

Key — Trail, Ski Lift, Building, Peak ▲

Wisp — 3080′ — Vertical drop 610′

Wisp's goals are ambitious and the resort's track record suggests that it may have a better chance than most to succeed. It already has fine skiing, golf, and summer lake recreation facilities at its perch beside Maryland's largest freshwater impoundment, Deep Creek Lake, in Garrett County. Wisp's first condo phase is complete; its second includes a brand-new base lodge and another 100 condo units for the winter of 1986–87. Development will continue from there.

Ultimately, the $50-million convention complex is projected to include 500 condominium units, convention facilities and a large exhibition space, four restaurants, snack bars, lounges, a theater, racquetball and tennis courts, indoor and outdoor heated pools and Jacuzzis, and a parklike atrium with indoor ice skating and retail shops.

The modern Wisp Condominiums now completed rival any slope-side lodging in the region. A spacious indoor pool facility includes a sauna and Jacuzzi, and a nicely designed lobby makes elevators, the pool, and dining and game room facilities easily accessible. The après-ski atmosphere of The Gathering Restaurant and Shenanigans Lounge is excellent. The multilevel dining facility serves three meals a day and features live evening entertainment on weekends. Inexpensive package prices include lift tickets, breakfast, dinner, and use of the pool, sauna, and Jacuzzi.

In addition to the facilities right at Wisp, many other accommodations are found in the Garrett County area.

Slope-side lodging is the emerging story at Wisp, but quality skiing is a longstanding forte. Wisp is as big as any southern slope in acreage, and its 2-mile trail, Possum, is the longest run in the region. The resort's 610-foot vertical drop is medium sized by southern standards, but 14 miles of skiing on sixteen slopes is substantial terrain.

Viewed from the base lodge, Wisp's outstanding features are The Face and Squirrel Cage, harrowing expert slopes that seem to stand on end. With steepest grades of 60 degrees, these often heavily moguled slopes are probably the best expert runs in the region. The feeling that you're going to take off from the slope and land on the lodge is part of their appeal. Besides chairlifts, the region's longest and steepest surface lift serves both runs.

Wisp's three double chairlifts serve the rounded top of the mountain (3,080 feet), although they all end at different locations. Chair 1 climbs the mountain's far left side, looking up, and lets you ski the entire length of Possum. Back toward the lodge, the terrain is gradual. Muskrat follows the lift line back down. On the far left, Bobcat drops steeper than Muskrat, but both intermediate slopes join at the bench where the gradual summit of Wisp drops abruptly. Boulder run is an arcing intermediate trail down this lip, and an expert run, Devil's Drop, takes the plummet more steeply, right beside The Face. Two wide, flat sections parallel the bottom of Chair 1, and a rope tow services this easy beginner area. (Future plans include five new slopes and three new lifts next to these slopes.)

Viewed from the base, chairs 2 and 3 sit side by side on the far right and climb the right side of Squirrel Cage, with The Face and its surface

lift to the left. Chair 3 reaches highest, tying into the easy trails, Possum and Wisp, both, from the top, going right on the longest, most gradual runs to the bottom. Chair 2 exits first, giving access to a variety of enjoyable intermediate connectors down to The Face, or to Possum and Wisp Trail, which make up the right edge of the resort. Views here offer spectacular glimpses of rolling mountains and snow-covered farms.

Wisp has daily ski sessions from 9:00 to 4:30 and night skiing on Tuesday, Wednesday, Thursday, and Friday from 6:00 to 10:00. Eighty percent of the slopes are lit for night skiing, including The Face and Possum.

Wisp's base lodge houses lift ticket sales, Rudy's Ski Shop—at Wisp for over thirty years—a cafeteria, ski rentals, a picnic area, The Bavarian Room for lunch and light evening après-ski entertainment, a warming area with a view of The Face, and the ski school, run by Austrian Dieter Baer. There are regularly scheduled races, and child care is available through the resort.

Wisp's big winter event comes just before the spring. The mid-March Winterfest is a longstanding annual event that benefits local charities. A Kickoff Party launches the fun. The two days that follow offer a variety of ski and fun races, sleigh and pony rides, snowmobile slope climbs, fireworks, and a torchlight parade, among other activities. Winterfest is a good time with much local participation.

For more information, contact

Wisp Resort, Marsh Hill Rd., McHenry, Maryland 21541.
　　301/387-5581.
Snow report: 301/387-4000.

West Virginia

Alpine Lake: Small on a Big Scale

Set amid the rolling uplands of snowy Preston County, near Terra Alta, W.Va., Alpine Lake has a designed-with-nature feel to it. A 2,500-acre residential development discretely blends into the forests that surround the 200-acre enlarged natural lake. The lake shore is undeveloped, one of many factors that helped earn the resort a state award for excellence in ecological planning. Twenty-four-hour security patrols and a gatehouse add an air of exclusivity, but Alpine Lake is not a subdivision for millionaires. The resort retains a middle class flavor that bolsters its appeal as a family ski area and summer vacation destination. Alpine Lake is unpretentious and comfortable . . . in an upscale sort of way.

The resort's ski area, like its other amenities, is part of an overall package: this isn't a Snowshoe, Wintergreen, Beech, or Sugar, where skiing on a grand scale carries the banner for the entire development. Skiing is one more activity for home owners, and the public is invited.

With suitable weather, skiing at Alpine Lake usually starts by Christmas, with daily operation and night skiing through the holidays. Snow making is most energetic, and the skiing at its best, in January and February, when the area receives the bulk of its annual 80-plus inches of natural snow.

Alpine Lake's slopes are open only on Saturday and Sunday, with night skiing on Friday and Saturday. The resort attracts day skiers from surrounding towns, but the nearby Canaan Valley and Wisp ski areas draw the crowds.

The slopes offer a 400-foot vertical drop on a 2,200-foot main advanced slope. A platter-pull tow services this major run, which starts at a 3,300-foot elevation. There are also a 700-foot intermediate slope and a 300-foot

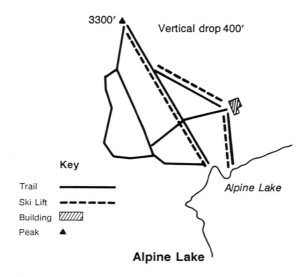

Alpine Lake

beginner slope, both served by tows. All slopes are covered by snow making and grooming, except for a half-mile, natural snow, unlit trail that descends through the woods from the top of the advanced slope. All these runs face a stunning view of frozen Alpine Lake and the advanced and intermediate slopes end at the shore line.

Downhill ski rentals and lessons are available, and there is also a cross-country ski center and an ice skating rink with rentals.

Alpine Lake's ski facilities are perfect for the family or beginner group who doesn't need or want the challenges of a major resort. Luckily, any big ski resort would be proud of Alpine Lake's amenities.

Ambience, atmosphere, and après-ski are where Alpine Lake really shines. Off-slope facilities center on a rustic, Swiss-style lodge with eight rooms, one of them a suite. Other lodging is located in a modern thirty-five-room motel. Each room has a porch and a color satellite TV; ice and snacks are available all night; and there is a laundry facility for guests.

The main lodge houses the 200-seat dining room, with a view of the lake. The food is quite good and diverse. Nearby is a bar and lounge, with a big screen TV and nighttime entertainment on weekends. Downstairs is another daytime dining area frequented by skiers. Beer, wine, and mixed drinks are available at Alpine Lake.

An Olympic-size, heated indoor pool with a diving board is located on the lower level of the lodge near the cafe. A well-equipped health/exercise room adjoins the pool, and two large Jacuzzi hot tubs dominate the entrance to the locker rooms. A sauna is nearby.

These attractive offerings, along with three nicely appointed meeting rooms and group rates, make Alpine Lake a favorite spot for skiers. A very inexpensive ski package features two nights' lodging for up to four people, unlimited skiing for two, and all amenities and activities. And if the skiing at Alpine Lake isn't what it should be, the resort will substitute a lift ticket at Wisp, forty minutes away.

Alpine Lake, after a period of decline, is a resurgent resort with style. If the positive changes continue, skiing at Alpine Lake will no doubt also improve. As it is, Alpine Lake is an attractive resort experience, especially for families and novice groups that want a lot of fun for their dollar.

In summer, Alpine Lake offers all of the above amenities with an emphasis on golf (twelve holes and a driving range), tennis (four hardsurface, day-use courts), fishing in a stocked lake, boating (canoe, sail, paddle, and row boat rentals), and a miniature golf course. In late September, Preston County—"The Buckwheat Capital of the World"—stages its Buckwheat Festival in Kingwood. Alpine Lake serves the area's most delicious buckwheat pancakes all year.

For more information, contact

Alpine Lake Resort & Conference Center, Terra Alta, WV 26764.
304/789-2481.

Canaan Valley Area: Introduction

In the late 1800s, they called this high, sparsely settled valley Canada. Today, the climate that spawned that name has made Canaan Valley a developing winter sports area of regional significance. Average snowfall varies from 100 inches on the valley floor to perhaps 150 on surrounding ridges.

One of the first surprises to emerge from a trip to Canaan is that locals don't pronounce the name with the Biblical emphasis on the first syllable, but with the second syllable stressed: kha-NANE.

Canaan is easily one of the South's top winter destinations, especially for the cross-country skier and winter hiker/backpacker. The winter scene at Canaan easily conjures a stanza from a poem by Joe Gray used in an early 1950s film about the first organized skiing in the valley: "Above the Valley called Canaan, / Rises a slope where all may go, / It's West Virginia's Sky Terrain / A wonder 'Driftland' deep in snow."

The valley is reached via W.Va. 32, north from Harman, south from Thomas. The road runs the valley floor with the undulating crest of Cabin Mountain and the Dolly Sods to the east and Canaan Mountain on the west, both evergreen covered ridges are in the Monongahela National Forest.

From its southern end, where it gains the high valley at Canaan Valley Resort State Park and ski area, W.Va. 32 passes White Grass Ski Touring Center and Mount Timberline, another ski area. There are a number of restaurants, shops, and lodging developments along the road. W.Va. 32 rises from the valley floor and crests Canaan Mountain, with fine views at Canaan Heights, then rolls to the quaint lumber town of Davis (3,200 feet) and the entrance to Blackwater Falls State Park.

Everything is easily accessible and compact in Canaan, with no need for long drives to distant towns or resorts. When Tory Mountain opens in Harman, it too will be close. In fact, even more northerly state parks in West Virginia and Garrett County, Md., are easy to reach on day trips from Canaan. Check other entries for possible ski sites, lodging, and dining.

Access from population centers is more problematical. West Virginia's famous country roads are the primary routes. From the east, the state's rippled ridges are a tedious washboard of ups and downs. The best routes enter the state low or high and run up or down the valleys. Good access routes into the area include Route U.S. 219, 33, 32 from Elkins and south, U.S. 50 from the northeast, and for Washington D.C. area residents, Interstates 70, 40, and U.S. 220, 50 south from Cumberland Md., or U.S. 219 through Garrett County. Dining and lodging at both Canaan Valley and Blackwater Falls state parks are quite good. See those entries for details.

Recommended private accommodations are various and in Davis include the homey atmosphere and hearty food of the Victorian Twisted Thistle Inn, a bed and breakfast. The Best Western Alpine Lodge has the Sawmill Restaurant and an indoor pool. The Mountain Aire Lodge in Davis and the Village Inn Motel in Canaan Village are also good choices. There are condominium accommodations in Davis at Pendletonheim, and in Canaan Valley at Mount Timberline and airstrip-equipped Talheim Resort Village, where units include Jacuzzis. Canaan Realty offers a variety of accommodations, and there are other condomium and real estate services. Call ahead for lodging. Many valley accommodations require two-night rentals for weekend stays.

Between Canaan Valley and Garrett County, 12 miles north of Davis on U.S. 219, Mountain Village Inn offers fine dining, lodging and a rental cabin. See the Cathedral State Park for details.

Private restaurants are many. The Oriskany Inn, just north of Canaan Valley State Park, is the valley's favorite gourmet restaurant, with fine views of surrounding summits and ski areas from picture windows. The menu runs from steak to veal, including excellent broiled seafood like a delicious sampler and a variety of kabobs. Diners enjoy padded reclining chairs, and the Gemstone Lounge is cozy and quiet. The Sawmill Restaurant at Best Western in Davis has an excellent preski breakfast.

Other options in the same area include family dining with good Italian specialties at Peter Christian's in Blackwater Center and Big John's Family Fixin's in Canaan Village. Gas 'n Grub is a convenience store and deli with fried chicken and baked pastries. Canaan Village, north of the park, is a battery of shops, and Davis has a pharmacy, grocery store, and other services.

Alcohol is widely available in the valley, and live music is available at Canaan Valley State Park on weekends.

A number of ski shops operate in the valley, including Weiss Knob Ski Shop, owned by early Canaan Valley ski pioneer Bob Barton, in Blackwater Center. Cabin Mountain Sports is located in Canaan Village, just north of Canaan Valley ski area, The Inside Edge Ski Shop has one outlet at Canaan Heights and another at Canaan Valley ski area.

TransMontane Outfitters in Davis was the area's first cross-country ski outfitter. They have complete rentals, and tours. The Davis shop stays open until late Friday evening, with a wine and cheese party and free waxing clinic, to rent skis for Saturday. Children under ten get free rentals when their parents pay. TransMontane is a backpacker's source for rental snowshoes, unusual in the South, and the skiers best bet for information on snow conditions in the Canaan Mountain area, where boggy terrain can make for poor skiing even with substantial snow. TransMontane runs extensive summer programs, for families and professional groups, in backpacking, whitewater sports, and caving.

Winter recreation can include visits to Smoke Hole Caverns, open daily, and weekend stops at Seneca Rocks Visitor Center in Mouth of Seneca. Winter events include cross-country and downhill ski races, and there is a festival in the early spring. Throughout the summer and fall, the Alpine Visual Arts Painting & Photography Workshops feature nationally known photographers and artists in seminars based in Davis.

For more information, contact

Potomac Highland Travel Council, PO Box 1459, Elkins, WV 26241.
  304/636-8400.
TransMontane Outfitters, PO Box 325, Davis, WV 26260.
  304-259-5117.

Canaan Valley Resort State Park Ski Area

For some years, the ski area at Canaan Valley Resort State Park has borne the image of a second choice to West Virginia's biggest ski area, Snowshoe. Isolation plays a part. A Canaan skier once said, "when you're at Canaan, you're at Canaan." Unlike the North Carolina high country, the neighborhood doesn't include four or five resort towns, and unlike Snowshoe, the area is less colored by the more glamorous après side of skiing—hot tubs and discos, for instance, are not as readily available. This situation is changing, though, as the area becomes more popular. For many skiers, Canaan Valley may become a favorite among southern slopes.

Canaan Valley, as the publicists say, is "Big Snow Country." Today's Canaan Valley ski area is on the exact spot where West Virginia's first commercial ski area opened in 1955. That early ski area relied on natural snow, and the valley called Canaan is one of a handful of spots in the South where natural snow is plentiful enough to do without snowmaking. The ski slopes climb Cabin Mountain, the highest peak above West Virginia's highest valley. Conservative snow estimates here are 120 to 140 inches a year. The resort claims 180. And much of that is real powder snow. For years, Canaan continued to rely mostly on natural snow, and conditions were often better at other resorts with big snowmaking systems. But after a massive recent increase in snow-making, Canaan now covers 90 percent of its terrain with machine made snow. Add that to its ample natural accumulation, and Canaan's skiing conditions are among the best in the South.

Canaan isn't the biggest southern resort, but with twenty-one slopes and trails it is among the largest. Its excellent design creates a satisfying variety of terrain. Want a long run? Unlike some resorts where the longest run is one top to bottom route through the middle of the slopes, Canaan offers two long, meandering trails, each in a different direction from the summit chairlifts and with a different appeal. Timber Trail, remote, and scenic, recalls the easiest runs at Killington. Dark Side of the Moon brushes the top of Weiss Meadows and offers a western feel for intermediates. Each is over a mile long.

Experts have the heart-stopping Gravity, a new, often heavily moguled slope that is among the steepest and most sustained drops in the region. Spruce Run is another expert trail with substantial vertical drop. Tucked all over the mountain are shorter expert pitches, many, like The Chute, narrow and exciting.

Canaan's is scenic skiing, with open views and runs that often wind through evergreen glades. The beginner area is completely separated from the other slopes and offers a great mix of flat learning slopes and alternative runs, some of them quite long. Beginners have their own double chair, surface tow, and slope-side building where lift tickets are available.

Although not all of the slopes are lit, night skiing offers something for everyone. Most beginner slopes are lit. Canaan's slopes weren't always easily accessible. For quite some time, only a double chairlift reached the top of the mountain's 850-foot vertical drop. Now, the double chair and a new triple chair serve the 4,280-foot summit, making long lift lines a thing of the past.

From the two main buildings at the bottom of the slope, Valley Haus and Weiss Haus, even the separated beginner area is accessible. This two building base facility faces an enclosed, snow-covered courtyard with ski storage racks. For food, skiers can choose between a cafeteria and a snack bar/lunch room with an outdoor deck. There's also a warming area with a fireplace, and the pub is a popular late afternoon gathering spot for both visitors and local ski pros.

The two lodges also house ski rentals, a ski shop, a repair shop, and lockers, as well as the ski school office. Canaan's ski school is a member of the Professional Ski Instructors of America system and widely noted for its special emphasis on skiing instruction for the blind, and the physically challenged, including amputees. The school also focuses on children, with a nursery for toddlers eighteen months to six years old and a Ski-N-Play program for youngsters three to six years old. The ski school offers video taping of skiers as part of its lesson plan.

Racers of all ages can get special instruction, and recreational races are held at midweek and on the weekend. Anyone can enter. The racing slope has a new, permanent timing system with dual competition capability. Serious local racers often compete at Canaan. There are United States Ski Association-sanctioned races during the season, and in March The Governor's Cup Race caps the many special races the resort features throughout the winter.

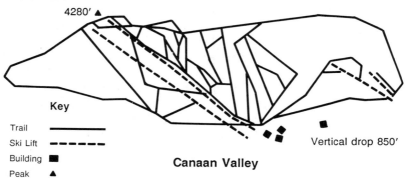

4280'

Key

Trail ——————
Ski Lift – – – – –
Building ◼
Peak ▲

Canaan Valley

Vertical drop 850'

Cannan offers much more than skiing, too. The slopes are one part of a 6,000-acre park where the scenery and climate resemble Canada's. This spot may be the best in the South for winter sports. With its pronounced alpine, tundralike aspect, the area has a very wild, North Country feel. Visitors routinely glimpse sheltering herds of deer amid the spruce.

The facilities are hardly primitive, though. Across W.Va. 32 from the ski area, a winding access road leads to the heart of Canaan's resort ambience. Five modern two-story lodges offer 250 rooms, each with telephone, color satellite TV, two double or king-size beds, and climate control. Six efficiency apartments are also available, and all accommodations are connected to the main resort lodge by covered walkways. Fifteen two- to four-bedroom cabins with fireplaces are nearby. Many packages offer substantial savings, and information, reservations, and a snow report are available toll free at the number listed at the end of this entry.

For dining, the main lodge offers two alternatives. A snack bar is open all day and late into the evening. The Aspen Room is Canaan's main dining room, and it is indeed an achievement. The modern, open decor isn't particularly warm or intimate, but the big windows look out on a sweeping view of the valley, surrounded by snow-covered peaks. According-ing to a resort publication, the dining room offers "moderately priced dishes" but "gourmet foods are not featured." Both of these statements are not really true. The Aspen Room may render the best combination of reasonable prices and excellent food at any southern ski resort. In fact, the Aspen Room's prices can only be called unbelievably inexpensive. Granted, as for gourmet foods, the menu includes few exotic dishes, but it offers diversity. Everything is well prepared using fresh ingredients. Many gourmet restaurants would be proud of the consistent high quality of the Aspen Room's satisfying meals. Wine, beer, and mixed drinks can complement your meal, and for children under twelve, a portion of any entree is half the menu price.

A lounge/pub is downstairs in the main lodge, and on weekends throughout the ski season, diverse live musical entertainment and dancing take place in the lodge. During the week, the lack of live music may limit Canaan's appeal for the hard-core nightlife crowd.

If these diversions aren't enough, Canaan adds others. A full size, lighted ice rink adjoins the lodge, and skate rentals and lessons are available. With natural snow, a special sledding/tobogganing hill is maintained, complete with rentals. The park operates a year-round recreation program, headquartered in the lodge with daily activities, craft classes, evening movies, and slide programs, all listed in a weekly booklet. A gift shop, and video game room are also located in the lodge.

Canaan can be a good choice for groups, especially meetings and conventions. A Convention Services Department handles arrangements for up to 500 people. There are five meeting rooms, and sessions can be video taped.

With all this going on at the resort, even Canaan's image of isolation isn't holding up. In fact, the resort may be easier to reach than Snowshoe for some skiers. And once you arrive, you can do without your car by riding the frequent shuttle buses between the lodge and the ski area.

If you don't mind driving, Canaan's environs offer other diversions, including other places to ski. The new Timberline ski area, although closed recently, will likely reopen, and that resort offers a very different skiing experience from Canaan's and promises to become a major resort itself. Also expected to open soon is the new Tory Mountain Ski Area, near Harman, W.Va. In addition, Alpine Lake ski area, near Terra Alta, W.Va., and Wisp ski resort in Maryland are not too far away.

If you'd like to sample Nordic skiing, there are more cross-country opportunities within and near Canaan Valley State Park than anywhere else in the South. Several public park and private Nordic ski centers exist. Nordic is so popular in the Canaan area that the ski area has become a favorite slope for telemark skiers. In fact, a good many of Canaan's downhill ski patrollers make their rounds on cross-country skis.

Recommended dining opportunities outside the park include Big John's Family Fix'ins and The Oriskany Inn, both near the park, and the lodge at Blackwater Falls State Park, north of Canaan at Davis, W.Va. Other restaurants and grocery stores, as well as motel and condominium lodging, some with sauna facilities, are all available close to Canaan Valley State Park, many near the towns of Thomas and Davis (see the preceding entry). Elkins, W.Va., thirty-five miles away, also offers entertainment, dining, lodging, and air service from major cities via Wheeler Airlines.

Canaan's season usually runs from December 1, weather permitting, to late March or early April. The valley's heavy snow and the park's annual, late March Spring Thing Celebration, which includes pond jumping on skis, make this area a fine spring skiing destination.

Summer offers a large swimming pool facility, a championship eighteen-hole golf course, six lighted tennis courts, miniature golf, and naturalist-led hikes.

For more information, contact

Canaan Valley Resort State Park, Rte. 1, Box 39, Davis, WV 26260
304/866-4121.
Snow report, reservations, and information: 800/CALLWVA.

Silver Creek: A Flair for Style

The first things you notice about Silver Creek are the lodge, the view, and the slopes. All differ greatly from those at other southern ski areas.

The lodge is served by the Silver Creek Access road, which leaves Snowshoe Drive just before Snowshoe ski resort. Both resorts are on the crest of Cheat Mountain.

Pulling up to the Silver Creek Lodge is indeed a shock. Besides being surprised by valet parking, the visitor is confronted by a futuristic building resembling a space-age settlement on some faraway planet. The nine-story facility spreads ramp-like wings around a central atrium.

Inside, the lodge is even more impressive. Sun beams into a huge central cavity and people flow between multilevel decks, listening to live music during a break from skiing as glass-walled, talking elevators move up and down, serving accommodations in the Ice Castle and the Crystal Wings.

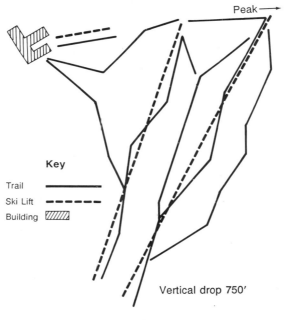

Peak ⟶

Key

Trail ▬▬▬▬
Ski Lift ▬ ▬ ▬ ▬
Building ▨▨▨

Vertical drop 750′

Silver Creek

In essence, the lodge at Silver Creek is a village under one roof. Amenities match the startling architecture. Lodging ranges from efficiency apartments to one-, two-, and three-bedroom condominiums, all completely sound proofed, with a color cable TV, wet bar, regrigerator, climate control, phone, and fireplace in each unit. Only the efficiencies don't have fireplaces. The rates are reasonable, and there are special rates for groups, early- and late-season skiing, and packages for individuals.

The lodge also houses an indoor/outdoor heated pool and spa, an ice skating rink, a grocery-equipped gift shop, a boutique, and a cafeteria, restaurant, lounge, and bar. Lodge guests have free slope-side ski storage at the rental shop. All facilities are easy to reach by phone using the resort's concise directory of services. Overall, the Silver Creek Lodge is one of southern skiing's single most impressive resort structures.

Outside, the view stretches across a high plateau that is scarcely distinguishable from landscapes in Vermont, New Hampshire, or Maine. The direction of view is critical to Silver Creek's fine skiing: the slopes face north, unlike those at Snowshoe, which face east and west and encompass a view of valleys and ridgetops. Silver Creek's north-facing slopes drop 750 feet onto a high crest, a vertical descent comparable to that of Snowshoe's bowl slopes. When the spring sun has melted the white from between Snowshoe's runs, snow still chokes the woods between Silver Creek's slopes.

The northern exposure means that Silver Creek keeps the maximum amount of natural snow, with an annual average of at least 180 inches. To that northern scene and snowfall, Silver Creek has added slopes that are a real pleasure to ski. All ten existing slopes (twenty-four are planned) are wide, drop directly down the fall line, or steepest part of the slope, and are designed to follow the most interesting terrain available. In many places, skiers can exit a slope and enjoy the deep powder in the birch and spruce forest glades that line the trails. The longest run is three-quarters of a mile. Silver Creek is a favorite area among telemark skiers, and telemark lessons are offered through Elk River Ski Touring Center.

The lodge sits in the middle of the slopes. The double chairlift for beginners, Tenderfoot, whisks novices to a large beginner area beside the lodge, and other easy slopes descend away from the lodge to the base of the mountain. Beginners reaching the base's triple chair, Mountaineer, ride up to a point well above the lodge and take another easy slope back down to the Tenderfoot lift.

More advanced skiers following the same pattern can choose a variety of intermediate routes down from Mountaineer, many reaching a second triple chair, Cascade. From this lift's summit, other slopes, including the expert Fox Chase, are accessible. This slope design segregates the beginners from the experts and gives first-time skiers an excellent, lodge-side start as well as the opportunity to descend below the lodge, ascend back above it, see the whole mountain and return on yet another easy run.

Good beginner terrain reflects Silver Creek's family emphasis. The resort provides babysitting at a group location, in-room private babysitting, special ski instruction for children under four, and a special two-hour afternoon ski school for children four to twelve, so parents can ski on their own. Adults have a full complement of group, private, and guided ski lessons as well as daily NASTAR races, and Silver Creek boasts instruction and races for the physically challenged.

Intelligent design, proper orientation of the slopes, and aggressive grooming make Silver Creek one of the most satisfying skiing experiences in the Southeast. Unfortunately, though, like nearby Snowshoe, Silver Creek has experienced bankruptcies since its opening and is still less than stable financially. Plans for future development may change, but the essential physical attractiveness of Silver Creek should remain intact, no matter how the resort continues operation.

Current plans include two new lodge wings, a tennis center, a golf course/cross-country ski area, and residential development. How quickly expansion occurs, and how soon the resort realizes its planned twenty-four slopes and 1,200 feet of vertical drop, remain to be seen. It seems likely, though, that Silver Creek will continue to operate, despite its problems. Contact the resort for year-to-year changes that may complement the description in this book.

Of course, its closeness to Snowshoe adds substantially to Silver Creek's appeal, whether you want skiing, dining, or nightlife. Together, these resorts may be the South's most attractive ski resort combination. And excellent nearby cross-country skiing contributes to that appeal.

For further information, contact

Silver Creek Ski Resort, One Silver Creek Parkway, Silver Creek, WV 26291. 800/624-2119, 304/572-4000.
Snow Report: 800/CALLWVA.

Snowshoe: New England in the South

Snowshoe, W. Va., symbolizes southern skiing. The resort is one of the largest southern ski areas and is easily the most diverse in terrain, lodging, and amenities. Too distant from urban areas to be a day skiing area, Snowshoe is a multiday destination where ski vacationers find some of the region's best skiing and entertainment.

Despite the resort's financial ups and downs, Snowshoe's basic offerings are so attractive that even variations in management haven't prevented the slope from opening year after year. Snowshoe's advertising slogan, "The Island in the Sky," is apt. Capping the region's first

inverted ski area, the resort facilities cover the nearly 5,000-foot crest of
Cheat Mountain, West Virginia's second-highest summit. Snowshoe averages more than 180 inches of annual snowfall, much of it light powder.
That accumulation accounts for the presence of the snowshoe hare, a New
England resident that reaches its southernmost range here. Snowshoe's
slopes start amid groves of snow-draped red spruce that contrast with
hardwood summit forests at most ski areas in the region.

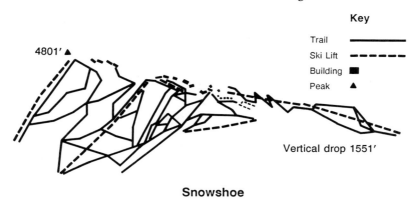

Key

Trail	——————
Ski Lift	– – – – – –
Building	■
Peak	▲

4801' ▲

Vertical drop 1551'

Snowshoe

Fifteen feet of natural snow amply enhances machine-made cover on
the slopes and adds a very northern atmosphere to the resort, complete
with snow drifts reaching to second-story windows. Snowshoe skiers
should have their cars prepared for snowy roads and cold temperatures.

Skiing is Snowshoe's forte. Even though the resort recently closed a
trail network—the Hawthorne slope system—Snowshoe still boasts
twenty-nine separate slopes and trails that descend both sides of the
mountain, including the South's premier ski trail, Cupp Run. Unlike
other large southern ski areas, which favor fewer and wider slopes,
Snowshoe follows the "ski trail" philosophy, with more and narrower
runs. This is one southern resort where first timers will frequently
consult a trail map. Beginner, intermediate, advanced, and expert slope
categories each claim 25 percent of the resort's 85 acres.

On the northeast side of Cheat Mountain, the Basin Slopes spread
horizontally under the ridge-top road and adjacent lodging and resort
facilities. A variety of linking trails allow all levels of skiers to use the five
triple chairlifts. The gradual Skidder slope and lift is beginner terrain that
traverses the ridge top in front of the main lodges. Other slopes drop

down the 650-foot vertical descent, all bearing names from the logging operations that denuded the peak in the early 1900s.

Advanced skiers will like Upper Ball Hooter, a steep and moguled slope under the lift of the same name. Widowmaker and Grab Hammer are other exciting runs for the expert, while Gandy Dancer, J-Hook, and Spruce Glades are intermediate slopes with interesting variety. Powder Monkey, Whiffle Tree, Whistle Punk, and the long, gradual Flume and Hootenanny give beginners miles of cruising all over the mountainside.

Across Snowshoe Drive from the top of the Powder Monkey lift is Cupp Run, which Jean Claude Killy in 1975 named as one of his favorite slopes in the world. Although that accolade may have been enhanced by a promotional arrangement, Cupp is a regional favorite and not unlike runs in the North and West. The mile-and-a-half intermediate/advanced slope plummets 1,500 vertical feet, the biggest drop in Dixie. Steep drops alternate with more gradual sections to provide excitement, interest, and a fine view. For less-accomplished skiers, Cupp Cake meanders down to a midstation on the 6,000-foot Cupp triple chair for the ride back up.

Snowshoe's facilities, reached by Snowshoe Drive from U.S. 219 near Slatyfork, lie perpendicular to the slope systems along the very crest of the ridge. Views stretch in all directions and the wind and snow bear down fiercely at times. Flatlanders can find the almost arctic scene awe inspiring.

The first stop for skiers will be the Welcome Centre at the base of Snowshoe Drive. All resort lodging and lift tickets are dispensed there. The ride up the mountain passes Cupp Run Overlook and the entrance to Silver Creek Ski Area. At times, the combination of snow, clouds, wind-borne spindrift, and a fairyland frosting of rime ice can make summit destinations elusive. Newly added numbered road signs work with a Welcome Centre handout to help travelers locate lodging and facilities.

Snowshoe's diverse lodging, most of it slope-side, can accommodate 6,000 skiers. Nightspots, spas, and satellite television offer evening entertainment after the lifts stop. Snowshoe does not offer night skiing. The resort's televised information channel is a comprehensive directory to services and entertainment.

The hub is Shaver's Centre, a large, warm-toned wooden building on Skidder slope that includes a variety of cafeteria and fast-food eateries, nightly live entertainment at the Connection Night Club, gift and fudge shops, two ski schools, property sales, a U.S. Post Office, the ski patrol/medical center, and Mountain View Photography, the first photo service in the South to offer slope photography of skiers.

South of Shaver's Centre is the slope-side Spruce Lodge, the resort's 100-room, economy accommodations. Just behind Spruce Lodge is the administration building, a T-shirt shop, and bordering the parking lot, Auntie Pasta's Ristorante & Bistro, Snowshoe's best breakfast/brunch spot. Auntie's features Italian food and is also open late as a cozy pub. Edelweiss Ski Shop and Snowshoe's ski rental and lift ticket sales fill the slope-side building beside Auntie's and Spruce Lodge. Next is Timberline Lodge, with fifty large rooms, a lobby, and enclosed access to a large, slope-side dining area that has a fine view and now houses Skidder Pub. Downstairs, The Comedy Cellar offers live entertainment.

Just South of Timberline Lodge and slope-side is Resort Spas, with saunas and hot tubs. An athletic club with an indoor pool and weight room is nearby. The Mountain Lodge dominates the view from Ballhooter lift. This lodge contains 228 one- or two-bedroom suites and lodge rooms, all linked by spacious, modern atria and public spaces. The Mountain Conference Center occupies the lower level with 20,000 square feet of meeting space in 10 rooms, including a two-tiered lecture hall and seating for 514. On the same level are Good Time Bobby's Eating Emporium and a similarly named nightclub and pub. A day-care center and babysitting service is located in the lodge also.

Next to Mountain Lodge, the General Store offers basic condo cooking supplies and other items, including gas and auto services. Adjacent condo complexes are Wabasso, Leatherbark, and Treetop.

The major facilities farthest up on the summit include the Top of the World Centre, the highest lodging in the state, at the top of the Widowmaker lift. This huge building has 84 one-bedroom condos above a gift shop, a Sportin' Life Ski Shop, a nightclub, and a spa. Snowcrest Village, 96 one- and two-bedroom condos with a central courtyard and spa, abuts the spruce forest that shelters Snowshoe's 4,848-foot summit.

Other accommodations are located on the way up Snowshoe Drive north of Shaver's Center. Sundown Hutches, three-bedroom round houses, cluster slope-side on Cupp Run. Powderidge consists of 84 one- and two-bedroom condos with master-bath spas in the two-bedroom units. Mountain Crest Villas are economy efficiency apartments with lofts. Single-family homes and more condominiums line West Ridge Road.

The Overlook efficiency condominiums and the Inn at Snowshoe, with

500 rooms, an indoor pool and spa, and a restaurant and lounge, are clustered at the base of the mountain near U.S. 219. The Ski Barn ski/rental shop and a general store/restaurant are also located at the U.S. 219 junction. Misty Mountain Stables, 1 mile up Snowshoe Drive from the Welcome Centre, offers winter horseback riding and instruction. Sleigh rides are available in the nearby town of Mingo.

The most distinctive lodging and dining at Snowshoe is Whistlepunk Village and Inn, a luxurious complex with forty-eight condominiums and an inn. The Whistlepunk Spa is the best on the mountain, with a complete Nautilus center, a heated pool, men's and women's saunas, and an outdoor Jacuzzi overlooking the slope. Massage is offered, and limited public use of the spa is available for a fee.

Snowshoe's best restaurant, The Red Fox, is slope-side in Whistlepunk's Slaymacher's Square and serves continental cuisine. Its exotic game dishes at times include boar and venison. Braised duckling with raspberry sauce is a favorite. The arched, antique-decorated dining room adds to the old world atmosphere. Upstairs is Yodeler's Pub.

Most of the dining, lodging, and entertainment on the summit can be reached on skis by choosing the right lift. On foot, the full range of facilities are out of reach, but most lodging is close to a variety of services, and Snowshoe's longstanding free shuttle/van service, which covers the entire length of the resort, makes it possible to park your car for the length of your stay. Guests can call for van service at any time, but check new brochures for the latest schedule first.

Snowshoe's Skidder slope isn't the best teaching slope in the region but the resort attracts beginners for its fine ski school and long, diverse novice slopes. Snowshoe's ski school has a wide variety of plans, including group lessons, private lessons, and a beginner's program of three consecutive lessons with no lift ticket required for the first. A block of lessons can be purchased at a discount, and the Family Ski Plan combines instruction with a tour of the mountain. For racers, clinics and NASTAR races are held daily.

The Brr-Rabbit Ski School offers half- and all-day ski instruction, games, and indoor warm-ups, with or without lunch, for kids five to ten years old. Day care and in-room babysitting are also available. Snowshoe offers teacher-supervised classes for students from grades 1 to 8. Your child's teacher at home can assign work in the student's own school books, and Snowshoe's tutors will issue a certificate of completion.

Snowshoe's appeal is due in part to its proximity to both Silver Creek

Ski Resort, also on the Snowshoe Road, and Elk River Ski Touring Center, on U.S. 219 south of Snowshoe Road junction.

Because of its size, climate, and sophisticated offerings, Snowshoe may be the best resort in the region for multiday skiers wanting to take a midweek or week-long ski vacation. Discounted midweek rates are available for all accommodations, and substantial savings can be had early and late in the season.

Wild, Wonderful Season runs from the resort's opening to December 15, with lift tickets, ski lessons, rentals, and lodging discounted 35 percent below normal rates. Almost Heaven Season, from March 8 to closing, offers unbelievable 50-percent discounts on the above items. Snowshoe's season frequently runs through mid-April, and substantial snowfall and winter conditions often continue through March. With Almost Heaven discounts, all the resort's slopes open, warmish days, and continued snow, Snowshoe is the spring skier's vacation choice among southern resorts. Many find it to be the best choice all winter long.

Recently, the only consistent thing at Snowshoe has been change. The mountain's fine facilities seem likely to endure, although a new restaurant may turn up in this niche or a different bar in that. Interested skiers can easily update specifics with the resort's latest brochure.

Snowshoe is a quiet place for a summer vacation. Its very high elevation makes it cool. Area attractions include the Cass Scenic Railroad, easily the South's best steam train attraction. In early August, the Annual Hillbilly Chili Cookoff awards prizes to the best competing chili chefs. The festivities also include parties, a hollerin' contest, and crafts demonstrations.

For further information, contact

Snowshoe Mountain Resort, Box 10, Snowshoe, WV 26209
    304/572-1000. Reservations, 304/572-5252.
Snow report: 304/572-4636 or 800/CALLWVA out of state.
Whistlepunk Village and Inn, PO Box 70, Snowshoe, WV 26209,
    304/572-1126, or 800/624-2757 out of state.

WinterPlace: Easiest Access in the Region

Among West Virginia's isolated ski areas, quick access is a key to prominence. WinterPlace is the South's only slope reached entirely by interstate highway. It is brand new and modern in style, and 90 percent of its slopes are lit at night, making it clearly visible from Interstate 77. For skiers living in the deep South and for piedmont Carolinians, WinterPlace is an easy-to-reach, attractive alternative to North Carolina's High-Country slopes. For residents of Roanoke and West Virginia cities like Beckley, Bluefield, Huntington, and Charleston, WinterPlace has almost single-handedly made the sport convenient. In fact, the resort's seven nights of skiing a week have made it an after-work spot for thousands who'd never drive to Snowshoe or points north.

WinterPlace's 600 feet of vertical drop, between 3,000 and 3,600 feet, lie just inside the southern end of West Virginia's snow zone, near Beckley. Don't expect Snowshoe-type accumulations, but most years WinterPlace claims and probably receives 100 inches of snow. The trail map lists twenty trails, but most of those qualify as parts of larger runs. Total skiing area is 75 acres with the easy Ridgerunner trail giving a 1¼-mile run from the summit.

The slopes descend from the peak of Flat Top mountain within sight of one of West Virginia's earliest ski areas, Bald Knob, which closed many years ago. Starting at the level area in front of the base lodge, beginners go right to the first double chairlift and the easy Highland slope beside Winterhaven Condominiums. Left of the lodge, beginners descend a steeper slope served by a rope tow back to the lodge. Better skiers can take this steeper pitch to the left and ride the second double chair to the next highest knob above the condominiums.

Exiting to the right from this second chairlift, skiers can cruise down Ridgerunner, past the condos and onto the base of the beginner slope at the lodge. Also going right, better skiers can make another right off Ridgerunner and drop under the triple chair they'd just ridden up to the start of the next and highest triple chairlift, or they can bear left under the chairs and descend back to the base of the second chair and the rope tow back to the lodge. Experts can avoid Ridgerunner by going left off the second lift to tackle the open meadows and deep drifts of Drop Off and Snow Bowl, intermediate to advanced skiing that also ends up at the start of the highest triple chairlift.

The loftiest peak, like the bald knob at the top of the second chairlift, recalls western ski resorts where lifts reach rounded open summits. At these big resorts, a graded, road-like easy trail often goes in one direction, and the experts turn sharply and drop into steep bowls from cornices. At both triple chairs, the WinterPlace experience is similar. The easy

Ridgerunner trail goes right and the steepest plummets drop left. On Flat Top's summit, just under a forest fire look-out tower, Ridgerunner starts its mile-and-a-half gradual descent on the right. Plunge and Nose Dive, both very steep trails, go left. The lift line, dubbed Night Mare, is skiable for experts after deep natural snow.

The two-level, modern base lodge is well designed, with easy traffic flow. The upstairs cafeteria, run by the concessionaire who served the 1980 Winter Olympics in Lake Placid, offers three meals a day. Across the hall is the cozy Snowdrift lounge, serving hard and soft drinks and snacks with a slope-side view. Ski rentals are downstairs and removed from food-service traffic. The Apple Crate gift shop and Snow Tracks skier photo service also occupy the lodge. The ski school has temporary quarters near the building.

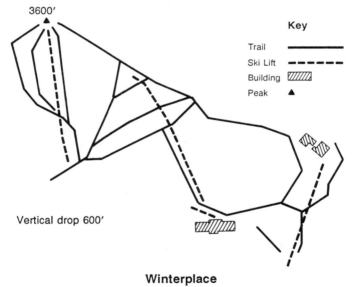

Winterplace

Expect WinterPlace to grow in the next few years. The newest building flanking the lodge parking lot houses Billy Joe's, a full-service restaurant and lounge with a prime rib specialty, and downstairs, a Sportin' Life Ski Shop.

One-day skiing is the emphasis now at WinterPlace, but multiday skiers won't be disappointed. Current lodging includes the Winterhaven condominium complex and the first few Snowpine Village condos. Both are reached by road from the base lodge and flank the double chairlift and beginners' slope, Highland Run. Guests can easily ski home on the

Ridgerunner trail from the top of the mountain, and breakfast at the lodge is a short run down the beginner slope.

Winterhaven Condos are very well appointed, each having a telephone, a color cable TV, a "designer kitchen" with a microwave oven, a fireplace, two bedrooms, a bunkroom, a porch with a slope-side view and access, and two private baths.

Situated between the two Winterhaven wings is The Fireside Loft, a two-story deli and lounge. Sofas surround a roaring fire downstairs. Upstairs, suspended catwalks back the bar with tables that offer views of the slopes. An indoor sauna/Jacuzzi and an outdoor hot tub are part of the The Fireside Loft's atmosphere. The resort thus offers a nice variety of evening options for those not needing live music.

Nearby accommodations also offer ski package plans, among them the Best Western Motel and Econo Lodge in Beckley and the Holiday Inn at Bluefield, a 159-unit motel with an indoor pool and Jacuzzi, a lounge with live entertainment, and some rooms with kitchenettes.

WinterPlace has a number of programs to encourage first-time skiers. Youngsters can attend the nationally standardized *Ski Magazine* SKIwee Program for children four to ten years old. SKIwee lessons combine indoor and outdoor games with on-snow instruction. The child's progress is charted on a parent's report that can be given to another SKIwee instructor anywhere in the country where the program is available. For adults, on Sunday nights and Monday and Tuesday mornings WinterPlace offers a "Try Skiing" plan that includes an hour-and-a-half group ski lesson, three hours of ski rental, and a three-hour novice slope pass, all for $15 per person. NASTAR recreational racing is available at WinterPlace on Sundays and Wednesdays. In late January, the weekend WinterPlace Winter Carnival features a Pro-Am race, and the annual St. Patrick's Day Celebration and Spring Fling takes place in mid-March.

For further information, contact

WinterPlace Resort, Box 1, Flat Top, WV 25841. 304/787-3221. *Snow Report:* 304/787-3965 or 800/CALLWVA.

Mount Timberline: Back-country Downhill

Among southern slopes, Timberline has a special feel. The Canaan Valley resort, located 3 miles north of the state park, has been closed sporadically since its early 1980s opening and has never operated with a chairlift to the top of its slopes. An admittedly long surface lift and occasional snowcat rides to the summit have limited the extent of skiing at Timberline.

The situation is expected to change, however. New owners will reportedly reopen the resort, add a summit chairlift, and again begin marching Timberline toward the major resort status it could enjoy. Although with proper funding Timberline might quickly become a multilift ski area, ski resort development is notorious for being slower and less ambitious than developers originally predict. For the moment, the most likely changes upon reopening will be a new name and adjustments in base offerings to suit the new owners.

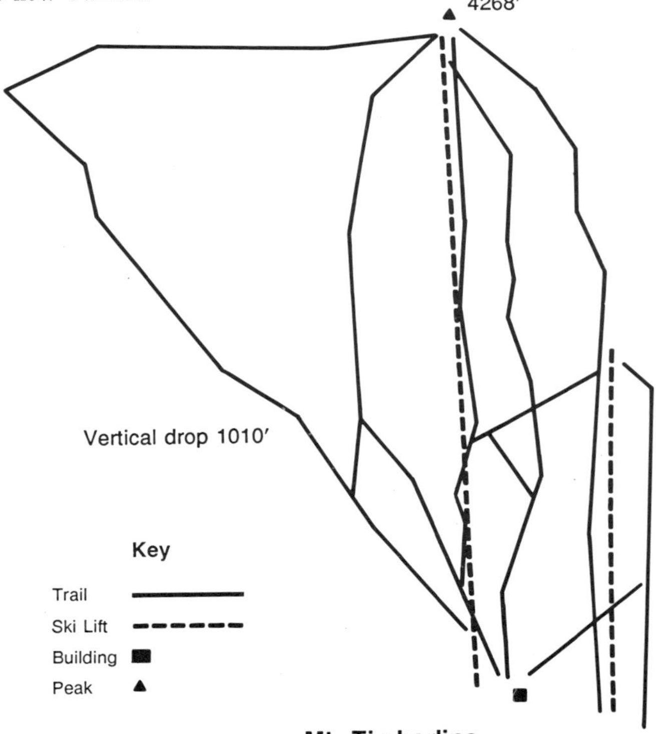

▲ 4268'

Vertical drop 1010'

Key

Trail	————
Ski Lift	- - - - -
Building	■
Peak	▲

Mt. Timberline

Any added slopes in the vicinity of the downhill ski area at Canaan Valley Resort State Park will be a plus for skiers. With Timberline and

Doc Brigham's Tory Mountain in the same area as Canaan, northern West Virginia will come into its own as an attraction for skiers.

Timberline will add to the area in a distinctive way. Like those at Canaan Valley ski area, Timberline's slopes crest atop Cabin Mountain, adjacent to the Dolly Sods Wilderness on the edge of Canaan Valley. But unlike the state park ski area, with its many shelves or benches, all of Timberline's summit slopes drop out of the evergreen forest zone on fall-line plummets that are consistently steep, much like Canaan's Gravity, only with twice the vertical drop. Timberline's main slopes drop 1,000 vertical feet, from 4,268 to 3,258 feet. Even if the resort reopens with the addition of only one chairlift, Timberline will be a worthwhile place to ski.

Unlike other southern ski areas, Timberline is pursuing a style of development that gives it a back-country feel. The impresssive summit view encompasses the entire sweep of Canaan Valley's evergreen forests and frozen lakes. The more than 3,000-acre second-home development that surrounds the ski area is low density, with undeveloped tracts dedicated as nature preserves.

Likely or existing facilities include a base lodge with rentals, a Professional Ski Instructors of America ski school, and a cafeteria, evening restaurant, and pub with some entertainment. Chalets and some slopeside condominiums are already available for rent.

Viewed from the base, Timberline's slopes center around a beginner area on the lower right of the slope system. A T-bar surface lift serves this slope's 375-foot vertical drop. Four routes run to the bottom from the T-bar, as well as a few crossovers and interesting gladed areas. A beautiful forest and artful slope design sustain the back-country feel of this novice area.

A planned chair will serve three main runs from the top, all between 3,500 and 4,300 feet long. More fall-line slopes and a long switchbacking beginner/intermediate trail from the top are possible additions when and if the chair goes in. Eventually, Timberline could encompass at least 200 acres of skiing.

For more information, contact

Timberline Resort, Canaan Valley, WV 26260. 304/866-4433 or
   304/866-4144.
Snow report: 800/CALLWVA.

Virginia

Bryce: Outstanding Racing in a Family Atmosphere

Nestled under the towering Alleghenies in northwestern Virginia on the West Virginia state line, Bryce Resort is modest in size and sophisticated in its offerings. Bryce enjoys a reputation for quality, excellent skiing instruction, a superb, nationally known citizen's racing program, and a family atmosphere.

With a summit elevation of 1,750 feet, Bryce's four slopes and cross-over trail drop 500 vertical feet before flattening out to a broad beginner's area, easily seen from the deck and picture windows of an expansive base facility. One building houses the Copper Kettle lounge—offering mixed drinks and, on weekends, live evening entertainment—a restaurant, and a gift shop. A second large slope-side building houses a ski lodge, a cafeteria, ski rental and repair facilities, and a ski shop.

The resort has about 20 acres of skiing terrain. An annual accumulation of 30 inches of natural snow supplements 100-percent snow-making coverage.

Two rope tows and two double chairlifts service the slopes. Both chairs climb to the summit and allow skiers to reach all the runs, which fan out horizontally across the mountain. The one easiest and three more difficult runs are generally uninterrupted by congested junctions with other trails: whether the slope is gradual like Red Eye or steep like White Lightning, each trail offers better skiers a chance to ski the entire vertical. All four slopes are approximately 3,500 feet in length.

Bryce is noted for an exceptional Professional Ski Instructors of America member ski school, a real plus considering the resort pursues a sound policy of suggesting that first-time skiers take a lesson. Group and private instruction are available seven days a week and at night.

Bryce Resort's most outstanding feature is its racing program. Nation-

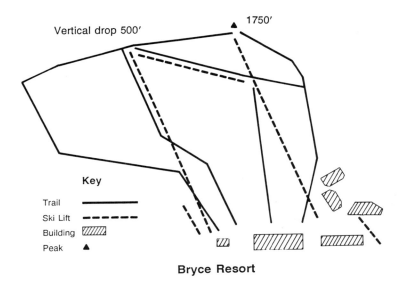

Bryce Resort

wide, citizen and club racing programs are proving that you needn't be young or world class to enjoy the challenge of racing. In the South, Bryce is among a few leading that trend. Every weekend, Bryce stages racing clinics before the lifts open, and the resort hosts a nationally sanctioned racing camp each winter. A variety of races are scheduled throughout the winter, including regular weekend and holiday NASTAR and Equitable Family Ski Challenge races; both are open to visiting members of the public and are very popular with families and skiers of all ages and abilities. Fine videotape-assisted coaching and regular racing routinely place Bryce skiers at the very top of national family, age-group, and club-style racing. Bryce is one of the South's best places for skiers of any age to sample the improved ski technique that is possible through contact with a racing program. Parents of children and teen-agers who ski with plenty of abandon but not enough discipline would do well to make Bryce and its racing clinics a destination.

Bryce also emphasizes its group and package plans, another plus for vacationing families and for students at the many nearby universities. Group rates for twenty or more people cover lift tickets, lessons, and ski rentals but are not offered on holidays or weekends. Similarly, the resort's "Ski" and "Learn to Ski" packages cover weekdays only—Sunday through Thursday. Both packages offer substantial savings for a stay of two days and nights, double adult occupancy, with additional charges for other nights and for children. In addition, each package includes unlimited day and night skiing and two dinners and breakfasts. The "Learn to Ski" package also includes lessons and rentals. The resort can accommodate meetings and conferences of up to 200 participants at any time of year.

Accommodations are available in the slope-side Aspen East Condominiums or the nearby Stony Court Townhouses. Each unit has a kitchen, fireplace, and balcony. There are a grocery store and drug store at the resort. Private chalets are available for rent at Bryce and there is a Best Western Motel 10 miles away in Mt. Jackson.

Transportation to Bryce is among the easiest of any ski resort in the region. The resort is only 11 miles off Interstate 81, exit 69, via Va. 263 from Mt. Jackson. Unlike any other ski area in the South, Bryce maintains a lighted airport with a 2,500-foot runway only feet from the slopes. The airport is well used during ski season.

Cross-country skiing is permitted on Bryce's golf course and bridal trails. Fine cross-country ski routes (and motorized winter sightseeing) are also found in Shenandoah National Park. See the Shenandoah entries in Part 3. Other nearby points of interest include historic sites and battlefields and caverns.

In the summer, grass skiing gets the "most unusual" award. Invented in Europe as a summer training method for skiers, grass skiing mimics snow skiing but substitutes tank-tread-like skates for skis. Horst Locher, Bryce's ski school and ski area director, brought the sport to America in 1975, and in 1979, the World Grass Ski Championships were held at Bryce. Locally, the sport is popular. Bryce offers rentals, lessons, and grass skiing on Sundays from Memorial Day through the fall, with special expanded schedules, including evening hours, in midsummer.

For more information, contact

Bryce Resort, PO Box 3, Basye, VA 22810. 703/856-2121.
Snow report: 703/856-2151.

Cascade: Virginia's Newest

Cascade is a compact, three-slope ski area just inside Virginia and only a stone's throw from Interstate 77. Winston-Salem, other piedmont

Carolina and southwestern Virginia cities, and towns like Elkins and Hillsville are the primary market for Cascade's slopes.

The resort perches atop the escarpment of the Blue Ridge, a crest to which Interstate 77 climbs dramatically from the South. From the flatlands of the Winston-Salem area, the four-lane highway leaps above surrounding farmlands and offers spectacular vistas. After snowfall, skiers arriving from this direction usually have easy driving until they reach the high elevation near the ski area, an advantage not enjoyed by skiers heading deeper into neighboring high country on loftier highways.

Cascade was but one amenity of a vacation-home development until purchased as a separate ski area in 1984. Because of its isolation from major resorts and its easy accessibility from nearby population centers, Cascade has only night, or "after work" skiing during the week. This format creates an excellent opportunity for nearby skiers. Weekend hours are from 9:30 to 4:00, with night sessions on Friday and Saturday from 6:00 to 10:00. Half-day tickets from 12:30 to 4:00 are available either day.

Arriving skiers disembark at the bottom of the slope for ski rentals. The base facility includes the ski school and a light-snack shop. On the far left, looking up, is the easiest-rated Fancy Free, a run of more than half a mile. To the right of Fancy Free is Express, a 2,000-foot intermediate slope; and to the right of that, Zuma, the slope rated most difficult, runs 1,500 feet. These three slopes come together at the bottom, 253 vertical feet below the 3,000-foot summit. At the mountaintop, a full-service, hot-food snack bar serving chili, hamburgers, soups, and the like, makes a great lunch stop.

At the bottom, a wide rope-tow slope, Flat Foot, serves the ski school and beginners. The Flat Foot Special is a ski school program that makes Cascade particularly appealing to groups and first-time skiers. For only $15, a skier receives rental skis, a lesson, and three hours of rope-tow use.

Accommodations are also attractive for nearby groups wanting a first ski trip. Cascade Mountain Inn, just inside the development's 24-hour security gate on Va. 608, has a twenty-person, eight-room "Skier's Apartment," in addition to twenty large, carpeted motel rooms, each with two double beds, and a one-bedroom efficiency apartment, all with color TV. Rates are inexpensive. The on-premises restaurant at the inn serves home-cooked meals. Hours are flexible, with breakfast available anytime. Guests of the inn are the usual customers, but day skiers are welcome. The management requests that if you plan on a Saturday or Sunday evening meal—before driving home, for instance—you make a

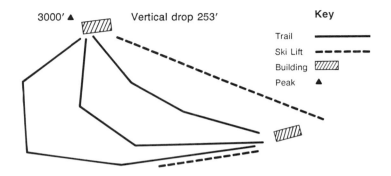

3000' ▲   Vertical drop 253'

Key

Trail
Ski Lift
Building
Peak ▲

Cascade Mtn.

dinner reservation before skiing. The inn is open seven days a week all year.

Another motel, The Stables Inn, is located near Interstate 77. The small, antique-filled rooms feature color cable TV and in-room coffee.

For more information, contact

Ski Cascade, Fancy Gap, VA 24328. 703/728-3161.
Snow report: 703/728-3351.
Cascade Mountain Inn, Stables Inn, Fancy Gap, VA, 24328.
   703/728-2300.

The Homestead: Five-star Skiing

The Homestead is the South's most distinctive ski resort.

Although not huge, its 40 slope acres offer ample, diverse, and high-quality skiing. This area was the region's first to rely solely on a complete snow-making system. Southern ski legend Sepp Kober still runs the slopes and his ski school, staffed by young Europeans. Austrian accents were once the norm at southern slopes. Now the cosmopolitan flavor of The Homestead's ski school is uniquely in tune with the resort's Old World luxury hotel.

For families wanting to learn to ski and for serious skiers with relaxation in mind, the Homestead is hard to beat, especially when winter package rates greatly reduce the price of luxury.

The resort's massive and dignified main building hints at its two-century status as a retreat for the rich and famous. Earth-heated waters still bubble from the Allegheny Mountain location near Virginia's Warm Springs, Hot Springs, and Healing Springs. Inside the resort, the waters flow through a century-old marble swimming pool and health spa. Cavernous hallways give way to ornate sitting rooms complemented by beautiful works of art and the strains of a distant string ensemble. Tea and cakes accompany the music every afternoon at 4. Various shops fill the lobby.

The 600 rooms and suites are impeccably decorated and have cable TV. A chocolate on the pillow and turned-down covers greet guests returning from dinner. The modern and mammoth convention-center wing of the hotel is a state-of-the-art facility able to accommodate the largest meetings.

Dining at the Homestead is best appreciated after a day on the slopes. Few skiers will remember even one previous ski vacation repast to rival the Homestead's meals. The resort's food is simply among the best served in this country. Variety is astounding, and flown-in fresh ingredients make the most minor part of breakfast or dinner a taste treat. The service is so subtle that you almost don't realize your water glass is being refilled. In the evening, there are dancing, swimming, bowling, and nightly movies. The Homestead is not the place to find intense après-ski party spots. At this resort the fun is far more refined.

Active alternatives to alpine skiing include an Olympic-sized, slope-side ice skating rink and cross-country skiing or sleigh rides (with sufficient natural snow). The resort maintains miles of hiking trails.

The Homestead's five slopes and three trails drop 700 vertical feet from a 3,200-foot summit. The main double chairlift, with a midstation, reaches the peak, and after a short advanced pitch, the lift line runs as the main intermediate slope for just under a mile down to the lodge. Branching right as the skier leaves the top of the intermediate slope, two advanced trails veer down and into the woods. One shortly rejoins the main slope. The other is a long meandering jaunt to the bottom. An intermediate connector joins the two advanced trails. A variety of links connect the woods runs and greatly expand the interest of the main slope.

Beginners start at the bottom left, and have a large learning area served by three surface lifts. The area includes an intermediate run that advanced skiers will use after skiing the advanced trails down from the summit.

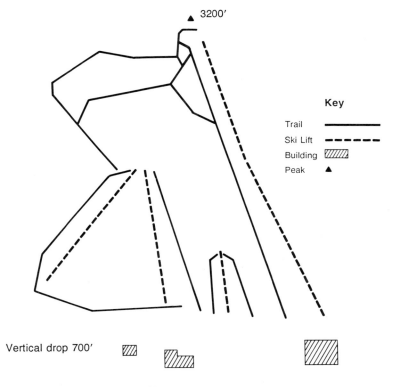

3200'

Key

Trail ───────

Ski Lift ━ ━ ━ ━ ━

Building ▨▨▨

Peak ▲

Vertical drop 700'

Homestead

The Sepp Kober Ski School offers group, private, and children's lessons, available in discount books. There are weekend ski races and daily racing clinics. The Homestead offers no night skiing, but expanded daytime hours run from 9:00 to 5:00 on weekdays and from 8:00 to 5:00 on weekends and holidays. Half-day rates are available seven days a week, A.M. or P.M. Day skiers pay more for lift tickets than hotel guests, but package plans make the resort's lodging affordable. Packages include Modified American Plan lodging and meals (breakfast and dinner daily, lunch on your own) and a variety of combinations of lifts, lessons, and rentals, depending on the skier's needs. Lessons are also available for ice skaters. A free shuttle links the hotel and the slopes.

The base lodge is open, airy, and sunlit through large picture windows. The ski shop, ski school, and ski/skate rental shops are downstairs.

An upstairs grill serves a wide variety of lunch choices, and the outdoor deck is backed by plexiglass that breaks the wind.

The Homestead is north of Interstate 64, via U.S. 220 from Covington, Va. Skiers can reach The Homestead by flying Piedmont Airlines to Lewisburg, W. Va., just 35 miles away, and renting a car.

For more information, contact

The Homestead, Hot Springs, VA 24445. 703/839-5500, or 703/839-5079 for the ski lodge.
Information, reservations, and snow report: 800/542-5734 in Va., 800/336-5771 out of state.

Massanutten: Shenandoah Valley Skiing

Massanutten, situated on the mountain of the same name in the heart of the Shenandoah Valley, is Virginia's second biggest ski area. Just 13 miles from Harrisonburg and Interstate 81, Massanutten is easily accessible, especially for Washington, D.C., residents.

The resort's nine slopes and 40 acres of skiing fan out along the ridge above a three-story base lodge that is among the more beautiful at Dixie slopes. An average of just over 30 inches of snow annually covers the slopes. The 795 feet of vertical drop ranges from 1,730 feet at the base to 2,525 feet at the summit observation deck. The longest run is just over a mile.

The interesting slope design is built around Southern Comfort, a gradual beginner slope running by the base lodge and served by a double chair lift. Along the ridge's length, three separate slope systems rise left, served by two chairlifts and a J-bar surface lift. These slopes, Whim Wham, Turkey Trot, and the two-slope area of Tail Feather and Geronimo, are all novice and low-intermediate runs with vertical drops between 125 and 190 feet. With Southern Comfort, these small side slopes lend variety to the lower half of the mountain and disperse skiers.

Advanced skiers will want to ride chairlift 5 to the ridge top. This chair serves the 600 feet of vertical drop covered by Massanutten's big slopes. On the right exiting the chair is Rebel Yell, an aptly named, wide and cruising advanced slope. Intermediates can ride to midstation and ski the lower, easier half of Rebel Yell. Going left off the top chair ramp,

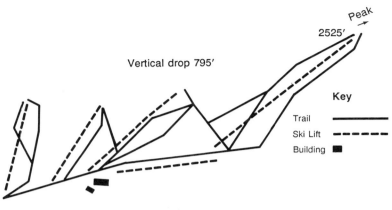

Massanutten Village

Dixie Dare is a narrower expert-rated run that drops the entire 600 vertical feet. An intermediate side slope, Pacesetter, goes right on the way down and joins another easy slope, Crossover, on its way from the top of Geronimo to the base of chair 5.

Five slopes are lit for night skiing every night from 6:00 to 10:00, and day and twilight sessions run from 9:00 to 4:30 and 12:30 to 10:00, with half-day rates on weekdays. Special rates apply before Christmas and in March.

Massanutten's striking base lodge houses a cafeteria, more formal dining in The Shenandoah Room, a game room, a slope-side deck, and a ski shop. The third-floor Peak Lounge has nightly live entertainment and dancing. Both dining areas serve hard and soft drinks.

Lodging at Massanutten is a time-sharing arrangement with hotel units for rent. Rooms, each with a Jacuzzi tub, are spacious and within walking distance of the lodge. Available packages include unlimited skiing and a variety of options for families, beginners, and serious skiers.

Massanutten's Professional Ski Instructors of America ski school features a "Fast Cat" program for children four to five and six to twelve years old. The classes start after 9:00 and include skis, lifts, lessons, lunch, a snack, and other activities before ending just before 2:00. Family and recreational races are scheduled throughout the week, with frequent college and other contests, including the Virginia Governor's Cup. In late February, Massanutten holds a Winter Carnival.

Harrisonburg offers extensive lodging and dining and some nightlife.

One of the most popular nightspots is Scruples Lounge at the Harrisonburg Sheraton Inn.

For more information, contact

Massanutten Village, PO Box 1227, Harrisonburg, VA 22801.
703/289-9441.
Snow report: 703/289-9441.

Wintergreen: Best in the South?

Wintergreen may be the South's best ski resort. Few people who've skied there would disagree. Wintergreen is about 45 miles from both Charlottesville and Lynchburg via U.S. 29. From Lynchburg, take Route 151 north 21 miles to Route 664, Wintergreen's access road. From the north, take Route 6 to 151 south for 14 miles to Route 664. Wintergreen's entrance is 4.5 miles on Route 664.

From beginning to end, the Wintergreen resort experience is impressive in its consistent quality. Begun only in 1975, the entire facility is new, modern in style, and scrupulously maintained. Services and amenities recall the very best, poshest ski resorts in the country. Wintergreen impresses the skier with its comparability to Utah's Deer Valley or Colorado's Keystone.

Style and convenience are the key words here. The style starts with the visible fact that much of this 11,000-acre valley-to-mountaintop development is untouched: large natural areas and 20 miles of beautiful hiking trails, many suitable for jogging, are part of the ambience. The Appalachian Trail winds through the resort.

Wintergreen is a summit ski area, with accommodations and facilities at the top of the slopes. Skiers start there, and lifts bring them back. The road up is well-designed on an easy grade, offsetting the need to drive to the top. The slope-top resort center and condominium complexes offer astounding views up the spine of the Blue Ridge and off to each side. To the west is the Shenandoah Valley. To the east, the foothills tumble to the flat horizon of Virginia's piedmont. The view east is especially panoramic from Wintergreen Overlook, a Blue Ridge Parkway-style pulloff on Wintergreen Drive above the ski slopes.

Convenience starts at check-in. The Mountain Inn is a one-stop

Key

Trail ——————

Ski Lift — — — — —

Building ■

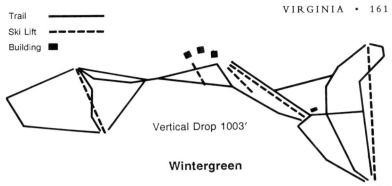

Vertical Drop 1003′

Wintergreen

entrance to the resort, where a guest gets everything, including a colorful Activities Guide, before going to a chalet or condominium, either in the Mountain Inn itself or elsewhere across the resort's 3,400-to-3,800-foot Blue Ridge crest. The Trillium House, a beautiful bed and breakfast inn, rounds out lodging.

You can park your car for the duration of your stay. Shuttle buses regularly serve all the lodging complexes from 8:00 A.M. to midnight. Bus stop signs bear a shuttle schedule that is also available in brochure form. Perhaps most appealing is the ease of walking to the slopes. The ski runs are spread out horizontally under the summit ridge line, so that most lodging is close to at least one slope. Simply ski away onto the nearest run in the morning and catch the lift back home whenever the urge strikes.

Wintergreen entices beginners and families—or anyone on a tight budget—with a variety of package plans that cover weekends, weekdays, and early- and late-season stays, all at considerable savings, with unlimited, guaranteed skiing. Overnight guests, whether on package plans or not, have free access to the beautiful new Wintergarden recreation complex, which includes indoor and outdoor pools, saunas, Jacuzzis, hot tubs, and an exercise room. For added convenience, overnight guests can rent their skis the night before skiing.

Children are well taken care of at Wintergreen. Those under four receive a special lift ticket rate when they ski with their parents, but two separate programs offer supervised activities and lunch, with or without skiing, for youngsters up to seven years old. Babysitting is also available.

In addition, the average "This Week at Wintergreen . . ." activity list usually includes a few kids' items, like a "Soda Straw Painting Workshop." There is also a video game room. And there are movies—normally, weekend skiing films and Saturday-night feature films in the convention

center ballroom. But, as the cliché goes, that's just the beginning. Bingo games, classes on interior decorating, exercise classes, beginning swimming lessons, and "Hands-on computer seminars" can be among the diverse offerings of a given week at Wintergreen.

The glossy Activities Guide indexes extensive activities and just about any other amenity you could want, with phone numbers to call for details. Wintergreen is a resort where comprehensive information on just about anything is only a phone call away.

Shopping near the slopes is diverse. The Mountain Inn contains a shopping gallery that includes a Blue Ridge Mountain Sports branch, a confectionary, and stores for clothing, gifts, crafts, and other specialty items. The nearby Blackrock Village Center has a grocery store.

Dining is exceptional. Besides recreational facilities, the Wintergarden complex offers very fine food and an extraordinary Sunday Brunch in the Garden Terrace Restaurant. Three daily meals are served at the slope-side Coppermine Restaurant, with an evening emphasis on Continental cuisine. The Gristmill Restaurant in the Mountain Inn features popularly priced meals. Cost-conscious skiers can eat all their meals inexpensively at Wimmydiddles cafeteria, near the slopes at Blackrock Center.

A very special family-style restaurant is The Rodes Farm Inn. Located "in the valley" and housed in a quaint, mid-1800s farmhouse, Rodes Farm serves huge bowls of delicious, home-cooked Virginia cuisine, a fine counterpoint to the more formal fare served on top of the mountain. The inn got its start when local school bus driver Marguerite Wade served a welcome lunch to Wintergreen's developers on one of their trips to the area. The food was so good, and Mrs. Wade's infectious good humor was so appealing, that Wintergreen asked her to operate an inn at the Rodes Farm. She agreed, and she still entertains guests as they enjoy any of the three daily meals served. Autographed photos of presidents and governors line the entry hall, attesting to the inn's good food. One guest register sheet on the wall documents the day when Mick Jagger of the Rolling Stones and the late John Lennon dropped in for lunch!

Nightlife is plentiful. The Gristmill Lounge and Coppermine Lounge are perky night spots with live music or comedy. The Garden Terrace Lounge offers pool-side cocktails amid a jungle of indoor greenery. Special concerts are often scheduled, and there are special events like the Winter Carnival in early March, one more reason to enjoy Wintergreen's fine spring skiing. Together, the many amenities explain why Wintergreen operates a successful, 9,000-square-foot conference center for groups up to 450.

Luckily, the skiing matches the rest of the resort. With 85 acres of slopes, Wintergreen is among the four southern resorts that lead the region with over 100,000 annual skier visits each. In some ways, the intelligent design of Wintergreen's runs makes the area seem larger.

When the ski resort opened, the center part of a three-section slope layout was the beginner area, a broad, gently sloping, three-run system just under the Mountain Inn. This big beginning area is one of the best in the South, in part because it is amply served by three chairlifts—two triples and one double.

Parents and experts will love the way the rest of Wintergreen is segregated from this novice area. To reach the other two slope systems, skiers must exit bottlenecks with warnings that beginners should remain in beginner areas.

The Big Acorn Area, served by a triple chairlift, consists of two intermediate and two advanced slopes, all with a vertical drop of 525 feet. One of the advanced runs is divided to let intermediates enjoy a groomed surface while the experts tackle an exciting mogul field.

The 1982 opening of the Highlands slope system really put Wintergreen in the big league of southern slopes. Designed by ski area manager Uel Gardner and served by a double chairlift, the Highlands slopes represent some of the region's best advanced skiing. Highlands boasts a vertical drop of 1,003 feet on 4,200-foot runs like Cliffhanger and Wild Turkey. Unlike those at other ski areas with similar vertical drops, Wintergreen's consistently steep Highlands slopes are uninterrupted by easy terrain. When you head down, the entire vertical drop can be taken in one run, and beginners are not likely to be in the way.

Access to the Highlands area is at the bottom of the easy slopes and is closely supervised. Not only is there a "No Beginners" sign, but a ski patroller is stationed at the site to enforce the rules and administer the "Ski Test." Yes, the ski test. From an observation point, the ski patroller watches the first-time Highlands skier take the plunge on the top of Cliffhanger. If you carve and don't skid your turns, the patroller marks your ticket and you stay. If you're sloppy, you're invited to return to the easy slopes. Although this screening process may sound overly stringent to some, the test isn't really all that hard, and it protects the only place in the South where the advanced skier can be sure of skiing without the interference of the novice, thanks both to creative design and policy. Bravo to Wintergreen.

Another unique slope feature is the Checkerberry Cabin. Located at the bottom of the easier slopes at the access to the Highlands, Checkerberry is the South's only on-mountain, parking-lot-free restaurant, where beginners and experts can conveniently meet for lunch in an on-slope facility like those at world class resorts such as Killington, Keystone, Park City, and Squaw Valley.

The final touch at Wintergreen is a slope-grooming effort second to none in the South. The resort's grooming fleet is constantly at work. Wintergreen boosts its attractiveness as a spring skiing destination through March because continuous grooming in the spring keeps the softer snow compacted for a more enjoyable skiing experience.

Speaking of snow, don't expect Wintergreen to have as much natural snow as slopes in West Virginia or North Carolina. The resort receives about 40 inches annually. Cross-country enthusiasts will find the best bets near Wintergreen on the Blue Ridge Parkway.

For more information, contact

Wintergreen Resort, Wintergreen, VA 22958. 804/325-2200.
Reservations and information: 800/325-2200.
Snow report: 804/325-2100.

North Carolina

North Carolina High Country: Introduction

When most people think of the Southern Appalachians, the Smokies spring to mind. But since the dawn of skiing, the northwestern corner of North Carolina has become known as the landmass with the highest average elevation east of the Rockies. The Deep South's snowiest winters and coolest summers are in Avery and Watauga counties, called the North Carolina high country by travel and tourism literature. Average annual snowfall varies from 45 inches upwards to about 100 inches on the very highest summits.

The six, expected to be seven, ski areas in the two counties represent the region's greatest concentration of ski facilities. In the small town of Banner Elk, N.C., license plates say "Ski Capital of the South." When snow covered, these mountains rival highland scenery anywhere in the East. The combination of spectacular scenery and sophisticated skiing flanked by a handful of century-old resort towns qualifies this snowy corner of North Carolina as one of the South's best winter sports destinations.

Boone is the hub of the high country. The large campus of Appalachian State University makes the town, the Watauga County seat, a cultural, academic, and entertainment center. Boone has all the area's movie theaters, diverse craft shopping, and at ASU, visiting lecturers and artists.

East of Boone on U.S. 321 lie Appalachian Ski Mountain and the Blue Ridge Parkway town of Blowing Rock. South of Boone, N.C. 105 dips past Hound Ears and Mill Ridge ski areas in the Watauga River Valley. It then rises past Hawksnest ski area and the lofty resort town of Seven Devils and enters Avery County. Under massive Grandfather Mountain, N.C. 184 branches west past Sugar Mountain and into Banner Elk and a junction with N.C. 194. To the right, north of Banner Elk, 194 winds down into Valle Crucis and joins other roads to Boone.

South of Banner Elk, N.C. 194 passes the Parkway up to Beech Mountain ski area and reaches the town of Elk Park, near Roan Mountain on the Tennessee state line. Further south on 194 is Newland, the highest county seat east of the Rockies. East of Newland, N.C. 181 reaches Linville and N.C. 105 just south of Grandfather Mountain. Linville Falls and Linville Gorge are further south. Like Blowing Rock, they cling to the 3,000-foot crest of the Blue Ridge.

Road elevations change dramatically, and at these altitudes, snow can be locally heavy in one place and nonexistent in another. Boone is only 20 miles from Banner Elk, but there are few four-lane roads, so travel can be slow. Despite that, some visitors roam the entire area, skiing, dining, and sleeping in different towns. Others choose one resort setting and enjoy concentrated amenities.

Access from outside the area could certainly be better, but from any direction, interstates are just over an hour away. U.S. 321 and 421 give the best western access from Interstate 81 and Johnson City or Bristol. From Interstate 40 and cities to the east like Hickory and Winston-Salem, U.S. 421 and 321 are again good routes. From the south, U.S. 221 from Marion at Interstate 40 or, from Asheville, U.S. 19/23 to 19 are acceptable. Most of these roads are two lanes with some three- and four-lane sections.

High-country towns are home to historic districts and sites. Some, like the 100-year-old Mast General Store in Valle Crucis, and the Victorian hotel, Green Park Inn in Blowing Rock, serve today's visitors and are attractions in themselves. Many summer attractions are open in winter, among them are Grandfather Mountain, Mystery Hill, Blue Ridge Lifestyle Museum of mountain antiques, and Linville Caverns, the state's only commercial cave.

Natural attractions include trails, Nordic skiing, and sightseeing on the Blue Ridge Parkway's plowed section at Blowing Rock. Surrounding mountains like Roan, Grandfather, Mitchell, and Beech offer more cross-country skiing and hiking, some on the Appalachian Trail.

The appeal of high-country ski resorts, trails, and other recreation sites is bolstered by the wide variety of dining and lodging in surrounding towns. But be forewarned: the availability of alcohol, with or without meals, varies widely according to local option and is in a state of change. Most restaurants permit brown-bagging or carrying in beer, wine, or liquor purchased elsewhere.

As of this printing, Banner Elk offers wine for on- and off-premises consumption and a state ABC Store for liquor. Blowing Rock, like Beech Mountain, has liquor by the drink and sells on- and off-premises beer and wine. Blowing Rock also has an ABC Store. Boone currently sells on- and off-premises beer and wine and has an ABC Store. Seven Devils has beer and wine, and Sugar Mountain may have both soon. Restaurants outside these towns may offer no alcoholic drinks. If in doubt, call ahead.

Conference facilities and inexpensive group accommodations are close at hand, particularly around Boone. These are described under Appalachian Ski Mountain because of that resort's group orientation.

Accommodations in the area run a wide spectrum. Chalets, four-star country inns, mammoth mountaintop condos, and timesharing resorts are available at various ski resorts and in surrounding towns through rental agencies. Read the resort entries that follow for details. The lodging described below is in addition to that covered in the resort descriptions.

One bed and breakfast inn is Banner Elk's inexpensive Wapiti Lodge. The warm, relaxed atmosphere includes an ornate interior with winding stairs and a parlor fireplace surrounded by overstuffed sofas. The Mast Farm Inn in Valle Crucis is a distinctive mountain farmhouse. Archer's Inn is halfway up Beech Mountain. In Linville, Hampton Lodge is a fine choice for groups wanting a bed and breakfast experience. Blowing Rock's best include Gideon Ridge Inn and the Sunshine Inn.

Chain and independent motels and hotels are plentiful, some with very fine facilities. In Boone, the Mountain Villa Motor Lodge offers an outdoor Jacuzzi, and the High Country Inn boasts a complete spa and indoor pool. The inn's frozen waterwheel is a roadside landmark in Boone. The Cabana Motel, Plaza Motel, and Boone Holiday Inn and Convention Center are also attractive. The new Sheraton Appalachian Inn and the ASU Center for Continuing Education, two very attractive facilities, are described under Appalachian Ski Mountain.

Blowing Rock's lodging boasts the unmatched atmosphere, elegance, and history of the Green Park Inn. The elegant Meadowbrook Inn is a new addition. Other good motels are The Appalachian, Azalea Garden, and the Alpine Village Inn.

Adams Apple Racquet Club features condos and a rustic outdoor hot tub. The recently renovated Holiday Inn of Banner Elk is located between Beech and Sugar Mountains. The Linville Falls Motel and Cottages in

Linville Falls, Shady Lawn in Newland and Times Square in Elk Park are outlyers.

Dining is a high point of the high country. Most fast food chains are represented, but good independent restaurants with varied price ranges exist, many at the above lodging facilities and at ski resorts. Besides those described elsewhere, recommended independent eateries include several options. In Boone, Sollecito's has held the high ground for Italian-food lovers despite a wealth of pizza chain competitors (the proprietor sings along with Sinatra records). The Mountain House is a favorite breakfast spot, and Makoto's is an entertaining Japanese steak house. The Peddler and Chuck's are other steak restaurants with fine reputations. Boone Drug has good food and is a gathering spot for locals. The popular Daniel Boone Inn serves huge bowls of traditional mountain cooking, including country ham and biscuits—be hungry.

Blowing Rock's Coffey's Restaurant and Bar offers a diverse and delicious menu and the area's best service and widest beer and wine list, all at reasonable prices. Woodland's Barbecue features excellent and inexpensive barbecue and Mexican food with live bluegrass and mountain music. Downtown, at Sonny's Grill, excellent breakfasts and lunches are served amid the area's largest collection of weird sayings.

The Banner Elk area has a seasonal ebb and flow of eating establishments. Long-term fixtures with fine food include both the eclectic decor and soft, live music of Galt's, at the traffic light, and Jeremiah's, known for native trout. New faces include Stone Wall's, Cajun cooking at Lousiana Purchase, and authentic Swiss Cuisine at Heidi's Swiss Inn. The Sunrise Restaurant is inexpensive and good, and Woodberry's is a late-night stop for a quick pizza or sub.

Ski shops seem to be on every corner. The best include the Alpine Ski Center at the entrance to Sugar Mountain, the High Country Ski Shop in Pineola, Foxfire Sports and Highland House at Invershiel, Powder Haus in Banner Elk, and Farmer's Hardware, First Tracks, and Footsloggers in Boone. High Country Ski Shop in Pineola, Edge of the World Outfitters, and Fred's General Mercantile in Banner Elk also rent cross-country skis. Edge of the World is a complete outfitter in one of Banner Elk's most beautiful buildings. The shop is not a ski center, but guided tours and lessons take place on nearby trails. Summer offerings include hiking, backpacking, and a variety of whitewater canoeing options. Army/Navy of Boone is another good stop for the backpacker or cross-country skier.

The attractions, resorts, and listed outdoor sites have year-round appeal, but summer recreation also focuses on seasonal activities of interest, like the Boone outdoor drama "Horn in the West," the story of the Revolutionary Battle of King's Mountain. Whitewater rafting and canoeing outfitters are available, and the Grandfather Mountain Highland Games and Gathering of Scottish Clans is an internationally known spectacle.

For free snow reports on all High Country downhill and cross-country areas, information on all of the area's attractions, and a free Area Guide Map, contact N.C. High Country Host, 800/222-7515 from inside N.C., or 800/438-7500 from elsewhere in the eastern U.S. N.C. HCH, 701 Blowing Rock Rd., Boone, N.C. 28607.

The multicounty organization's Regional Visitor Information Center in Boone is an excellent stop for the latest details on area resources.

Appalachian: The Place to Learn

For all of Appalachian Ski Mountain's attractive qualities, its value to beginners stands out above the rest. To complement its excellent existing beginner terrain, the mountain has undergone major expansion. Intermediate and advanced slopes are now available, and North Carolina's only quad, or four-person chairlift, has virtually eliminated lift lines. Appalachian boasts a massive snow-making system. And its French-Swiss Ski College is the region's premier teacher of new skiers, especially groups.

Few ski areas in the South are run as professionally or successfully. Appalachian takes great pride in its spotless facility and family atmosphere.

The large, recently expanded base lodge files skiers past ski ticket windows, ski school desks, and a full-service ski shop and into a streamlined ski rental facility, all slope-side on the lower level. The lodge's upper level has cafeteria-style fast food and also more substantial meals, each eating area has its own separate and smooth traffic flow. The main dining room has a slope-side view, and a huge fireplace is always ablaze with 4-foot logs. Just outside, skiers stretch on a sunny deck overlooking the slopes. Other dining areas adjoin the cafeteria, which opens an hour before the start of the nine-to-four daytime skiing session and remains open through the six-to-ten night session. The lodge also contains meeting space, a lounge, the Ski Patrol room, and a gift shop that offers parka, bib, glove, and goggle rentals.

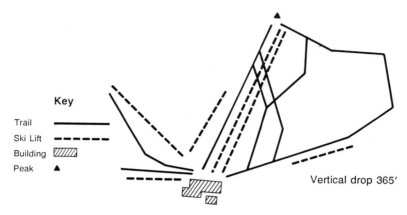

Key

Trail

Ski Lift

Building

Peak

Vertical drop 365′

Appalachian

Above the lodge, the slopes rise to a vertical drop of 365 feet. Farthest left, looking up, a rope tow serves the easiest, shortest novice slope, Appaltizer. Next is a short double chair that reaches the highest part of this left slope, the intermediate Strudel.

Just right of this lift is the main or right-hand slope, Big Appal. The Lower Big Appal is intermediate and is reached on the left by a tow taking skiers halfway up. The same midslope starting point can be reached from midstation on the double chairlift that climbs the right side of the slope. Riding the chair all the way up and going left takes skiers down the advanced-rated Upper Big Appal, usually moguled.

Looking up from the base, Appalachian's new quad chairlift is to the right of the longer double chair. Skiers can go left to Big Appal from either lift, or to the right down another intermediate slope, the switchbacking Orchard Run. At the base of Orchard Run is another, recently enlarged rope-tow area, which is reserved for the ski school. Heading down at the top of Orchard Run, Hard Core and Thin Slice, two advanced trails, drop to the right and rejoin Orchard Run at the bottom. All slopes are lit for night skiing seven nights a week.

To its fine terrain for beginning as well as intermediate skiers Appalachian adds the French-Swiss Ski College, probably the most visited southern ski school and the region's recognized group specialist. Each year, thousands of people learn to ski with French-Swiss instruction, many of them in church, youth, civic, school, business, and other groups. Appalachian's large parking areas offer ample bus parking near the slopes, and electrical hookups are available for RVs. A parking fee is charged for autos. French-Swiss offers a ski trip planning service for group or family vacations at Appalachian and other area resorts.

Excellent group accommodations are available on either side of Appalachian. In Blowing Rock, The Blowing Rock Assembly Ground (BRAG) is a full-service group conference center and American Youth Hostel. Although BRAG focuses on church groups, families can take advantage of the facility's inexpensive rooms, cabins, suites, and cottages. An indoor pool is one of many amenities. In Boone, Appalachian State University's Broyhill Center for Continuing Education is a more luxurious setting, with state-of-the-art audio-visual equipment for conferees, but is still reasonably priced. Appalachian's Winter Special Olympics is based at Broyhill. Boone's new Sheraton Appalachian Inn has rooms, suites, and convenient ski storage lockers just inside the auto entrance. The Mission School Conference Center and Camp Broadstone, both in Valle Crucis, and Hampton Lodge in Linville also offer inexpensive group lodging.

At Appalachian Ski Mountain, private and group lessons are available, for individuals and organized parties at all levels of ability. Special clinics, some lasting all day, focus on various skills, including racing, and some feature video analysis of the skier's technique.

Appalachian's premier event is the Southeastern Winter Special Olympics in early January. Handicapped athletes from nine states come to Appalachian and other area sites for downhill and cross-country ski racing. Cross-country telemark skiing is not permitted at Appalachian.

For further information, contact

Appalachian Ski Mountain, PO Box 106, Blowing Rock, NC 28605. 704/295-7828.

Ski Beech: Skiing on Top of the World

Beech Mountain's 5,505-foot summit rises higher into the winter air than any other ski resort in eastern America. And in 1982, Beech Mountain became the highest town east of the Rockies. Like Sugar Mountain, the other behemoth of northwestern North Carolina's high country, Beech annually attracts over 100,000 skiers.

From Banner Elk, skiers climb the winding Beech Mountain Parkway to the mile-high plateau of The Beech. At the crest, a conical summit rises on the left, covered with slopes and houses. A twisting ride down the other side of the mountain leads to the resort's alpine village, easily accessible from large parking areas. The town fans out around the ski resort.

Beech's appeal begins with its elevation. When altitude is a deciding factor in how cold it is or whether snow or rain falls, Beech usually has more going for it than adjacent high-country resorts. Although temperature inversions do occur, Beech is the first major summit above Tennessee's rippling foothills, so the mountain gets the most snow of any high-country ski resort, between 80 and 100 inches annually. Clouds often keep the peak encased in a fairyland coating of rime ice. And clear-day views stretch west across Tennessee, north to Virginia, and east to massive Grandfather Mountain.

Recent changes at Beech have bolstered its status as one of North Carolina's and the South's best ski areas. Massive expansions of the mountain's snow-making system make it among the region's best at opening an entire top-to-bottom slope in one day of snow making. Major lift overhauls, a new upper mountain lift, and plans to boost a double chair to a quad should keep lift lines as short here as at any of the major resorts.

Beech was the region's first "big" ski area. Since its midsixties opening, new slopes have expanded the skiing terrain to about 70 acres. The most popular slope at Beech is Shawneehaw, separated into an upper and lower section with each served by a chairlift. Lower Shawneehaw is rated intermediate, the upper part is advanced, and together they permit a long descent of the mountain's 830 vertical feet of drop.

Beginners have a small learning area served by a J-bar tow and a huge open area of two slopes, Freestyle and The Beech, served by two double chairs. Accomplished novices can enjoy the longest run on the mountain, about a mile and a half, and beat the longer lift line to Lower Shawneehaw by taking a summit lift and winding down Snow Road. This trail angles across the entire face of the mountain to the intersection at the top of Lower Shawneehaw and then down to the base. Since this route crosses advanced terrain, beginners should keep an eye open for descending skiers at junctions.

Experts enjoy Beech's newest slopes, Tri-South, Southern Star, and Upper and Lower White Lightning. These descents tackle the steeper face of Beech, to the right of Shawneehaw as you look up the slopes. Tri-South, the farthest left, drops at the most consistent grade. Southern Star

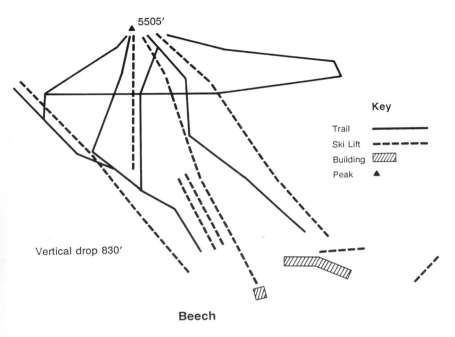

5505'

Vertical drop 830'

Key

Trail ———
Ski Lift – – – – –
Building ▨
Peak ▲

Beech

is similarly steep, and both of these slopes feed into the mountain's newest chairlift to the summit. The excellent placement of this lift lets experts ski the upper steeps, including Shawneehaw's intermediate upper section, without having to venture through beginner areas to catch another chairlift ride.

White Lightning is the really steep run at Beech. The slope starts at the top and drops gently at first, then gets steeper, reaching Snow Road, where "mere intermediates" can bail out. From there down, Lower White Lightning is steep enough to produce the same butterfly feeling associated with a steep, high run in New England or the West. The almost endless view is enough to stimulate acrophobia. After the plummet, the slope becomes gradual and stays separated from beginners all the way to its own lift at the bottom, the chair furthest to the right looking up from the base. This slope offers the advanced skier the one, uninterrupted top-to-bottom run of the mountain's entire vertical drop.

For first-time skiers, Beech maintains a large, Professional Ski Instructors of America ski school. The resort's children's program is exceptional. For infants to three-year-olds, the Land of Oz Nursery provides day care.

For four-to-twelve-year-olds, *Ski Magazine*'s SKIWee Program offers standardized instruction that can be meshed with other SKIWee program schools around the country. Beech also emphasizes racing. Special clinics and a full schedule of NASTAR races are available. Many of the races at Beech are regional showdowns between major ski clubs. Recreational skiers can also arrange to run race gates on an electronically timed course.

Beech excels where atmosphere is concerned. Unlike West Virginia's Snowshoe or Virginia's Wintergreen, where resort life also takes place on the ridge top, Beech seems intimate. Granted, the town is so high that one feels somehow separated from the world, a feeling that recalls the summit locations of Snowshoe and Wintergreen. But Beech is different. The peak is loftily there, especially when lit for night skiing, but the town nestles snugly around the snow-covered summit, offering a focus that other, more stretched-out summit resorts lack. Beech feels like a community with much more to it than resort-run facilities.

Even the resort itself has a community focus: a picturesque alpine village surrounds the base of the slopes. Every niche is taken by a separate shop. Crafts, ski accessories, specialty foods, lunch, and even video games are available, all wrapped around an ice skating rink offering rental skates and professional lessons. At night or during the day, at Christmas or in February, the maze of paths are festively lit, glimpses between the European-style buildings net views of distant peaks or lodges on the mountain side, the smell of wood smoke is in the air, snow is on the ground, the trees are caked in frost, and Beech can feel like a little town far above a gratefully forgotten world. This is Ski Beech at its best.

Near the slopes, the alpine village reverses its inward orientation and turns out, facing the slopes. The slope-side Viewhaus Cafeteria offers a fine view and a huge, sunny porch. An adjoining building houses the ski school, lockers, a rental shop, and a ski shop with its own deck and picnic tables. The Viewhaus, and a slope-side pub both offer beer, mixed drinks, and wine.

Below the village and also slope-side is the Beech Tree Inn, perhaps the mountain's best restaurant. Downstairs is the Red Baron Room, the oldest name in nightlife on Beech Mountain, now infused with new life by the 1985 passage of a liquor-by-the-drink referendum. Both facilities serve drinks, and evening entertainment is the norm most nights of the week.

Although not solely responsible, the availability of beer and wine, and now of liquor, has helped Beech establish the most diverse on-mountain nightlife in North Carolina. Fred's General Mercantile serves light meals and deli fare with live music. Rascals and Moguls are the emerging nightlife leaders if you like music and dancing. Rascals has reasonably priced informal meals, especially chicken, beef, and pork barbecue. Moguls is more expensive. Both have good atmosphere.

Special events add to the fun at Beech. Every February, the mountain stages its Winterfest, a nearly two-week celebration that has been featured on national TV. Special entertainment events, bathing suit contests on skis, broom hockey tournaments, ski races, snow sculpture, torchlight parades, fireworks, ice skating shows, and the elaborate sleds and exciting action of the Great Cardboard Box Derby add up to one of the South's top snow festivals. The event is staged when weather statistics say natural snow is most likely. Winterfest makes the first two weeks of February a great time to plan a Beech Mountain ski trip or vacation. Even nonskiers will have a lot to do.

Lodging on Beech includes single-family chalets, as well as modern condo complexes. Slope-side accommodations are situated beside Upper Shawneehaw and boast one of the South's best ski resort views. Hotel-style lodges offer single rooms, and the massive Pinnacle Inn and Country Club includes spa facilities with indoor and outdoor Jacuzzis, a sauna and steam room, and an indoor heated pool.

Various independent rental agencies handle accommodations on Beech Mountain. To simplify booking arrangements, Ski Beech provides a toll-free central reservation service for "one phone call" convenience. Although Beech offers no packages that include lodging, resort packages feature single or multiday savings on lift tickets, rentals, and lessons for individuals and families. Groups of fifteen or more receive group rates.

A number of stores in town sell beer and wine, groceries for renters of kitchen-equipped accommodations, clothing, and other retail items. Diverse dining and lodging, including modern accommodations and country-inn bed and breakfasts, and an ABC liquor store are located in Banner Elk, just 4 miles "down the mountain." Other high-country towns add to those offerings.

The altitude that wraps Beech in its winter wonderland of snowfall and frosted trees can also mean severe weather both on and off the slopes. At times, local enforcement agencies require tire chains on cars climbing the road to Beech. The town of Beech Mountain mounts an effective snow removal effort, and like the best New England and western resorts, Beech offers shuttle bus service from early morning to midnight during January and February. The buses link the resort with the neighboring town of Boone and with the town and ski resort of Sugar Mountain. Best of all, within Beech Mountain most major lodging, the slopes, and other points of interest and business are connected by three bus routes. Even cross-country ski rentals and trails are accessible by bus.

In the warm months, if you can call them that, Beech offers a swimming pool, a golf course, tennis courts, and summer and fall festivals.

For more information, contact

Ski Beech, PO Box 1118, Beech Mountain, NC 28604. 704/387-2011. *Snow report:* 800/222-2293 in N.C., 800/438-2093 outside N.C.

Cataloochee: Skiing in the Great Smokies

North Carolina's first ski resort has become the largest in the southwestern part of the state and the biggest of the Deep South's slopes. Among North Carolina ski areas, Cataloochee has the easiest access. The drive to the resort is almost entirely on Interstate 40.

Cataloochee's slopes reach to 5,400 feet on the Cataloochee Divide of the Great Smoky Mountains, just outside the National Park in Maggie Valley. The high elevation nets 50 inches of annual snowfall. Snow making covers 90 percent of Cataloochee's eight slopes, about 70 acres of skiing terrain with a 740-foot vertical drop.

From the summit chair, skiers have fine views of the massive Great Smokies. Picnic tables make the summit a great lunch stop on a sunny day. At the top, experts head left for Omigosh, the resort's premier expert run. Intermediates ski the two right-side switchbacks of Upper and Lower Snowbird or another advanced run intended for racing, Subaru Trail. All these slopes funnel into intermediate-rated Lower Omigosh for the return to the lodge. A 600-foot surface lift serves Rabbit Hill, and a rope tow serves the large teaching slope, Wolf Creek Hollow.

The entire mountain, except Lower Snowbird Trail, is lit for night skiing Monday, Wednesday, Friday, and Saturday from 6:30 to 10:00. Day hours are 9:00 to 4:30. Cataloochee charges half the normal day rate from opening day to mid-December, then only weekday rates until December 20 and after March 1. Another good deal for skiers going home Sunday afternoon is an A.M. lift ticket from 9:00 to 1:00. Cataloochee also offers another rarity, a P.M. weekend ticket.

From the top of the mountain, skiers can go right, onto High Meadow Run, when there is sufficient natural snow. No machine-made snow covers the 80-acre meadow, but when the big storms strike, High Meadow Run makes Cataloochee the South's biggest ski area, with 150 acres of terrain. Cataloochee is the only slope in the South that offers such open-meadow skiing.

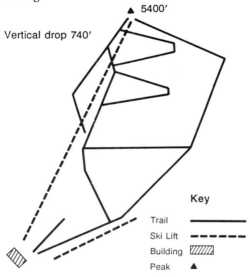

Cataloochee

The lodge is 4 miles from U.S. 19 in Maggie Valley on a paved state road, Fie Top Road. In snowy weather, the free Snowflake Express shuttles skiers to the large lodge. The base facility houses a cafeteria, rental shop, ski shop, warming areas, a big deck facing the slopes, and lockers. The lodge serves alcohol, so brown bagging isn't permitted. Nearby, the resort's summer facility, Cataloochee Ranch, offers limited winter lodging.

In 1986, Cataloochee merged with Southeast Holding Co. of Charlotte, and slope-side lodging, ice skating, and substantial slope expansions should come to the resort in the near future.

Cataloochee's large Professional Ski Instructors of America (PSIA) ski school offers a variety of lesson plans as well as the Catt Trackers program for kids four to seven years old. The two-hour program includes a snack break.

Racing is an emerging focus at Cataloochee. In conjunction with Subaru, Cataloochee offers team racing programs for high schoolers and the Subaru Alpine Classic Series for various teams and individuals. An annual downhill cross-country telemark race is also held. Cataloochee is routinely chosen as the site of PSIA instructor training courses.

The Alpine Classic Series concludes on the first weekend in March during Cataloochee's premier ski season event, Spring Frolic. All types of fun and serious races, costume contests, and other events make Spring Frolic the best end-of-season celebration at the southernmost slopes.

Another very attractive ski season event at Cataloochee is Christmas in the Valley, a month-long celebration that includes special dinners at local restaurants, a torchlight ski parade, caroling, special concerts, parties, and dances.

Maggie Valley is one of the Carolina's most popular summertime mountain vacation areas. That means that in winter, Cataloochee ski vacationers can choose from a wealth of nearby accommodations, dining, and nightlife. Lodging includes the Holiday Inn-Maggie Valley; the Laurel Park Inn; Mountainbrook Inn; Heart of the Valley Motel, which offers shuttle service; Creek Wood Village, where cabins have fireplaces; and the Waynesville Country Club. Most of these lodgings offer cable TV, movie channels, and group rates or package plans.

Dining in the valley ranges from spaghetti at Country Vittles, to steak and seafood at J. Arthur's, to Angelo's Family Pizza. Michael's specializes in steak and provides live entertainment Thursday through Saturday evenings. Beer, wine, and liquor by the drink are available.

Cross-country skiers aren't left out at Cataloochee. No Nordic skis are rented, but a free Cataloochee Ranch map shows a number of mostly road-width trails for those who bring skis. A favorite tour is a 2.5-mile gradual climb past Pine Tree Gap to spectacular views at 5,600-foot Hemphill Bald on the National Park boundary. Soco Gap on the Blue Ridge Parkway is another nearby Nordic site.

Summer and fall are popular seasons to visit Cataloochee Ranch, a 1,000-acre, mile-high guest ranch with a rustic lodge, cabins, a tennis court, lawn games, stables, trail rides, and cool summer days. Excellent, garden-fresh food served family style and a quaint rustic setting characterize the fifty-year-old ranch. Day and overnight trail rides explore private land and Great Smoky Mountains National Park. Down in Maggie, craft shopping and golf are other diversions.

Asheville, only 35 miles away on Interstate 40, offers a wealth of dining, lodging, and attractions. Christmas skiers at Cataloochee won't want to miss Christmas at Biltmore House and Gardens, the massive, late nineteenth-century summer home of the Vanderbilts that is styled like a sixteenth-century French Renaissance chateau. This National Historic Landmark is a museum of spectacular proportions, all the more impressive when decorated for Christmas. Roving carolers and chamber ensembles make candlelit evening tours a truly stirring experience. Fine dining and tours of Biltmore's winery make the trip even more memorable.

Asheville's nightlife and many restaurants, hotels, and motels, many with full spa and convention facilities, make the largest city in western North Carolina a good place to stay while skiing Cataloochee or Wolf Laurel. See the latter resort's entry for more on Asheville.

For more information, contact

Cataloochee Ski Area, Rte. 1, Box 500, Maggie Valley, NC 28751. 704/926-0285.
Snow report: 704/926-3588.
Maggie Valley Chamber of Commerce, PO Box 87, Maggie Valley, NC 28751. 704/926-1686.
Asheville Travel and Tourism Office, PO Box 1011, Asheville, NC 28802. 800/257-1300 in the eastern US, 800/548-1300 in N.C.

Hawksnest: The Skier's Mountain

Ski Hawksnest, formerly Seven Devils ski area, is unique among southern resorts. There is some beginner terrain, especially learning slopes, but Hawksnest is a skier's mountain designed for the intermediate.

Recently, under the ownership of Jon Reynolds, the resort has been undergoing rapid improvement and change. Substantial easy terrain is likely to be added, perhaps in the near future. Until then, Hawksnest is one resort where the never-ever skier, adult or child, can learn, while mom, dad, or friends enjoy some of the region's most interesting and challenging intermediate skiing. Hawksnest is a favorite ski area among high-country locals.

The resort is in the town of Seven Devils, high above the Watauga River Valley, between Boone and the turnoff to Banner Elk on N.C. 105. In bad weather, a free shuttle ferries skiers from parking on 105 to the slopes.

Besides its exciting, difficult-rated runs, Hawksnest is noted for its downright inexpensive lift tickets. The resort also gives skiers an hour of free morning skiing to inspect conditions.

Hawksnest's slopes begin behind an attractive, alpine-style lodge at 4,200 feet. The 7 slopes and 20 acres of skiable terrain top out at 4,819 feet, for 619 feet of vertical drop.

Beginners will focus on Kitty Hawk, the teaching slope, or First Flight, an undulating, entertaining 500-foot run for better beginners; both are below the lodge and served by rope tows. Above the lodge, beginners have a rope tow to Red Tail's Run. Hawksnest offers a special low-priced ticket on weekdays for skiers using only the three beginner slopes. Other ticket options are day skiing from 9:00 to 4:00, twilight skiing from 1:30 to 10:00 all days but Saturday, and night skiing from 5:00 to 10:00. With all of Hawksnest's slopes lit and the area's inexpensive prices, night skiing is very attractive for better skiers.

Low intermediates can ride the shorter chair to reach a steep challenge on lower Raven's Run or to cross the slope and switchback through the woods when snow permits. Above this run, Hawksnest is for good skiers.

The main chairlift bisects the oval of summit slopes and arrives at picnic tables with views of Grandfather Mountain. From there, the scenic trails offer expansive views dominated by the conical, frosted summit of Hanging Rock. To the left, Sock-Em-Dog winds its twisting, steepening way past a spectacular rock pinnacle to the top of Raven's Run. This segment is a Hawksnest classic. Going right from the lift, a narrow, curving access drops to the top of The Right Stuff, the major right-side slope looking up from the lodge. This half-mile trail periodically shelves into steep drops on an otherwise fast cruising slope that advanced skiers will really love. The curvy first stretch from the lift can be avoided by going left on Sock-Em-Dog, then left under the lift to The Right Stuff. Here also is a natural snow glade called Narrow Gauge.

The Hawksnest Lodge is a three-story, heavily windowed building with fine views, big fireplaces, cozy, private niches, and an enclosed greenhouse lunch deck. Flags snap on poles surrounding the outside deck with its picnic tables. Lift ticket sales, the Ski Patrol, the ski school, ski rentals and repair, a ski shop, and a cafeteria/lunchroom occupy the first two floors. Upstairs, in the Hawksbill Lounge, beer and wine are sold owing to the recent passage of a referendum in Seven Devils, as are meals. The lounge features periodic live entertainment.

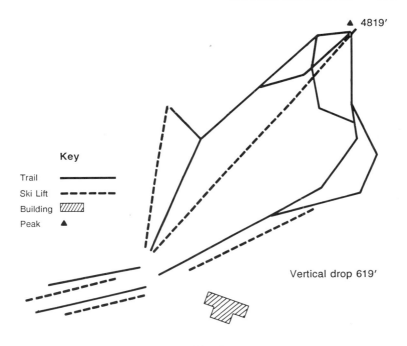

Key

Trail
Ski Lift
Building
Peak

▲ 4819'

Vertical drop 619'

Hawksnest

Hawksnest's Professional Ski Instructors of America ski school offers a special children's program called the Kiddy Hawk Ski School for kids five to twelve years old. The plan includes all-day instruction, lunch, and supervision.

On the first weekend in March, Hawksnest celebrates its Spring Carnival, a fest that starts Saturday night with fireworks and a torchlight parade and continues Sunday with crazy ski races and other events. Costumed skiers get a special lift ticket price. Check local papers for Hawksnest specials. The resort often offers good deals and offbeat promotions—like all-night skiing!

At present, most lodging and dining for Hawksnest skiers is off the mountain. Hound Ears Club and Adam's Apple Racquet Club are located on N.C. 105 near the resort. And just north of the turn for Hawksnest on 105 is the Grandview Restaurant. This local favorite serves inexpensive, hearty meals, especially breakfasts, with a great view of Grandfather Mountain.

For more information, contact

Hawksnest Ski Area, Rte 1, Box 256, Banner Elk, NC 28604.
   704/963-6561.
Snow report: 704/963-6563.

Hound Ears: Four-star Skiing

Hound Ears is best known as an exclusive warm weather resort with six-figure second homes, an outstanding golf course, swimming pool, and tennis courts, and . . . a ski area.

Hound Ears was the North Carolina high country's first posh second-home development. The resort occupies the flat bottom land beside the Watauga River, 6 miles south of Boone on N.C. 105, just north of the community of Foscoe. Homes and condos climb the surrounding mountain sides. Hound Ears' elevation is 3,000 feet, so the weather is milder and there is less natural snowfall than at the highest local slopes.

The Hound Ears' ski area can only be described as small. There are two slopes. The "learning run" is very gradual, 200 feet long, and served by a rope tow that starts in front of the ski lodge. The "big slope" is a 1,200-foot curving run, accessible by a double chairlift. This slope starts narrow at the top of the lift and fans out to a width of 200 feet, then narrows again to the chairlift entrance. Although relatively short, the slope's width and shape permit a variety of routes down the hill's 107 feet of vertical drop.

In the South, saying a resort is small is not the same as saying it is unappealing. Hound Ears epitomizes the attractiveness of many small Dixie ski areas. What the resort gives away in size, it compensates for in quality. Hound Ears is never crowded, so lift lines are very short and skiers spend a maximum of time on the slopes. The easy terrain makes Hound Ears a perfect place for a family outing, especially for beginners who want a very low-stress skiing situation. Professional instruction is always available, although the teaching program is not a large ski school as is the case at larger ski areas. And among high-country resorts, Hound Ears may be the most suitable for cross-country skiers learning the telemark turn. Telemark clinics have been held at the slope by local cross-country ski schools, and the gentle hills, the slope-perimeter areas, and a flat section at the base of the slopes make Hound Ears attractive for

Nordic skiers, whether they want downhill practice or just to get on skis early in the season. Even if you don't use the lift, be prepared to buy a slope ticket to pay your share of the snow-making expenses.

The Ski Haus, or base lodge, is homey, with seating in front of a large fireplace. Ski rentals and instruction are also available at the lodge.

When you're ready for lunch, be ready for the best. Just across the parking lot is the Hound Ears Clubhouse. The atmosphere is warm and luxurious. The richly paneled walls create a cozy respite from the winter air. And lunch for winter skiers is the resort's only meal during the entire year at which the public can be served without staying in the lodge. Breakfast and dinner at the club and use of the lounge are included in the lodge's Modified American Plan package prices for accommodations in the twenty-two lodge rooms. In winter only, Hound Ears also offers accommodations on the European Plan (accommodations only), so that skiers can dine at other restaurants, perhaps after skiing at another resort, and still enjoy Hound Ears' luxurious lodging. The slopes, lodge, and clubhouse are a short walk apart. Together, these facilities are called The Hound Ears Lodge and Club, and they make up a dining/lodging combination that has earned Mobil's four-star rating of quality.

In winter, the ski slopes, lodge, and dining facilities are open on weekends only, Friday through Sunday. The ski season usually runs from mid-December to early March, and the slopes are open daily during the Christmas-to-New Year holidays, except for Christmas Day. There is no night skiing.

From January on, Hound Ears offers half-price lift tickets on Friday. That program takes the cost of skiing well below $10. Besides the savings, the sparse crowds make that day the best time for Nordic skiers to practice their turns.

In winter, the public is invited to use the slopes whether or not they are staying at the lodge. In summer, Hound Ears offers the amenities described above, but only to resort residents and members of the public who are lodge guests. In summer or winter, all the offerings of the high country, including other ski areas, are easily accessible from Hound Ears.

For more information, contact

Hound Ears Lodge and Club, PO Box 188, Blowing Rock, NC 28605. 704/963-4321.

Mill Ridge: The South's Biggest Little Slope

For skiers who don't want the region's longest runs—or its longest lift lines—the smaller slopes often fill the bill.

Unfortunately, some skiers routinely spend the most crowded weekends at the biggest ski areas when they'd be having more fun at a smaller one. For some reason, the image of smallness keeps them away, and managers and owners of resorts that writers and skiers call small are sensitive to the negative implication.

At Mill Ridge, skiers see the positive side of a less-than-large ski area. In fact, Mill Ridge may be the biggest little ski area in the South. That characterization is much more than a turn of phrase. From N.C. 105, about 8 miles south of Boone, Mill Ridge looks compact to say the least. But the ski area's longest run is over half a mile. And Mill Ridge may come closer than any small ski area in the region to being a miniature replica of the largest southern ski areas. Usually, the smaller areas offer one or two beginner slopes. Mill Ridge's offerings run the gamut from easy to bona fide expert terrain.

A major slope redesign took place in 1985 and made the resort's terrain even better. Beginners have a flat lower area served by a pony lift, and novice skiers can use another surface tow to enjoy the wider, steeper grade of the Bowl. The next step for beginner and intermediate skiers is a ride up the double chairlift to the top of the mountain's 275 vertical feet. To the left, looking up from the lodge, Easy Flyer takes a long looping run out and back before reaching the top of the Bowl.

Better skiers can exit Easy Flyer at the Chute, an exciting narrow run. The really good advanced terrain is short but hair raising. For the experts, Go For It has always been the pride of Mill Ridge. Going right from the top of the lift, the terrain drops steeply, offers an escape route called Cut Back, and then plummets over a short but nearly vertical face into a runout beside the Bowl. An advanced alternative to Go For It skirts the main drop and offers another way down for better skiers.

Mill Ridge is fun for better telemark skiers, and the new slope design makes the often uncrowded slopes a good place to learn. Whatever kind of skis you're using, lift lines are rare and always short.

Mill Ridge is also a great family place because the resort's instructors can give skiers the basics and the terrain does the rest. In fact, if you've ever watched athletic teen-agers take their first ski lesson and then quickly work up to challenging slopes, you'll know why Mill Ridge is a fine family ski area. The kids can advance quickly from novice areas to more exciting runs, but they'll never be far from their parents' watchful eyes. Make sure, though, that before skiing Go For It, a youngster has had a lesson. This little ski area is diverse, not just easy, and therein lies its distinction.

Mill Ridge's ski school has about five instructors. During the week, any skier buying a lift ticket can take a free ski lesson at 10:00 or 2:00. Also during the week, any child under twelve receives a free lift ticket when accompanying an adult who buys a lift ticket.

The lodge continues the variety of the slopes. Over the years, the lodge at Mill Ridge has been added to in more ways than would have seemed imaginable. The result is a very successful blend of diverse facilities and intimate, homey charm. Downstairs, ski rentals, lift tickets, and a warming area with a fireplace exit directly to the open slope. Upstairs, a separate and recently expanded food-service area serves three meals a day and offers up to 150 people a sunny, glass-enclosed view of the slopes. The ski area has in the past experimented with BYOB evening entertainment. The recent restaurant expansion should make that option even more practical. There are two ski shops, one upstairs and one down. Beside the lodge is the Mill Ridge National Ski Patrol building. The facility is small but one of the most modern and efficient in the South.

The resort is closed Tuesday. Day skiing, twilight skiing, night skiing, and half-day rates are offered every other day of the week. Recently, Mill Ridge has followed the biggest slopes into a Thanksgiving opening and usually stays open until early March. The area's design and size make it attractive to groups. Special rates are available.

At 3,200 feet elevation, Mill Ridge receives about 30 inches of natural snow per year. The temperatures and weather conditions at that elevation are never as severe as they are at the highest nearby ski areas. But at night, when the cold settles into the Foscoe Valley, temperatures can be better for snow making at Mill Ridge than higher up. The management is aggressive and effective at snow making and grooming.

Part of Mill Ridge's appeal lies around the resort: the North Carolina high country. Five other ski areas, including the two biggest in the state, are all within a twenty-minute drive of Mill Ridge. Chalet rentals are available throughout the area and also at Mill Ridge itself. Smoketree Lodge, a popular dining spot/timeshare resort with rental accommodations, is only a few miles toward Linville from Mill Ridge. In Foscoe, The Village Cafe serves gourmet breakfasts. The Hidden Valley Motel in Foscoe provides the least expensive lodging near the ski resort.

For more information, contact

Mill Ridge Ski Mountain, Rte. 1, Box 367, Hwy. 105, Banner Elk, NC 28604. 704/963-4500.

Fairfield/Sapphire Valley: Resort Setting with Skiing

Fairfield/Sapphire Valley is a 5,400-acre southwestern North Carolina resort community that boasts year-round recreation and amenities, including skiing. The resort has earned the Mobil four-star rating. It is located on U.S. 64E, 3 miles from Cashiers, N.C., and it centers on beautiful Fairfield Lake beneath the towering cliffs of Bald Rock Mountain.

At just over 3,000 feet, the ski area has 425 feet of vertical drop, about 5 acres of skiing, and a longest run of half a mile. There are four slopes, from beginner to advanced, a double chairlift, and two rope tows.

The chairlift begins by the base lodge, where hot food, ski rentals, and a ski shop are located. Beside the lodge, the ski school has a small teaching area with one of the two rope tows. The chair bisects a two-slope area and ends where the slopes join. To the right off the chairlift, an advanced run descends back to the lowest rope tow. To the left, a wider intermediate slope does the same. A second rope tow starts at the top of the chairlift and serves an expert slope that drops from the area's high point.

Although not big, the slopes are well groomed and have adequate snow making. Skiing is daily from 9:00 to 4:30; half-day sessions last from 1:00 to 4:30, and there is night skiing every night except Sunday. The Professional Ski Instructors of America ski school has group and private lessons. A child's lesson program and babysitting are available.

Primary skier accommodations are in motel-type rooms or in condominiums near the slopes. The resort offers a variety of packages, some for groups, that feature lodging, lift tickets, and ski rentals. Dining at Fairfield/Sapphire Valley includes a warm atmosphere and good food at the new Mica's Restaurant, open for three meals daily. When the restaurant closes at 10:00 on Friday and Saturday, the After Hours lounge offers live music. If you want alcohol, you must bring your own.

Future plans include a new Fairfield Inn built on the site of the original Fairfield Inn, which was nearly a century old when razed. The new inn is expected to have 60 rooms, 9 suites, conference space for 150 people, and

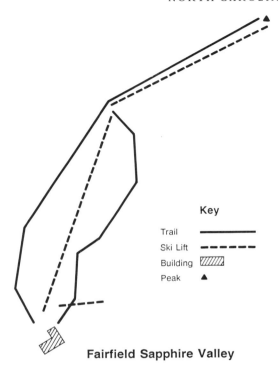

Key

Trail	————
Ski Lift	– – – – –
Building	▨
Peak	▲

Fairfield Sapphire Valley

dining facilities. Woodwork and fixtures from the old inn will recreate a turn-of-the-century atmosphere.

A new recreation center is expected to be open for winter 1986–87 with indoor swimming, a sauna and Jacuzzi, exercise equipment, and a video game room. The stables and horseback riding are available year-round. Fine hiking and sightseeing trips in the "Land of Waterfalls" area are close by, many offered under the resort's diverse winter recreation program.

A recreation director coordinates a full calendar of social and recreational activities, including holiday-related events and all types of workshops, clinics, and gatherings. The program greatly expands the resort's appeal as a winter vacation spot. Even though natural snow doesn't often blanket the resort, tobogganing is a popular activity with families and youngsters. Fairfield/Sapphire Valley has the region's only organized sledding on machine-made snow.

In summer, Fairfield has a swimming pool, tennis, golf, and a variety of boat rentals for use on the lake.

For more information, contact

Fairfield/Sapphire Valley Resort, Sapphire, NC 28774. 704/743-3441, or 800/222-1057 in N.C., 800/438-3421 in the eastern U.S.
Snow report is extension 3150.

Ski Scaly: North Carolina's Southernmost Slopes

Hugging the Georgia border, Ski Scaly is North Carolina's southernmost and newest ski area. The slopes pull people from nearby cities in South Carolina and Georgia, including Atlanta, which is just over two hours away.

From the top of the double chairlift, skiers look down the wide-open hillside to a two-story base lodge, 225 vertical feet below. Runs range from a beginner slope served by a 300-foot rope tow to three routes down from the crest.

From the chairlift, the summit runs go to the right. The 1,800-foot beginner trail follows the edge of the woods on a gradual grade, while the 1,600-foot, often bumpy intermediate trail descends more abruptly beside and under the lift. Nothing separates the runs, so downhillers and telemarkers can take the whole hillside if they like. A 1,200-foot trail, rated advanced, passes the top of both beginner and intermediate slopes and follows a route down through the woods to emerge at the lodge. Natural snow opens runs to the left of the lift.

The snow-covered hillside stands out prominently in the view from the access road, parking lot, and slope-side deck of the lodge. A big wood stove, a sandwich grill serving hamburgers, hot dogs, soup, and chili, an accessory counter, a warming area, and a deck take up the upper floor. The Ski Patrol room and equipment rental fill the lower floor. There's a general store across the street.

Scaly doesn't claim to be a destination for multiday vacations. The single-season recreation area is well run, modern, and a perfect place for deep southerners to take a lesson and see if they like skiing—without a long drive. A family-fun atmosphere prevails at Scaly, an ambience appreciated by the many school groups that learn to ski at the slope. Rarely does this uncrowded area reach its 450-skier capacity.

In Scaly Mountain, chalets can be rented at Scaly Mountain Chalets and Wood Alley Chalets. Other accommodations are 15 minutes away in Highlands, N.C., or Dillard Ga., each 7 miles distant via N.C. 106.

In Dillard, the Best Western, with John & Earl's Restaurant, is popular. Jacuzzis are available at Earl's Chalets, rented through Best Western. In Highlands, a high-elevation resort town of considerable character, the Townhouse Motel and Colonial Pines Bed & Breakfast are recommended. During substantial cold spells, lights are strung beside ponds in Highlands, a fire is lit on shore, and the public can rent skates to use in the Currier & Ives setting.

Scaly Mountain will supply brochures on area accommodations and dining to those who write.

For more information, contact

Ski Scaly Mountain, PO Box 339, Hwy. 106, Scaly Mountain, NC
    28775. 704/526-3737.
Highlands Chamber of Commerce, Highlands, NC 28741.

Sugar Mountain: North Carolina's Behemoth

In many ways, Sugar Mountain is the kingpin of North Carolina's high-country and southern skiing. For a decade, mammoth Sugar has been a stable and expanding center for skiing in the Deep South.

The Banner Elk resort is the first of the two major high-country slopes reached from Boone and Linville on N.C. 105. The ski resort starts at the elevation of Banner Elk, making it easier to reach than Beech. But Sugar has more than accessibility to recommend it. The mountain boasts the biggest vertical drop in North Carolina and the Deep South, 1,200 feet, just 300 feet shy of Snowshoe's Cup Run in West Virginia. With Sugar's branching side trails, the slopes impress as being the most diverse in the high country. Sugar's uphill lift capacity of nearly 9,000 people per hour makes it the region's fastest people mover as well. The mountain's massive snow-making system seems to open slopes overnight, and manager Gunther Jochl is known for aggressive snow-making and slope grooming. Routinely, Sugar claims the earliest opening date in the region, often in November.

Sugar's appeal can add up to crowds, but the resort has expanded steadily to relieve the pressure. Sugar is one of many southern slopes where the skier should consider a weekday ski vacation to enjoy a fine mountain when the slopes are least crowded. But weekend skiers need not dismay. Recent lift and slope expansions have made Sugar better able than ever to handle its popularity. Night skiing is offered seven nights a week starting in December. With most of the mountain lit, Sugar offers the largest night skiing area in the region.

Sugar's 16 slopes and 100 skiable acres rise from 4,100 feet to the 5,300-foot summit, rendering spectacular views of Grandfather Mountain and three states. From the top of the two summit double chairs, most slopes follow the center of the mountain down to the huge lodge. Left off the lift, Boulder Dash and Tom Terrific plummet for 700-foot runs that are easily among the steepest in the South. Going right, intermediates wind down Switchback, the start of Sugar's 1.5-mile longest run. Switchback has fine views and joins the center mountain slopes again under Boulder Dash and Tom, named for Tom Brigham, slope designer and southern skiing pioneer.

Two slopes take up the next downward stretch. Sugar Slalom, on the left, is served by its own surface lift, and Upper Flying Mile drops to rejoin Sugar Slalom at midstation on the summit lifts.

Looking up the mountain at midstation, Dead End slope and its surface lift drop right. Rising left is the popular New Slope, a wide, cruising run that rises up to the left, the top of its double chairlift circled by slope-side condominiums in the gap between Sugar summit and Little Sugar Mountain, where the ten-story Sugar Top condominium perches on the peak.

From midstation, the main slope continues down as Lower Flying Mile. To its left, the intermediate run Big Birch, served by a triple chair, is usually the mountain's first slope to open. A connector off the top of Big Birch drops to the lower lift terminal of the New Slope. Big Birch and Lower Flying Mile fuse at the bottom in front of the lodge where both summit lifts and the Big Birch triple chair start.

Back at midstation, skiers going right on Dead End can enter an entire beginner slope system. Easy Street Extension connects Dead End to Easy Street and Little Nell, two fine beginner runs that drop to the bottom of the mountain and are served by a double chair reached by going right from the lodge.

Because of the frequent junctions and a varying grade, experts may find Sugar's top-to-bottom run less dramatic than Snowshoe's Cup Run or Wintergreen's Highland slopes. But the skiing is diverse, interesting, and able to please a wide range of skiers.

Base facilities are centered in a big lodge with a cafeteria serving three

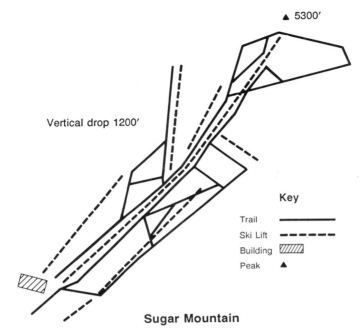

▲ 5300'

Vertical drop 1200'

Key

Trail ——————
Ski Lift ▬ ▬ ▬ ▬ ▬
Building ▨
Peak ▲

Sugar Mountain

meals a day, the Sugar Mountain Sports ski shop, the Sugar Shop for other items, and the Sugar Hollow Club, a cavernous but cozy dining room with good food, live music, a view of the slopes, and a brown-bagging bar. Administrative offices, lift ticket and group sales, lodging check-in, lockers, and an extensive game room are also under this one roof.

In addition, the base lodge houses the Ski Patrol, ski rental, and the ski school programs. Sugar's Professional Ski Instructors of America member ski school is among the largest in the region, with four group sessions a day, including one at night. Services include video-tape analysis and racing clinics. The Sugar Bear Ski School gives children five to ten years old a supervised five-hour session including lessons, rentals, lunch, and supervision. A nursery is available for those too young to ski. Children four and under and adults seventy and over ski free at Sugar.

Sugar's yearly race program includes NASTAR races as well as a variety of exciting professional and amateur contests, including the locals' race, The Hometown Advantage, sponsored by the area newspaper the *Mountain Times*.

Within walking distance of the base lodge is the Sugar Mountain Lodge beside Big Birch slope, a thirty-two-room slope-side hotel with round slope-side houses above it. Other lodging on the mountain is diverse. Some is available, like the lodge rooms, with one-stop check-in through the resort's rental pool. Sugar is a well-developed resort community with hundreds of condominiums, single-family homes, and chalets available for rent through various agencies. Timesharing facilities also offer rentals, and many accommodations include use of pools and Jacuzzis.

Sugar Top and Sugar Ski and Country Club are two striking and controversial summit facilities that may offer the region's most unique ski lodging.

Sugar Top is a ten story, monolithic high-rise tower erected on the flattened top of Little Sugar Mountain. National news coverage accompanied its construction and North Carolina passed a ridge law restricting similar building projects. The 230-unit luxury residence has an active rental program and a hotel-like ambience. Valet parking sets the tone. The view from either side of the structure is simply staggering. There is a central pool and an excercise, sauna, and Jacuzzi facility. An on-premises general store carries groceries, crafts, and other items. A separate drive-through entrance offers access to The Tack Room, arguably the high country's best restaurant. Fine dining, as well as a bar and sandwich grill, are the restaurant's fare. A deli is open at times in the lobby, and guests can get room service. Ski lockers in the lobby and a shuttle bus to the slopes are other amenities. All this adds up to a complete resort, but it seems a galling spectacle to those who prefer their mountains unadorned.

A sister development to Sugar Top, but far more rustic, is Sugar Ski & Country Club. The eight-building, three-story condo complex is located in the gap under Sugar Top and offers fine views and a spa center. A chairlift and the New Slope reach into the development, making for ski-from-your-door convenience. There are even slope-side, bubble-enclosed Jacuzzis. Both summit complexes are reached by paved road, but be prepared for snowy, high-elevation driving.

Sugar's food and evening facilities are likely to expand and be joined by new businesses if alcohol sales become legal in the recently incorporated village of Sugar Mountain. That seems likely, so the diversity of Sugar Mountain dining and nightlife may grow substantially in the near future.

March brings Sugar's major festival, Spring Fling. Awards for the best costumes and crazy ski races are among the attractions.

Summer facilities at Sugar include an eighteen-hole executive golf course, tennis courts, a swimming complex, stables with trail rides, and conference facilities for 250 people.

For more information, contact

Sugar Mountain Resort, Inc., PO Box 369, Banner Elk, NC 28604.
   704/898-4521.
Snow report: 704/898-5256.

Wolf Laurel: "Ski the Wolf"

Tucked under the Appalachian Trail and the bulking, meadow-covered summit of Big Bald Mountain, Wolf Laurel is a 4,000-acre, four-season mountain resort on the North Carolina/Tennessee state line. Although medium sized, the ski area boasts a mile-long trail, two of the steeper expert slopes in the South, and wide, open, easier slopes.

Wolf Laurel is a family-type resort with many rustic second homes. The ski area is at the center of the development, and skiers park just below the two, rough-cut timber buildings at the base of the slopes. Lift ticket sales and ski rentals occupy the first building. The second houses a grill, a large warming area with a fireplace, and the ski shop. Both buildings are rustic and informal. The Wolf is no modern, chrome-plated ski resort.

For many years, Wolf Laurel limited its snow-making system to the main runs, Broadway, Sideslip, Eagle, and The Chute, all intermediate runs reached from the midstation or top of the resort's one double chairlift. These slopes offer a 500-foot vertical drop to the base lodge, which is at an elevation of 4,000 feet. Left of these runs is a natural snow slope called The Flyer. All these runs descend a natural bowl where sheep used to graze before the ski area was built.

Recent years have brought continued expansion and improvement. From the top of the chairlift, a platter-pull surface lift takes skiers another 200 vertical feet higher to the top of the relatively new Flame Out and Wolf Ridge, both steep expert slopes that now have snow making and are lit for night skiing. But not only experts can take the tow to the top of Wolf Laurel's 700 feet of vertical drop. Novices can skirt the top of the expert drops and take the winding Wolf's Crossing more than a mile

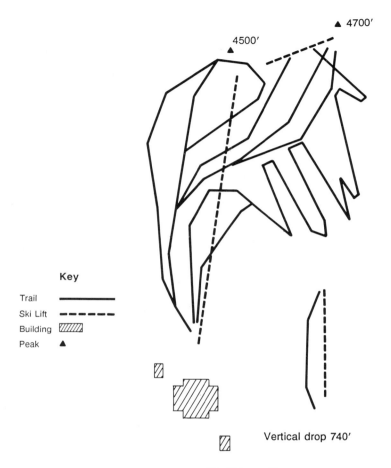

▲ 4700'

▲ 4500'

Key

Trail ————
Ski Lift — — —
Building ▨
Peak ▲

Vertical drop 740'

Wolf Laurel

down to the lodge. Wolf's Crossing is one of the three of Wolf Laurel's nine slopes that aren't lit for night skiing.

The Wolf Laurel ski school teaches on a 300-foot beginner slope served by a rope tow and lit for skiing at night.

Skiers needn't leave after a day on the slopes. The Wolf Laurel Inn, only 2 miles from the slopes, has seventy-five rooms, each with color TV. A big fireplace graces the main lobby. Winter rates, especially midweek, are inexpensive. Many of the resort's second homes can also be rented.

The Mountain Top Restaurant, next door to Wolf Laurel Inn, serves three meals a day every day of the year. The Timberwolf Lounge has live weekend music and a BYOB bar.

Wolf Laurel can accommodate conferences of up to 150 people, and group rates are available for skiing.

During Wolf Laurel's mid-December to early March season, night skiing is available every night except Christmas Day and New Year's Eve. Weekdays, the lifts start at 10:00 with half-day rates from 1:00 to 4:30 and night skiing from 6:30 to 10:00. On weekends, the resort offers half-day rates only on Sunday afternoons. A twilight ticket is good on weekends from 1:00 until the end of night skiing.

Wolf Laurel qualifies as the closest ski resort to Asheville, recently published in *The Places Rated Almanac* (Rand McNally) as one of the most "livable" cities in America. The Wolf is just a 27-mile, forty-five-minute drive from Asheville, mostly on four-lane highways. Signs are easy to follow on the short stretch of two-lane road. Besides ski vacationers, the easy access brings in Asheville residents for night skiing after work. Wolf Laurel is popular with local telemark skiers.

Asheville is a premier convention and tourism city and the place to stay if nightlife and an urban setting are desired. Major hotels offer large meeting facilities, and there is direct service by Piedmont and other major airlines. Nearby attractions include the beautiful Biltmore House, the largest private home in America—a castle and museum filled with art. The Thomas Wolfe Home is another site of historic interest. Pubs and night spots are numerous, and liquor by the drink is available.

Suggested dining and nightspots include Bill Stanley's Barbecue and Pickin Parlour and a variety of restaurants at the Inn on the Plaza. Stanley's offers good food and live mountain music and dancing. The Grove Park Inn is noteworthy for fine food and for its 100-year-old history as a popular mountain inn.

In summer, Wolf Laurel boasts one of western North Carolina's best golf courses, a pool, tennis courts and a variety of trails. The Appalachian Trail borders the resort.

For more information, contact

Wolf Laurel Resort, Rte. 3, Mars Hill, NC 28754. 704/689-4111. *Snow report:* 704/689-2222.

Tennessee, Alabama, and Georgia

Gatlinburg, Tennessee: No one sits looking out the window

Ober Gatlinburg is one of the most diverse and unique ski resorts in the South. As one Gatlinburg fan has phrased it, "At Ober Gatlinburg, no one has to just sit looking out the window of the lodge."

Of course, all ski resorts try to offer alternative activities for nonskiing family members and for skiers after the slopes close. Many southern resorts do so successfuly. None does it like Ober Gatlinburg.

Just getting to the slopes is an experience, in the positive sense. The resort's name, Ober Gatlinburg, gives a clue. Ober means "over" in German, and the slopes lie on Mount Harrison, 1,000 feet above the streets of Gatlinburg. That wouldn't be unusual if skiers simply drove up to the resort, and they can. But unlike patrons at other resorts that lie at the end of a winding, sometimes icy two-lane road, most at Gatlinburg reach the ski lodge in one of two 120-passenger aerial tram cars that start in the town itself. Aerial tramways of this kind are most often found in Europe. In eastern America, only Cannon Mountain in New Hampshire has one, and it is much smaller than Ober Gatlinburg's. And the exciting ride is free to all skiers who purchase a lift ticket.

The ride, featuring views of a vertical mile up into the Smokies, is spectacularly scenic; and by parking below, skiers can reach the slopes by driving exclusively on interstates and four-lane highways. At the top of the tram, you needn't worry about exiting into a snow storm. Skiers and sightseers alike disembark inside a huge and astoundingly diverse base lodge facility. But the term base lodge doesn't do this emporium justice.

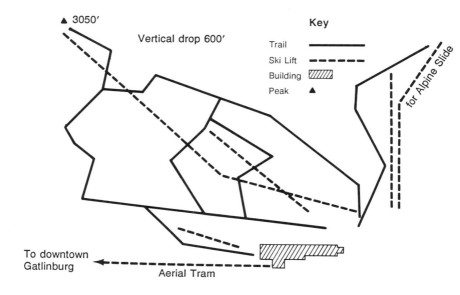

Ober Gatlinburg

One part of the facility is a huge, 60,000-square-foot, 1½-acre shopping and crafts mall. The center of this cavernous, multilevel open space is a 140-by-75-foot ice skating rink complemented by a complete program of skate rentals, lessons, and exhibitions. Specialty shops, craft outlets, and an open-air cafe surround the rink.

Nearby, a municipal black bear habitat lets visitors watch the Smokies' native animals in a natural setting. A museum and slide show accompany the habitat. And if you have any time left over, and don't want to ski, try the 1,800-foot alpine slide from the summit of Mount Harrison. This ride is normally a summertime attraction but is also open during the skiing season when weather permits. People of all ages enjoy the ride down a concrete chute, resembling a bobsled run, in wheeled carts with speed-control handles. No other southern ski resort operates an alpine slide.

Having encountered all these diversions, remember you're still just arriving at the slopes. The real base lodge includes the usual ski rental operation, ski school, ski retail shops, snack bar, and large warming room with big, open fireplaces. Upstairs, the Old Heidelberg Restaurant, styled like a Bavarian Hofbrauhaus, features Swiss, German, and American food accompanied in the evening by "oom-pah-pah" music from the colorfully costumed Bavarian Fun Maker Band. The food is excellent. Dancing, too, is encouraged, but not just at the Old Heidelberg. Nearby, the Studio 2000 Disco opens at 9:00 nightly, except on Sundays. The disco, a lounge, a snack bar, and the Old Heidelberg serve alcoholic beverages.

From the lodge you can look up Gatlinburg's ten slopes. The mountain's 25 acres of skiing terrain make it medium sized by Dixie standards. The thing you'll notice most is another Gatlinburg first, two quad (four-person) chairlifts. Gatlinburg was the first resort in the South to have a quad and is the only one to have two. With these lifts and another double chair, Gatlinburg's lift lines are never very long.

One of the quad chairs reaches the 3,050-foot elevation on Mount Harrison, 600 vertical feet above the lodge. From there, Ober Chute tests advanced skiers and allows a 1-mile run, Gatlinburg's longest. Grizzly, a steep, shaded, 3,800-foot slope is the most difficult. Except for Grizzly, all of Gatlinburg's slopes are lit every night except Sunday. Just above the lodge, a quad chairlift serves beginner's slopes like Bear Paw, Cub Way, Edelweiss, and the steepest of the easy slopes, Castle Run. Ober Gatlinburg averages about 25 inches of snow a year. On the streets of Gatlinburg, at just under 1,500 feet, snowfall averages 12 inches a year.

Like the best of the region's resorts, Gatlinburg expertly and effectively makes snow and grooms the slopes. The ski school is certified by the Professional Ski Instructors of America. Children are taught in groups, and although there is no resort nursery, area accommodations will refer parents to licensed babysitting services in town. Overall, Gatlinburg is a particularly good destination for families, especially when not everyone will be skiing.

That family appeal continues off the mountain. Gatlinburg, its downtown known nationwide as a premier tourist venue, may be the most bustling ski resort town in the South, especially on weekends. There are craft and specialty shops of all varieties, many situated in clusters around open plazas. Dozens of attractions offer winter hours, including the American Historical Wax Museum, Ripley's Believe It or Not Museum, and Christus Gardens, where wax figure dioramas depict the life of Christ. In summer, Gatlinburg's popularity as a vacation spot is unmatched in the Southern Appalachians. Besides its alpine slide, Ober Gatlinburg even has skiing in the summer, thanks to a 5-acre Astro-Turf slope that is covered with polyurethane beads and sprayed with a water/silicone solution.

Few ski resorts in the country besides Ober Gatlinburg can boast 150 nearby motels with an overnight capacity of 30,000. Amenities include indoor pools, spas, exercise rooms and ample convention and meeting facilities. Winter's off-season status in this summer mecca and Gatlinburg's wide variety of accommodations make remarkable bargains easy to find. Restaurants and nightlife are as varied as lodging, and all these services span a spectrum of expense. Among all the choices, the Open Hearth Restaurant is one favorite Gatlinburg dining spot.

Package plan savings are widely available in Gatlinburg. Many motels and other lodging facilities offer packages that include lodging and skiing. Specific assistance with package information can be obtained by calling the ski resort or the Chamber of Commerce. In fact, the best course of action for skiers bound for Ober Gatlinburg is to contact one of the Chamber of Commerce's toll free numbers and request the information packet and the many additional brochures put out by chamber members.

Because of Gatlinburg's summer prominence as a bus tour destination, the ski area, lodging businesses, and restaurants are among the best prepared in the South to offer good prices and smooth service for all kinds of groups. Groups of twenty or more are offered greatly reduced rates.

Also, don't forget the Great Smoky Mountains National Park. The Smokies' rise above Gatlinburg equals the Rockies' dramatic thrust above Denver. Cross-country skiing, winter hiking, and sightseeing by car are all possible.

For more information, contact

Ober Gatlinburg, 1001 Parkway, Gatlinburg, TN 37738. 615/436-5423. *Snow report and information after Nov. 1:* 800/251-9202 outside Tenn., 800/843-6237 inside Tenn.

Gatlinburg Chamber of Commerce, 520 Parkway, PO Box 527, Gatlinburg, TN 37738. 615/436-4178, or 800/251-9868 outside Tenn., 800/824-4766 inside Tenn.

Cloudmont, Alabama: Southernmost Snow

Cloudmont is Alabama's only ski area and the East's southernmost slope. The ski area's peak is 1,800 feet high on Lookout Mountain. Cloudmont brochures exhort skiers to "Ski 'Bama!"

Cloudmont's small but professionally run facilities provide a fine place to sample skiing for nearby Alabamans, Georgians, and deep southerners. With the purchase of a lift ticket and ski rentals, a ski lesson is free.

The area's two slopes rise 150 vertical feet above a surrounding golf course and pond. Two tows, on the left side of the slopes, serve wide, 1,000-foot runs. The left slope, looking up, is the most difficult. The gradual slope on the right is the choice for beginners. Skiing is open seven days a week 9:00 to 4:00, with half-day rates after 1:00. There is night skiing every night from 6:00 to 10:00, and until midnight on Friday and Saturday nights.

Cloudmont's base lodge includes ski rentals, a round fireplace, and a snack bar serving sandwiches, soups, and chili. Six chalets, each with two bedrooms and a loft, provide lodging at the resort. Nearby, DeSota State Park has motel rooms, cabins, and chalets, and there is a Quality Inn and Best Western in Fort Payne, 8 miles distant. The resort is easily reached by taking Ala. 117 from Interstate 59.

In summer, Cloudmont has tennis and a nine-hole executive golf course. The slopes are the site of a popular weekend grass skiing program.

For more information, contact

Cloudmont Ski and Golf Resort, Mentone, AL 35984.
Details and snow report: 205/634-3841.

Sky Valley: Georgia's Only Ski Resort

Sky Valley, Ga., is a resort community and ski area in Rabun County, one of the coolest, most mountainous corners of a state noted for its sultry climate.

The nearly 2500-acre resort is 5 miles from Dillard on Ga. 246, about 100 miles from Atlanta.

The ski area has just under 10 acres of skiing on four slopes. A rope tow serves a 400-foot beginner run, and a double chairlift takes skiers up to 3,325 feet and an 800-foot advanced slope, a 2,200-foot beginner run, and a 2,000-foot intermediate slope. The 250 feet of vertical drop overlooks the resort's picturesque valley and large, gabled lodge. Slopes are open daily from 9:00 to 4:30, and three slopes are open at night from 6:00 to 10:00, except on Sundays. Half-day tickets are available after 1:00 weekends only. Special arrangements are only required to receive skiing

instruction for children under twelve and at night. Babysitting is available.

The beautiful lodge includes ski rentals, ski lockers, the ski school, a ski shop, and The Fireside Dining Room, a three-meal-a-day facility. A third floor lounge is open daily and at night, some nights with live music. The Ski and Tee Cafe, adjacent to the lodge, serves breakfast and lunch daily.

Ski accommodations range from one- to four-bedroom condominiums and chalets, all privately owned and in a rental pool. Many have cable TV. Package rates for skiers include skis and lift tickets, but not lodging.

Warm weather amenities include golf on a twenty-seven-hole championship course, tennis, swimming, and horseback riding. Special events are Oktoberfest in the fall and summer day camps for children and teen-agers.

For more information, contact

Sky Valley Resort, PO Box 1, Sky Valley, GA 30537.
Snow report and information: 404/746-5301.

Part Three

CROSS-COUNTRY,
HIKING AND
MOUNTAINEERING
AREAS

Maryland

Swallow Falls State Park: Maryland's Highest Waterfall

Swallow Falls State Park contains Maryland's highest waterfall, 64-foot Muddy Creek Falls. The park, within Garrett State Forest, is on Swallow Falls Road, 3 miles north of Herrington Manor State Park. In summer, Swallow Falls Park offers a deluxe developed campground with hot showers, a youth group camp, an interpretive center with guided hikes, and campfire programs.

CROSS-COUNTRY TRAILS AT SWALLOW FALLS

The primary cross-country ski trail accessible at Swallow Falls is the intermediate linking trail that runs 6 miles to Herrington Manor State Park. The trail begins at a youth camping area past the main parking lot for waterfall hikes.

WINTER HIKING

Swallow Falls offers a short, spectacular winter loop hike past waterfalls, virgin timber, and the Youghiogheny (Yock-a-gain-ee) River Gorge.

Park at the main parking area, .25 mile inside the park. A short distance from the trailhead is a spectacular overlook of Muddy Creek Falls and the Youghiogheny Gorge. From the first view, snowy steps descend 75 feet to a ledge trail along the river and past Swallow Falls to a right turn along Tolliver Creek. Here the trail enters the 40-acre Youghiogheny Grove, Maryland's biggest stand of virgin forest. Many of these hemlocks are 350 years old. In the grove, the trail parallels the park entrance road and ends at the parking lot in 0.6 mile.

For more information, contact

Swallow Falls State Park, RFD 5, Box 122, Oakland, MD 21550.
301/334-9180.

Herrington Manor State Park: Popular Nordic Park

Herrington Manor State Park is one of two fine cross-country skiing state parks in Maryland's Garrett County. (The other major area is New Germany, covered next.) There are 6 miles of Nordic trails and 10 miles of snowmobile trails.

Herrington Manor and nearby Swallow Falls are Maryland's oldest state parks. Herrington's nearly 500 acres surround a 55-acre lake in 7,500-acre Garrett State Forest. The park is located 5 miles from Oakland on Herrington Manor Road, Md. 20.

There are 20 fully-equipped cabins, 13 are available for winter use with a minimum two-night stay. Since Herrington Lake is shallow and spring fed, walking on winter ice is prohibited. Skiers must be off the trails by 4:00.

A skier trail fee is expected beginning in winter 1986–87. Skiers and snowmobilers start at the main parking area near the beach on Herrington Lake—take the right fork of the park entrance road. The park's beautiful new lodge building will house the winter warming facility, with a fireplace and possibly ski rentals and hot-food service. Contact the park for the latest services.

Snowmobile trails lead north into the state forest. Cross-country trails lead south past the lake and fan into five loops and an out-and-back tour. Herrington's trails explore the park's mixed hardwood and evergreen forests, including scattered and scenic evergreen plantations containing a wide variety of conifer species.

Herrington has gentle but interesting beginner trails. The road-width trails cross easy, rolling terrain. Bridges span streams. Junction signs clearly mark the trails, which rangers regularly groom with machine-set tracks. Annually, the park is the site of a Nordic citizens race in the Allegheny Mountain Race Series.

The park has a beach, bathhouse, and concession area for swimmers, paddle and rowboat rentals for pleasure and fishing, a picnic shelter, tables, and an interpretive center. Evening campfire and nature walks are conducted in summer.

Cross-Country Trails at Herrington Manor

Loop A, the longest, is the outer ring of trail, 3.5 miles round trip. Loop B is 2.8 miles. Loop B/C is 1.8 miles, loop D is 1.8, and loop E is

1.2. The Pine Patch out-and-back trail branches in the cabin area and is 1.0 mile round trip.

North from the main parking area, a 6.0-mile, hillier intermediate trail links Herrington Manor with Swallow Falls State Park. Parts of this trail are narrow compared with Herrington's wide paths. The trail twice crosses highways.

For more information, contact

Herrington Manor State Park, RFD 5, Box 122, Oakland, MD 21550. 301/334-9180.
Snow report: 301/768-0895.

New Germany State Park: Maryland's Best

For intermediate cross-country skiers, New Germany State Park is western Maryland's main attraction. New Germany offers easy, streamside trails, but numerous trail loops climb to ridges above Poplar Lick and provide exciting downhill runs.

The park is 5 miles southeast of Grantsville with easy access from U.S. 48 for skiers from either the Pittsburgh or the Baltimore area. From U.S. 48, take exit 24 and follow the signs for New Germany. Turn right at Twin Churches Road, then left on New Germany Road and left into the park at about 3 miles. Just outside the park, a large white farmhouse, Dubansky's, offers ski rentals and lessons.

From McHenry, where Deep Creek Outfitters rents skis, New Germany is 18.5 miles from U.S. 219. Take Bumble Bee Road, then right on Mosser Road, left on Rock Lodge Road at 3.5 miles, then right on Md. 495 (Bettinger Road) at Brenneman's Store at 7.8 miles, then left on New Germany Road at 10.7 miles, and right into the park at 18.5 miles.

Skiers pause just inside New Germany to pay a $2 trail fee and pick up a map. Large parking areas branch left, but keep going straight unless the park is packed. Skiers prefer parking lot 4, on the left beside the recreation building/warming hut, and lot 5, on the right at the trailhead.

New Germany is popular with outdoor programs because instructors have ideal teaching terrain: a variety of flats and gradual hills beside the warming hut, which has heated rest rooms, as well as across the road beside lot 5. With sufficient snow, rangers maintain machine-set tracks.

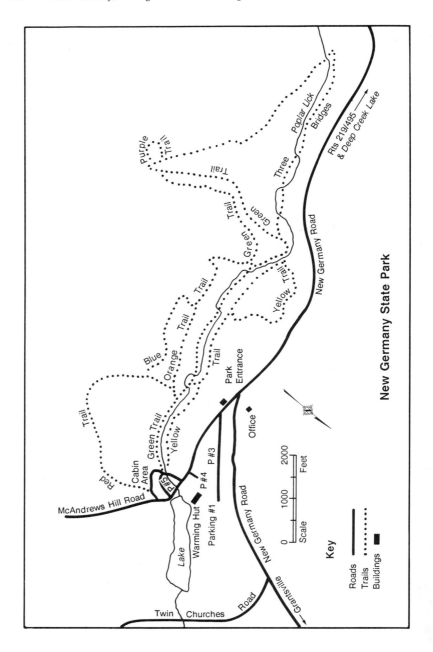

New Germany State Park

Key

Roads
Trails
Buildings

The warming hut serves hot drinks and snacks beside a roaring fire. Rangers mingle on weekends and can answer questions. Seven heated cabins are available for rent at New Germany.

The forest around the cabins and warming hut has a New England feel. Evergreens tower over the stream. Trails follow the 2,400-foot elevation of Poplar Lick and climb to 2,600 feet with views of Meadow Mountain.

Several trails make up New Germany's touring network. All are color coded on a map and trail junctions are nicely marked with a map and difficulty-rating symbols.

GREEN TRAIL

This two-section, 3.2-mile trail leaves lot 5 and follows a road grade on the south side of Poplar Lick. The first 1.5 miles are flat and cross bridges in a beautiful setting. The second section, a loop, climbs up to the trail system's high point at a junction with Three Bridges Trail. From there it descends. In either direction, it's steep and rocky, requiring a bit more snow cover than the lower section, and it demands a strong snowplow.

YELLOW TRAIL

This is a second two-section trail with easy stream-side skiing on the first part and again with a steeper end loop. Together, the two sections cover 1.6 miles on the north side of Poplar Lick. The Yellow Trail connects to the Green at a small rest bench at the start of the latter's end loop. Taking the Yellow and Green trails stream side, avoiding both end loops, makes for a fantastic easy tour of about 3 miles.

THREE BRIDGES TRAIL

Three Bridges is a 1-mile route that leaves the Green Trail beside Poplar Lick and runs flat over bridges into a climbing left turn. It then ascends to the evergreen-forested high point and reaches junctions with the Green Trail and a 0.4-mile intermediate side loop, the Purple Trail. The 1-mile trail is easy on the way up and intermediate on the run down. Seeps across the trail and some rocks require cold weather and 6 inches of snow. Combining the lower, flat section of this trail with the stream-side Yellow and Green trails makes a fine easy tour.

BLUE TRAIL/ORANGE TRAIL

These two routes form short loops above the Green Trail to which they are joined by a small stretch of the Red Trail, the first to the left off

the Green. The Orange Trail is 0.4 miles long, and the Blue is 0.9 miles. Both are undulating, interesting routes through evergreens. Intermediates will enjoy them.

RED TRAIL

This advanced, one-way trail leaves the upper cabin area, climbs to a crest, and drops down to join the Blue, Orange, and finally the Green trails. A Red, Orange, Blue combination offers many nice turns for the trail telemarker.

Eleven cabins for summer use require a minimum one-week stay and are assigned by lottery upon application after January 1. A winter cabin stay requires a two-night minimum, and cabins are assigned on a first-come, first-served basis. See the Garrett County Introduction in Part II for more cabin information.

For more information, contact

New Germany State Park, Rte. 2, Grantsville, MD 21536. 301/895-5453.

Wisp Ski Touring Center: Rolling Beginner Terrain

From its facility beside the Wisp ski resort, Deep Creek Outfitters runs a ski touring center on the Village Green golf course in McHenry. The shop has skis and accessories for rent and sale.

For a $2 trail fee, skiers use two loops of machine-set tracks over rolling hills and through tree-lined areas and can also ski on the rest of the course. The inner loop is 0.6 mile and the outer loop is 2.5 miles. Skiers should avoid greens and ponds. Wisp resort lodging and services are a short walk away.

For more information or a snow report, contact

Wisp Ski Touring Center, PO Box 172, Deep Creek Drive, McHenry, MD 21541 301/387-6825, or 301/387-5581, ext. 123. Deep Creek Outfitters' main store is in downtown McHenry at the same address. 301/387-6977.

West Virginia

Alpine Lake Resort: Terra Alta Ski Touring

Alpine Lake resort's downhill slopes and excellent accommodations, dining, and après-ski opportunities are further complemented by a cross-country skiing center. The center is based in the lodge and offers ski rentals, some retail items, beginner lessons, and some machine-set tracks. See the Alpine Lake entry in Part 2 for details on resort amenities.

The approximately 14 miles of skiing covers three areas. The Lakeside Loop around Alpine Lake is a 2.5-mile shore-line trail, half of which is machine-set track. The resort's golf course is set with five or six loops of machine-set tracks totaling 2.5 miles. The ridge-top Castle Rocks Trail leaves the fairway trails and climbs along a summer bridle trail through woods set aside as a natural area. The route, untracked, reaches good views at Castle Rocks and descends along Burchinal Road until, at 4.5 miles, it joins the Lakeside Loop at the lake's inlet brook. Other skiing possibilities include unplowed roads in the resort's undeveloped subdivisions.

Although it's in West Virginia, Alpine Lake is close to a cross-country-ski-oriented Maryland State Park, Herrington Manor. The resort's future plans include a 1.0-mile link to Herrington Manor's trails using a power company right-of-way across the state line. The link would branch from the Castle Rocks Trail.

For further information, contact

Terra Alta Ski Touring at Alpine Lake Resort, Terra Alta, WV 26764. 304/789-2481.

Babcock State Park: Ski to an Historic Mill

Located north of Beckley, W.Va., Babcock State Park features a working grist mill created from the ruins of many West Virginia mills. On a snowy day, the scene recalls a Currier & Ives painting.

The park contains a 20-acre lake and a large stream that cascades through a natural area on its way to the nearby New River.

In winter, cross-country skiers enter the park at the main entrance, 32 miles from Beckley on W.Va. 41. The road is plowed as far as the park office and two parking areas near the Glade Creek Grist Mill, which is always open on weekends. If weekday winter visitors inquire at headquarters, the mill will be opened.

Paddle, sail, and rowboats are rented in the summer. Other warm weather facilities include a swimming pool, 20 miles of trails, a campground, tennis and game courts with rental equipment, picnicking, a restaurant, and the mill, where stone-ground cornmeal and buckwheat flour are sold.

PICNIC AREA

On the way in, the first road to the right is unplowed. Skiers can use the road to reach Manns Creek Picnic Area loop and a fine view to the New River Canyon. The round trip is 5.0 miles.

WILDERNESS TRAIL

This trail runs a scenic ridge line above the park's natural-area canyon. Skiers leave south from the mill parking area and ski up the road toward the lake to the start of the Wilderness Trail and a junction with Island in the Sky Trail. The Wilderness Trail is 3.0 miles out to a dead end, 6.0 miles round trip. Beyond the trailhead, the road to the lake is also skiable.

Winter Hiking

ISLAND IN THE SKY TRAIL

This 0.25-mile trail begins at the Grist Mill but can also be reached via the Wilderness Trail access on the lake road. The trail, which is icy, leads to a photogenic canyon view.

For more information, contact

Babcock State Park, Rte. 1, Box 150, Clifftop, WV 25822. *Information, reservations, or snow report:* 304/438-6205 or 304/438-5662.

Blackwater Falls State Park: Spectacular Ski Site

Blackwater Falls State Park, south of Davis on W.Va. 32, is one of West Virginia's most scenic areas. The 1,700-acre park, which straddles Blackwater Gorge and includes its namesake falls, may be the South's best destination for cross-country skiers.

Like nearby Canaan Valley State Park, Blackwater is in the state's heavy snow zone. Its thick red spruce forests are magical when hung with snow. Annual average snowfall is 126 inches.

For winter use, the park offers 25 two-, four- and eight-person cabins with fireplaces. Rustic, year-round Blackwater Lodge has 55 rooms and a restaurant at its spectacular perch on the canyon rim. Especially in winter, the atmosphere is cozy and isolated. The lodge offers standard amenities like color TV and room phones, but unlike Canaan Lodge, with its Aspen Dining Room, Blackwater Lodge only serves alcohol in the lounge. For socially oriented skiers, Canaan Lodge may be a better choice. But Blackwater was planned to offer the relaxing, remote side of a ski trip. Scenic overlooks punctuate the park's roads.

There are miles of cross-country trails, including one that links Blackwater to Canaan Valley State Park for lodge-to-lodge tours. The park's fine cross-country skiing center is affiliated with White Grass Ski Touring Center and is located in the recreation building at Pendleton Lake. Professional Ski Instructors of America members give daily lessons. Rentals and tours are also offered daily, and the shop carries retail ski equipment. Blackwater's program includes an annual cross-country ski workshop sponsored by the state and seminars in back-country skiing and racing technique. An Allegheny Mountain Series race is held at Blackwater every winter. Inexpensive package plans are available. The first six skiing sites and trails listed below offer 4.0 miles of machine-set tracks. A sledding slope served by a rope tow is available to skiers wanting to pursue telemark instruction or practice.

The nearby town of Davis, the state's highest, offers dining and lodging, as well as the private ski center TransMontane Outfitters, another source of ski rentals, lessons, and tours on nearby public trails.

Cross-Country Trails

PENDLETON LAKE DRIVING RANGE

The driving range is an easy open meadow, with set track, near the skiing center.

CAMPGROUND LOOPS

These loops offer good beginner practice and are accessible from the driving range and the skiing center.

NORTH RIM ROAD TRAIL

This trail follows the unplowed road that loops left from the skiing center access road. One trailhead is opposite the campground entrance and the other starts where the skiing center road goes right. This 1.0-mile, evergreen-forested novice loop has double set track and many picnic tables.

SPUDDER TRACK

This 0.75-mile novice trail runs through the middle of the North Rim Road loop, leaving that trail at the shelter and rejoining it near the campground entrance.

GEE-HAW TRAIL

This 0.25-mile novice trail links the driving range to Spudder Track through the middle of North Rim Road Loop.

PENDLETON TRACE/PENDLETON POINT OVERLOOK

Pendleton Trace leaves the west side of the skiing center parking lot and climbs to a parking lot on North Rim Road. It then leaves that lot and reaches the overlook at Pendleton Point and other canyon-side rock outcrops. Pendleton Trace is a 0.5-mile, intermediate-rated trail.

DOBBIN HOUSE TRAIL SYSTEM

This newly opened 5.0-mile trail network branches from Pendleton Trace and crosses the dam of Pendleton Lake into Monongahela National Forest.

The 3.5-mile Dobbin House loop is intermediate to advanced. It follows tunnels in the rhododendron and passes spruce forests, meadows, ponds, and strip mine benches. It takes about two hours to ski the loop. Dinky Jumpoff and Woodcock Trails, both 0.5 mile and intermediate rated, bisect the Dobbin Loop and join each other to create three possible loop tours.

The easiest tour in the Dobbin House area is an out-and-back trip using the leftward leg of Dobbin House and the Pase Point Trail, a 0.5-mile trail that branches left to a view from the canyon rim.

DAVIS TRAIL

This trail, marked by blue diamonds, starts at the park stables and is the first leg of the 7.8-mile Blackwater/Canaan Cross-Country Trail, a connector trail (see the entry on Canaan Valley State Park a few pages ahead). In 1.75 miles, the Davis Trail reaches a crossing with the Plantation Trail (see the next entry, on Canaan Mountain). A six-person shelter is 200 feet to the right on the Plantation Trail. Skiers can use the Davis Trail as an out-and-back route or as the start for loop trips on Canaan Mountain trails.

RED SPRUCE TRAIL/WATER TANK TRAIL

Like the Davis Trail, Red Spruce Trail begins at the stables. From there, it reaches the cabin access road near cabin 1 in 2.0 miles. The Red Spruce Trail is rated intermediate and ventures through impressive evergreens.

Just under halfway to the cabin road on Red Spruce Trail, The Water Tank Trail branches right and in 0.25 mile reaches a park spur road, a short walk from Blackwater Lodge. Skiers touring from Canaan Valley State Park can take the Red Spruce Trail, then Water Tank Trail to the lodge. Rangers ask that skiers descending the Tank Trail stop on the flat and walk the last 20 yards to a dangerous junction with the park road.

STEMWINDER GRADE

This is a 1.0-mile, intermediate-to-advanced connector beteen the Red Spruce Trail and Davis Trail. Stemwinder Grade leaves to the right from Davis Trail near the park boundary, and it enters Red Spruce Trail on the left 0.2 mile west of Water Tank Trail. This connector allows loop skiing from a number of trailheads.

CHERRY LANE TRAIL

Starting across the road from the end of the Red Spruce Trail, near cabin 1, Cherry Lane Trail winds level past the sledding hill and loops back on itself near the circle at the end of the cabin road. The trail is 1.5 miles long and rated intermediate to advanced.

SHAY TRACE

This trail leaves the park road at the west entrance to the lodge parking area near the stream, Shay Run. Shay Trace crosses the Red Spruce Trail between Water Tank Trail and the cabin road, then crosses cabin road between cabins 4 and 5 on one side of the road, and 2 and 6 on the other, and ends at the warming hut on Sled Run Trail. Shay Trace is 2.0 miles long and intermediate rated.

SLED RUN

This is a good downhill practice area with a rustic, truck-powered rope tow reminiscent of skiing's early days.

Winter Hiking

FALLS VIEW TRAIL

A 2.0-mile linking trail between Blackwater Lodge and the Hemlock Trail, with its views of Blackwater Falls. Only heavy snow makes this hike difficult. The trail begins on the south side of the park road where it enters the lodge parking lots.

The easiest view of falls is from a short trail for the handicapped that starts at the parking area, 1.1 miles east of lodge.

HEMLOCK TRAIL

If snow is deep or there isn't much time, hike to Blackwater Falls on the 0.5-mile Hemlock Trail. Park in the lot on the right just past the bridge over the Blackwater River on the way to the lodge. Avoid the trail's longer loop by going left at the first junction, reaching the falls overlook in 0.3 mile, and retracing your steps.

EKLALA TRAIL

This easy, highly scenic trail leaves the south side of Blackwater Lodge, crosses a waterfall on a footbridge, and reaches a view of the canyon only 0.5 mile from the lodge. The trail intersects the main park road 0.5 mile south of the lodge, just before a scenic overlook on the right side of the road.

BALANCED ROCK TRAIL

Starting 0.5 mile south of the lodge across the park road from the Eklala Trail, the Balanced Rock Trail leads to a uniquely balanced rock and a good view. It then continues to a junction on the right with the Rhododendron Trail and terminates in the cabin area between cabins 12 and 13. The total distance is 1.5 miles. Start at the cabins for the fastest route to the balanced rock.

RHODODENDRON TRAIL

This 0.5-mile trail branches left from the Balanced Rock Trail behind cabin 12. After threading between rhododendron, the trail ends beside cabin 9.

For more information, contact

Blackwater Lodge, PO Drawer 490, Davis, WV 26260. 800/CALLWVA.

Canaan Mountain Area: Skiing between State Parks

Between Blackwater Falls and Canaan Valley state parks lies Canaan Mountain, a long flat ridge of National Forest land that reaches elevations of 3,700 feet. This is very northern country. A large part of this tract consists of an 80-year-old spruce plantation that can only be called Canadian in character.

Through the heart of this area runs the Blackwater/Canaan Cross-Country Ski Trail. Many other trails and road grades in the area offer extensive loop skiing, best accomplished from Blackwater Falls State Park, the Canaan Loop Road, or trailheads on W.Va. 32, the main highway between the two adjoining state parks. Unlike the parks, the Canaan Mountain area is less well marked and trails can at times be wet and rocky. Two shelters and many tent sites make the Canaan Mountain area a prime target for experienced ski campers. Deep snow, a map, and conservative skiing should be prerequisites for using this very beautfiul area. Because of their isolation, trails here require at least intermediate skills.

Cross-Country Trails

CANAAN LOOP ROAD (CLR)

This 12-mile Forest Service fire road is unplowed in winter and forms a long, looping traverse of Canaan Mountain. The road starts on the west side of W.Va. 32, 3.1 miles south of the river bridge in Davis at the road sign, Canaan Mtn., Elev. 3702'. The road terminates just beyond the parking area for Sled Run in Blackwater Falls State Park.

For some of its distance, the road serves as a link in the Blackwater/Canaan Cross Country Trail. Although rutted by summer travel, the road is mostly level. It skis best in deep snow.

PLANTATION TRAIL

This beautiful trail is gradual as it passes through spruce and rhododendron forests. Plantation Trail leaves the west side of W.Va. 32, 2.6 miles south of Davis, at a prominent sign and small parking area. The trail descends, then rises to a signed junction on the left, at 1.0 mile, with Fire Trail 3, a 0.75-mile, expert-rated connector to parking lot 9 on CLR.

Plantation Trail crosses a bridge soon after the junction, and at 1.7 miles it crosses a gas pipeline. At 2.5 miles, it crosses another dam/bridge, and at 2.7 miles it crosses the Davis Trail (right to Blackwater Falls State Park; left to Canaan Valley State Park and CLR; see Davis Trail, Blackwater/Canaan Cross-Country Trail). To Davis Trail, Plantation Trail is easily skiable for intermediates. Some 200 feet past the junction on Plantation Trail is a six-person shelter on the right.

After that, the trail continues level, crossing streams at 3.7 and 4.0 miles and a dam at 4.5 miles. At 4.7 miles, the intermediate to advanced Fire Trail 6 goes left and runs 1.3 miles to CLR, which it joins about 4 miles from W.Va. 32. The Plantation Trail crosses another dam at 5.0 miles, and then the trail becomes rockier and narrow. At 5.75 miles, the trail descends steeply to a junction with Lindy Run Trail, then it climbs back up to flat touring and a junction with Railroad Grade Trail at 6.6 miles. Gradual grades through evergreens, open areas and bogs characterize the last stretch to CLR at 8.5 miles.

FIRE LANE

A Fire Lane runs roughly parallel to but south of the Plantation Trail between the Lindy Run Trail and the gas pipeline. The Fire Lane can be used as a connector between Lindy Run, Fire Trail 6, and Davis Trail. Beyond Davis Trail, it deteriorates.

The unsigned Fire Lane leaves the east side of Lindy Run Trail, 0.5 mile north of CLR. It crosses Fire Trail 6, 0.5 mile north of CLR at a sign and reaches Davis Trail at an unsigned junction 0.7 mile north of CLR. This trail is quite level. However, Fire Trail 6 is rated intermediate to advanced.

LINDY RUN TRAIL

From Plantation Trail, the southern section of Lindy Run Trail is very skiable to CLR. The Fire Lane Trail branches east 1.0 mile south of the Plantation Trail. Lindy Run Trail ends 0.5 mile later at a signed junction with CLR.

RAILROAD GRADE TRAIL

This is an excellent trail to use in a loop trip. The trail begins 2.0 miles west from the Sled Run parking area in Blackwater Falls State Park. Ski to the trailhead on CLR. The trail follows an old railroad grade gradually up to the Plantation Trail, at 1.5 miles, and then widens and descends as it goes south. A six-person shelter is located at 2.2 miles, and the signed CLR junction is at 3.5 miles.

MOUNTAIN SIDE TRAIL

This excellent, skiable route branches from CLR about 1.0 mile north of the latter's junction with the Plantation Trail. The Mountain Side Trail gradually slabs Canaan Mountain with fine views, rejoining CLR as a Forest Service road about 2.0 miles west of the southern end of the Railroad Grade Trail.

For more information, contact

District Ranger, U.S. Forest Service, Cheat Ranger District, PO Box 368, Parsons, WV 26287. 304/478-3251.

Canaan Valley Resort State Park: A Park for Watching Wildlife

Canaan Valley Resort State Park is one of many facilities that make this high West Virginia valley a cross-country skier's paradise. Besides ample

Nordic facilities right in Canaan Valley State Park, the immediate area includes the private White Grass Ski Touring Center, another cross-country center at Blackwater Falls State Park, and other trails at Cathedral State Park and the Dolly Sods National Forest lands. Snowfall here is among the deepest in the South. Skiing at this 3,200-foot elevation can be expected from late December to late March.

For information on Canaan Valley State Park's lodge, downhill ski area, and other substantial amenities open to Nordic skiers, see the resort's entry in Part 2.

Canaan Valley State Park operates a cross-country ski center at its nature center. In all, 18 miles of ungroomed ski trails and an eighteen-hole golf course are available in the park, all marked with ski ratings and with caution signs at difficult areas. The center is open daily when there is skiing and offers retail goods, rentals skis, group and private ski lessons, and guided tours.

The park has four enjoyable loop trails for skiers, most of which afford views of northern scenery, including beaver ponds. There are many open meadows, some on roadsides. One of Canaan's advanced ski trails connects in 7.8 miles to Blackwater Falls State Park, enabling skiers to tour lodge to lodge for an overnight trail experience.

Although designated for skiing and marked, trails are not patrolled. Let the ski center or lodge personnel know your plans before skiing.

Cross-Country Trails

BLACKWATER RIVER TRAIL

This beginner trail starts in the golf clubhouse parking lot. The trail, marked with red circles, follows an old railroad grade on a 1.0-mile, level tour along the Blackwater River.

GOLF COURSE

This large area is fine for both beginners and advanced skiers. The tundra-like bogs, the beaver ponds, and the spectacular views make great surroundings in which to learn.

CLUB RUN TRAIL

Starting opposite the end of the last loop of cabins (across from cabin 15), this loop trail can be skied either way from the junction just after the start. Going right, another trail comes in on the right, the intermediate-rated, white-circle-marked Ridge Top Trail to the Middle Ridge Trail loop. Near Club Run, the Club Run Trail bears left past beaver ponds and returns along the stream to the first junction. Club Run Trail is 1.5 miles long, marked with red circles, and rated intermediate.

MIDDLE RIDGE TRAIL

This 2.5-mile loop starts on the left below the lodge on the road to the golf course near Balsam Swamp Overlook. The trail reaches a junction and, taking a right, follows an old logging road to near Club Run. Take the left near the stream to return along Middle Ridge with views of beaver ponds. (Keeping straight at the second junction leads to Blackwater Falls State Park.) At the third junction, the Ridge Top Trail goes right to join Club Run Trail. Take a left and return to your car at the overlook.

The trail is rated intermediate to advanced, has some steep ups and downs, and is marked with yellow circles.

RAILROAD GRADE TRAIL

Although not a loop itself, this trail allows skiers to make a large loop from shorter trails. The trail is rated intermediate to advanced, with some steep ups and downs.

Railroad Grade Trail is reached on the Middle Ridge Trail. Go straight at the second junction on that trail. Cross two streams, Club Run and Enoch Run, come to another junction. Go left on Railroad Grade Trail, marked with blue circles, for 2.5 miles on a scenic old railroad grade. At the next junction, take Chimney Rock Trail left, following green circles, to the last bend in the cabin access road. The whole loop is 5.0 miles. To the right at the last junction, upper Chimney Rock Trail is unskiable.

To return to parking at the overlook, skiers can ski alongside the road to Club Run Trail, take that to Ridge Top Trail, and proceed back to the overlook. Another option is to park between the Chimney Rock and Club Run trailheads and make 5.0-mile circuit from there. The three loops described can be connected in many ways.

DEER RUN TRAIL

This summer nature trail is a 1.5-mile connector between the lodge recreation area and the nature center/campground that runs through the heart of the park's wildlife observation area. For skiing, the trail is rated intermediate and is marked by orange squares. It crosses boardwalks over boggy areas, and deer are a frequent sight here and from the nearby lodge access road. Meadows and evergreen glades surround this area and offer scenic exploring on skis.

BLACKWATER/CANAAN CROSS-COUNTRY SKI TRAIL

This 7.8-mile park-to-park trail is rated intermediate to expert and is marked with blue diamonds, yellow paint blazes, and caution signs at steeper sections. The trail crests Canaan Mountain between the two parks at 3,600 feet. Rangers recommend that there be 15 inches of snow on the ground before you try this trail. Skiing time, including a break, ranges between three and six hours. Over the trail's length, a skier touring from Canaan to Blackwater will encounter 39 percent downhill, 26 percent uphill, and 35 percent level.

From Canaan, the trail begins from the second junction on the Middle Ridge Trail, which starts at Balsam Swamp Overlook. The Blackwater/Canaan Trail crosses Club and Enoch runs, passes a junction with Railroad Grade Trail, which leaves left, and climbs to the park boundary at 2.6 miles. Continuing in the Monongahela National Forest, the trail reaches the wide CLR at 3.8 miles. Turn right on the CLR and ski 1.2 miles to a left turn onto the Davis Trail. After the turn, cross a fire lane at 0.5 mile, and 1.0 mile after the turn, the Plantation Trail is crossed. (A six-person shelter is located 200 feet left on Plantation Trail). In another 1.8 miles, the trail reaches the Blackwater Falls State Park trailhead. Of this last stretch from the CLR, 75 percent is downhill. The trailhead at Blackwater Falls is at the park's stables, 0.7 mile from the lodge. To reach the lodge, take Red Spruce Trail, described under Blackwater Falls State Park.

From either park, this trail can be an out-and-back day tour that climbs on the way out, and descends on the way back.

For more information, see the list of contacts in the Canaan Valley Resort State Park Ski Area entry in Part 2.

Cathedral State Park: Virgin Timber Trails

This 140-acre state park contains the only remaining virgin timber in West Virginia. The state's biggest tree is here: a 100-foot hemlock 26 feet in circumference. The big trees here are said to be 350 years old.

Skiers will find this park aptly named. Photographers should take their cameras.

At 2,500 feet in snowy Preston County, the park's flat terrain makes its 5.0 miles of trails remarkably skiable. Eight rustic bridges carry skiers over Rhine Creek as they glide through the silent, massive forest. Huge rhododendrons form the understory, tangling the banks of the rushing stream.

From the parking lot at park headquarters on the north side of U.S. 50, a half-mile east of Aurora, W.Va., the Cathedral Trail forms a loop through the park. Five other loops are created by the Giant Hemlock Trail, Wood Thrush Trail, Partridge Berry Trail, Trillium Trail, and Cardinal Trail as they branch to form smaller side loops, a few requiring a short ski along an unpaved country lane. A picnic shelter and grills are provided adjacent to the parking area.

Although it does not offer a lengthy tour, beginning cross-country skiers will find that this park yields an inspiring and forgiving afternoon of skiing. For advanced skiers, the forest creates an enjoyable backdrop for fast, flat-track skiing.

The Mountain Village Inn and Cabin Lodge are fine nearby accommodations for skiers at Cathedral as well as for those at Canaan Valley. Cabin Lodge, in Aurora, is an antique-furnished spruce-log cabin amidst streamside hemlocks and is rented like a condominium. Mountain Village Inn, 12 miles north of Davis and 10 miles south of Cathedral, offers three guest rooms with a shared bath, fine dining, and a cozy lounge. A 1.0-mile loop trail for cross-country skiers circles Silver Lake, just outside the inn.

For more information, contact

Superintendent, Cathedral State Park, Aurora, WV 26705.
    800/CALLWVA.
For Mountain Village Inn and Cabin Lodge, contact Mountain Village
    Inn, Route 219, Horseshoe Run, WV 26769. 304/735-6344.

Cooper's Rock State Forest: Touring near Morgantown

Cooper's Rock combines a large recreation area and a West Virginia University forest into a 13,000-acre preserve on the banks of the Cheat

River near Morgantown, 6 miles west of Bruceton Mills. West Virginia's largest state forest is a day-use area with increasingly popular cross-country ski trails, ice skating, and 90 inches of annual snowfall among its attractions. Summer amenities include a campground, picnicking, a souvenir shop, and a playground.

With Morgantown and West Virginia State University only 13 miles away, this park is heavily used for winter sports. The closest cross-country ski rental is at The Pathfinder outdoor shop and the WVU Student Union in Morgantown. The Pathfinder's multiday rental rates are very inexpensive.

Ice skating is popular at Cooper's Rock on Messinger Lake near the forest headquarters and at a small skating pond near a now closed slope and rope tow at Chestnut Ridge Camp. Plans for the park include, in the near future, a warming hut at the ski trailhead and machine-set tracks. Most of the Cooper's Rock ski trails are old logging grades.

The closest lodging is at the Sheraton Lakeview Resort and Conference Center, just outside Cooper's Rock State Forest and an excellent base of operations for winter vacationers. Other skiing sites close by include trails at West Virginia's Cathedral State Park and slopes and a Nordic center at Alpine Lake Resort. Nearby are Maryland's two fine cross-country state parks, New Germany and Herrington Manor, and the Wisp ski resort, all less than one hour away on four-lane U.S. 48. Canaan Valley is two hours away.

Sheraton Lakeview permits cross-country skiing on its scenic golf course overlooking Cheat Lake, a popular summer destination for water sports. The resort has condominiums and lodge rooms, fine dining, a coffee shop, a lounge and live entertainment, a spa and fitness center, tennis, swimming, and boating. Ski packages offer savings on regular rates and shuttle service is available to nearby ski areas.

Cross-Country Trails

SKI LOOPS

Starting south of U.S. 48, there are three ski trail loops, each rated at a different level of difficulty. A plowed parking area and rest rooms are available at the trailhead.

The 1.0-mile beginner loop uses part of a gated road. The 1.5-mile intermediate trail has easy ups and downs and crosses bridges. The 5.5-mile advanced loop offers steeper climbs and long downhill runs and can be extended to 7.0 miles by skiing a larger loop on an unplowed road. The two advanced loops split near an early-1800s iron furnace in the park's interior. Beyond the parking area on the road in, skiers can also ski past the plow line and reach the fine view from Cooper's Rock, an overlook on the Cheat River.

WEST VIRGINIA UNIVERSITY FOREST

North of four-lane U.S. 48, the WVU Forest side of Cooper's Rock contains miles of rarely used, very scenic trails suitable for intermediate skiers. From park headquarters, go east on W.Va. 73, then turn north toward Chestnut Ridge Camp to the intersection at the superintendent's residence.

GLADE RUN HOLLOW

This 1.5-mile trail begins beside the superintendent's residence and follows Glade Run to Messinger Lake.

INTERPRETIVE TRAIL NETWORK

Opposite the residence, the Interpretive Trail goes east. A trail branches right, crosses the park road and descends the Glade Run drainage to Messinger Lake. The Interpretive Trail continues to Laurel Run and branches. The right fork goes south through a grove of towering hemlocks to a parking area on the north side of W.Va. 73 toward the town of Bruceton Mills. The left fork, north from the Interpretive Trail, is Ken's Run Trail and follows Little Laurel Creek to a fire road and left turn to Sand Springs Fire Tower. Continuing past the tower, the grade joins an unplowed park road that goes south, completing a loop at a gate where the Interpretive Trail starts opposite the superintendent's residence. These trail options exceed 12 miles.

For more information, contact

Cooper's Rock State Forest, Rte. 1, Box 270, Bruceton Mills, WV, 26525. 304/594-1561.

The Pathfinder, 182 Willey St., Morgantown, WV 26505. 304/296-0076.

Sheraton Lakeview Resort & Conference Center, Rte. 6, Box 88A, Morgantown, WV 26505. 304/594-1111.

The Dolly Sods: Alpine Scenery

The Dolly Sods is a 13,000-acre U.S. Forest Service Wilderness and Scenic Area east of Canaan Valley. However, the name *Dolly Sods* has come to be generally used to describe the high, open ridge crests in the area. This is some of West Virginia's most alpine scenery. Besides the spruce-covered Red Creek drainage of the Wilderness proper, 6,000 acres of adjoining private lands create a huge upland area of treeless alpine scenery.

The area is immensely popular with backpackers in summer, and tourists flock to Forest Service Road (FSR) 75 that crosses the area. Visitors are attracted by activities like car camping at Red Creek Campground, sightseeing, blueberry picking, and watching the noteworthy hawk migration from Bear Rocks.

South of FSR, another 12,000 acres of USFS land covers similar terrain on Roaring, Flatrock, and Rohrbaugh plains, areas as scenic but far less visited than the Dolly Sods proper. The local term *Sods* applies to all these crest zones. After turn-of-the-century logging, fires cleared the summits, and tundralike plains remain today. The early Dahle family name is probably the source of the modern spelling of Dolly Sods.

Summer access is easy. In winter, skiers and winter mountaineers can reach the Sods at only a few areas. However, most sections can be accessible for ambitious, well-equipped parties. In this area, skill with map and compass is essential. Although USGS topo maps do not accurately represent trails, carry them in addition to a trail map for topographic detail. Very deep snow can obscure all signs of a trail, and often, travel is essentially cross-country, with or without skis. Experienced Sods adventurers stress the changeable weather and severe winds. Most snow storms are windy, causing shallow cover to alternate with the state's deepest drifts.

No wilderness permit is needed, but a permit is required to use private railroad land along Cabin Mountain north of White Grass Ski Touring Center (described later in this section). White Grass owner Chip Chase can guide users to the permit outlet in Davis and can also offer valuable advice on access and snow conditions.

Cabin Mountain/Northern Sods

This is one of the Sods' most scenic areas and the terrain is very suitable for skiers. Meadows alternate with spruce stands. Access is easiest from FSR 80 at White Grass Ski Touring Center or from Canaan Valley ski area via the chairlift. Skiers and snowshoe mountaineers can traverse the open areas to Blackbird Knob and beyond to Red Creek Campground on FSR 75, the crest of the Sods area. FSR 75 goes north to Bear Rocks, then drops east to the vicinity of Petersburg, a remote access not recommended in winter. South from the Red Creek Campground area, FSR 75 joins FSR 19, which reaches a plowed public road at Laneville that is easily accessible from W.Va. 32 south of Canaan Valley State Park.

Skiers and backpackers should approach Cabin Mountain on FSR 80, which starts just past White Grass Ski Touring on Freeland Road. FSR 80 crests a ridge and slabs east of the Cabin Mountain summit to a common trailhead of Breathed Mountain Trail and Big Stonecoal Trail. North of these designated trails, old railroad grades and jeep roads offer many open routes.

BREATHED MOUNTAIN TRAIL

From the FSR 80 trailhead, Breathed Mountain Trail goes east across open fields and past beaver ponds to a junction in 2.0 miles with Red Creek Trail, which forms a connector left to Blackbird Knob Trail and private land.

BLACKBIRD KNOB TRAIL

From the Wilderness boundary on Red Creek Trail, Blackbird Knob Trail goes north then east to Blackbird Knob. The trail reaches a large outcrop, then ends, after a total of 2.0 miles, at Red Creek Campground on FSR 75. From the area of Blackbird Knob, it is possible to leave the trail and head overland, staying north of the Wilderness boundary, back to Cabin Mountain.

BIG STONECOAL TRAIL

This trail follows many railroad grades on its descent from high meadows to the Red Creek Trail 1.5 miles above FSR 19 at Laneville. The trail crosses Big Stonecoal Run four times and passes numerous beaver ponds in its 4.5 miles. On the way, the Dunkenbarger Trail leaves to the right and the Rocky Point Trail goes left.

Laneville/Southern Sods

The town of Laneville offers the best access to the Dolly Sods Wilderness. Because of their frequent stream crossings, trails in this part of the

Wilderness are most suitable for backpackers. High-water crosssings here can be dangerous. The massive damage of the 1985 West Virginia flood is easily visible as one approaches Laneville on county road 45, 5.0 miles from a well-signed junction just south of Canaan Valley State Park on W.Va. 32.

RED CREEK TRAIL

This trail starts at the Laneville ranger cabin just across the Laneville bridge at the start of FSR 19. The trail passes Little Stonecoal Trail at 0.5 mile and Big Stonecoal Trail at 1.5 miles, both on the left. Climbing the drainage, the Fisher Spring Run Trail goes right and the Rocky Point Trail leads left. Leveling out, the Red Creek Trail is joined on the left by the Breathed Mountain Trail and ends at Blackbird Knob Trail after a total of 6.0 miles. Red Creek Trail was skiable before the flood, but there is now substantial damage between the Little and Big Stonecoal trails.

DUNKENBARGER AND ROCKY POINT TRAILS

These very scenic trails link the drainage trails to form loops in the lower Red Creek area. The Dunkenbarger Trail links Little Stonecoal Trail, which dead ends at the Wilderness boundary, to Big Stonecoal Trail. Dunkenbarger is a very scenic 1.5 miles.

Rocky Point Trail crosses the ridge between Big Stonecoal and Red Creek trails. The nearly 2-mile trail is level with great views of the Red Creek drainage at an outcrop near Big Stonecoal Trail.

ROHRBAUGH PLAINS AND FISHER SPRING RUN TRAILS

These trails link the Red Creek Trail with the least accessible parts of FSR 75. Snowshoe backpackers carrying skis could traverse the Wilderness and ski back to Laneville on FSRs 75 and 19.

The Fisher Spring Run Trail leads in 2.0 miles from the Red Creek Trail to FSR 75, 0.5 mile north of old Bell Knob firetower road. The Rohrbaugh Plains Trail leaves Fisher Spring Run and crosses the very rocky edge of the plateau to FSR 19 at the Dolly Sods picnic ground. Although some railroad grades are used, skiers might opt to join the Wildlife Trail, a skiable road grade to wildlife feeding areas that quickly gets skiers out to FSR 75.

FSR 19/75

From Laneville, the unplowed FSR 19 rises to meet FSR 75, offering access to many trails. Although this is a road, ski backpackers could make good use of this route in reaching the high scenery and trails in the Flatrock Plains area.

The easiest access to these isolated plateaus is by hiking or skiing FSR 19 to either the strenuous Boar's Nest Trail or FSR 70, a road, gated most of the year, that makes a fine skiing route to the high crest. At the most distant reaches of these plains lies Mount Porte Crayon, the sixth highest peak in West Virginia at 4,770 feet. The name, literally "pencil carrier," is the pen name of David Strother, a mid-1800s illustrator and writer. No maintained trails reach the summit.

BOAR'S NEST TRAIL

This trail begins, with the South Prong Trail, above Laneville on the south side of FSR 19 where a logging road goes steeply downhill. The trail is best suited for backpackers. It then crosses the South Fork of Red Creek and switchbacks steeply up to the edge of Flatrock Plains, which it then crosses to FSR 70, a total of 3.0 miles. To the south, 0.3 mile down FSR 70, is the start of Roaring Plains Trail at a gas pipe swath.

ROARING PLAINS/FLATROCK RUN TRAIL

Where FSR 70 meets the gas pipe swath, the Roaring Plains Trail begins. The trail climbs briefly, then winds through rhododendron thickets and across open meadows to its terminus at 3.0 miles. It ends atop Roaring Plains, from which the Flatrock Run Trail descends steeply to Laneville.

FSR 70

From its start on FSR 19, FSR 70 reaches the gas pipe in 3.6 miles, enabling skiers to easily reach the high, isolated Roaring Plains plateau. Park at Laneville, ski up to the gated start of FSR 70, and go right to connections with the Roaring Plains Trail or overland skiing on the open meadows.

For more information, contact

Potomac District Ranger, USDA Forest Service, Petersburg, WV 26847. 304/257-4488.

Elk River Ski Touring Center: Set-track Skiing

Elk River is the major ski touring center in the vicinity of Snowshoe and Silver Creek downhill ski areas.

The ski center and The Willis Farm, a rustic overnight lodge, perch on the banks of the Elk River 5 miles south of the turn for Snowshoe and Silver Creek on W.Va. 219. The center and lodge are operated by Gil and Mary Willis and partner Al McKinnon. A variety of trails and 3 miles of machine-set tracks explore the meadows and forests around the center. One trail is lit for night skiing. Under a U.S. Forest Service permit, Elk River marks and maintains another 20 miles of trails 9 miles south of the center on the eastern end of the Highland Scenic Highway. New trails open regularly. A $2 weekday and $3 weekend trail fee is charged. A free map is available with letters that correspond to junction signs on the various trails.

Elk River maintains a Professional Ski Instructors of America member ski school with flat track lessons at the center and telemark downhill lessons at Silver Creek ski resort. Guided ski tours are available, and the trails are patrolled by a Nordic unit of the National Ski Patrol System. The center houses a complete rental and retail ski shop with a wide variety of ski equipment, clothing, and literature. Across the parking area, the Willis Farm is a cozy country inn that sleeps eighteen in four private rooms with two shared baths. There is a dining room and a living room with a big open-front wood stove. A nearby cabin sleeps five, with kitchen and bath. The farm offers tasty morning and evening meals prepared by Mary Willis.

In summer, Elk River becomes a gathering place for hikers and mountain bicyclists. Mountain-bike rentals and guided bike tours on the 72-mile Greenbrier River Trail are offered. Additional accommodations and services are available at Snowshoe and Silver Creek ski areas to the north, and at Marlinton, W. Va., 16 miles south of Elk River. See the Richwood entry later in this part for Marlinton dining and lodging information.

Cross-Country Trails at Elk River

THE MEADOW

A large meadow flanks the ski center, offering nearly a mile-long learning and lesson area with set track and a sloping practice hill.

MINNIE'S LOOP

Starting in front of the center, Minnie's Loop is an easiest-rated 1.5-mile loop of set track that follows the Elk River and circles the meadow. It is lit for night skiing. At Blue Hole, skiers view a large pool in the river. Nearby, the open door of an ancient outhouse offers a glimpse into the past.

DRUM'S BEAT

This 0.5-mile intermediate trail climbs from behind the ski center to a junction with River Trail, then passes a house and leads to a lettered intersection and, beyond, to a dead-end view at Lookout Meadow.

HEART ATTACK

Aptly named, this 0.75-mile uphill trail for experts runs from the end of Minnie's Loop to a lettered intersection with Drum's Beat below Lookout Meadow.

RIVER TRAIL

This intermediate to advanced trail branches left from Drum's Beat below the house and climbs through evergreens past lettered intersections with Sheep's Trail and Springhouse Trail. Some steep up- and downhill stretches here may require sidestepping. The last descent ends at the bank of Elk River and leads into two long loops of beautiful stream-side skiing. These snowy trails, separated by two lettered intersections, are very skiable for the intermediate and may be the best trails at Elk River. The total loop is 5.0 miles.

SHEEP TRAIL

This intermediate trail climbs 0.5 mile through oaks from the first lettered intersection on River Trail to Drum's Beat.

SPRING HOUSE TRAIL

This trail is a steep 0.5-mile climb from Minnie's Loop, behind Willis Farm, to a lettered junction on the high point of River Trail. It's advanced if skied downhill.

Cross-Country Trails on the Highland Scenic Highway

HIGHWAY

The highway offers miles of easy touring with expansive views. It is an out-and-back tour, and forms the primary access to the many miles of touring trails, marked by Elk River Center, that fan out on both sides of the road.

GAY SHARP TRAIL

This novice to intermediate trail leaves the east side of U.S. 219 just south of the junction with the Highland Scenic Highway. The trail makes two loops past lettered intersections. Meadows here are called Tele Fever for their exciting downhill runs.

WOLFPEN ROCKS TRAIL

This fire road trail begins south of the Scenic Highway on the west side of U.S. 219. From this starting point, eastern views at Wolfpen Rocks are most accessible. The trail, intermediate, passes rocks and bears right at two lettered intersections to join Shearer's Run at a lettered trailhead beside the Scenic Highway just 100 yards from U.S. 219. The total distance is 2.5 miles.

SHEARER'S RUN

Shearer's Run is a 1.5-mile, two-loop trail system starting at a lettered trailhead 100 yards west of U.S. 219 on the Scenic Highway. One leg of Shearer's Run rejoins the Scenic Highway 0.7 mile west of U.S. 219.

BLACKBERRY JAM

Blackberry Jam consists of two easy to intermediate trail loops north of the Scenic Highway, with two lettered intersections. The trail, 2.0 miles total, goes right from the Scenic Highway at 0.7 mile and reenters at 1.6 miles from U.S. 219.

RED LICK LOOP

This short intermediate loop through snowy hardwoods leaves north from the Scenic Highway at 3.9 miles from U.S. 219.

RED SPRUCE RUN

A very gradual loop south of the Scenic Highway, this trail circles 4,703-foot Red Spruce Knob. From the highway, the forest road leaves left, under the peak, at a point 4.4 miles west of U.S. 219. It reaches the Scenic Highway again 5.7 miles from U.S. 219. This easy trail is 3.0 miles long.

GAULEY MOUNTAIN TRAIL

This intermediate to advanced trail leaves the Highland Scenic Highway on the right atop Gauley Mountain. The trail starts in a field opposite an overlook about 5.8 miles from U.S. 219. The trail runs a gradual ridge top for 5.6 miles and then joins the Sharp's Knob Mining Road (State Road 219/1) near the top of Gauley Mountain. A very aggressive day tour would involve skiing the highway to the Gauley Mountain Trail and then continuing to U.S. 219, just south of Elk River, on the Sharp's Knob Road. This mining road leg is 4.0 miles long.

For more information, contact

Elk River Ski Touring Center, Slatyfork, WV 26291. 304/572-3771.
Marlinton Chamber of Commerce, 805 4th Avenue, Marlinton, WV 24954. 304/799-4990.
Marlinton Ranger Station, USDA Forest Service, PO Box 210, Marlinton, WV 24954. 304/799-4334.

Kumbrabow State Forest: West Virginia's Highest

Pronounced Koom-BRAY-boe, this state forest is West Virginia's highest. The skiing is on ridge-top fire roads from 3,000 to 3,800 feet in elevation. The nearly 10,000-acre park contains a small campground, five rustic cabins, a picnic area, and a playground for summer use. The closest ski rental is at Elk River Ski Touring Center in Slatyfork.

Although two gravel roads reach Kumbrabow, the best winter access is via secondary county road 45, 5 miles north from Monterville or 8 miles southeast from the town of Pickens, West Virginia's snowiest weather recording station. Where this road runs through Kumbrabow, a side road branches into the park's interior and runs past park headquarters to the cabin area, where it leaves the park and reaches U.S. 219 in 4 miles. Most often, the park road is plowed only from county road 45 to park head-quarters, making the U.S. 219 access more difficult.

When unplowed past headquarters, the park road can be skied. The park's best ski trail is the gated Rich Mountain Fire Trail, which begins at a sign on the north side of road 45 toward Pickens from the road to park headquarters. This road-width trail, Kumbrabow's high point, follows a ridge with numerous dead-end grades branching left and right. Round-trip distance on the main trail is about 10 miles.

Toward Pickens from the Rich Mountain Trail, two other fire roads begin on the same side of the road. Inside the park boundary, a grade descends to Phillips Camp Run and forms a loop of about 5 miles. Just outside the park boundary, the out-and-back Piney Ridge Fire Trail dead ends in 3.0 miles. As with the Mill Ridge Fire Trail that begins outside the park near the camping area, permission from private landowners may be needed before skiing Piney Ridge. The best policy is to contact the park superintendent before skiing these two fire roads.

Attractive winter accommodations are available near Kumbrabow in Helvetia, a quaint and isolated village settled by Swiss families, about 12 miles from the park. The charming, antique-furnished Beekeeper Inn has four bedrooms, two baths, a common room, and a kitchen, and reasonable rates that include breakfast. The entire inn can be rented for one low nightly price. Nearby, the Hutte Restaurant serves authentic Swiss cuisine at modest prices. Make inn reservations as far in advance as possible. Owner Eleanor Mailloux can suggest other ski trails convenient to town.

For more information, contact

Superintendent, Kumbrabow State Forest, Huttonsville, WV 26273. 304/335-2219.
Beekeeper Inn, Helvetia, WV 26224. 304/924-6435 or 924-5467.

Pipestem State Park: Complete Resort Facilities

Pipestem, straddling the 1000-foot gorge of Bluestone River, may be West Virginia's most complete resort state park. Its 4,000 acres include miles of hiking, horseback riding, and cross-country ski trails, a sled run with a rope tow, stables, indoor and outdoor pools and saunas, conference facilities, two restaurants, a snack bar, thirty campsites with all hook-ups and twenty with electricity only, twenty-five cabins, tennis courts, a nine-hole par 3 golf course and an 18-hole championship course, miniature golf, a gift and craft shop, and two lodges, one in Bluestone Gorge reached by aerial tramway. There are even hay rides and overnight horsepacking trips to a log cabin in this summer vacation state park.

Pipestem is also an attractive and accessible destination for cross-country and downhill skiers. The park is less than 15 miles from Interstate 77 at the Athens Road exit, and although there is no downhill skiing within the park, it is less than forty-five minutes from WinterPlace Ski Resort, also on the interstate. Downhill and cross-country ski packages are available.

Pipestem Lodge is open in winter with dining, a pool and saunas, and suites as well as rooms. The cabins are close by, clustered above Long Branch Lake. Pipestem rents cross-country skis.

Cross-Country Trails

THE GOLF COURSES

Beginning and even advanced skiers will enjoy the golf courses at Pipestem, which cover rolling, interesting terrain with scattered evergreens. The 18-hole course flanks spectacular views along the canyon rim.

LAKE SHORE TRAIL

This road-width gradual trail circles 16-acre Long Branch Lake in 3.0 miles. Cabin guests can ski this easy trail almost from their front door.

COTTAGE TRAIL

A 0.5-mile trail that begins behind cabin 1 and ends at Long Branch Lake, this is a good access to Lake Shore Trail.

RIVER TRAIL

This intermediate to advanced trail leaves the west side of the main park road near Pipestem Lodge. In 3.0 miles, the orange-marked River Trail reaches the shore of Bluestone River in the gorge. In the last 1.5 of its 6.0 miles, the trail gradually descends 900 feet on a road-width track.

COUNTY LINE TRAIL

Starting at the nature center, the advanced-rated County Line Trail follows red blazes along the outer edge of the looping nature trail, then branches to a junction with the River Trail at 2.5 miles. A short side trail offers a walk, too steep to ski, to Indian Branch Falls. Connecting County Line, River, Lakeshore, and Lake View trails allows a loop of about 7 miles.

LAKE VIEW TRAIL

This 0.75 road-grade trail links the nature center area and the Lake Shore Trail. It starts on the north side of the park road beyond the vista near the nature center.

Hiking Trails

Of course, any of the ski trails can be hiking paths if there is insufficient snow for skiing. The Canyon Rim Trail is a steeper path to the edge of Bluestone Canyon at Heritage Point. This 1.0-mile, blue-diamond-marked trail begins at the Canyon Rim Center, the summer tram terminal. Round trip is 2.0 miles.

For more information, contact

Pipestem Resort State Park, Pipestem, WV 25979. 304/466-1800 or 304/466-2780.

Richwood Area: Winter Adventure

(Cranberry Backcountry and Wilderness and Highland Scenic Highway)

Just east of Richwood, W.Va., is one of the Mountain State's most attractive winter sports areas. The Monongahela National Forest's Gauley Ranger District includes the 26,000-acre Cranberry Backcountry and the 35,000-acre Cranberry Wilderness, both flanked by the beautiful Highland Scenic Highway.

This section of the Allegheny Plateau rises from rushing streams in deep valleys to nearly 5,000-foot ridges covered in red spruce. Frost occurs here even in summer, and in winter, the settling effect of cold air turns the area's 100-plus inches of annual snowfall into what is often the best snowpack in the state.

The scenic and natural significance of the area matches the fine snow conditions. Tucked between the Backcountry and Wilderness is Cranberry Glades, five bogs similar to muskegs on the Canadian tundra. These wetlands contain sedge grasses, carnivorous plants, and rare wildflowers. A boardwalk trail leads into the bogs and a modern visitor center interprets this famous botanical area.

Winter is fast becoming a popular time to visit the Richwood area. Cross-country skiing on miles of beautiful forest roads and snowmobiling on the Highland Scenic Highway are the two main sports. The Richwood Chamber of Commerce, Richwood Ski Club, and U.S. Forest Service have joined to expertly mark 75 miles of trails for Nordic skiing and provide a recorded snow report. The town of Richwood, very reminiscent of a quaint northern New England town, provides lodging and dining, as does Marlinton, just south of Snowshoe and Silver Creek ski resorts.

The best winter access to the Cranberry area is via W.Va. 39/55, which connects Richwood to U.S. 219 south of Marlinton. From Richwood to the Cranberry Mountain Visitor Center, 23 miles, 39/55 is a year-round part of the Highland Scenic Highway. On its climb from Richwood to the crest at the visitor center, the road passes trailheads and often crosses the icy North Fork of the Cherry River. This high-quality, isolated highway has wide shoulders and is well plowed on its way through solemnly snowy forests of spruce and birch. The scene is as beautiful as any forest drive in a northern New England National Forest.

From the Cranberry Mountain Visitor Center, W.Va. 39/55 drops east in 6 miles to U.S. 219, while the Scenic Highway goes north another 24 miles to U.S. 219 on Elk Mountain, nearer still to Snowshoe and Elk River Ski Touring Center. This ridge-running section of the highway is the only U.S. Forest Service Parkway in the country. There are overlooks, one picnic area and some of West Virginia's most spectacular scenery, most above 4,000 feet. In winter this part of the road is closed to traffic, hence its popularity with snowmobilers and skiers. After repeated midwinter storms, incredible snow drifts make this a dangerous travel alternative for even big trucks.

Although trails and fire roads in this area are extensive, access is difficult in snow because even open forest roads are plowed only when needed by logging or other operations. Unfortunately, many of the Cranberry Wilderness trails and some Backcountry trails are thus off limits most of the time. For details on road conditions, call or visit the Gauley Ranger District office between 8:00 and 5:00 on weekdays. It's 1.9 miles from the light in Richwood on W.Va. 39/55.

Cross-Country Trails in the Cranberry Backcountry

In both the Backcountry and the adjacent Forest Service lands along W.Va. 39/55, cross-country skiing is the primary winter sport. Level trails and gated forest roads are the focus for skiers. Seven 3-sided shelters that sleep six to ten line the most popular ski route, Forest Service Road (FSR) 102, and make this area one of the South's prime overnight ski backpacking spots.

On weekends, the Cranberry Glades Visitor Center is partially open as a warming hut and Nordic Ski Patrol office. The closest ski rentals are at Elk River Ski Touring Center, about an hour away. In Dunbar, near Charleston, Mountain State Outfitters also rents skis. It appears likely that Richwood will have a ski rental shop or cross-country center of some kind in the near future, so check with the Chamber of Commerce for the latest developments and a map of the location.

Cranberry Mountain Visitor Center

From the visitor center, the easy Pocahontas Trail switchbacks for 2.5 miles up to fine views at Blue Knob, a 5-mile out-and-back tour. At Blue Knob, the Kennison Mountain Trail descends gradually in 0.9 mile to W.Va. 39/55, 0.3 mile east of the Dogway Road. Two cars make this a pleasant 3.4-mile tour. Continuing past Blue Knob, the Pocahontas Trail reaches Fork Mountain Trail at 4.0 miles from the visitor center and then drops steeply to 39/55 at 5.5 miles. The drop to the highway is for advanced skiers. Turning around before the plummet makes this an easy to intermediate out-and-back trip of 9.0 miles.

HIGHLAND SCENIC HIGHWAY

From the Cranberry Mountain Visitor Center, the Scenic Highway runs north, passing many overlooks and trailheads. An easy day tour to a fine view reaches the Cranberry Glades Overlook Trail parking area at about 4.5 miles from the start of the highway. From the lot, a 0.25-mile graded trail climbs to an excellent view of the Cranberry Glades. The round trip is about 10 miles.

CRANBERRY RIVER ROAD (FSR 102)

This road starts on W.Va. 39/55, 0.6 mile south of the Cranberry Mountain Visitor Center. FSR 102 leaves the highway, passes the start of the Cow Pasture Trail and the Cranberry Glades Trail and reaches a

circular parking lot and gate at 2.3 miles. From that gate, this easy road enters the Cranberry Backcountry, crossing the Cranberry River and side streams on bridges as it makes its way gradually down the scenic drainage. South Fork Shelter is at 2.5 miles, North Fork Shelter is at 4.5, Tumbling Rock Shelter is at 6.0, Houselog Shelter is at 7.5, and Dogway Shelter is at 9.0. Continuing straight, the road becomes FSR 76 and Pheasant Hollow Shelter is at 11.0 miles, Queer Branch Shelter is at 14.0, and the trail reaches a gate at developed Cranberry Campground at 16.0 miles. From the campground, FSR 76 is an ungated, open but unplowed road back to W.Va. 39/55, just north of Richwood at the Gale's Supper Club intersection.

CRANBERRY GLADES TRAIL

This flat, 0.5-mile boardwalk loop explores a natural area first designated in 1949. The trail branches right from FSR 102 at a parking area 1.4 miles from FSR 102's start on W.Va. 39/55. At times, the unplowed FSR 102 will be driveable to the Glades trailhead and to other very popular trails nearby. When the road is undriveable, the Glades Trail is an easy 3.5-mile round trip from W.Va. 39/55.

COW PASTURE TRAIL

This 7.0-mile intermediate trail leaves the right side of FSR 102 1.3 miles from FSR 102's start at W.Va. 39/55 (before the road reaches the Glades Boardwalk area). The trail goes east, then north and west, circling Cranberry Glades with good views before rejoining FSR 102 about 2.8 miles north of W.Va. 39/55. Skiing left on FSR 102 past the first trailhead and back to the starting point at W.Va. 39/55 yields a loop of 11.1 miles.

A shorter, 9-mile version of this loop can be had by starting on the Highland Scenic Highway and going left on a gated FSR at 100 yards. Go right on Cow Pasture Trail around Glades, then left on FSR 102 and back to Cow Pasture trailhead on the left, 0.1 mile past the Glades trailhead. Go left on Cow Pasture Trail then right on the FSR back up to the Scenic Highway.

DOGWAY ROAD (FSR 232)

This easy forest road enters the Cranberry Backcountry on the left from W.Va. 39/55, 20 miles from Richwood. Vehicular access ends 1.0 mile uphill from the highway where FSR branches left; the Frosty Gap

Trail crosses the road and a gate is reached. Beyond the gate, the road continues downhill along Dogway Fork. FSR 78 branches left at about 8.5 miles and Dogway Road reaches Cranberry River Road (FSR 102) near Dogway Shelter at 10.0 miles. FSR 78 provides a link uphill to forest road and trail loops near Summit Lake and Mike's Knob.

FROSTY GAP TRAIL

Facing the gate on Dogway Road, the Frosty Gap Trail going left passes ice-covered rock outcrops in 0.5 mile. The trail continues on a 10.0-mile advanced out-and-back tour from the gate to the Mike's Knob area and the Pocahontas Trail, reached about 5.0 miles from Dogway Road. To end on W.Va. 39/55, using two vehicles, take the Frosty Gap Trail to the area of Mike's Knob, go left on the Pocohontas Trail, pass the Eagle Camp Trail turnoff and descend to W.Va. 39/55 on the Pocohontas Trail for a 9.0-mile tour. The Pocohontas trailhead is on W.Va. 39/55, 2.25 miles toward Richwood from the turn off for Dogway Road. For a shorter 8.0-mile tour, turn right onto the Eagle Camp Trail from Pocohontas Trail and descend to W.Va. 39/55, 4.3 miles toward Richwood from the turnoff for Dogway Road.

Just before reaching the Frosty Gap Trail, the new FR 731 goes left 4.0 miles to a dead end offering fine views and easy skiing.

KENNISON MOUNTAIN TRAIL

This intermediate ridge-top trail is quite level, with good views, until it drops steeply to the Cranberry River. The easiest access is to take the Frosty Gap Trail to the right when facing the gate on Dogway Road. This trail reaches the Kennison Mountain Trail in 0.6 mile. Going left, the blue-blazed Kennison Trail crosses the spruce-covered summit of Kennison Mountain with only brief steep sections. This out-and-back tour can be up to 15 miles long, round trip. Snow should be deep to cover wet spots.

SUMMIT LAKE ROAD

At times, the 2.0-mile uphill road to 43-acre Summit Lake (3,400 feet) is driveable even when roads and trails at the lake are skiable. When skiers can't drive, the lake road is an easy ski tour. It starts on the left side of W.Va. 39/55, 7.7 miles from Richwood, 0.1 mile past the North Bend Picnic Area on the left.

Taking the Forest Service Road to the right just before reaching Summit Lake allows two loop tours that begin at Forest Service gates:

A. At the gated intersection, 1.0 mile uphill from Summit Lake, FSR 99 and the Pocohontas Trail go left roughly parallel from the locked gate. For an enjoyable 3.0-mile loop, follow FSR 99 west about 1.5 miles. As the road crests and drops, offering views of the Cranberry River drainage, a logging road comes in on the left (FSR 786). Go left on FSR 786 to the crossing of the Pocohontas Trail. Take Pocohontas Trail to the left, uphill to Hanging Rock, then east, back to FSR 99 and downhill to the locked gate.

    Beyond FSR 786, FSR 99 continues to a second gate. This gate is also reached from Richwood by skiing east on FSR 99 from Cherry Hills Golf Course in Richwood.

B. Going right at the Summit Lake trailhead, gated FSR 77 and the ridge-top Pocahontas Trail form a 10.0-mile loop offering fine views near Mike's Knob. This tour can be enlarged by following FSR 77 to its end near the site of a former firetower. A short crossover trail and two junctions between FSR 77 and the Pocahontas Trail allow many circuits. On this tour, FSR 77 also connects to FSR 78 to the Dogway Road and Cranberry River Road.

CHERRY HILL COUNTRY CLUB

This 9-hole mountaintop golf course offers fine views and easy skiing terrain as well as access to Summit Lake on FSR 99. The course is 3.0 miles from W.Va. 39/55 on FSR 76 from the junction near Gale's Restaurant and Supper Club just north of Richwood. Ski on fairways only.

Winter Hiking in the Cranberry Backcountry and Wilderness

Under heavy snow, winter hikers will find it very difficult to reach the interiors of the Cranberry Backcountry and, especially, the Cranberry Wilderness. Major perimeter roads like the Highland Scenic Highway and FSR 86 bear most of the trailheads and neither is plowed. Other trailheads lie along the Cranberry River Road (FSR 102), but these make for a long ski tour or snowshoe to interior trails that are generally unskiable.

The serious winter backpacker will need to ski into the Backcountry or

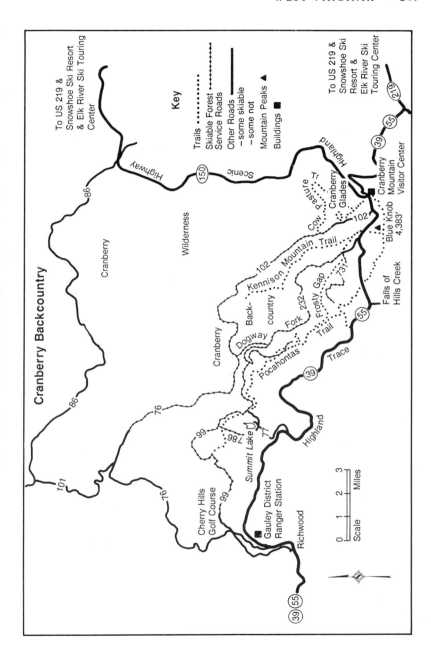

Cranberry Backcountry

To US 219 & Snowshoe Ski Resort & Elk River Ski Touring Center

To US 219 & Snowshoe Ski Resort & Elk River Ski Touring Center

Key

Trails
Skiable Forest Service Roads
Other Roads
– some skiable
– some not
Mountain Peaks ▲
Buildings ■

Highway

Scenic

150

86

Cranberry

Wilderness

Cranberry

Back-country

Dogway

Fork

232

Pocahontas

Trace

101

86

76

99

99

98

77

76

Summit Lake

Cherry Hills Golf Course

Gauley District Ranger Station

Richwood

Highland

39

55

Highland

Cow Pasture

Tr

Cranberry Glades

Kennison Mountain Trail

102

102

731

Frosty Gap

Trail

Blue Knob 4,383'

Cranberry Mountain Visitor Center

Falls of Hills Creek

39

55

39

219

55

39

Scale

0 1 2 3

Miles

along the Scenic Highway and then switch to snowshoes for looping treks on hiking trails. Generally, trails in both wild areas are very well marked. The Forest Service publishes an excellent trail and road map that is available free from the Gauley Ranger District.

No permit is required for wilderness use. Forest Service rules state that parties be smaller than ten people, that camp sites be no closer to water than 100 feet, and that camp sites be used no longer than two consecutive nights and no structures be built. No motor vehicles are allowed in either the Backcountry or the Wilderness, although bicycles are allowed on gated forest roads within the Cranberry Backcountry (mountain bikes are particularly suitable).

FALLS OF HILLS CREEK

Falls of Hills Creek Scenic Area is a good choice for the day hiker who is prepared for steep, icy terrain. This 0.75-mile hike descends into a gorge containing West Virginia's second-highest waterfall. The side road to the trail head is 17 miles north of Richwood. The wooden walkways on part of the trail are in disrepair but are likely to be improved in the near future.

RICHWOOD RESOURCES

The closest base of operations for skiers and backpackers in the Cranberry area is Richwood. The Watergate Inn is on W.Va. 39/55 in town and has 30 rooms with cable TV and telephone. Inexpensive ski packages are available with some meals included.

Dining runs from fast food and pizza to finer dining. What may be Richwood's best restaurant is conveniently located just outside of town on the way to the Cranberry. A small diner and larger, more formal dining rooms make up Gale's Restaurant and Supper Club. Gale's features all beverages and a diverse dinner menu with a broad price range for good food. Pieri's Restaurant has authentic Italian food, including homemade pasta. Richwood Pub and Deli is a bar with a mostly sandwich menu and a good atmosphere in a turn-of-the-century building. There are other family restaurants, including a Pizza Hut and a Dairy Queen.

In Marlinton, the Marlinton Motor Inn offers seventy-five modern rooms with TV and telephone, and a restaurant, coffee shop, and lounge with live ski season entertainment. In downtown Marlinton, French's Diner is a widely known and popular eatery with good food.

Richwood's warm seasons feature special events, the foremost being the Feast of the Ramson, less formally known as the Ramp Feed. The April event offers huge servings of ramps, pungent mountain onions that are so strong their aroma stays on the breath for days. In early May, the Spring Nature Tour focuses tours on the Cranberry Glades area.

For more information, contact

Richwood Chamber of Commerce, Box 587, Richwood, WV 26261. 24-hour snow report: 304/846-6790.

Gauley Ranger Station, USDA Forest Service, PO Box 110, Richwood, WVA 26261. 304/846-2695. Request the "Recreation Guide for the Gauley District."

Watergate Inn, Richwood, WV 26261. 304/846-2632.

Marlinton Motor Inn, Rte. 219 North, Box 25, Marlinton, WV 24954. 304/799-4711.

White Grass Ski Touring Center: Plenty of Machine-Groomed Trails

White Grass, in Canaan Valley, may be the premier private Nordic ski center in the South. Owner-operator Chip Chase is certainly the region's reigning cross-country character and a very experienced skier and teacher. The Blackwater Nordic Center in the nearby state park is a state park concession of White Grass.

Chase's center at White Grass occupies the base lodge for the old Weiss Knob ski area, West Virginia's second commercial ski area, opened by the same man who christened the first, Bob Barton. Today, as then, the building sits beneath the old ski slope, tucked under the snowy northern side of Cabin Mountain beneath the alpine beauty of the Dolly Sods. Snow fences pile the snow up on a series of easy learning loops boasting 10 miles of often double-tracked, machine-groomed trails. This is the region's biggest trail-grooming operation and a $3 weekday and $4 weekend trail fee is charged, with special rates for children and groups.

From the flat bottomland at 3,200 feet, the 25-mile Weiss Knob trail system reaches up and onto the 4,400-foot summits along the Dolly Sods; there are trails connecting to Canaan Valley and Timberline ski areas, as well as high trails across the Sods plateau. Director Chase knows this wild area as well as anyone, and guided day and overnight Sods tours reach isolated wilderness cabins, and in spring, huge drifts of corn snow tucked among the rolling plains and evergreen stands. White Grass often opens new trails and even serious mountaineers would do well to consider a tour or advice from White Grass before attempting the Sods in winter.

Tours can feature naturalist guides, outdoor skills experts, ski instruction, or headlamp trips after dark. Chase is a fully certified Professional Ski Instructors of America (PSIA) teacher, and his ski school is often the site of PSIA instructor training courses, United States Ski Association Nordic citizen races, and North American Telemark Organization (NATO) clinics and downhill races. A rope tow for the old Weiss Knob ski slope is planned. White Grass offers expert instruction for all levels of skiers. A two-night, guided lodge-to-lodge tour goes from White Grass to Canaan and on to Blackwater Falls State Park, the only such experience in the South. Events include a telemark festival in early February and a Nordic spring festival in early March.

The White Grass Center features a full rental and retail ski shop with free demo use of equipment before purchase. A popular natural foods cafe serves homemade breads and cakes, soups, sandwiches, hot drinks, and beer. A big wood stove sits on an unusual and effectively dry gravel floor. Evening entertainment is offered on weekends.

White Grass is located on Freeland Road, the first junction north of Canaan Valley State Park and ski area. The intersection is the site of Buena Chapel and is marked with an international cross-country skier symbol. The ski center is open daily from December to March.

Cross-Country Trails

BEGINNER SKIING

Near the ski center, most beginner trails have machine-set tracks. The Meadows loop and adjoining stream-side trails, Freeland Run and Freeland Wood, are good for beginners. Longer easy tours reach west of the center to Springer Orchard with a return on Gandalf's Glade, a one-hour loop of 2.0 miles. Northeast from the center, the Timberline Trail follows an old railroad grade over easy, rolling terrain, a fine out-and-back tour.

East of the center, Three Mile Trail follows easy logging grades up to Cabin Mountain, where beginners can go left on Blackbird's Wing to Forest Service Road (FSR) 80, descend the road, and return to White Grass on the easy Timberline Trail, a three-hour loop. Many other tours are possible that link both sides of the old downhill slope, one with a fine waterfall view.

INTERMEDIATE TO ADVANCED SKIING

Between the above easier trails, intermediate and advanced trails connect to the ski slope and to overland trails and pipeline swaths to neighboring ski areas and summits. White Grass trails are well maintained. Skiers bound for distant summits should take a USGS topo map and compass and ought to be proficient orienteers.

Two extended tours are popular. Skiing up Three Mile Trail, Blackbird's Wing goes left, joins FSR 80, and climbs to the edge of the Dolly Sods. Return to White Grass by circling back across the Sods side of Cabin Knob and reentering the Three Mile Trail. Skiers also often ride the chairlift to the summit of Canaan Valley ski area, ski off into the evergreens on a trail to a pipeline swath, and continue on to spectacular views at Bald Knob, a short distance from White Grass' trails. From White Grass, skiers can reach the Canaan Valley ski area on a maintained trail, making the above tour a loop.

White Grass is developing a new trail system on the Dolly Sods side of Weiss Knob, the summit of Canaan Valley ski area. From the higher White Grass trails, advanced skiers can enjoy a 500-foot vertical drop on the old ski slope and telemark runs through open glades.

For more information, contact

White Grass Ski Touring Center, Rte. 1, Box 299, Davis WV 26260. 304/866-4114.

Virginia

Peaks of Otter: Enjoy a Wide Variety of Trails

North of Roanoke, the Blue Ridge Parkway reaches its Virginia high point and passes one of the state's most distinctive summits. Sharp Top (3,875 feet) certainly lives up to its name. The conical peak is a landmark visible for many miles to the east and west of the Blue Ridge.

Sharp Top and Flat Top (4,004 feet) are collectively known as the Peaks of Otter, probably owing to the proximity of the nearby Otter River. This 4,200-acre Parkway recreation area is located between mileposts 84 and 87. In the high valley between the peaks are a 24-acre lake, a 144-site campground (open in winter with chemical toilets and water), a 62-site picnic area, and summer amenities that include a camp store, service station and visitor center, a restored mountain farm, an amphitheater for naturalist programs, and a number of trails. A road reaches the summit of Sharp Top, and the public can pay a small fee for the bus ride (no private autos allowed). Peaks of Otter Lodge, located beside the lake, is a year-round modern accommodation with fifty-eight rooms, three suites, a restaurant, and a lounge serving all beverages.

Peaks of Otter is one of the best, non–ski resort sites for a winter vacation in the southern mountains. Whether or not snow is on the ground, the lodge and campground provide a memorable setting that is still much as it was when "Polly Wood's Ordinary" became the area's first hostelry in the 1830s. A larger hotel followed, and guests rode up Sharp Top in horse-drawn carriages.

The lodge's winter season allows hikers and cross-country skiers to enjoy a wide variety of trails in an isolated atmosphere with all the comforts of home. Even if active outdoor pursuits are not your goal, Peaks of Otter is a fine place to just relax. The lodge encourages winter stays with room rates that include some complimentary meals. At 2,500 feet, the lodge averages about 30 inches of snow annually. The summits get more.

The lodge and trails are easily accessible because Va. 43 makes a "staggered crossing" of the Parkway at Peaks of Otter between the towns of Buchanan (Buck-annon) and Bedford. The lodge is 10 miles from both Interstate 81 on the west, and Bedford at U.S. 221 on the east. Because Va. 43 follows the Parkway for 5 miles in its crossing of the mountain, the Parkway is plowed there for public use. North of that 5-mile stretch, the Parkway is also plowed to allow employee access to a Federal Aviation Administration facility near milepost 76. Ski trails here are near the Parkway's highest point in Virginia, 3,950 feet.

Cross-Country Trails

JOHNSON FARM LOOP

This 2.2-mile trail is a skiable portion of the larger Harkening Hill Loop (see the section on hiking trails that follows). The Johnson Farm Loop leaves the Parkway at the north end of the visitor center parking area. The isolated old farmstead, reached in 1.1 miles, is an inspiring sight in the snow. This trail is rated intermediate.

ELK RUN TRAIL

This easiest-rated trail is 0.75 mile long and begins behind the visitor center. Written exhibits along the trail interpret the forest ecology.

LODGE VICINITY

Skiers can follow many paths that link the facilities at Peaks of Otter. A shore-line trail crosses the dam, circles the scenic lake, with fine views, and offers touring connections to the campground, picnic area, and large meadows surrounding the lodge and bordering the Parkway.

APPALACHIAN TRAIL/PARKWAY

At milepost 91, where Va. 43 leaves the Parkway, the Parkway to the south is gated in snow and makes a fine ski tour for beginners. The Appalachian Trail (AT) is also accessible from this point. For about 7 miles south of the gate, the AT is gradual and a very enjoyable ski tour for intermediates. In that approximately 7 miles to Blackhorse Gap, the trail crosses the Parkway three times, allowing a variety of Parkway/AT circuits.

SHARP TOP ROAD

Under snow cover, skiers are permitted to ski on the bus road to Sharp Top's 3,875-foot summit. The 3.3-mile one-way trip is steep with abrupt turns. Advanced skiers will find this to be an exciting day tour. Because of the road's paved surface, this route is best in deep snow. Sledders are also permitted to use the road, but no hiking is allowed. Hikers must use the Sharp Top Trail.

FLAT TOP MOUNTAIN TRAIL

The skiable leg of this trail begins at a parking area 2.3 miles north on the plowed Parkway from the visitor center (milepost 83.6). The northern part of this strenuous trail is skiable for experts.

U.S. FOREST SERVICE ROAD

Between mileposts 83.1, at Fallingwater Cascades Overlook, and milepost 80.5, Floyd Fields, a USFS timber road parallels the Parkway, offering easiest-rated skiing.

RADAR ROAD

From milepost 78.4 on the plowed Parkway north of Peaks of Otter, a Forest Service road parallels the west side of the Parkway to milepost 76.6, the Parkway's limit of plowing at the FAA access road. This tour is just over 1.5 miles one way. Without two cars, start at milepost 78.4 by parking in Sunset Fields Overlook and take the USFS road to the right, just beyond the overlook. The route is gradually uphill, with the return being down. This is an easy tour that crosses the Parkway's highest point in Virginia on a road that retains snow well.

PARKWAY

When gated at milepost 76.6, the snowy Parkway is designated for skiers north to another gate at milepost 71. From milepost 71 north, the Parkway drops in 7.3 miles from 2,361 feet to its lowest point, 649 feet on the James River, and a junction with U.S. 501. Skiers can also reach milepost 71 from that area, approximately 22 miles from Lynchburg.

Winter Hiking

SHARP TOP TRAIL

This trail starts at the camp store, across the Parkway from the visitor center. The trail climbs 1,400 feet, steeply at times, reaching the peak in 1.5 miles. A short loop threads among the summit boulders offering spectacular vistas. Just below the peak in a gap, a spur trail leads right to Buzzards Roost, a series of interesting boulders. This is a strenuous hike.

HARKENING HILL LOOP

This 3.3-mile loop begins behind the visitor center and climbs steeply to a viewpoint where the Johnson Farm is visible. The trail descends to a spur path reaching a balanced rock and then drops to a junction with the Johnson Farm ski loop. Harkening Hill hikers should go right at the junction to return to the trailhead. This is a strenuous hike.

FLAT TOP TRAIL

This trail connects with the Fallingwater Cascades Trail, forming a National Recreation Trail designated in 1982. Trailheads are located at a Parkway parking area 2.3 miles north of the visitor center (milepost 83.6) and at the first major road fork in the picnic area. From trailhead to trailhead, the total distance is 4.4 miles and includes a 1,600-foot gain to the summit at 4,004 feet. From the Parkway trailhead, hikers pass a short, steep leftward spur trail to Cross Rock, and then reach The Pinnacle on the main trail. This is a strenuous hike and far less traveled than the Sharp Top Trail.

FALLINGWATER CASCADES TRAIL

This trail connects to the Flat Top Trail across the Parkway from that trailhead, but it begins at its own parking area at milepost 83.2. The trail is a 1.6-mile loop that drops to Fallingwater Creek amidst huge boulders, hemlocks, and rhododendron. The elevation gain back to the car is 260 feet. In snow and ice, this can be a very slippery hike.

For more information, contact

District Ranger, Blue Ridge Parkway, Rte. 2, Box 163, Bedford, VA 24523.

Peaks of Otter Lodge, PO Box 489, Bedford, VA 24523, or call 704/586-1081.

For sources of snow reports and general Parkway information, see the Introduction in the Blue Ridge Parkway section.

Mountain Lake Wilderness and Resort: A Lake atop a Mountain

Mountain Lake is both a federally designated 8,253-acre wilderness and a distinctive resort more than a century old. The area's central feature is 250-acre Mountain Lake at 3,875 feet, one of only two natural lakes in Virginia and a mountain rarity south of New England. In fact, Mountain Lake looks much like a highland pond in Vermont, New Hampshire, or Maine.

The Mountain Lake area is a 4,000-foot plateau of the southwestern Virginia Alleghenies near the border with West Virginia. The rhododendron, red spruce, hemlock, birch, and beech forest that covers this crest characterizes the highlands of North Carolina and West Virginia more than it resembles the surrounding Virginia countryside.

Cool in summer and quite snowy in winter, Mountain Lake is an extension of West Virginia's weather that is perched high above the Great Valley of Virginia. Just the 16 miles between Blacksburg, at 2,000 feet, and Mountain Lake, at 4,000, frequently means a transition from rain or flurries to substantial snow and cold.

Tucked away in this unique setting is the Mountain Lake Hotel, a huge stone edifice dating from the 1930s when it replaced a frame structure with roots in the mid-1800s. Rustic cabins and modern lodge accommodations augment the fine dining and lodging of the hotel, center of a 2,500-acre private nature preserve. Summer attractions include boating, swimming, golf, tennis, and a wide variety of private trails as well as those of Jefferson National Forest. In winter, those trails and Mountain Lake Hotel make an attractive destination for cross-country skiers, hikers, and vacationers.

Mountain Lake Hotel offers a winter season with memorable lodging and dining in the hotel and a huge fireplace blazing in the lobby. Ice skaters glide in a Currier & Ives setting on the frozen lake, and horse-drawn sleigh rides are available. Cross-country skiing is encouraged on a system of newly expanded and well-signed Nordic ski trails. Skiers should check in at the lodge. Although unblazed, trails are wide and easy to follow. The best ski report for the area would come from the hotel or Back Country Ski and Sports in Blacksburg (see the end of this entry).

Mountain Lake is easy to reach. The area is only 7 miles from U.S. 460, a four-lane highway that links Interstate 81 in Virginia with Interstate 77 in West Virginia. The road to Mountain Lake is Va. 700, a right turn from U.S. 460 10 miles from Blacksburg. Va. 700 begins with views of an old covered bridge to the left of the road and stays very scenic and gradual to the road's crest beside the hotel. Beware of the hill on the other side of the crest. If your car is poorly equipped, park nearby and don't descend. In very icy, slippery conditions, getting back over the crest can be tricky. Beyond the crest, Va. 700 drops gradually down along the west side of the lake and becomes unpaved Va. 613 at a lake-shore building. Va. 613 then proceeds across the Mountain Lake crest, into the next valley, passing wilderness area trailheads on the way.

Besides Mountain Lake Hotel, diverse winter accommodations, including a wide variety of restaurants and some nightlife, are available in nearby Blacksburg. Cross-country ski rentals, too, are available in Blacksburg at Back Country Ski and Sports. Virginia Polytechnic Institute students can rent skis and hiking equipment at VPI's Squires Student Center.

Cross-Country Trails

GOLF COURSE AND ACCESS ROAD

For beginners or experts, the golf course is one of the best ski tours at Mountain Lake. But the tour is more than just golf course skiing. Skiers start west of the lodge at a metal gate barring motor access to the golf course access road. Where Va. 700 crests at the hotel, skiers walk left uphill between cabins to the gate.

The first 1.5 miles of this tour follow a gradually graded woods road through mixed evergreen and hardwood forests that ascends to 4,100 feet at the nine-hole golf course. The course includes undulating terrain and north-facing hills for downhill runs. A cliff-top stone warming hut at the course offers fine views. Just 0.1 mile from the start of the access road tour, a short side road goes right to the 4,100-foot summit and a fine view of the hotel and surrounding area.

A number of additional trails connect to the golf course access road, making it a focus of Mountain Lake Nordic skiing. The area is a nature preserve and skiers occasionally see deer huddled in the frozen forests.

JUNGLE TRAIL

This trail links the lodge with the golf course access road, forming a 3.0-mile loop around the lake. The trail leaves east from beside the lake-side cabin on the paved loop road around the lodge. Slabbing above the lake, the trail reaches open meadows at a former "fur farm" where mink and fox were once raised. The Jungle Trail then descends to Va. 613, where skiers have to walk or ski north on the road before taking a left on the next Jungle Trail section. This next part of the trail is steep and can be avoided by not descending to Va. 613 from the fur farm. Instead, go left to a lake-shore building on Va. 613. Crossing the road from the building, skiers descend a road grade, then make a left turn back onto the Jungle Trail. After crossing another old road grade and ascending, the Jungle Trail joins the golf course access road 0.3 mile above the metal gate near Va. 700. The Jungle Trail is beginner-rated.

THE WHITE DOT TRAIL

This trail forms a 1.5-mile, intermediate-rated loop that branches right from the golf course access road, descends, and reaches the golf course below the loop at the end of the course.

THE BLUEBERRY LOOP

This 0.25-mile novice trail loops left from the access road on the way to the golf course.

BALD KNOB

At 4,363 feet, Bald Knob is the highest elevation in the Mountain Lake area. The intermediate trail to the peak leaves the south side of the lodge, soon joins a road grade to the peak, and reaches spectacular summit views approximately 0.8 mile from the lodge.

NATIONAL FOREST SKI TRAILS

After a deep snow, one of the best trails at Mountain Lake may be Va. 613. From Mountain Lake Hotel, the road descends and bears left at the University of Virginia Biological Research Station. If unplowed, Va. 613 is usually quickly chewed up by four-wheel-drive vehicles, so skiing is limited. If the road is plowed, though, skiers can drive to two good touring sites.

CHESTNUT TRAIL

This trail begins on the right side of Va. 613, coming from Mountain Lake, about 1.5 miles from the UVA Research Station. Leaving the parking area, Chestnut Trail follows a ridge crest. Where Chestnut Trail goes left, a side trail continues to War Spur Overlook. Round trip for a novice tour to the overlook is approximately 2 miles.

Skiers who choose to descend the Chestnut Trail where it goes left will find an expert-rated run through a very scenic grove of virgin hemlocks. Reaching the junction with the Link Trail at just over 2 miles, skiers can go left 0.3 mile to the parking lot, for a 2.5-mile, partly advanced loop.

LINK TRAIL

From the scenic area parking lot, the Link Trail bears left and continues gradually for 1.5 miles, then it drops steeply to a junction with the Appalachian Trail. If you return when the trail begins to drop, this is a very scenic, easy out-and-back tour of 3.0 miles. In summer, much of the Link Trail is a level, grassy lane bordered by profuse ferns.

BUTT MOUNTAIN FIRE ROAD AND TOWER

The Appalachian Trail crosses Va. 613 3.5 miles beyond the scenic area trailhead of the Link Trail. At this junction, just before Va. 613 drops toward the town of Kire, a Jefferson National Forest fire road goes left to the summit of Butt Mountain. The approximately 6-mile, intermediate-rated tour (12 miles round trip) involves a descent from 4,000 to 3,600 feet and then a climb back to the firetower on the peak at 4,200 feet.

An alternative approach to reaching this tour requires turning right from U.S. 460 onto Va. 635 19.5 miles from Blacksburg. Just over 16 miles from 460, past Kire, turn right from Va. 635 onto Va. 613 for the climb to the fire road.

Winter Hiking in Mountain Lake and Vicinity

INDIAN TRAIL

This hike around the shore-line of Mountain Lake is very beautiful in snow when ice covers the lake. The trail begins on the lake side of the main lodge near the gazebo and circles the lake in 1.75 miles.

THE CASCADES

This National Recreation Trail is one of the most scenic winter hikes in southwestern Virginia. The 70-foot waterfall plummets over a ledge and falls onto a fan-shaped outcrop and into a large pool. The shaded stream-side trail retains snow, and the cliff-enclosed waterfall freezes into awesome ice flows, some of which experienced and properly equipped ice climbers have been known to take on during severe cold.

The 2.0-mile hike to the falls passes under the cliffs of Barney's Wall, to the left. The route can follow an old jeep trail or a footpath, or both to form a loop. In deep, fresh snow, advanced skiers might be able to ski the road grade. In warm summer weather, the Cascades pool is a fine place to cool off. The trail is very popular with students from Virginia Polytechnic Institute in Blacksburg.

To get to the trailhead, follow U.S. 460 just over 17 miles from Blacksburg, then turn right on Va. 623 at Pembroke. The road ends 3.0 miles north at the Cascades Recreation Area and trailhead. In warm months, the site offers picnicking, fishing, and rest rooms.

For more information, contact

District Ranger, Blacksburg Ranger District, U.S. Forest Service, Rte. 1, Box 404, Blacksburg, VA 24060. 703/552-4641. Office located 3 miles outside Blacksburg on U.S. 460.

Mountain Lake Hotel, Mountain Lake, VA 24136. 703/626-7121.

Back Country Ski and Sports, 3710 South Main St., Blacksburg, VA 24060. 703/552-6400.

Blue Ridge Outdoors, 211 Draper Rd., Blacksburg, VA 24060.

Virginia Tech Outing Club, PO Box 538, Blacksburg, VA 24060. 703/961-6712.

Mount Rogers National Recreation Area: The Rooftop of Virginia

Mount Rogers is the "Rooftop of Virginia." It can be argued that this nearly 6,000-foot highest peak in the Old Dominion is the state's most scenic, most significant mountain mass.

If you're looking for an experience like that out West, Rogers' combination of evergreen-zone forests and high open meadows thrusting rocky peaks at racing clouds may be as close as you'll find in the Southeast. The mountain signals the rise of the major Blue Ridge peaks in North Carolina.

Rogers' exposed crest zone offers one of the region's best venues for experiencing mountaineering in a setting like that above the timberline.

Trail routes, including the Appalachian Trail (AT), have been altered on Mount Rogers in the last ten years, so older maps may be inaccurate. Even when well marked, trails in this snowy, open setting may be hard to find, especially in the whiteout snow storms that buffet the high balds. Be prepared and proficient with map and compass. Larry Landrum of Blacksburg, Va., privately publishes a highly recommended map of Mount Rogers (see the end of this entry for the address).

Compared with Roan Mountain, on the North Carolina/Tennessee border, Mount Rogers sees relatively few skiers, although the mountain can be called a popular skiing site. Ski rating symbols are in place on most trails listed here. The mountain is not near major population centers, but access by interstate is remarkably direct, especially from Interstate 81 on the west. From the southeast, the fastest access is Interstate 77, then U.S. 58 west, unless you are starting in the Boone area. In that case, U.S. 421, Tenn. 91 and then east on U.S. 58 from Damascus is a faster, although less scenic route than smaller roads through Ashe County, N.C.

Heavy snow trails are concentrated on the crest zone of Mount Rogers, which includes White Top, Virginia's second highest summit, and Pine Mountain, a double for High Sierra summits. The crest zone lies within the Jefferson National Forest's Mount Rogers National Recreation Area (NRA). Virginia highways circle this 114,000-acre mass and cross it at Elk Garden Gap (4,450 feet) between the Rogers and White Top summits. Abutting the southern side of Mount Rogers is Virginia's highest state park, Grayson Highlands. Across a valley north of Mount Rogers, the Iron Mountains and the Feathercamp area have trails up to 4,500 feet in elevation.

Trailheads are reached via highways that run the perimeter of Mount Rogers. From Interstate 81, Va. 16 and 600 cross intervening ridges and join a road net around the mountain that includes U.S. 58 on the south, Va. 16 on the east, Va. 600 on the west, and Va. 603, north of Rogers and south of the Iron Mountains. Just south of Elk Garden Gap, the White Top Road climbs through forest to the open balds of White Top. This ungated road can be skied but is best considered a four-wheel-drive experience.

Area accommodations are few in the vicinity of the mountain but diverse a short distance away. The Mount Rogers Inn on Interstate 81 at Marion is a fine place to spend the night after a long drive to the area. The modern motel is located on a major access to the NRA, Va. 16, and includes a restaurant. Abingdon, Va., on Interstate 81, is an hour or so from the NRA via U.S. 58. This beautiful town has the fine lodging and dining of the Martha Washington Inn and a variety of good restaurants, including The Tavern.

Cross-Country Trails

VIRGINIA HIGHLANDS HORSE TRAIL

This orange-blazed trail begins at 4,450-foot Elk Garden Gap on Va. 600. The popular Nordic trail starts east across the balds in a road bed that usually fills with snow even when the balds blow clear. The trail bears left around a peak where snow drifts very deeply, and skiers often practice downhill techniques in the sunny bowl. The trail then enters the woods and deeper snow in a climb to Deep Gap at 2.0 miles. This is an easy, rewarding day tour with a great lunch stop at Deep Gap Shelter on the AT.

Past Deep Gap, the old grade continues, only steeper, another mile to meadows at Brier Ridge. Only in the deepest snow is the meadow skiable. Open views make this point a great turnaround for a 6.0-mile round-trip tour for intermediates. Past the meadows, the Horse Trail continues on the other side of the meadow and remains graded and very skiable to Wilburn Ridge balds and access from Grayson Highlands State Park at 6.0 miles from the start. The trail is hard to locate in the woods across the meadows at Brier Ridge, but it provides a fine tour for those who explore and continue. Snow gets shallow in meadows but is usually deeply drifted in the woods.

HELTON CREEK AND SUGAR MAPLE LOOPS

Two skiable loop trails, one in the meadows at the start of the Virginia Highlands Horse Trail, and one in the woods on the way to Deep Gap, branch right and descend into the Helton Creek drainage. The second right, in the woods, is the easiest to find, so start there. The top, purple-blazed loop is rated most difficult and is 5.0 miles long. The 4.5-mile bottom loop is purple blazed on the west side and dark-blue blazed on the east side. Both loops are rocky, with stream crossings, so snow should be deep. A low-elevation trailhead for the lower loop can be reached from U.S. 58 on plowed Va. 783, a side road from U.S. 58 between White Top Post Office (at the junction of U.S. 58 and Va. 600) and Grayson Highlands State Park.

MOUNT ROGERS NATIONAL RECREATION TRAIL (NRT)

From Va. 603 north of the mountain, the Mount Rogers NRT is a graded, switchbacking 4.5-mile climb from Grindstone Campground to Deep Gap Shelter. This light-blue-blazed, blue-diamond-marked ski trail runs through the heart of the Mount Rogers Scenic Area and its massive northern-hardwood forest. Snow is usually deep, and the run back to the car is refreshing.

With two cars and a start at Elk Garden Gap, the Virginia Highlands Horse Trail and Mount Rogers NRT make a fine 7.0-mile traverse of the state's highest peak. The NRT starts just east of the campground entrance.

GRASSY BRANCH TRAIL

This dark-blue-blazed trail starts just west of Grindstone Campground on Va. 603 and climbs gradually through the Lewis Fork Wilderness to Va. 600. The 3.0-mile trip ascends only 500 feet and is steepest at the very top. This is a good out-and-back trip or two-car downhill tour.

LEWIS FORK TRAIL

This trail for strong intermediates is rarely used, and on it, wildlife is often much in evidence. Lewis Fork is the first trail east of Grindstone Campground and the Mount Rogers NRT on Va. 603 at a meadow.

The trail crosses a fence, field, and stream, then enters woods and climbs over a few smaller streams. Just past these streams, skiers go left in a meadow on a graded trail. (If you miss this turn, the stream-side trail becomes a steep uphill climb but does eventually exit again on the graded Lewis Fork Trail.)

Taking the left, the Lewis Fork Trail reaches a junction/switchback. To the left is the Old Orchard Shelter and the AT. To the right, the gray-blazed Lewis Fork Trail follows a prominent grade into a snowy northern bowl, crosses a stream at a missing bridge, and reaches a junction. To the left is a rugged dead end, to the right the trail seems to disappear in a snowy, gladed forest. Use a map here and gradually ascend around the ridge to join the Mount Rogers NRT at 3.5 miles. Down the NRT to 603 makes for a 7.0-mile loop from the start of the Lewis Fork Trail.

APPALACHIAN TRAIL FROM VA. 603

The AT intersects Va. 603 about 4 miles west of Troutdale and 2 miles east of the Mount Rogers NRT. The white-blazed trail climbs to the Old

Orchard Shelter in 1.7 miles. Then it becomes graded to the crest, reaches a junction at 3.6 miles, and then continues across the flank of Mount Rogers to Scales (the site of a former cattle weighing station), at 4,600 feet, and spectacular views on Pine Mountain. This 5.5-mile tour (11.0 miles out and back) is rated more difficult.

RHODODENDRON GAP TRAIL

This 2.0-mile, blue-blazed trail branches from the AT 2.0 miles above Old Orchard Shelter and runs southwest to Rhododendron Gap, where it rejoins the AT on one of the South's most spectacular balds. From Rhododendron Gap, the AT goes west to Deep Gap and south on a loop to Scales that passes awesome summits with easy access to Massie Gap and a plowed trailhead in Grayson Highlands State Park (see below, AT to Rhododendron Gap). Deeper snow is needed for skiing across the open balds. From Va. 603, Rhododendron Gap is a good high-point ending for a day tour. Round trip is about 12 miles.

HORSE TRAIL FROM VA. 603 TO SCALES

The Virginia Highlands Horse Trail is another route to the crest zone and a possible part of a loop using the AT or the Lewis Fork Trail. The orange-blazed Horse Trail leaves Va. 603 opposite the junction of Va. 603 and 741, just east of the AT parking area. The 3.0-mile trail climbs gradually to the Scales.

OTHER HORSE TRAILS

Many other horse trails begin near the Livery, just east of the Highlands Horse trailhead on Va. 603. A variety of loops can be formed, some reaching high onto the crest zone and joining the AT and Grayson Highlands State Park on the spectacular Wilburn Ridge. (For more on this network, see Landrum's map, the USFS horse brochure, and the NRA Sportman's Map; addresses are at the end of the entry.)

Cross-Country Trails in Grayson Highlands State Park

This beautiful state park has a reliably plowed road right to the flank of Mount Rogers' crest zone. The road enters the park from U.S. 58 about 9 miles west of the Va. 16 junction at Volney. The park road climbs into the high country offering some of the South's most stirring views of alpinelike summits. The road is gated at Massie Gap, blocking access to the visitor center near the top of Haw Orchard Mountain, the park's summit.

From Massie Gap, the meadows start immediately. Here hikers often see herds of ponies standing in the lee of spruce thickets, their manes matted with hoarfrost. In very deep snow, these meadows can recall ski touring in the Sierra Nevada of California. With less snow, mountaineers can easily reach high, open country. However, the variation in snow depth between the balds and the woods recommends that even backpackers take skis or snowshoes when they intend to hike long loops. At times, drifted snow around the rocky summits permits snow-cave camping and igloo construction.

ROAD TO HAW ORCHARD MOUNTAIN

The gated, paved road from Massie Gap to the picnic area/visitor center atop Haw Orchard Mountain is a good beginner tour of just over 2.0 miles round trip.

RHODODENDRON TRAIL

This 0.5-mile blue-blazed trail leaves the road at Massie Gap and reaches the AT on the meadow crest above the road.

APPALACHIAN TRAIL TO RHODODENDRON GAP

At the crest above Massie Gap, the AT runs north through meadows skirting the big rocky pinnacles of the Wilburn Ridge. At Rhododendron Gap, the trail goes west to Deep Gap Shelter just above the Virginia Highlands Horse Trail. The AT from Deep Gap to Rhododendron Gap is skiable, although the easternmost, open end requires deep snow. Some skiers who take the Virginia Highlands Horse Trail from Deep Gap actually end up on the AT at Brier Ridge by leaving the top of the meadow.

In deep snow, ambitious experts starting from Deep Gap or Grayson Highlands could form an AT/Horse Trail loop. The Horse Trail crosses the AT just above Massie Gap at a fence line/USFS boundary. From Massie Gap, a left goes toward Deep Gap and a right takes the Horse Trail to the Scales, above the AT.

Iron Mountain Area

This major ridge north of Mount Rogers has a shelter and a number of fine graded trails and unplowed forest roads for skiers. The ridge-top Iron Mountain Trail used to be the AT.

FLAT TOP TRAIL/FLAT TOP ROAD

This combination trail/forest road begins opposite the Mount Rogers NRT on Va. 603. The trail climbs gradually to the road and Flat Top Mountain. Left on the gated road—Forest Service Road (FSR) 285—near the top leads to the Cherry Tree Shelter on the Iron Mountain Trail. This blue-blazed, 2.0-mile tour is rated easiest.

Beginners can continue east along the Iron Mountain Trail for another 2.5 miles to the AT, and then return. Or, better skiers can descend the AT, which makes the tour more difficult.

APPALACHIAN TRAIL TO IRON MOUNTAIN

The AT is skiable north of Va. 603 to the Iron Mountain Trail, a distance of 2.0 miles. The AT crosses Va. 603 about 4 miles west of Troutdale.

IRON MOUNTAIN TRAIL

Whether reached from the AT or Flat Top Trail/Road, the Iron Mountain Trail is skiable east (to the AT, see above) and west of the shelter on Flat Top.

IRON MOUNTAIN TRAIL/FSR 84

From Flat Top Road, go left on FSR 285 past the shelter to the trail's junction with the yellow-blazed Iron Mountain Trail. The two trails run together for a while. Go west and take FSR 285 when it branches right. Descend to FSR 84 and return west. FSR 84 eventually joins FSR 828, the Flat Top Road, on the opposite side of the ridge. Take FSR 828 south to Flat Top and the vicinity of the shelter for a 9.0-mile easy-rated loop. This could be a very long day tour (13.0 miles round trip from Va. 603) or a fine day tour on a ski backpacking/camping trip using the shelter.

Winter Hiking in Mount Rogers NRA

Hikers and mountaineers can use any of the trails already described, but they should use snowshoes when appropriate. Popular backpacking routes include favorite ski trails like the Virginia Highlands Horse Trail to Deep Gap Shelter, and it is not uncommon to see two or four weekend backpackers post holing the snow cover in ski tracks created by dozens of Nordic skiers. On open balds, bushwhack mountaineering can circumvent this conflict (see Chapters 5 and 6 for more on hiker/skier trail etiquette).

APPALACHIAN TRAIL TO DEEP GAP SHELTER

The AT leaves Elk Garden Gap at the Virginia Highlands Horse Trail, but instead of slabbing the bald, the AT climbs over the bald and joins the more gradual ski trail at the shelter. Many overnight backpackers camp at Deep Gap Shelter and do little if any day hiking. Hikers without snowshoes should use the AT to avoid spoiling the ski tracks on the horse trail and to make the hike easier: snow is usually much shallower on the AT.

WILBURN RIDGE/GRAYSON HIGHLANDS

A good day hike for casual visitors to Grayson Highlands is the Big Pinnacle Trail to Twin Pinnacles Trail. The trail starts at Massie Gap and quickly climbs 400 feet to a 1.5-mile loop across pinnacles of Haw Orchard Mountain with great views of the crest zone.

CABIN CREEK TRAIL

From the east side of Massie Gap, this trail descends to some waterfalls and returns in 2.0 miles on an old grade. Skiers could go out and back on the graded section of this trail.

APPALACHIAN TRAIL/BALDS

From Massie Gap, the biggest balds in Virginia open up across the Wilburn Ridge. Map- and compass-hiking or backpacking in this area offer truly alpine mountaineering experiences. The lower section of the AT to the Scales could be included in a multiday loop featuring exposed camping and even snow caves. Evergreen groves offer shelter. Be prepared for windy, arctic conditions.

In summer, Mount Rogers is extremely popular with backpackers. Circuit trips can be up to 50 miles long. A variety of car campgrounds and a very active horseback program are also offered. Sightseeing in the area includes high-altitude views at Grayson Highlands and the 2-mile White Top Road, highest in Virginia. In Troutdale, near the NRA, the Troutdale Dining Room is a recommended spot, and in summer and fall, the widely known Barter Theatre stages plays.

For more information, contact

Mount Rogers NRA, Rte. 1, Box 303, Marion, VA 24354. 703/783-5196, weekdays. To receive an NRA Sportman's Map, send $1.

Grayson Highlands State Park, Volney, VA 24379.
Mount Rogers Map, write to Larry Landrum, PO Box 247,
  Blacksburg, VA 24060. Send $2.95. During the winter, the map can
  be obtained at Osborne's General Store, a few miles east of Grayson
  Highlands State Park entrance on U.S. 58.

Ramsey's Draft: Easily Accessible

The Ramsey's Draft Natural Area is a 7,000-acre watershed hemmed
in by a horseshoe of ridges and named for the stream that drains it.
U.S. 250 borders the open side of the basin, offering easy access to
winter walkers and cross-country skiers. But more than accessibility
recommends the Draft. At its lower, stream-side elevations, Ramsey's
Draft harbors thousands of acres of Virginia's most impressive virgin
forest. No doubt, many of the huge hemlocks, white pines, and tulip
poplars that tower over the trail were growing here when George
Washington surveyed this domain for Lord Fairfax. This is a forest of
stereotypical proportions.

Ramsey's Draft lies in the George Washington National Forest on the
Allegheny Front, just west of the Shenandoah Valley and about 20 miles
west of Staunton (pronounced Stanton) Va., and the same distance east of
Monterey, Va., in Highland County. The area lies in one of Virginia's
highest snowfall zones, east of and bordering on West Virginia's snowiest
counties. The Allegheny Front is often white when the Shenandoah
Valley is snowless.

Winter trails in the Draft area focus on two main routes, the ridge-
top Shenandoah Mountain Trail and the Ramsey's Draft Trail that
follows the stream. Skiers will favor the flat Shenandoah Mountain
Trail, and hikers will prefer the equally flat Draft Trail with its
unskiable stream crossings.

Cross-Country Skiing

From U.S. 250, the Shenandoah Mountain Trail runs north and south
with either choice offering fine Nordic skiing. North, the Shenandoah
Mountain Trail, like most Draft area trails, is marked with blue blazes.
South, the trail is orange blazed. The trail ranges in elevation from 3,000
to 4,000 feet.

SHENANDOAH MOUNTAIN TRAIL/NORTH

The northern leg begins at the Confederate Breastworks, a ridge-top Civil War observation point on U.S. 250 18 miles east of Monterey and just under 17 miles west of Churchville.

For nearly 10 miles, the Shenandoah Mountain Trail runs the ridge of Shenandoah Mountain at very easy, skiable grades. The trail begins on the north side of the U.S. 250 parking area as one leg of a loop trail around the Breastworks (a good short winter hike that starts on the parking lot's west side). The Mountain Trail then goes right and away from the loop trail. There is fine skiing as the gradual route snakes back and forth on the ridge with good winter views into West Virginia.

The last mile of this trail drops off the ridge sharply to a Forest Service road that may be impassable under deeper snow. For that reason, and to use your ski tracks, make this an out-and-back tour. Fine campsites abound, and a connecting trail reaches a Potomac Appalachian Trail Club (PATC) cabin, which is a destination for overnight skiers who could make their total tour up to 18 miles long.

At almost 3.0 miles from the start of the Shenandoah Mountain Trail, the Jerry's Run Trail enters from the right. This trail drops in 2.0 miles through virgin forest to the Ramsey's Draft Trail in the drainage to the east. To reach the PATC's locked and enclosed, bunk- and woodstove-equipped cabin, Sexton Cabin, and a spring, ski 0.3 mile down the Jerry's Run Trail from the Shenandoah Mountain Trail. Since this is now a Wilderness Area, the rustic cabin is controversial and could, regrettably, be dismantled.

At about 8.0 miles on the Shenandoah Mountain Trail, the Ramsey's Draft Trail joins from the right in a glade of big trees under the area's second highest peak, Tearjacket Knob (4,229 feet). To the right, the Ramsey's Draft Trail is skiable into the gap between Tearjacket and the Draft's highest summit, Hardscrabble Knob (4,282). At the gap, a spur trail branches right up to Hardscrabble and the Draft Trail descends. A short walk down the Draft Trail reaches Hiner Spring, on the right, but in deep snow a longer walk might be needed to reach water.

Beyond the Ramsey's Draft Trail, the Shenandoah Mountain Trail passes scenic ridge-top settings and good campsites. At the point where the trail drops abruptly west off the ridge, at about 9 miles, turn around and return.

SHENANDOAH MOUNTAIN TRAIL/SOUTH

The southern section of this trail begins at a gated fire road, 1,000 feet east and downhill from the Confederate Breastworks parking area on U.S. 250. The fire road is open to hunter's vehicles in the fall but is gated in other seasons.

For skiers seeking solitude and wanting to avoid hikers this is the best, least-traveled choice. The trail climbs gradually as a fire road for the first 2.6 miles, then the Shenandoah Mountain Trail branches left as a ridge-top trail. Skiers will prefer to go right on the old road, which gradually reaches, then follows, Benson Run Creek. This trout stream tumbles over falls through a forest of hemlock and birch with fine back-country campsites. The old road reaches Forest Development road (FDR) 173 at a gated T-junction in 3.0 miles. The total one-way distance is nearly 6.0 miles, making about a 12.0-mile round trip.

Taking FDR 173 left and uphill at the gated junction leads to the Shenandoah Mountain Trail at the ridge. Expert skiers could form a loop by linking the 4.4-mile ridge-top part of the Shenandoah Mountain Trail, FDR 173, and the old road along Benson Run Creek.

Winter Hiking

RAMSEY'S DRAFT TRAIL

Without skis, winter hikers can venture across the nearly twenty stream crossings of the Ramsey's Draft Trail into the heart of the virgin forest. Unlike the cold, often breezy ridge top of the Shenandoah Mountain Trail, the Draft Trail is chilled by the sinking of cold air and the deep shade of the towering trees. Although snow on this trail isn't as deep as it is higher up, it stays. Icicles often cover the stream-side cliffs.

The trail begins near the Mountain House Picnic Area, 13.8 miles west of Churchville, Va., at just over 2,000 feet in elevation. The picnic area marks the site of an old ordinary, a rustic overnight lodge for early travelers crossing the mountains. Entering the picnic area, drive 0.8 mile to parking slips near the first ford.

Be forewarned. In high water or icy conditions, the Draft Trail can be a challenge, with some uncrossable fords forcing stream-side bush-whacks that can lead above icy cliffs. Waterproof boots, high, water-proof gaiters, and instep crampons are useful. In severe cold, the stream may be frozen enough to make walking and even skiing over the Draft crossings possible, but this condition is rare, and trekkers should always be cautious. Be prepared with warm, dry clothes, and expect temperatures in the woods' interior to be 15 degrees colder than at the parking lot. Except in very high water, summer hiking in this area is easy and memorable.

After the first ford, a 0.5-mile nature trail leaves and returns to the old road of the Ramsey's Draft Trail on the right. Built in 1940 by the Augusta, Va., Garden Club, the self-guiding thirty-minute walk is a fine winter stroll through virgin timber.

In its 6.5-mile climb to the Shenandoah Mountain Trail, the old road grade crosses the stream often and follows the ever-narrowing valley. Many fords are avoidable, so explore. At 1.7 miles, the Jerry's Run Trail leaves left and follows the stream of that name for 2.0 miles to the Shenandoah Mountain Trail, 0.3 mile past Sexton Cabin (see Shenandoah Mountain Trail/North).

Past the junction with Jerry's Run Trail, the Draft Trail continues with Freezland Flat rising to the left, a peak of more than 4,000 feet with a natural meadow at its summit. The grade is nearly level to the 3.5-mile mark. The roadbed ends where the Left Prong of Ramsey's Draft flows in from the left from between Freezland Flat and Hardscrabble Knob. No trail follows this left fork, but the virgin timber and silence are impressive.

The trail leaves the road grade at 2,900 feet and climbs steeply as a foot trail along the Right Prong of Ramsey's Draft. The Springhouse Ridge Trail leaves right at 5.4 miles, just below Hiner Spring on the left, and reaches the gap between Hardscrabble and Tearjacket knobs and the Hardscrabble Knob Trail, also to the left, at about 6 miles. From this camping area, the trail descends gently to the Shenandoah Mountain Trail at 6.5 miles.

For more information, contact

Deerfield Ranger District, USFS, 2304 West Beverly St., Staunton, VA 24401. 703/885-8028.

For details about Sexton Shelter and other Potomac Appalachian Trail Club cabins and maps, see the next entry, introducing Shenandoah National Park.

Shenandoah National Park: A Park with a History

Shenandoah National Park is a 300-square-mile strip of land encompassing the northern Virginia spine of the Blue Ridge Mountains. The ridge, almost a single perpendicular mass, rises east of the Great Valley of Virginia and is the first line of mountains seen on a drive west across Virginia's piedmont.

Although not as snowy as some higher, more western mountains, Shenandoah annually receives substantial snow storms. Rangers say an average winter supplies just over a month of snow cover. Luckily, many Shenandoah Valley cross-country skiers and winter hikers live close by. The more distant residents of the eastern urban corridor from Richmond to Baltimore all have excellent, high-speed highway access to the park. For these reasons, cross-country skiing is becoming very popular.

When dedicated in 1936 by President Franklin Roosevelt, Shenandoah had the distinction of being the first Southern Appalachian national park. Action was taken here first because the park was close to the nation's capital and accessible to millions. Unlike government-owned western land, Shenandoah was wrested from private ownership only at great expense and after substantial legal action. The state and citizens of Virginia contributed millions of dollars to this precedent-setting effort.

The park's nearly 200,000 acres have a history of heavy human impact. Native Americans periodically burned the high plateau now known as Big Meadows to create better hunting opportunities. After colonization, the rich Shenandoah Valley quickly became settled and prosperous. Timber harvesting and mining came to the mountains, and the growing population sparked movement into the high valleys and hollows of what was to become the park. These isolated communities were, in some cases, separate societies. As such, they were among the most defiant of outside authority and the most colorful in Appalachia. Today, winter sky provides an eery canopy for cabin ruins glimpsed in the Old Rag Valley or in Nicholson Hollow, known as Free State Hollow during its rebellious heyday.

By the twenties, tourism was on the rise. That trend included Shenandoah's popular Skyland Lodge, started in 1894 by George Freeman Pollock who was instrumental in efforts to create Shenandoah National Park.

Skiers and hikers now see Shenandoah's forest in an impressive maturity. Oaks, maples, and hemlocks abound. There are dozens of trails, including over 100 miles of the Appalachian Trail. More than twenty shelters include three impressive stone shelters built by Harry F. Byrd, Governor of Virginia, while money was being raised to buy the park. The Civilian Conservation Corps built many trails and the Potomac Appalachian Trail Club (PATC) maintains five enclosed cabins. All can be rented for winter use, as discussed at the end of this introduction.

The park's central feature is the 105-mile Skyline Drive, finished during the 1930s as a counterpart to the Blue Ridge Parkway that links Shenandoah with Great Smoky Mountains National Park in North Carolina. The road travels the crest of the Blue Ridge with views of the piedmont and Shenandoah Valley. Access is at four points where highways cross the ridge. Two highways sever the park into three sections. In winter, skiing, hiking, and motorized sightseeing focus on the rugged central section, where the park's highest peaks and biggest recreation area are.

During periods of snow, plowing of the park begins at Thornton Gap, the northern end of the central section. U.S. 211 reaches the park entrance station near Luray. Most winter days, a ranger is stationed here to charge the $2-per-car admission fee, issue the required back-country camping permit, and otherwise inform visitors. The road is first plowed to Big Meadows, giving hikers and skiers many trail options. Later, the central section will open to Big Meadows from Swift Run Gap at U.S. 33. When the central section is clear, the northern and southern sections of Shenandoah open as soon as possible.

When any section of the park is closed due to heavy snow, gates will be in place and skiers may ski on the road if plowing is not in progress. A sign at each gate informs skiers when they can and cannot ski the road.

Even with snow on the ground, backpackers with permits can leave their cars on the Drive overnight. The only overnight closure of the Drive, except in very heavy snow, occurs during hunting season in the southern and northern sections, from mid-November to early January. During winter months, when heavy snow is predicted or is beginning, rangers will try to contact backpackers, skiers, and hikers who are parked on Skyline Drive. If they can't, they will leave a note, and cars will be freed as soon as possible. To avoid being trapped, hikers and skiers should return to their cars and be prepared to leave the park at the onset of heavy snow or inclement weather. Backpackers parking on the Drive should have extra food and be prepared for this contingency.

Shenandoah pursues a camping policy of "dispersion," meaning there are no designated campsites. To ensure that no sites become overused, people must camp out of view of trails, fire roads, developed facilities of all kinds, and other campers. Shelters are also off limits for camping. Shelter fireplaces or fire rings may be used for cooking and other activities, but no camping is allowed in the shelters, except in emergencies. All winter backpackers are expected to carry the proper tent and other gear and to be prepared for snow. Only the destruction of a tent, a massive snow storm, or a medical emergency constitutes a reason to use a shelter. Certain other areas are off limits for camping, like the summits of Old Rag and Hawksbill. Ask rangers for the latest policies when applying for overnight permits.

Besides the Thornton Gap Entrance Station, the best place to contact park rangers is the Byrd Visitor Center at Big Meadows, which also posts snow conditions for a variety of trails. The center is open five days a week, including both weekend days, from 9:00 to 5:00. The facility is closed two days during the week.

Other park facilities are closed during the winter, including the Skyland Lodge, Big Meadows Lodge, the restaurant and store at Big Meadows Wayside, and Big Meadows Campground, all in the central section. The campground closes January 1.

Most designated trails in Shenandoah begin at parking areas or overlooks. When using those that don't, visitors should park as far to the side of Skyline Drive as possible, in particular, far enough off the road surface so as not to interfere with snow plows. And remember that plowing could trap your car.

Many places in Shenandoah can be reached by climbing up fire roads or trails from valleys on both sides of the ridge. The recommended start for the Old Rag trip is an example. Many of these accesses are usable even under heavy snow, and the PATC series of Shenandoah sectional maps are a good resource for finding these isolated trailheads. Most of the time, skiers will want to start at the higher elevation of Skyline Drive to take advantage of deeper snow.

Shenandoah is a popular vacation destination. Spring, summer and fall have their rewards, but trails can be crowded. Midweek visits are recommended. There are five major campgrounds on the Drive and seven picnic areas. Tent and motor home campers may take advantage of shower and laundry facilties, evening programs, and self-guiding nature trails. Concession services are extensive. Park concessionaire ARA-Virginia Skyline Company, Inc., also operates lodge and cabin accommodations and dining facilities (alcohol available) at Big Meadows, Skyland, Lewis Mountain, and the Panorama Restaurant, and a service station and gift shop at the Thornton Gap entrance to the park. As with park facilities, these services usually run from May to October, but schedules do vary. Limited meeting space is available at Big Meadows and Skyland. Details may be requested from the concessionaire (address below).

PATC maps and cabins are available to the public. The club maintains five cabins in Shenandoah and many more in the vicinity. The general public must file a responsibility statement with the club (address below) and fulfill certain requirements and pay minimal fees. The cabins are very inexpensive and very popular, so reserve well in advance. The club suggests phone reservations after the initial forms have been filed. PATC maps cover many prime winter hiking areas, especially Shenandoah. Ask for the order form.

For more information, contact

Superintendent, Shenandoah National Park, Rte. 4, Box 292, Luray, VA 22835-9051. 703/999-2243 (weekdays only). 24-hour recorded snow report: 703/999-2266.

ARA-Virginia Skyline Company, Inc., Box 727, Luray, VA 22835. 703/743-5108.

Potomac Appalachian Trail Club, 1718 N St., N.W., Washington, DC 20036. 202/638-5306 (weeknights only 7-10 P.M.)

Cross-Country Trails

The trails recommended here are in the central section of the park due to its heavier snow and plowing priority. Use the PATC's central section map.

THE LIMBERLOST

This romantic sounding name is appropriate to Shenandoah's most impressive remnant of virgin forest. Some of the mammoth hemlocks on this trail are said to be between 400 and 500 years old. Few experiences in the park inspire more awe than a snowy ski tour through the Limberlost.

Two starting points are possible: the White Oak Canyon parking lot at Drive milepost 42.6, or the small road-side parking lot at the start of the Old Rag fire road at milepost 43. This smaller lot can sometimes be closed by snow, requiring parking at the edge of the road.

From the White Oak Canyon parking area, descend that trail a little more than 0.5 mile (intermediate) to the Old Rag fire road. Take the road to the right, pass the gate at the milepost 43 parking lot, and immediately turn left on the Limberlost Trail. Halfway through the 1.2-mile loop, be sure to bear left at the junction with Crescent Rock Trail. Further on, at the junction with the White Oak Canyon Trail, bear left and follow that trail back to White Oak Canyon parking area on Skyline Drive. This loop tour is a little over 2.0 miles and, except for the intermediate start, is mostly beginner rated.

The trip is shorter and easier if you begin at the small lot at milepost 43 where the Limberlost Trail really starts. Most of this ski tour is at 3,300 feet. Both parking areas are only a short distance from Skyline Drive's highest point, 3,680 feet, near the entrance to Skyland Lodge.

BIG MEADOWS CAMPGROUND

Although a campground and not a trail, this site's many loops and cross-trails are a fine learning area that is rated easiest. Many of the loops offer nice views, especially Z loop where views reach to the Shenandoah Valley. Some loops offer steeper grades, and other trails tie in here. Depending on plowing, the campground can be reached by driving or skiing down the access road or taking the roadside trail between Skyline Drive mileposts 51 and 52 that connects Big Meadows Wayside and the lodge, campground, stables, and picnic area.

NATURE TRAIL

This 2.0-mile round trip explores the high-mountain swamp and bog at Big Meadows. The trail begins at a trailhead in Big Meadows picnic area beside the amphitheater. The trail is a loop.

THE MEADOW/RAPIDAN FIRE ROAD

The recreation area at Big Meadows was named for a large meadow at the 3,500-foot elevation. The 300-acre opening boasts the park's greatest diversity of plant life.

Just across from Byrd Visitor Center, the Rapidan fire road leaves the east side of Skyline Drive at a gate. As at Big Meadows Campground, numerous easy routes are possible. A perimeter tour yields fine views, including distant Old Rag, and there are hillsides for downhill runs. The meadows are best with at least 6 inches of snow. The fire road itself crosses the meadow, entering the woods, and a horse trail branches right

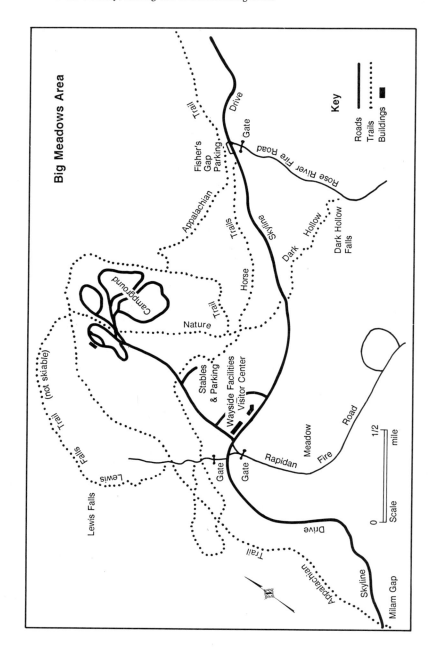

Big Meadows Area

Key

Roads
Trails
Buildings

just over a mile from Skyline Drive. Return from here or continue on the Rapidan fire road as it drops off the ridge.

Under deep snow, the Hoover Camp can be a good destination for advanced skiers with back-country skiing experience and equipment and plenty of ambition. The cabins are the restored fishing retreat of President Herbert Hoover. Informative signs interpret the camp for skiers. The route descends from Big Meadows down the Rapidan fire road, with fine views, to a junction in the fire road. To the left, the fire road continues a descent to a gate at the park boundary. To the right, the fire road climbs, after crossing a bridge, to Hoover Camp, about 6.0 miles total from Big Meadows. The return climb rises about 1,200 feet from the initial descent, so allow plenty of time for this tour, or turn around after you've enjoyed the higher part of the route at the beginning.

TANNER'S RIDGE LOOP

This 2.0-mile loop, a horse trail, requires at least 8 inches of snow or a very solid base. Starting at the Big Meadows Stables parking lot, head southwest through the open field, and at the posted horse crossing, cross the paved access road to the stables from the Wayside. After a gradual downhill run, the trail passes a connector left that goes to Skyline Drive and then on to the Rapidan fire road at the meadow. Just beyond the junction, the Tanner's Ridge trail forks into a loop that can be followed either way. After this yellow-blazed trail branches into its loop, it crosses the Lewis Spring fire road and then the Appalachian Trail (AT). The loop is intermediate rated.

HORSE TRAIL FROM BIG MEADOWS TO FISHERS GAP

Leaving right (east) toward the stables from the parking lot, skiers encounter a sign and take the trail to Skyland. The descent from here to Fishers Gap, Drive milepost 49.4, is rated intermediate to expert, with hills at the top and bottom. Use care to avoid some rocky sections. The distance one way is 1.3 miles. This route can be connected to the Rose River fire road to make a 5.0-mile out-and-back round trip.

ROSE RIVER FIRE ROAD

From Fishers Gap, Skyline Drive milepost 49.4, the easiest-rated Rose River fire road gradually descends 1.1 miles to a steel bridge crossing Hogcamp Branch. Beautiful Dark Hollow Falls is only a few hundred yards upstream, but do not try to ski. Follow the short side trail on foot.

This is a fine beginner ski trip. You may go past the bridge, but unless you've placed a car about 5 miles away at the park boundary, be prepared to ski back up.

WEAKLEY HOLLOW FIRE ROAD

This easy ski trip through the Old Rag Valley begins in the town of Nethers, east of the park. See the description of Old Rag later in this section for details.

WHITE OAK FIRE ROAD

This 1.8-mile tour to views of White Oak Falls is for advanced skiers with back-country equipment. The total route, including return on the same trail, is 3.6 miles. The fire road, a combined hiking and horse trail, departs the east side of the Skyline Drive in a sharp turn at milepost 45. There is little parking space. The fire road joins the horse trail, and skiers turn left. The trail descends gradually, then more steeply in an exciting run to White Oak Canyon. Cross at the stream, or use the bridge just uphill. Skiers should cross, then hike, not ski, down the 200 feet to an overlook on White Oak Falls. The return trip gains 900 feet.

HAWKSBILL MOUNTAIN

This is Shenandoah National Park's highest peak (4,049 feet). An observation deck, the stone Byrd's Nest #2 shelter (no camping), privies, and fire pits mark the summit. Four separate trails make the peak skiable, and a fifth is a fine winter hiking route (see the following description of hiking trails for details).

Except for easy sections of trail from the Upper Hawksbill parking area and on much of the AT from Hawksbill Gap, the skiing on Hawksbill is imtermediate to advanced and warrants back-country equipment and skillful turning and snowplowing. Hawksbill is a scenic, exciting destination for experts.

There are two trailheads that allow out-and-back tours to the summit. From Hawksbill Gap, between Skyline Drive mileposts 45 and 46, the white-blazed AT heads west across the shaded northern slopes of the mountain, passing between open scree slopes. At about 1.0 mile, the Hawksbill Trail leads left, climbing to the summit in just under a mile. Return on this route for a 4.0-mile round trip, or link to the fire road described below at Hawksbill summit.

From Upper Hawksbill Parking Area, milepost 46.7, take the easiest-

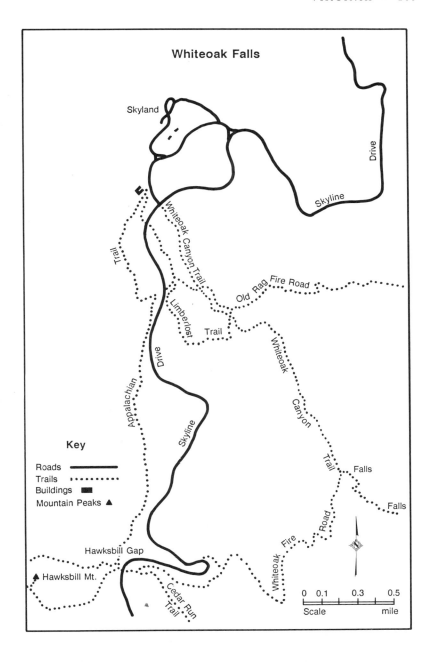

Whiteoak Falls

rated Upper Hawksbill Trail 0.6 mile to a junction with the Hawksbill fire road. Beginners can return to the car from the junction for a 1.2-mile round trip. Advanced skiers can descend left to milepost 47 on Skyline Drive or turn right on the fire road for an expert climb of less than 0.5 mile to the Hawksbill summit. The last stretch of the fire road to the summit parallels Hawksbill Trail coming up from the AT, as described above. The round trip from Upper Hawksbill parking area to the summit and back is roughly 2.3 miles.

A circuit tour allows you to park at one trailhead and ski most of the trails, but unfortunately it requires skiing beside the Skyline Drive for nearly a mile. Skiers starting at Hawksbill Gap can descend either the entire expert fire road to milepost 47, or the fire road/Upper Hawksbill Trail combination, also to Skyline Drive, and then ski down the road side just over a mile back to Hawksbill Gap for the circuit. This route passes the Old Rag Overlook, a fine Skyline Drive view whether on skis or in a car. This circuit is approximately 4.5 miles.

APPALACHIAN TRAIL: BIG MEADOWS CAMPGROUND TO MILAM GAP

From the west end of Big Meadows' Y loop, at a concrete trail-marker post, a side path reaches the AT. Take the AT south, following white blazes, past Big Meadows' picnic area, lodge, and viewpoints. The trail has occasional steep descents on its way to Lewis Spring Road. After crossing the road, the AT regains an easy grade, crosses two legs of the Tanner's Ridge Loop—a horse and ski trail—and then the Tanner's Ridge fire road. It reaches Skyline Drive at Milam Gap. One-way distance is 3.0 miles. This intermediate trail would be suitable for beginners if skied from Milam Gap north.

A fine Big Meadows loop can be formed by starting at the stables, connecting to the campground on the Nature Trail, joining the AT at Y loop, skiing to Lewis Spring Road, then through the Tanner's Ridge Loop and back to the stables. Creative skiers could also start at other places and make similar loops.

APPALACHIAN TRAIL: SKYLAND TO FISHERS GAP

This 6.5-mile section of the Appalachian Trail includes the portion around Hawksbill and offers all levels of skiing difficulty. There are many access points with which to break the trip up, but the entire tour is a good one for a party of skiers with two vehicles. Advanced skiers could enjoy a 12.0-mile round trip.

Access is easy from a parking area just inside the south entrance to Skyland and at the Fishers Gap parking area near the Redgate fire road.

APPALACHIAN TRAIL: SADDLEBACK MOUNTAIN AREA

This tour explores the Blue Ridge in the more southerly part of Shenandoah's central section, near one of the park's most popular waterfalls. Elevations here are about 3,000 feet, 400 to 500 feet lower than Big Meadows.

Leave South River picnic area, milepost 62.8, on South River Falls Trail. In a short distance, turn right and go south on the white-blazed AT. Go left on the first fire road to South River maintenance hut (no camping, privie and fire pit available). Continuing past the hut, take the blue-blazed Saddleback Trail gradually uphill, then down to a junction with the AT. Turn right and follow the AT north across a fire road and back to the picnic area. Round trip on this loop tour is about 4.0 miles.

The trip could be lengthened by parking at an overlook north of the entrance to the picnic area, skiing north on the South River fire road to the AT, then south to connect with the tour described above. This approach might be best if the the picnic area is unplowed. A shorter trip could also be made by starting at the fire road to the maintenance hut, leaving out the first leg of the AT. Parking to start on that fire road would be just north of milepost 63 on the east side of Skyline Drive. (A longer expert ski tour near South River picnic area is described in the following description of winter hiking, under South River Falls.)

Tours that begin at South River picnic area are good options if the Drive is closed by snow—when skiers can't reach Big Meadows and skiing on the road is permitted. From U.S. 33, a plowed highway in Swift Run Gap, the starting points for these tours are less than 3 miles north on the unplowed Skyline Drive, much of it sheltered from the sun by a ridge on the east side of the road. A road and trail combination tour would be a little less than 10 miles with the last 3 miles downhill.

Even when the Drive is plowed in snowy weather, this tour allows access from a primary public highway for those who don't want to motor the nearly 20 miles of high, snow-covered Drive to Big Meadows.

Winter Hiking

HAWKSBILL MOUNTAIN

This highest peak in the park (4,049 feet) offers spectacular views from rocky cliffs and a stone observation platform. The Shenandoah Valley to the west and Old Rag and the foothills to the east create one of Shenandoah's most impressive views. At night, cities spangle the surrounding valleys 3,000 feet below. A stone shelter (no camping), privies, and fire sites are all in the summit area. Luckily, the summit is quickly accessible on a short trail, which is not suitable for use by cross-country skiers. The PATC's map of the park's central section is recommended.

From Hawksbill Gap parking area on Skyline Drive between mileposts 45 and 46, the Old Hawksbill Trail climbs to the summit, at times steeply. About 0.3 mile up from Hawksbill Gap, a side trail leads left to a spring about 100 feet off the trail. The trail climbs from there and reaches the summit, about 0.8 mile from Hawksbill Gap. This is a fine winter day hike.

Camping is not permitted on the Hawksbill summit and campers should not expect to use the shelter. Like others in the park, this one, called Byrd's Nest #2, is off limits except in emergencies (see the introduction at the start of this entry for specifics about camping). The open shelter faces into the winter wind anyway, an uncomfortable prospect without the canvas curtains that once covered the front. When applying for an overnight permit, campers should ask rangers about current camping options at the Hawksbill area.

SOUTH RIVER FALLS

Starting at the east side of the South River picnic area, hike on the South River Falls Trail through beautiful stream-side forest past the rim of the falls. At about 1.0 mile, you reach a viewpoint. Hiking back from this spot makes an easy 2.0-mile day hike.

Continuing a few tenths of a mile past the view, turn right at the next junction and descend 0.5 mile to where a rough trail ascends the last few hundred feet to the base of the falls. Returning from this point makes a longer, nearly 4.0-mile day hike. Exercise extreme caution on ice near the falls.

An alternate return for the second, longer hike involves taking a right at the junction on the return from the base of the falls and going about 0.5 mile to the South River fire road. A left on the road leads to the AT in a little less than a mile. A left on the AT leads to the South River Falls Trail at the picnic area starting point in 0.5 mile. This is a 4.5-mile loop.

Backpackers and energetic day hikers may add another loop to this first falls loop to create a 10.0-mile circuit. Expert cross-country skiers can make a long deep snow tour out of this loop by avoiding the falls trail and staying on the AT, fire roads, and horse trail described here.

Starting as above, turn left on the AT, crossing the South River fire road in 0.5 mile and continuing up the AT a little more than 3 miles to the Pocosin fire road. Turn right and descend past the Pocosin cabin, available for rent through the PATC and more directly accessible on the Pocosin fire road from a gate on Skyline Drive between mileposts 59 and 60. After a mile, turn right onto a signed horse trail, which shortly reaches the ruins of the Upper Pocosin Mission. Bear right in a flat area about 1.2 miles from the junction with the horse trail. One-tenth of a mile later, join the South River fire road. After a little over a mile on this fire road, hikers and backpackers can turn left, descending to the falls and the South River Falls Trail. Skiers should stay on the road, rising to make a left on the AT back to the picnic area.

CEDAR RUN/WHITE OAK CANYON

This is another long day hike or overnight backpacking trip. Hikers will find deep clefts in the mountainsides where ice and snow hide from the warmth of the sun. Frozen waterfalls glisten on this strenuous, 8.0-mile circuit that loses and then regains more than 2,000 vertical feet. But as on the summit of Hawksbill, overnight camping is not permitted in the canyons. Refer to the PATC map for the park's central section, and ask rangers for details when applying for an overnight permit.

Start at Hawksbill Gap, on the east side of Skyline Drive between mileposts 45 and 46. Descend on the blue-blazed Cedar Run Trail. After staying left of the stream for 1.5 miles, the trail crosses to the right side, with views of a cascade and cliffs across the stream. Descend for about another 0.5 mile, and then be alert because the trail crosses to the left side of the stream and slabs the ridge line, leaving Cedar Run.

At the next junction, go left upstream on the blue-blazed White Oak Canyon Trail. After crossing another stream, the climb passes waterfalls and icy cliffs.

At a little over 2.0 miles on the Canyon Trail, go left on the White Oak fire road, part of the Skyland–Big Meadows horse trail. Upstream a short distance is a bridge, which you can use if the rocks are too icy at the ford. From the stream, take the horse trail and go left at a junction after about 1.5 miles. This horse trail reaches the Cedar Run Trail in another 0.5 mile in Hawksbill Gap, your starting point.

From the stream in White Oak Canyon to the junction on the way back to the Cedar Run Trail, you may see cross-country skiers who start their tours on the Skyline Drive, to the right at the junction.

There are other fine hikes in Shenandoah. Near Old Rag, the Hazel Country hikes are popular, especially with backpackers, as are the Rocky Mountain–Brown Mountain area and Riprap Hollow, both in the park's southern section.

Winter Hiking and Cross-Country Skiing on Old Rag

Shenandoah National Park's Old Rag is arguably Virginia's most spectacular mountain. Lying east of the main Blue Ridge chain, the mountain stands alone, its rocky ridge line and prominent summits reaching to 3,291 feet. Old Rag's crags jut above its middle-elevation hardwood forests in a stereotypical alpine image. That classic scenic character has made the peak one of the park's most popular (some would say most crowded) destinations. Luckily, winter is the time when Old Rag is least visited.

Besides having a better chance for solitude, winter hikers and cross-country skiers see Old Rag in its starkest, most spectacular season. Even without snow, Old Rag is a winter hike worth taking.

For those wanting heavy snow, remember that Old Rag is just over 3,000 feet and lies to the east of the higher Blue Ridge, including Shenandoah's highest peak, Hawksbill. That ridge often gets more snow than Old Rag, and in fact, the Blue Ridge as a whole receives less snow than mountains farther west or even North Carolina's highest peaks. Still, finding Old Rag under snowy winter conditions may take close attention to weather reports and a phone call to park headquarters, but fine snow conditions do occur. And when they do, Old Rag's rocky ridge line becomes an unparalleled winter mountaineering location.

To get to and from the ridge line traverse, most Old Rag circuit hikers use the fire road that follows the valley between Old Rag and the main ridge. With good snow conditions, this is a fine ski tour by itself or in combination with a trip to the peak.

The trail begins near the tiny town of Nethers, about 14 miles from Sperryville, Va. The trailhead is reached by turning from Va. 231 at the

Hughes River between Sperryville and Madison, Va., onto a secondary road, Va. 602. Keeping to the left of the river, the road becomes Va. 601, 707, and then 600 before passing an overflow parking area on the left and climbing as a smaller road to a parking area at the park boundary. There, amid hemlocks and the tumbling Hughes River, the Old Rag Ridge Trail and the Weakley Hollow fire road begin.

The gated fire road will be the return for most winter hikers: the gradual grade makes a fine end to a rugged day hike. The blue-blazed Ridge Trail climbs through a hardwood forest at first, then takes numerous switchbacks to an intermittent spring at about the 1.5-mile mark. The spring is just to the right of the trail. A wooded saddle is reached 0.25 mile later, and the trail emerges onto the rocky ridge at about 2.0 miles.

In snow, follow the Ridge Trail blazes carefully. Experience in hiking on this trail without snow will be a help here. Remember, there is no substitute for proper equipment. Rope and even crampons, at least instep crampons, are necessary in ice and snow. A slide on the ridge could be fatal. Don't attempt this trail in icy conditions with just hiking boots.

The views on this trail are awesome. To the east, the flat Virginia piedmont stretches to Richmond. To the west, the main Blue Ridge rises. Between them, in the dark cleft of the Old Rag Valley, the Weakley Hollow fire road eludes the winter sun.

On this part of the trail, you will ascend steep-walled gullies, around house-sized boulders, above cliffs, and even through a tunnel-cave. At about 2.5 miles, a trail branches left to a wet-weather spring 100 yards away from the junction. This side trail passes the spring and rejoins the Ridge Trail just before the two rock summits, approximately 2.8 miles from the start. The ascent totals 2,200 feet.

Continuing past the peaks, the trail descends in 0.5 mile to Byrd's Nest #1, a scenic rock shelter built in 1962 by Virginia Senator Harry F. Byrd, Sr. Due to heavy use, camping has been prohibited at both shelters on this hike and on the Old Rag summit in general. Ask rangers for the latest policies when you apply for an overnight permit.

From the shelter, the Saddle Trail descends a little more than a mile, passing many fine views, to Old Rag Shelter, a six-bunk structure built in 1939. A good spring lies just below the shelter in the ravine. Just before the shelter, a fire road goes right, reaching the Weakley Hollow fire road in just under 0.5 mile. At this point, the hike has been about 4.5 miles.

To the left at this junction with the Weakley Hollow fire road, Berry

Hollow fire road goes left, or south, to the town of Syria. West, or straight across the junction, the Skyland–Old Rag fire road climbs to Skyline Drive, and to the right, or north, the Weakley Hollow fire road descends, with yellow blazes, to Nethers and the parking area in 2.5 miles. Returning to the parking area, the entire circuit is just over 7.0 miles and can take eight hours in deep snow; it generally takes five to six hours in little or no snow.

This is an excellent winter backpacking circuit, but carry water up the Ridge Trail.

Old Rag is not just a winter hike or mountaineering trip. Cross-country skiers can focus on the Weakley Hollow fire road and have a fine day or overnight tour. A ski trip up Weakley Hollow fire road, then over the access road to the Old Rag Shelter and back is about 6 miles. The shelter is a fine lunch stop and camping in the vicinity is good also. On either a day tour or an overnighter, skiers can hike the Saddle Trail route up to the peak, or just stop at the views below Byrd's Nest #1 Shelter. The walk from Old Rag Shelter to the summit is just under 3.0 miles round trip.

The PATC's map of the central section of Shenandoah National Park is recommended on this trip. See the contact information at the end of the introductory discussion of Shenandoah National Park.

North Carolina

The Appalachian Trail: Southern Balds Section

Betweeen Roan Mountain and the town of Elk Park, N.C., lies the greatest expanse of balds in the South. The Appalachian Trail (AT) crosses this 11 miles of ridge-top meadow with spectacular views of three states and the East's highest peaks.

Access is from Tenn. 143/N.C. 261 at Carver's Gap, where skiers gather for Roan Mountain trails, including the AT, and near Elk Park, where the trail crosses U.S. 19E and continues north into Tennessee. Another major access in the middle of this roadless section of trail is at Yellow Mountain Gap (see the entry on Yellow Mountain Gap later in this section).

The snowy climate and alpine character of this area make it one of the prime winter mountaineering sites in the South. Although winter backpackers and hikers will enjoy this section of the AT most, approximately 60 percent of the trail is skiable for those who would combine the two sports in a deep snow traverse of the ridge. Day skiers are most prevalent at Yellow Mountain Gap, where terrain is moderate. At the Carver's Gap trailhead, the first few miles of this trail offer day hikers an alternative to walking on the trails of Roan Mountain, which are usually popular with skiers.

Crossing the entire ridge requires two vehicles or a drop-off/pick-up plan. The trip is easiest from Carver's Gap (5,512 feet) to Elk Park (3,100 feet). Although there are many uphill interludes, this is the most "downhill" direction overall. The climb from Elk Park to the first major peak, Hump Mountain (5,587 feet) is truly daunting, especially in snow.

In either direction, the white AT blazes painted on rocks are often obscured by snow and no cairns exist across the meadows. Carrying and being able to use a USGS topo map and compass are essential to safety and accurate route finding. This is a windy area subject to severe weather.

The trail leaves the east side of Carver's Gap after crossing a stile over a wooden fence. A short, steep ascent of hundreds of wooden steps placed in 1976 by an Appalachian Mountain Club trail crew reaches Round Bald in 0.5 mile. This summit is a brief, often windy day hike with great views of Roan, Mount Mitchell, and other summits. Day hikers can go farther, turning back on any of the bald summits on this first section of trail.

From Round Bald (5,826 feet), the trail descends to Engine Gap, then climbs to Jane Bald (5,807 feet) at just over 1.0 mile. Continuing, the AT reaches a junction at 1.5 miles and goes left where a side trail leads straight to Grassy Ridge Bald. The AT continues across the north slope of Grassy Ridge to Low Gap and Roan Highlands Shelter at 3.0 miles. (The shelter was built by the U.S. Forest Service in 1976. It sleeps six, and water is located down a blue-blazed trail to the east of the shelter.)

From the shelter, the trail ascends gradually to a nearby viewpoint and switchbacks through the next two gaps, avoiding abandoned, very steep sections of the AT. After skirting a knob, the trail drops steeply more than 200 feet into Yellow Mountain Gap (4,682 feet) and a 1.0-mile side trail to auto access at Roaring Creek Road, SR 1132, 4.7 miles from U.S. 19E (see the entry on Yellow Mountain Gap later in this section).

From the gap, the AT climbs the fence line over meadows, enters Beech woods at 4.9 miles, and levels off on a road-width trail. At 5.4 miles, a meadow appears across the fence line on the left. The AT crosses a stile on the fence and gradually slabs to the west side of the meadow, with a tree line of stunted beeches on the left. (Straight at the stile, the Old Yellow Mountain Trail climbs to a dead end on the balds of Big Yellow. See the Yellow Mountain Gap entry.)

The AT crests the bald ridge and passes beside large rocks with an AT symbol to the summit of Little Hump Mountain (5,459 feet) at 5.9 miles. Past the peak, the rugged trail descends steeply to a gap, then ascends along the tree line on the left and skirts a bald peak. After gaining another crest, the AT dips into Bradley Gap, accessible from the west on a 1.5 mile gated dirt road from Shell Creek, Tenn., and from the east by a private road from the Horse Creek community.

The AT then ascends the rocky ridge line of Hump Mountain, with hundreds of acres of meadows to the right or east. This is some of the South's most alpine scenery, reminiscent of New Hampshire's Mount

Jefferson. These sunny expansive meadows frequently blow or melt free of snow, but general snow conditions can be found after storms and in the many snow bowls that pockmark the crest. After deep midwinter snow, on cloudy snow-flurry days, and in spring sun on a good snowpack, Hump can be an incredible day or overnight ski tour, best reached on old road grades to Bradley Gap.

From the Hump's summit, 7.6 miles from Carver's Gap, the AT drops steeply through woods to Doll Flats, a fine campsite amidst grassy fields at 8.7 miles. From there the AT follows an early 1980s reroute down switchbacks to 10.3 miles and the beginning of a narrow valley, Wilder Mine Hollow. At 11.3 miles, the trail emerges at U.S. 19E, 0.8 mile inside Tennessee from the Tennessee state line sign to the east. Downhill, the Roan Mountain Motel provides accommodations in the town of the same name, and uphill, the Times Square Motel and restaurant is 3.0 miles away in Elk Park. On the way to Carver's Gap, Roan Mountain State Park's cross-country ski center rents back-country skis and heavy boots suitable for ski-backpacking on the ridge (see the entry on Roan Mountain later in this section).

For more information on this section of the AT, contact

Toecane Ranger District, PO Box 128, Burnsville, NC 28714. 704/682-6146.

Beech Mountain: A Cross-Country Ski Center

Five miles of cross-country ski trails stretch across the mile-high plateau of Beech Mountain. Some wind through the gnarled Beech forests that gave the mountain its name. Others cross meadows with expansive views of Mount Mitchell and the Black Mountains, Grandfather Mountain, and even the downhill slopes of Ski Beech.

With few exceptions, the trails are road-width. Although the easiest routes, mostly through meadows, are generally flat, advanced skiers can choose from exciting undulating runs. Trails may be groomed with machine-set tracks so Fred's General Mercantile provides the ski-center services a short distance from the privately owned trails, which Fred's manages and maintains for the public at no charge.

Fred's is a new, tastefully designed "general store" at the mountain's crest on Beech Mountain Parkway. A downstairs ski shop offers some of the better-quality Nordic rental skis available in the South, as well as downhill equipment. The shop also rents gaitors and sells a variety of cross-country items. A two-and-a-half-hour guided lesson/tour is available that includes a hot snack on the trail. The staff will run a ski instruction video cassette at no charge if customers ask. The program is shown in Fred's adjoining Backside Deli, a source of sandwiches for skiers, as well as three daily meals and live evening music. Upstairs, Fred's is an eclectic general store that sells everything from books on cross-country skiing to beer and wine.

Before leaving Fred's for the trails, be sure to register with the staff; and sign out after skiing. Most skiers will want to drive to one of the three trailhead parking areas with bulletin boards. Trails aren't named, but junctions are signed with a number and trail difficulty rating symbol. The trail numbers coordinate with the map available at Fred's. Trails are marked with blue diamonds.

The trailhead closest to Fred's is Beechwood Realty, toward the downhill slopes on the right side of Beech Mountain Parkway and marked with a 1 on the map. From there, junctions 2 through 6 can be reached on a large loop and a small one, all rated easiest. An easy connector runs south to trailhead junction 7.

Most skiers will want to park at trailhead junction 7, reached by turning right onto the Pinnacle Inn access road 0.5 mile south of Fred's on the way back toward Banner Elk. Enter the Pinnacle Inn parking area at the guard house and keep right, parking near the bulletin board but not in the way of traffic.

Beginners can ski the obvious grade entering the woods past the tennis courts to reach junction 6 and the easy-rated loops near Beechwood Realty. Intermediates can enter the woods behind the bulletin board and take a rousing downhill run with turns from junctions 7 to 8 and 15. This shaded trail often has deep snow. Novice skiers should ski this trail uphill from junctions 15 to 7.

Beginners can turn right off this route near its start and ski to junctions 10, 9, and 16. Junction 16 is a trailhead reached by bearing right on the gravel road on the way into Pinnacle Inn. These easy trails, including a loop, can also be linked to the intermediate run at junction 8. Trails in this area cross meadows, receive the most wind and sun, and have the network's shallowest snow—from junctions 7 to 10, 9 to 11, 11 to 15, and 11 to 12. In fresh snow, these trails are most enjoyable.

The most distant trails form two loops past a fine view at Plateau Overlook. Better beginners and low intermediates can use these advanced trails if they go in the correct direction. From 11 to 15 and beyond, the trail is a gradual uphill grade that only gets steep and narrow as it climbs to 14. Going downhill, this last pitch would be tricky "tree skiing" even for experts, so virtually everyone should ski from 11 to 15 to 14 and descend from 14 to 11, a gradual, easy grade. The winding trail between 12 and 13 can be climbed by energetic intermediates, but from 13 to 12 it is an exciting, narrow, road-width downhill run with many turns. This trail is a satisfying challenge for a skilled telemarker.

For contact information, see page 347.

The Blue Ridge Parkway: Winter Appeal

The Blue Ridge Parkway is among the most scenic highways in North America. The 469-mile route connects Shenandoah National Park in Virginia with the Great Smoky Mountains National Park in North Carolina and Tennessee. Its winter appeal is elevation. Although the Parkway's low point at the James River in Virginia is at 649 feet, most of the road soars among the highest peaks in the Blue Ridge and adjoining mountain ranges. Heavy snow often closes the road for weeks, since only selected sections are consistently plowed to provide public transportation or recreation. Although driving the Parkway itself is an impractical goal in winter, public highways cross the road at intervals, providing access for skiers, sledders, and hikers. These access points give the Parkway its reputation for winter recreation. Skiers and hikers willing to take a 6- or 8-mile round trip can frequently reach higher elevations, deeper snow, and awesome views. The entries that follow describe the best Parkway trails and road sections for snow sports.

In early, late, and even midwinter, there can be snowless periods when Parkway motoring is as or more spectacular than in summer. Without the leaves, clear winter views are unbelievable and the ruggedness of these ancient peaks is apparent. This is a motor trail through the heart of the Southern Appalachian wilderness. The Parkway offers the closest thing to a trail experience that can be had through a windshield. Countless easy "leg-stetcher" trails beckon at scenic overlooks. Civilization hides in valleys far below. Restored mountaineer farms sit sagging in the eery mist, weathered testimony that America's first great mountain wilderness remained just that until the 1930s, when Parkway construction pierced these shadowed hollows. A few days on the Parkway can seem like a trip back in time. Under snowless conditions, take advantage of this national treasure.

However, the lodges, picnic areas, campgrounds, and service facilities that help make a Parkway trip memorable are closed in winter, although there are a few exceptions. In midwinter, safety should be a prime concern of Parkway visitors. From fall to late spring, sudden, substantial snow can arrive. Plowed roads that cross the Parkway can be difficult to reach if you have to go up hill on the unplowed Parkway to get to them.

Heed the warning signs that sprout beside Parkway entrances in the fall. Avoid this road in snow and ice or in fog and rain when colder temperatures are on the way. During active snowfall, even plowed parts of the Parkway will turn "warning" signs into "closed" signs. Some junctions where the Parkway joins public highways are gated to prevent access. Others are not, and with dependable vehicles, snow enthusiasts can motor onto the snowy road. Snowmobiles are prohibited.

Skiers, hikers, and sledders are advised to use only those sections of Parkway behind locked gates to avoid accidents with vehicles attempting to travel the snow-covered, ungated sections of the road. Rangers may not object to skiing on an ungated section of road if the route is a short trip to a nearby trail or, especially, if snow is so deep that the Parkway is impassable for four-wheel-drive vehicles. But the rules prohibit skiing or walking on traveled sections of the road, so plan to use trails or gated road sections. And whether or not the road is gated, backpack camping is prohibited in the Parkway corridor. Only winter campgrounds may be used (see the entries that follow).

If you choose to challenge the Parkway by car, remember that the road can be a sea of snowdrifts at the bottom of the next hill. It is easy to get stuck and stranded on the Blue Ridge Parkway. People have died of exposure in such situations. The best advice is be prepared for the worst if the Parkway is part of your winter travel plans. Have a well-equipped car and clothing for winter weather. Do not drive up from the lowlands in light clothing and tennis shoes, decide to drive on the snow-covered Parkway without snow tires, and get yourself stuck. See Chapter 3 for further winter driving precautions.

The entries that follow indicate where motor travel is permitted on the snowy Parkway. Enjoy those areas, but do so with caution. Parkway rangers say most accidents occur when unsuspecting motorists encounter hidden ice in a shaded curve. This can be a problem in fall and spring, when the road is mostly clear. Even local mountain residents fall prey to this hidden trap. When parts of the Parkway are clear, changes in elevation and exposure create downright freak fluctuations in road conditions. Often, the intelligent choice is to park and enjoy a gated Parkway section or a trail on foot.

In winter, up-to-date Parkway snow and road closure reports can be easily obtained seven days a week, from Parkway dispatchers who are in radio contact with the rangers. Although you can reach dispatchers at night, it is best to call during daylight hours. In North Carolina, call the Asheville dispatcher at 704/259-0701. In Virginia, call the Vinton dispatcher at 703/982-6490.

In the warmer months, the Parkway attracts millions of people. Temperatures are cool at these heights, an attraction for people used to baking lowland heat. Campgrounds, lodges, service stations, picnic areas, exhibits, overlooks, and visitor and craft centers are scattered along the entire road. The Parkway will easily allow a cool week of wandering among the clouds.

For more information, contact

Superintendent, Blue Ridge Parkway, 700 Northwestern Bank Bldg.,
    Asheville, NC 28801. Or call 704/259-0351, 8:00 to 5:00 weekdays.
Sources of information for specific areas on the Parkway are listed in
    the entries that follow.

Julian Price Memorial Park

Like Moses H. Cone Park on its northern border (covered in the next entry), Julian Price Memorial Park is a monument to a businessman whose beloved mountain retreat found its way into public hands. Both parks are among eleven major Blue Ridge Parkway recreation areas that bulge from the narrow boundaries of the high road.

Price, again like Cone, built a major business in the days after the Civil War. Price's Jefferson Standard Life became one of the biggest insurance companies in the country.

The 4,200-acre Price Park has fine cross-country opportunites and a number of good hiking trails.

The park, between mileposts 295 and 298, is located on the same stretch of Parkway as Cone Park, running from Blowing Rock to Grandfather Mountain. Price is on the southernmost section, where the Parkway reaches a barricade blocking traffic from travel on the uncompleted road around Grandfather Mountain, scheduled to open in late 1987. Traffic heading south exits right to a yield sign, where the paved Holloway Mountain Road serves as a Price Park access point and a link to U.S. 221, the Parkway-alternate route south around Grandfather Mountain. To the right at the yield sign, the unpaved and often snow-covered Church Road meanders to Foscoe and N.C. 105 between Boone and Linville.

This section of the Parkway is plowed for winter access to trailheads and the largest of the Blue Ridge Parkway's campgrounds. There are nearly 200 campsites at Price Park Campground, 35 of which are open at no charge in the winter. The restrooms are closed in winter, but the campground maintains pump water and privies for winter users. The winter campground loop sits on the shore line of Price Lake, a 47-acre, often frozen impoundment above which rises Grandfather Mountain.

This high, upland area is known for the grandness of its forest. Price Park's elevation is a snowy 3,500 feet. Since logging at the turn of the century, the forests have again grown to impressive size on the banks of Boone Fork Creek, named for Jesse Boone, nephew of Daniel, who settled in this area in the early 1800s. The headwaters of this fine trout stream can be seen as a huge bowl-shaped valley on the flank of distant Grandfather Mountain.

Cross-Country Trails

PRICE LAKE LOOP/PRICE PARK CAMPGROUND

The 2.4-mile Price lake Loop trail circles Price Lake from Price Lake parking area, about halfway between Parkway mileposts 296 and 297. A 0.5-mile portion of this trail south of the parking lot traverses the campground section that is open in winter. Skiing through the campground area can make the trail a loop tour whichever way one circles the lake. Start either across the dam north of the parking area for a clockwise tour, or drive south to the boat launch area (a left turn 0.2 mile past milepost 297) and start at the south end of that parking lot for a counterclockwise tour. Either way, you can turn around at any point and enjoy the speed of your tracks on the way back, for a tour of up to 4.0 miles or more. Strong beginners can ski this trail, and the views are very nice. Areas near the three bridged streams may be boggy, especially when a first snow has fallen on bare ground.

For the beginner, the many loops of Price Park Campground could be a good practice area.

OLD JOHNS RIVER ROAD

This old road begins at a gate on the west side of the Blue Ridge Parkway, just south of Sims Pond Overlook, immediately beyond milepost 296. It is an easy out-and-back tour. By taking the first left, about 1.5 miles out, skiers can visit the site on Boone Fork Creek where Julian Price originally intended to build a dam for a 350-acre lake, seven times the size of the one eventually built by the National Park Service. Continuing past the side trail to the dam site, the road reaches a gate at the graveled Old Shull's Mill Road, N.C. 1558, after a gradual descent from the 3,500-foot high point.

TANAWHA TRAIL

This trail parallels the Parkway, including the section to open in 1987, from Price Park Campground to Beacon Heights, south of Grandfather Mountain. The trail section constructed first, from Price Park Campground to the junction with the Grandfather Trail Extension on Grandfather Mountain, is the most skiable. This segment is nearly 6.0 miles long but can be skied in smaller sections.

The best access is at Price Park Campground. On the west side of the Parkway, opposite the entrance to the camp loop that is open in winter, park near but not blocking the gate to the closed campground. Ski behind the gate a short distance to where a small, paved spur goes left toward the Parkway. Tanawha Trail leaves this spur through open woods as the spur departs the campground area. The trail coincides with, then leaves the Boone Fork Trail, passes through meadows, then later coincides with a dirt road.

From the dirt road, the trail branches left and reaches unpaved Church Road. The gated end of the dirt road provides some parking on Church Road for skiers wanting to start there, but Church Road is a notoriously inaccessible route in winter. Skiers would do well to start at Price Park Campground, cross Church Road to the next section, which crosses meadows with fine views, and then return to the campground for a 5.0-mile round trip.

Skiers could also park at the Parkway construction barricade about 1.5 miles south of the campground and ski or walk 150 yards on the unopened road to a parking lot on the right, just past Cold Prong Pond.

The Tanawha Trail is accessible here in the woods just below the lot. This section, which continues on from the one described above, runs to Grandfather Mountain's Grandfather Trail Extension and is approximately 2.0 miles long. It crosses a number of bridges, including one very impressive span of Boone Fork, and has some steep grades, making it more suitable for advanced skiers. With deep snow, skiers can turn right onto the Grandfather Trail Extension and ski that route (permit required; for trail description, see the entry on winter hiking on Grandfather later in this section) up to the junction with the Cragway Trail. Here fine views of Boone Fork's headwaters bowl, Grandfather Mountain's highest peak, and Price Park are a short walk to the left on the Cragway Trail. The total round trip to Cragway is about 6.5 miles.

Winter Hiking

Price Park has two major trails whose steeper grades and rockier footing make them best suited to hiking.

BOONE FORK TRAIL

This trail makes a fine loop of about 5.0 miles near Price Park Campground, offering fine views of rugged Boone's Fork, a tumbling mountain stream.

Start at the Price Park picnic area, 0.5 mile south of milepost 296. If the area is gated, park at but not blocking the gate. If it is not gated, enter and park on the left beside the first comfort station, which is visible from the gate. The trail leaves the lot and crosses a creek, and then a branch goes left to the campground for a clockwise loop. From a high point just outside the campground, the trail descends past Bee Tree Creek to a lowpoint of 3,040 feet at the junction with the larger Boone Fork stream. Go right, upstream, staying on the right side of Boone Fork, to the picnic area, at just under 5.0 miles. Although easy in summer, this moderate hike can be strenuous in deep snow.

GREEN KNOB TRAIL

This 2.4-mile loop trail starts in the Sims Pond parking area at Parkway milepost 295.9, just north of Price Park picnic area.

The trail descends to a pond, crosses a dam, and ascends left along Sims Creek through virgin hemlock forest and under a Parkway span at 0.75 mile. A side trail reaches a Parkway pull-off at the bridge, 0.5 mile north of the Sims Pond parking area. Above the bridge, the trail continues gradually to the summit of Green Knob (3,930 feet) at 1.5 miles for dramatic views of North Carolina's high country. Dropping more steeply off the peak, the trail descends to the Parkway across from Sims Pond Overlook. This section from the summit to the pond is skiable.

Between May and October, Price Park Campground offers 133 tent and 63 trailer camping sites. There is a dump station for trailers but no electrical hookups. Each site has a picnic table and fire place. A fee is charged. There is a boat rental facility at Price Lake, and both Price Lake and Boone Fork are very popular with anglers.

Price Park information is available at the District Ranger address and phone number listed under Cone Park, covered next. During the summer, the Price Park Campground contact station can be reached at 704/295-7591.

Moses Cone Memorial Park

The Moses H. Cone Memorial Park is a 3,500-acre bulge from the Blue Ridge Parkway at Blowing Rock, N.C. Forming one of the Parkway's most beautiful parcels, these rolling uplands are an outstanding tribute to Moses H. Cone, the textile industrialist whose stewardship created the best cross-country ski area on the Blue Ridge Parkway.

After amassing a fortune as "The Denim King" in North Carolina's post-Civil War textile industry, Cone moved to the mountains at the turn of the century. With the heart of a preservationist and the mind of a forester, he built a mountaintop manor house, created lakes, and offered jobs in the new orchards and fields to original landowners still living on the property. More than 25 miles of carriage paths were lightly laid on the land.

Today, the massive white pine forests appear virgin in their size and grandeur. Under this cathedral-like canopy, cross-country skiers glide through a silent and beautiful setting, one of the sport's high points in the southeast.

Cone Park's location in Blowing Rock nets it about 40 inches of snow a year, not a lot when compared with nearby mountains like Beech, Roan, and Grandfather. Most years, Cone averages three weeks of cross-country skiing, usually from late January to mid-February. During good snow years, Cone has had anywhere from six to eight weeks of good skiing.

When deep, consistent snow prevails, the crowds flock to this park, and the carriage roads often develop three and four sets of tracks. The

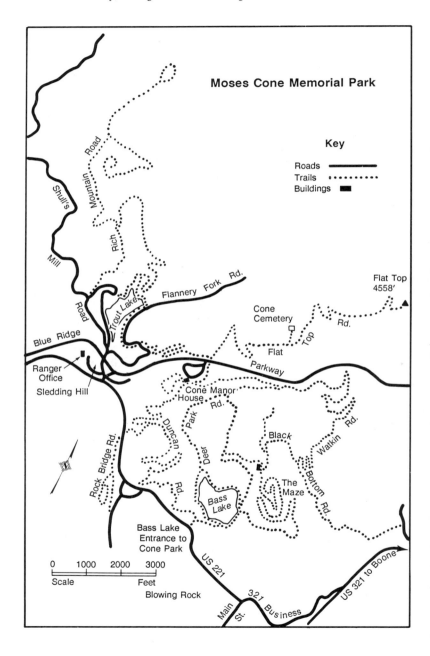

Moses Cone Memorial Park

National Park Service does little to encourage the sport: trails aren't marked for difficulty or even very well signed. The Manor House, Apple Barn, and privies are closed in winter. One realizes that were this park in New Hampshire, the heavy snowbelt of West Virginia, or just 40 miles away on top of Roan Mountain, it would surely be one of eastern America's premier cross-country destinations.

Even though more could be done to enhance the area's skiability, Cone's sheer physical suitability for Nordic skiing is unmatched in the Deep South. In the absence of a ranger-supervised weekend warming room inside the Manor House, skiers just eat lunch and enjoy the view from the veranda. Nearby lodging and dining are diverse and memorable. Ski rentals are plentiful. The entry introducing the North Carolina high country in Part 2 offers further details on services.

Primary skier access points are the Bass Lake entrance on U.S. 221, less than a mile south of Blowing Rock from the U.S. 221/Business 321 junction on Main Street. The other popular access point is the Cone Manor House and parking area at milepost 294 on the Blue Ridge Parkway.

The Parkway access point is easy to reach because this section of the road is plowed for winter use. The road is usually open from U.S. 321 between Boone and Blowing Rock (milepost 291) to the Holloway Mountain Road (milepost 298), a 1.0-mile side road to U.S. 221 south of Blowing Rock.

This section of plowed road takes in Cone Park and adjacent Julian Price Memorial Park (see the preceding entry).

Besides cross-country skiing and hiking, Cone Park offers a popular, north-facing sledding hill at the U.S. 221/Parkway junction, 0.5 mile south of the Cone Manor House on the Parkway and 2.0 miles south from the Main Street junction on U.S. 221. At the junction, follow the sign and go 100 feet to Shull's Mill Road and the ranger office. Most people park on the side of the ranger office or road and sled downhill toward the stone Parkway bridge.

Both of the access points described above allow skiers to enjoy the miles of forested trails between the Manor House and the town of Blowing Rock on the south side of the Blue Ridge Parkway. The Manor House perches on a high point overlooking the town and a deep basin containing frozen Bass Lake. Trails wander all through the forests, including the famous trail called The Maze.

Trail junctions are many, few are signed, and none offer mileages. This situation often confuses skiers, so the following descriptions recommend loop tours with carefully described junctions and turns. Experience on these loops provides a systematic introduction to trails that most skiers learn by trial and error. That error has at times involved unplanned after dark skiing. Although all the carriage path trails are very gradual, the longer tours will take more time, especially for an unskilled skier. For that reason, the longer tours are rated intermediate.

Some trails in Cone Park attract both skiers and hikers, so walkers should take care to create a hiking path along the trail side where snow is shallowest. Skiers can then break the drifts into skiable tracks.

BASS LAKE TRAIL

This is an easy loop suitable for first-time skiers. The scenic trail around Bass Lake begins at the Bass Lake entrance, just south of Blowing Rock on U.S. 221. From an iron gate, skiers gradually descend 100 yards to a T-junction with Duncan Road. A sign indicates the Manor House to the left (2.6 miles). Take the right turn and join the loop around the lake 0.2 mile from the junction. The Manor House is visible across the lake on a hill. Continuing in the same direction, skiers join the lake loop near the dam, crossing the lake's outlet on often shallow, windswept snow. Across the dam, keep left as a trail, marked "The Maze," bears right and then a second trail goes right. Continue left around the lake shore and return to where you first joined the lake loop. The loop itself is 0.95 mile, making a total round trip of just over 1.5 miles. This route is also popular with walkers.

MANOR HOUSE/MANOR HOUSE LOOP

Cone Manor House is a fine destination for a day tour. Skiers gather here on the porch for lunch and to watch hot doggers telemark the Manor's terraced front lawn. A snowy ramp beside the Manor, opposite the parking lot side of the house, offers an easy hill for beginners to practice their turns and access to an easy and interesting 0.5-mile figure-eight trail beside the house called the Craftsman's Trail. The Manor House Loop is easy terrain, but intermediate because of its length.

Starting at the Bass Lake entrance, just south of Blowing Rock on U.S. 221, turn left at the T-junction with Duncan Road at the bottom of the short descent from the parking lot. A sign here points left to the Manor House. On the 2.6-mile, gradually uphill tour to the house, two carriage paths branch left, and at each skiers go right. After a meandering stretch through huge hemlocks and rhododendron, the path passes meadows with views of the Manor House. Good skiers can practice turns here or descend the entire meadow to join the Bass Lake loop after a little bushwhack skiing. Beginners can ski just the first mile or so of this trail and return, avoiding the more crowded Bass Lake Loop.

From the Manor House, skiers descend on the path that branches right and follows a fence line gradually downhill toward Bass Lake. After 0.6 mile, skiers switchback hard to the right onto the Deer Park carriage path, avoiding the Watkin Road carriage path that goes left. Stay on the Deer Park path for the next 0.7 mile, avoiding one obscure old path that branches right. Near the bottom of this section, meadows appear on the right side of the trail and are similar to the meadows across the valley on the first stretch of Duncan Road up to the house. Again, good skiers can descend under deep-snow conditions. Just past this meadow, a carriage path enters on the left from The Maze. Continue to the right for 0.5 mile from this junction downhill through tall, stately white pines.

At the bottom the trail joins the Bass Lake loop. This junction is the second right from the Bass Lake loop after crossing the dam. Go left on the loop, passing The Maze entrance on the left, crossing the dam, and taking the first left up to the T-junction. Take a left to return to the parking area, about 0.4 mile after joining the lake loop. From the Manor back to car by this route is about 2.2 miles, mostly downhill, making the total Manor House loop 4.8 miles.

THE MAZE LOOP

The Maze twists and turns through a mixed forest of mature hardwoods and towering white pines. Most skiers on this trail are never really sure where they are until they emerge at viewpoints above Bass Lake.

The best access is at the Bass Lake entrance. Follow the directions above for the Bass Lake loop, but take the first right across the dam at the sign to The Maze. From this entrance, a carriage path loops around for 2.3 miles before reaching the Apple Barn. The carriage path that drops off to the right at the Apple Barn is Black Bottom Road. Go straight past that junction and the Apple Barn another 0.2 mile to a junction with Deer Park Road. This junction is just below where meadows border that path on the way down from the Manor House. Make a left at the junction and follow this last section of the Manor House loop to Bass Lake, across the dam, and back to the car. The total length is 3.8 miles.

BLACK BOTTOM/WATKIN ROAD LOOPS

The Maze and Manor House loops can be enlarged and connected by employing Black Bottom Road, which branches from the Apple Barn in The Maze, and Watkin Road, which branches from the sharp switchback below the Manor House on the Manor House Loop.

On The Maze loop, turn right at the Apple Barn onto Black Bottom Road and go for 0.5 mile to the junction with Watkin Road. Go left on Watkin Road for 2.3 miles to the switchback junction on the Manor House Loop, then proceed down to Bass Lake and back to the car. This turns the 3.8-mile Maze tour into a 7.1-mile trip. The same route added to the Manor House Loop turns that 4.8-mile trip into an 8.7-mile ski.

The Maze and the first section of the Manor House Loop can be avoided while still skiing the Black Bottom/Watkin Road Loop. This tour follows the first part of the Bass Lake Trail loop, takes the second right past the dam and up the lower return part of the Manor House Loop. A right on the Apple Barn connection, or a right on the Watkin Road higher up, can create a 5.5-mile loop.

Other combinations are available, especially if you avoid the popular Bass Lake entrance and use the start of Watkin Road, just off the south side of U.S. 321 between the Blue Ridge Parkway entrance and Blowing Rock, across the highway from the New River Inn, where food and lodging are available at trail side. This access is a 1.0-mile ski from the gate near U.S. 321 to the junction already described between Black Bottom and Watkin roads.

FLAT TOP ROAD

Flat Top Road and the Rich Mountain trail are located north of the Parkway and are basically out-and-back trails. Flat Top Road leaves the Parkway near the Manor House and, unlike trails on the south side of the road, climbs through open meadows to the Flat Top tower and a spectacular view of the North Carolina high country, with Grandfather Mountain as the focal point.

Park in either the Manor House parking lot or, when gated, at the entrance to the lot near the gate, but do not block the gate or Parkway. From the front of the Manor House, the trail leads to the Parkway by going left at the junction where the Manor House Loop descends the fence line to Bass Lake. Flat Top Road follows a tunnel under the Parkway (rarely skiable) and emerges in beautiful meadows at a junction.

If you park beside the Parkway, simply cross the road and descend the bank beside the tunnel to the junction. Turn right and go uphill. In 0.9 mile, Cone family graves are visible on a spur to the left, and 1.9 miles farther, the trail reaches the tower at 4,558 feet. One way is 2.8 miles; round trip is 5.6 miles.

This is an intermediate tour, due to some steeper grades and open windy areas. Snow is often drifted deep or blown shallow. Be prepared for Cone Park's severest weather.

RICH MOUNTAIN TRAIL

The trailhead is on Shull's Mill Road, best reached from the U.S. 221/Parkway junction 0.5 mile south of Cone Manor or 2.0 miles south of Blowing Rock on U.S. 221. At the junction, follow the signs to Shull's Mill Road, descend under the Parkway tunnel, and bear left to avoid unpaved Flannery Fork Road and the usually unplowed access to Trout Lake parking area, both on the right. From this low point, the road climbs less than 0.5 mile through snowy curves to a crest where a white fence and a pull-off on the right mark the start of the trail.

The trail climbs to Rich Mountain, locally called Nowhere Mountain, and good views at 4,370 feet. After the start, the trail reaches a junction at 0.6 mile. Go left 0.8 mile to a junction with an obscure road left. Go right 1.2 miles, and the trail reaches the summit after a spiraling ascent. The total one-way distance to the top is 2.6 miles, 5.4 miles round trip. On the way down, experts can cut out the long descent by dropping off the meadow to the southeast of the peak.

TROUT LAKE

A longer climb to Rich Mountain or a short lake-side tour can be made by starting at Trout Lake. Approach the trailhead by taking Shull's Mill Road, then turning right just past the Parkway bridge onto unpaved but plowed Flannery Fork Road. Park at the trailhead, on the left about 0.5 mile from the start of the unpaved road.

The trail crosses a dam and goes 0.3 mile to a junction. To the left, the trail continues around the lake to Trout Lake parking lot below the start of the Rich Mountain Trail. Going right, the trail climbs 1.4 miles to a gate, then another 0.3 mile to a junction with the Rich Mountain Trail. Go right to the Rich Mountain summit, or left back to Shull's Mill Road on the Rich Mountain trail. At that trailhead, you can descend into the rarely plowed Trout Lake parking lot to the lake-side path already mentioned that joins Trout Lake Trail at the first junction. From there it is 0.3 mile to the right back to the car.

Beginners can simply ski the lake-side trail out and back, or they can create a loop using the unplowed Trout Lake parking lot road, and then another link along the lake that starts within sight of the Parkway bridge and parallels Flannery Fork Road. This loop around Trout Lake is just over 1.0 mile.

Between May and October, Cone Manor is an impressive crafts center, visitor center, and gift shop with demonstrations by crafters scheduled daily. The seasonal visitor center phone number is 704/295-3782. Bass and Trout lakes are among the most popular fishing sites in the high-country area. Fishing licenses and information are available at Blowing Rock Hardware, at the junction of Business 321 and U.S. 221, a mile north of Bass Lake entrance.

For more information, contact

District Ranger, PO Box 565, Blowing Rock, NC 28605. Or call the Ranger Office, 704/295-7591, 8:00 to 5:00 weekdays.

For Cone Park cross-country ski reports, call the North Carolina High Country Host organization, 800/222-7515 from inside North Carolina or 800/438-7500 from elsewhere in the eastern U.S. The multicounty organization's Regional Visitor Information Center in Boone is an excellent stop for the latest details on area resources.

Linville Area

Nordic skiing opportunities near Linville, N.C., include a Parkway self-guiding nature trail, a stretch of Parkway across the newly completed Linn Cove Viaduct, and a short loop trail in town.

Cross-Country Trails

LENOIR PARK

This 0.8-mile beginner trail circles a virgin-hemlock-covered knob between the junction of U.S. 221 and N.C. 105 in the center of Linville. Turn east on U.S. 221, directed by a prominent sign to Grandfather Mountain. In 0.15 mile, turn left onto SR 1509, then go immediately left to the trailhead parking barriers. The loop goes right, passing quickly into virgin forest on its way around the knob. Views include possibly frozen Linville River on the right, then N.C. 105 through some trees. As the trail passes the road junction, it descends and returns to the car through less mature forest.

FLATROCK NATURE TRAIL

Turn onto SR 1511 in Linville; it is the only state road to the left driving south the from U.S. 221/N.C. 105/N.C. 181 intersection in town. The road leads five minutes up through scenic forest to a Parkway junction just north of milepost 308. Turn right and drive south on the Parkway 0.2 mile to the Flatrock parking lot on the right. If the Parkway is impassable, park and ski along the edge of the road to the lot.

Flatrock is a 1.0-mile loop trail that with fresh snow can be skied by beginners. Leave the lot, go left at the first junction, and ascend through mature forest with trail-side interpretive signs. Upon leaving the trees, turn right, going north, across open ledge with wind stunted trees and impressive views. The snow in this area is often compacted and drifted by wind. Rock cairns have devices for sighting distant peaks like Mount Mitchell, Roan, Hump, and very close, Grandfather. Leave the ledge at device for a nice downhill run to the loop-ending junction. Go left back to the car. The total distance from SR 1511 is 1.5 miles.

PARKWAY SKI TO VIADUCT

North from U.S. 221, the last link of the Blue Ridge Parkway is scheduled to open in late 1987 across the flank of Grandfather Mountain. At one point, the new road leaps away from the mountain and soars over huge boulders with views of peaks 2,000 feet above and the piedmont 3,000 feet below. The structure that accomplishes the preservation of this rocky area is the Linn Cove Viaduct, called the most complex highway construction project in the world. The viaduct is an easy and spectacular ski trip, especially in fresh, soft snow. When wind and sun make the snow icy at this site, the trip can be rated intermediate.

Taking U.S. 221 from the junction in Linville, pass the entrance to Grandfather Mountain and enter the Parkway to the left at 3.1 miles. Just inside the Parkway entrance, go north, left, through an open barricade on the new road. Continue 0.5 mile to a parking lot and locked barricade blocking northward travel. Ski beyond the gate and proceed to the viaduct. The shortest round trip is about 1.0 mile. If the Parkway entrance is impassable or if the first barricade, near 221, is closed due to heavy snow, park at the U.S. 221/Parkway junction and ski from there. That round trip is about 2.0 miles. After the new section of the Parkway opens, the description of this tour may change, depending on where the road is gated or whether it is plowed.

Winter Hiking

Of the two ski tours described, hikers can enjoy the Flatrock Nature Trail, but the Linn Cove Viaduct would be more enjoyable and is better able to accommodate both skiers and hikers.

BEACON HEIGHTS TRAIL

The Beacon Heights Trail is a satisfying and spectacular short hike with very good winter access. Families can enjoy this approximately half-mile hike.

The Beacon Heights parking lot is reached from Linville on U.S. 221. Go past Grandfather Mountain and enter the Parkway 3.1 miles from Linville, as you would to go to the Viaduct, but turn right at the barricade and go south. The parking lot is 0.3 mile from the entrance. If the Parkway is impassable, go past the Parkway entrance, under the bridge, and turn right at 3.25 miles from Linville on SR 1513. Go 0.1 mile to the Parkway Beacon Heights parking lot, on your right. The trail enters the woods on the left side of the road. If SR 1513 is unplowed, ski that road.

Entering the woods, the trail passes a junction with the Tanawha Trail, then climbs gradually in switchbacks to a bench at a junction. To the right, the trail exits on a dome with views of Grandmother Mountain and, to the south, to Mount Mitchell. To the left, the trail emerges on a rocky outcrop with spectacular views of Grandfather Mountain and its vertical-mile rise above the piedmont.

Linville Falls

Linville Falls is one of the most visited waterfalls in North Carolina. A developed Blue Ridge Parkway recreation area surrounds the head of the falls, and a U.S. Forest Service National Wilderness Area protects the Linville Gorge below.

The area was named for a father and son killed by Indians in the gorge in 1766. The unusual ruggedness of the canyon and falls area kept the lumber companies out until preservationist sentiment gained the upper hand. John D. Rockefeller donated the falls to the National Park Service, and today, skiers and hikers see this chasm much as it was centuries ago. Huge rhododendron flourish under towering evergreens. Virgin forest canopies the National Recreation Trails that reach viewpoints over the falls and primeval Linville Gorge.

With adequate snow cover, the Linville Falls area is a good base for a few days of ski touring. The town of Linville Falls offers a restaurant and accommodations at the Linville Falls Motel and Cottages. In winter, the Parkway's Linville Falls Campground offers sixty-nine campsites at no charge with privies and pump water. Besides the trails described here, skiing opportunities nearby include the Parkway at Little Switzerland, Grandfather Mountain, and the Parkway Flatrock Nature Trail in Linville, as well as other high-country sites.

The closest cross-country ski rentals are at North Cove Ski Rentals, ten minutes from Linville Falls on U.S. 221 toward Marion, N.C., and at High Country Ski Shop, near Linville Falls on U.S. 221 in Pineola. The latter offers a complete retail ski shop, with rentals, and guided cross-country tours and lessons by instructors affiliated with the Professional Ski Instructors of America. As for many Parkway sites, a snow report is available seven days a week from the Blue Ridge Parkway dispatcher in Asheville (704/259-0701; call during the day).

Cross-country ski trails and hiking trails at the falls are usually approached on a 1.4-mile spur road that leaves the Parkway between mileposts 316 and 317. In winter snow conditions, the easiest access will be from U.S. 221 in the town of Linville Falls. From this junction, the Parkway is often cleared 1.0 mile north to the spur road, the campground and the trail parking lot.

When the Parkway is heavily snowed in, the best access to the falls hiking and ski trails using a plowed public highway is the National Forest trailhead on SR 1238, 0.7 mile from the town of Linville Falls on N.C. 183. Although the state road is among the last to be plowed, the trail parking is only 0.1 mile away from plowed N.C. 183. Skiers can park on N.C. 183 where the sign directs National Forest visitors to Wiseman's View and can then ski or hike the short distance to the trail. This trail leaves Forest Service land 0.5 mile from the Forest Service trailhead and ties into the Parkway trail network around the falls.

Cross-Country Trails

PICNIC AREA

Leaving U.S. 221 and going north on the Parkway, a Parkway picnic area is 1.0 mile north. The long picnic loops pass through a forest of tall trees and offer fine views of the Linville River. Drive to this ski site, since rangers request that skiing take place on the Parkway only behind locked gates. If you park at the picnic area and thoroughly explore it, this is an easiest tour of about 1.5 miles.

FALLS TRAILS

Driving past the picnic area, turn right in 0.1 mile on the Linville Falls Spur Road and drive to the falls parking area. A sign board at the visitor center shows the trails. The open-sided center provides a heated unisex restroom and seating under a roof that shelters visitors from falling snow or rain.

Skiers will want to explore the trails across the Linville River from the visitor center. Trails on the same side as the visitor center are steep and better suited for hiking.

Crossing the Linville River on the trail to Erwin View, the path is road width and climbs in 0.15 mile to a crest and a fine north-facing meadow on the right for downhill practice. The trail then dips, crosses a stream bridge amidst huge timber, and at 0.3 mile a trail branches right to the National Forest parking area, 0.5 mile away on SR 1238. The main trail reaches a junction at 0.4 mile. Closed restrooms are on the right. To the left, a view of the Upper Falls is 500 feet away. Advanced skiers can ski down part of this trail.

Through the junction, the trail climbs, becomes steeper, and turns through a forest of massive, ancient trees. After a short descent of 0.6 mile, the trail reaches an open-sided, roofed shelter and a trail (not skiable) that descends left 100 feet to fine views of the main falls and gorge at Chimney View. Use extreme caution on the often steep steps that descend to these views.

To the right at this junction, the trail is skiable by intermediates to a bench beside the trail. Above this, the last 0.1 mile to Erwin's View and Gorge View is steeply uphill, eroded, and skiable only by experts and with deep snow. Even if you walk to these views, they are worth the effort. From the open shelter near Chimney View, skiers will need intermediate turning ability for the ski back down through the turns to the closed restrooms and junction. Experts will delight in the open areas under the huge trees.

If the Parkway is impassable, skiers and hikers will want to start near N.C. 183 at the U.S. Forest Service trailhead. From that trailhead, the first 0.1 mile is steeply downhill and the last 0.4 to the junction is easy.

PARKWAY SKI TO CHESTOA VIEW

At the Parkway entrance from U.S. 221 in Linville Falls, the Parkway is gated to the south. When snow conditions permit, this is a good tour to Chestoa View, about 3.3 miles south. The Parkway climbs, at times steeply, and reaches a left turn into the Chestoa parking lot between mileposts 320 and 321. The view is reached on a loop trail a little less than a mile long. The last section to the view is a group of steep steps. The panorama encompasses the piedmont, the deep cleft of North Cove, and the Linville Gorge. The total round trip—for intermediates—is about 8 miles. Beginners can start the tour and turn around when they tire. The return involves long downhill glides.

Winter Hikes

Start from the Linville Falls parking area on the Blue Ridge Parkway spur road (see the opening discussion of cross-country trails at Linville Falls for directions). Walk through the visitor center and go left to steeper, rugged trails. Easier trails, well-suited for cross-country skiing, are to right, across the Linville River. Hikers using these easy road-width trails should keep to one side so cross-country skiers can also enjoy the snow. When snow makes the Parkway inaccessible, the rugged Linville Falls hiking trails described below can be reached from a U.S. Forest Service parking lot near the junction of N.C. 183 and SR 1238. This route requires walking on the trails described for cross-country skiing. See that section for directions and trail descriptions.

Going left at the visitor center, a hiking trail leads up to a junction at 0.4 mile. To the right, the trail descends to a dramatic view of the falls at 0.5 mile. To the left at the junction, the trail drops to the bank of the Linville River at the head of Linville Gorge, 0.9 mile from the parking lot. Both hikes return on the same trail. Use caution on the steep steps, especially if they're icy.

Trails in the nearby Linville Gorge are also very popular. (Overnight camping permits are required for weekends and holidays from May to October; write to the District Ranger at the address below.) A favorite gorge view is from Wiseman's View, 4.0 miles on a dirt road beyond the U.S. Forest Service trailhead on SR 1238 for the trail to Linville Falls. Linville Caverns, the only commercial caverns in the state, are five minutes down U.S. 221 toward Marion.

For more information, contact

District Ranger, U.S. Forest Service, East Court Street, PO Box 519, Marion, NC 28752. 704/652-4841.

Shining Rock Wilderness

Although difficult to reach in winter snow, North Carolina's Shining Rock Wilderness is one of the South's most scenic highland areas and a fine destination for Nordic skiers and winter mountaineers.

The federally designated Wilderness Area is 13,600 acres. That acreage and Pisgah National Forest land between the wilderness and the Parkway make up an alpinelike zone of high open meadows and rocky pinnacles. In 1925, a 25,000-acre fire engulfed the logging camps then actively taking the virgin timber from these heights. Today's hikers traverse some of the treeless landscape that resulted. Because of the variety of trails and open terrain, visitors should purchase and carry the USFS Shining Rock trail map (see the end of this entry).

The most popular access to Shining Rock is the Art Loeb Trail, reached on a spur road from the Blue Ridge Parkway. The Loeb Trail is a 28-mile route from the Davidson River near Brevard; the last 7 miles traverse the crest of the Wilderness Area, taking hikers across the meadows of Black Balsam Knob and Tennent Mountain, crests reminiscent of the Scottish Highlands. Evergreen summits and gaps appear near the area's namesake, Shining Rock Mountain, a 6,000-foot peak capped by a solid outcrop of white quartz. The ridge then narrows and runs to Cold Mountain, a conical summit and the area's highest at 6,030 feet. Views reach to the Smokies and Mount Mitchell.

This lofty area, particularly the Art Loeb Trail corridor, is at times crowded in summer. Warm weather backpackers should come during the week and be prepared to spend time finding little used campsites away from gathering spots like Shining Rock Gap. No wilderness permit is required.

In winter, when the snowy Parkway is closed, mountaineers, backpackers, and day hikers find valley trailheads to be the most attractive because of shallower snow. Numerous trails climb to the summits from the west at SR 1129 and N.C. 215, and the east at U.S. 276.

Winter skiing access on the Parkway in heavy snow is popular. When conditions are right, Shining Rock is one of the region's best spots for mountaineering and backpacking on skis. With no snow, winter users can reach the Art Loeb Trailhead from the Parkway at milepost 420.2 on Forest Service Road (FSR) 816.

Cross-Country Skiing on the Parkway

In deep snow, cross-country skiers can most easily enjoy the Shining Rock area on the Parkway, starting at Beech Gap, milepost 423.2, elevation 5,340. This high gap is on N.C. 215, 17 miles north of Rosman and 18 miles south of U.S. 276 near Woodrow. This is a popular Parkway skiing site and is the home base for the Shining Rock unit of the National Nordic Ski Patrol.

South, the Parkway climbs toward Richland Balsam, the road's highpoint. North, the Parkway gradually gains elevation toward Shining Rock and in 0.8 mile reaches Devil's Courthouse Overlook, a view of a rocky outcrop, where an easy 0.8-mile trail to the rocky crag starts. At 1.1 miles from Beech Gap parking, skiers most often will walk through the 650 feet of Devil's Courthouse Tunnel. FSR 816 is reached 1.9 miles later at Balsam Spring Gap (5,550 feet) 3.0 miles from the car. Views on this section of Parkway are spectacular, and beginning skiers can turn around here or anywhere before this point.

GRAVEYARD FIELDS LOOP TRAIL

This trail starts at a parking area 1.4 miles farther north on the Parkway past FSR 816. Here, after examining the trail sign, skiers walk down a short steep stretch to Graveyard Fields Loop Trail. Skiers should go left, cross a stream to a junction at 0.9 mile, and continue to the right along the opposite bank to a connection on the right with a steeper trail back to the parking lot at 1.5 miles. Returning the way you skied in, this can be a 3.0-mile out-and-back trip through open areas with alpine views. Other trails, some unskiable, branch off to rewarding waterfall views.

In reaching Graveyard Fields, skiers from N.C. 215 should realize that the Parkway loses 400 feet of elevation from FSR 816 to the trailhead. A day tour to and including the fields will thus be at least 12 miles round trip with an uphill return. Exploring Graveyard Fields or entering Shining Rock Wilderness Area will be one-day excursions only for very strong skiers. For that reason and because camping is allowed on U.S. Forest Service land just outside the Parkway's no-camping zone, ski backpackers will find more ski options than day skiers. In fact, the 3.0- to 4.5-mile ski tour to Pisgah National Forest land beside FSR 816 makes this location very attractive for skiers who want to base camp and explore.

Cross-Country Skiing on USFS Land and in Shining Rock

Having skied 3.0 miles and reached FSR 816 at Balsam Spring Gap, day skiers may wish to ski into the National Forest on the 1.5-mile FSR 816. Ski backpackers taking this route can either venture into the Wilderness Area or base camp.

The road climbs in 1.0 mile to a parking area at the Art Loeb Trail crossing. To the right, the Loeb Trail follows the ridge to Ivestor Gap and the Wilderness boundary in 2.0 miles of intermediate to expert skiing or moderate hiking over windy meadows. Continuing on FSR 816, a final parking area is reached at 1.5 miles where a 0.5-mile connector to the Loeb Trail goes right and the Flat Laurel Creek horse trail goes left 3.7 miles to N.C. 215. The Ivestor Gap Trail continues straight on a contour below the ridge and the Loeb Trail.

IVESTOR GAP TRAIL

This old logging-grade trail has two sections, both very skiable. From the last parking lot on FSR 816, the trail slabs the northwest side of the ridge. In 1.6 miles the Fork Mountain Trail comes in from the left. The Ivestor Gap Trail continues 0.5 mile to Ivestor Gap and a junction with the Loeb Trail and the Greasy Cove Trail from U.S. 276 via the Big East Fork Trail. (The Loeb Trail again takes the high route over the next section of balds to a junction at 1.7 miles with the Ivestor Gap Trail at Shining Rock Gap.) The Gap Trail continues hard left 1.6 miles to a junction on the left with the Little East Fork Trail from the Scout Camp near Sunburst, N.C. The Ivestor Gap Trail continues 0.5 mile and ends at Shining Rock Gap, the heart of the Wilderness Area, 4.1 miles from FSR 816.

ART LOEB TRAIL

This trail is skiable for expert, although deep snow and some walking will be required. From FSR 816 to Ivestor Gap and on to Shining Rock

Gap is a combined one-way 4.0-mile ski or hike. Beyond the Shining Rock Gap junction (with the Old Butt Knob Trail and Shining Creek Trail from U.S. 276, and the Ivestor Gap Trail), the Loeb Trail runs a ridge with moderate grades and some steeper sections to Deep Gap (5,200 feet) at 2.6 miles, 6.6 miles from FSR 816.

The next 1.4 miles to Cold Mountain on the Loeb Trail have some steep spots. To the left at Deep Gap, a branch trail descends in 4.2 miles to the Scouts' Daniel Boone Camp at 3,300 feet. This trail starts at parking area SR 1129, 3.8 miles from N.C. 215. Although relatively gradual, the descent to the camp on SR 1129 quickly leaves the deep snow zone.

Overall, the skiability of the Loeb Trail depends on deep snow and your expertise. The open balds, when not blown free of snow, may be the best Loeb Trail skiing. Skiers can expect to see hikers on this trail along its entire length.

FORK MOUNTAIN TRAIL

From its junction with the Ivestor Gap Trail, 1.6 miles from FSR 816, the Fork Mountain Trail goes left and is gradual and skiable to the vicinity of Birdstand Mountain. Skiers may make this a day tour or camp on the trail away from the more popular Ivestor Gap.

Winter Hiking in Shining Rock Wilderness

For most day hikers, backpackers, and mountaineers who want to sample the views and weather of the Shining Rock summits, the Art Loeb Trail will be a favored destination. When Parkway access is closed by deep snow, walkers will want to gain the ridge from lower, more easily reached trailheads on SR 1129 or U.S. 276.

From the west side of Shining Rock Wilderness, the Art Loeb Trail/Deep Gap Trail climbs to Deep Gap from SR 1129 at the Scout camp (see the preceding description of the Art Loeb Trail).

LITTLE EAST FORK TRAIL

From the same trail parking at the Daniel Boone Scout Camp, cross to the right side of the river on an old road and ascend the drainage. Much of this trail climbs an old railroad grade, and it reaches the Ivestor Gap Trail in approximately 6.5 miles.

From the east side of Shining Rock Wilderness, four trails climb the 2,400 feet to the summits from Big East Fork parking area on U.S. 276

about 19 miles from Waynesville and 3 miles from the Blue Ridge Parkway. Linking these three trails with summit sections of the Art Loeb Trail can create a number of circuit loops.

BIG EAST FORK TRAIL/GREASY COVE TRAIL

From Big East Fork parking area, the trail climbs gradually along the Pigeon River to a junction at 3.4 miles. From there, the Greasy Cove Trail ascends steeply in another 3.5 miles to the Art Loeb Trail at Ivestor Gap.

SHINING CREEK TRAIL

From the Big East Fork parking area, follow the combined Shining Creek Trail/Old Butt Knob Trail for 0.7 mile; then go left at the junction for a steep 3.4-mile climb along Shining Creek to the Loeb Trail at Shining Rock Gap and a junction with the Old Butt Knob Trail, 4.1 miles from the parking area. The Shining Creek Trail is direct to Shining Rock Gap with minimum distance and elevation gain.

OLD BUTT KNOB TRAIL

Again, follow the combined trail from the Big East Fork parking area 0.7 mile to a right turn where Old Butt Knob Trail separates for a very steep 3.6-mile climb over Old Butt and Dog Loser knobs and Shining Rock. The trail descends to Shining Rock Gap at 4.3 miles.

For information, contact

District Ranger, Pisgah National Forest, Box 8, Pisgah Forest, N.C. 28768. 704/877-3265.

To receive a Wilderness Area hiking map, request the Shining Rock map from the U.S. Forest Service, PO Box 2750, Asheville, NC 28802. 704/253-2352. Send a $1 check payable to U.S. Forest Service.

Soco Gap

This is a favorite Parkway touring site near the Smokies and the Cataloochee Ski Area at Maggie Valley.

At 4,340 feet, Soco provides a lofty access point and gradual up-and-down skiing toward Cherokee for beginners. Better skiers may want to ski toward Asheville on the more consistent rise to Waterrock Knob overlook, a panoramic Parkway pull-off at 5,718 feet. The Waterrock Knob overlook is 4.5 miles from Soco Gap. The overlook offers a spectacular all-encompassing view of the major Southern Appalachian mountain ranges. From here, the Smokies are a massive wall to the west. Round trip is about 9 miles.

For expert skiers, or skiers who'd like a short hike, the Waterrock Knob Trail leaves the east side of the parking overlook and climbs in 0.5 mile to the summit (6,292 feet).

Soco Gap is located between Parkway mileposts 455 and 456, where U.S. 19 crosses the range, 12 miles north of Cherokee, 8 miles south of Dellwood, and 4 miles south of Maggie Valley. Park Service privies are located at the gap. Skiers should bring their own skis or rent at Mountaineering South or Black Dome Mountain Shop in Asheville. The nearby Cataloochee Ski Area has summer horseback and hiking trails that are popular with Nordic skiers. See the Cataloochee entry in Part 2 for the closest accommodations and services.

Craggy Gardens

For high-mountain scenery, Craggy Gardens is unmatched among Parkway ski tours. This Parkway recreation area lies between mileposts 364 and 367.

Elevation is the key. Craggy Gardens is the next Parkway recreation area south of the turn-off to Mount Mitchell State Park, between Parkway mileposts 355 and 356. Unlike Soco Gap near Maggie Valley where skiers start at a low-elevation highway crossing, skiers bound for the Great Craggy Mountains must enter the Parkway at N.C. 80 and drive 11 miles on the Parkway to a gate at milepost 355, where N.C. 128 leaves the Parkway and the Parkway climbs to Mount Mitchell State Park.

Access to the Craggies is only possible when the Parkway is plowed and open up to and into the state park. Plowing is done by the state park more to help its employees commute than for public use, so before the road is open, the weather will generally have moderated. Luckily, snowfall at these elevations is usually deep enough to keep skiing good for long periods.

The distance from the gate to Craggy Gardens Visitor Center is about 9.0 miles. Although some sections are consistent uphill grades, other areas are gradual and even level. The lower section of this tour is on the sunny, more sheltered side of the mountain. Scenery is very like that in the West as you pass under the spruce- and heath-covered cliff faces of the Black Mountain Range, with views into the Asheville watershed. From 5,100 feet at the gate, the road ascends to 5,677 feet, the Parkway's high point north of Asheville, and then descends again to just over 5,000 feet. Although this would surely be a good overnight ski mountaineering trip, the Parkway doesn't permit overnight camping.

Higher up, the road crosses to the northwest side of the ridge where snow accumulates in huge drifts. The ridge line narrows and vegetation declines, making the experience very alpine. Up in this zone, the Great Craggies rise in barren whalebacks to Craggy Dome (6,085 feet) and Craggy Pinnacle (5,892 feet). Just past milepost 364, the Craggy Dome parking overlook, at 5,640 feet, is the start of a trail less than 0.5 mile to views at the crest. The grassy lanes between the rhododendron shrubs at this site give the area a gardenlike appearance. Craggy Gardens is a popular late-June place to see the spectacular rhododendron bloom. Past this overlook, the road descends in 0.5 mile to Craggy Gardens Visitor Center, milepost 364.4, passing on the way through Craggy Pinnacle Tunnel, 176 feet long. Park Service privies are located at the visitor center.

This tour is a very long, 18.0-mile round trip, but most of the return is downhill. Even beginning skiers can start this trip, enjoy spectacular scenery, and turn around when energy wanes.

The closest rental skis are available in the high-country area and Asheville. Nearby accommodations and dining include the Pinebridge Center in Spruce Pine. The Parkway access at N.C. 80 is 8 miles from U.S. 70, between Marion and Old Fort, and 9 miles from Micaville and U.S. 19E, between Burnsville and Spruce Pine.

The Pink Beds: Named for its Mountain Flowers

One of southeastern North Carolina's best cross-country ski sites is located near Brevard in the Pisgah National Forest recreation site called Pink Beds. The name derives from the understory of mountain laurel, azalea, and rhododendron. A picnic area marks the site on U.S. 276, 4 miles south of the Blue Ridge Parkway, 10 miles north of the Pisgah District Ranger Station, and 2 miles from Brevard.

Skiers bound for the Blue Ridge Parkway at Shining Rock Wilderness will pass Pink Beds. With enough snow, the more accessible Pink Beds, at 3,300 feet, is an alternative to the higher-elevation Parkway.

At the northern end of the picnic area, a sign marks the start of the 5.0-mile Pink Beds Loop Trail. Leaving the lot, the trail crosses a stream and divides. Take the left fork through meadows and open forest to avoid stream crossings on the right fork. At the loop's midpoint, a side trail leads left to FSR 476, which is likely to be inaccessible in snow. Go right around the loop to the first stream crossing and the car to avoid streams, or, return for a 5.0-mile out-and-back tour. The trail is marked by a heel and sole hiking boot symbol. Many other logging grades intersect in the area, offering other options.

The nearby Davidson River Campground, just north of the ranger station, is closed in winter, and its loops offer flat touring.

For contact information, see page 347.

Roan Mountain: Southernmost Nordic Nirvana

Roan Mountain is one of the South's finest destinations for cross-country skiers.

Located on the state line, Roan is reached by North Carolina and Tennessee state highways that climb to Carver's Gap, a 5,600-foot notch between the bulk of "the Roan" and the 12-mile ridge composed of Grassy Bald, Yellow, and Hump mountains to the north (see the earlier entry on the Southern Balds section of the Appalachian Trail).

From Carver's Gap, a paved N.C. state highway and a gravel U.S. Forest Service Road (FSR) climb gradually to the more-than-6,000-foot crest of the mountain. Across this plateau covered by evergreen forest and meadows, these roads form a nearly level series of loops and parking lots. In late June, motorists crowd the summit roads and trails during the bloom of the mountain's natural rhododendron gardens, claimed to be the largest in the world. Native American legend has it that the Catawba Indians challenged all the tribes of the earth to a great battle to prove their invincibility. The Catawbas indeed won, and the red bloom of the rhododendron honors the blood of their slain warriors.

Early explorer Asa Gray called Roan, the "most beautiful mountain east of the Rockies." Rhododendron is only one part of that appeal. Interspersed among the mountain's dense, Canadian-like evergreen forests are natural meadows called balds. These sedge-grass-covered, high-altitude fields are unexplained by science.

One of the southern mountains' first resort hotels, Cloudland, stood atop Roan Mountain from 1885 to 1915, when it burned. Stage coaches climbed a "hackline road" to the 166-room, white-frame building.

Roan's gentle summit region of meadows and boreal forests is a rare southern island of spectacular northern scenery. Views encompass a virtual "Who's Who" of the Southern Appalachians. The scene reaches from neighboring bald, almost alpine ridges to the East's highest peaks. Meadows and two observation platforms offer views of the 4,000-foot drop into pastoral valleys.

The dramatic elevation change and the fact that Roan is the first major peak storms confront on their sweep from the west over the Tennessee flatlands creates an unusual snow-producing effect. (More insight into Roan's weather patterns is available in Chapter 1.)

Carver's Gap is the trailhead for cross-country skiers. When snow is deep enough to make driving up the summit road unsafe, the U.S. Forest Service gate is closed just above the gap. On snowy winter weekends, cars often line the summit road below the gate and the highways on both sides of the gap and fill the small adjacent parking lot, which has picnic tables, two privies, and an often snow-covered spring.

Weekdays offer solitude. Weekends usually do not. Although not prohibitively crowded on weekends, Roan is among the deep South's best Nordic sites so expect to see other people enjoying the sport. If you like people, the lively and exciting atmosphere can itself be enjoyable.

Although high and harsh in climate, Roan is popular with beginners because of its facilities, the usual presence of other skiers and instructors, and the regular presence of the high-country unit of the National Nordic Ski Patrol. Although Roan's biggest storms routinely stymie the snowplows, the state of Tennessee keeps the road to Carver's Gap well maintained. Roan Mountain State Park is the reason.

Located at the bottom of the long grade up to Roan from Tennessee, the state park offers a complete cross-country skiing center with over 100 sets of rental skis and retail offerings. Guided ski tours and lessons are available from the Center's Professional Ski Instructor of America-affiliated ski school, High South Nordic Guides. Located at 2,900 feet, the ski center and its adjoining state park trails are skiable an average of one month a winter. When they are snow-covered, ski lessons are offered at the park. The ski center may soon offer machine-made snow on a trail and teaching area at the park with machine-set tracks.

Another cross-country retail and rental shop, High-Country Nordic, is located in the town of Roan Mountain, a half mile after the turn onto Tenn. 143 from U.S. 19E, the most popular access to the mountain.

The park also has a 50-unit developed campground, with three heated bath houses open during the summer. In winter, the campground is open for self-contained campers only. However, a tent campground is also open in winter. Also available, and very popular, are twenty modern, inexpensive, fireplace-equipped cabins that each sleep six.

Additional accommodations, ski rental and retail shops, entertainment, and other services are available in the nearby high-country resort area. See the descriptions of the high-country and its resorts in Part 2.

Cross-Country Trails

THE SUMMIT ROAD

Starting behind the gate at Carver's Gap, the Roan summit road creates a 2.3-mile, gradually graded to level beginner ski trail that reaches up to and across the high plateau of the mountain. Three major parking lots and a loop at the end of the road provide skiing for novices amid the open meadows and evergreen forests. The road climbs gradually, passing a gated fire road on the left—the Old Balsam Road—at 0.85 mile, and a small Appalachian Trail parking area on the right, at 1.25 miles. On the left of this parking area, a picnic table sits in a sunny meadow with a spectacular view of Mount Mitchell.

Continuing up, often along a huge drift, the road levels out and skiers reach an open area, at 1.45 miles from the Carver's Gap gate with a meadow on the left, where the road is often blown almost bare of snow.

Just past this point, the road goes between evergreens, drifts deeply again, and swings to the right of a Forest Service gate, at 1.5 miles, into parking lot 1 (a 0.25-mile loop with an information board and a great view into Tennessee). Just as the road enters parking lot 1, the signed Cloudland Trail branches left at a stone water fountain (inoperative in winter). From this point on, major Cloudland Trail junctions with the summit road have been signed.

From the parking lot, the road continues uphill past the gate, cresting 1.8 miles from Carver's gap, where the Cloudland Trail emerges from the evergreens to the right of the road only a short distance from its start at parking lot 1. To the left is parking lot 2 and a small cabin used as a summer visitor contact station. The Rhododendron Gardens Trail begins to the right of the cabin. From this point, the road undulates across the mountain's crest with frequent connections to the Cloudland Trail. The first occurs just as parking lot 2 ends on the left, where the Cloudland Trail, which has followed the right edge of the parking lot in the trees, is accessible on the right at a "no vehicles" sign.

The road continues slightly downhill, and at 1.9 miles from Carver's Gap passes an entrance to parking lot 3 on the right. Continuing straight, the road branches at 1.95 miles left and right into its end loop. Going right, a second entrance to parking lot 3, and a Cloudland Trail crossing of the road is encountered at 2.0 miles. To the right, the Cloudland Trail parallels the north side of parking lot 3 back toward parking lots 1 and 2, and to the left, the trail bisects the end loop of the summit road.

Following the summit road to the right past the crossing of the Cloudland Trail, the road swings to the end of the loop at 2.3 miles. At this point, the Cloudland Trail again crosses the road from left to right, after bisecting the forest within the loop. (Caution: the trail runout onto the road is often blown clear of snow.) To the right, the Roan High Bluff Trail continues away from the end point of the summit road. Continuing past this trail junction, the summit road rounds its end and rejoins its loop junction with fine views of Mount Mitchell. Round trip from Carver's Gap is 6.6 miles.

Beginners should be aware that even the gradual lower part of the road can be a fast ride if the snow is particularly icy. The most unsure beginning skiers should descend the lower road only under good snow conditions. If it's too icy, ski on the drifted uphill side of the road, step turning uphill on the drift to stop or control your speed. Some skiers walk down, but to preserve the road's snowcover, do so where others have walked.

When snowfall is light, the Carver's Gap gate is often open and vehicles can drive the snowy road to parking lot 1. From there, the road is gated and beginners can start on the higher, more level summit road. Even when this lower road isn't gated, some skiers park at Carver's Gap and ski the roadsides to avoid the snowy drive. If you do this, watch for vehicles and keep an eye on children. To avoid the road when it's open to vehicles, imtermediate skiers should turn right at the lowest gate and ski up the Appalachian Trail (AT).

APPALACHIAN TRAIL

On Roan, the white-blazed AT is in two sections: one skiable, the other not. The popular skiable section has uphill and downhill stretches either way it is skied. Starting at Carver's Gap, below the gate, the first, hiking section of the trail is narrow, rocky, unskiable, and almost invisible in winter. Skiers should start behind the Forest Service gate, 0.25 mile above the Tenn. 143/summit road junction in Carver's Gap. A gradually ascending road grade—formerly the old stagecoach road to the summit hotel, Cloudland—leaves the summit road to the right just above the gate. In a few hundred yards, this becomes the AT when joined by the hiking trail on the right.

From this junction, the trail climbs in long switchbacks on the north side of the mountain through beautiful, dense forests of Fraser fir and red spruce. The snow stays on the AT longer than anywhere else on Roan, principally because the old road grade drifts in waves of snow, often 4 feet deep and more. At the last switchback, the trail straightens out and crests a height of land, about 1.25 miles from the summit road.

At the crest, an unskiable, blue-blazed side trail leads left 150 yards up to an enclosed log cabin, with a loft and porch, that comfortably accommodates twelve people. This is a fine overnight destination and is available on a first-come, first-served basis. The spring is downhill behind the cabin but is difficult to find in heavy snow. Melt snow for water.

Past the cabin trail junction, the AT descends 0.5 mile and intersects a small AT parking lot on the summit road directly across the road from a picnic table in a meadow with a spectacular view. Via the summit road, this lot is 1.25 miles above the gate where the AT access starts on the right.

Overnight ski backpackers will find the cabin most easily reached via the summit road to the AT parking lot and then up the shorter AT stretch to the cabin trail on the height of land.

Going up the AT switchbacks from Carver's Gap, the downhill sections have gradual turns and the trail can be taken by competent beginners. From the AT parking lot on the summit road, up the shorter stretch to the height of land, and then down the switchbacks, this trail is for strong intermediate and advanced skiers. Downhill speeds are great, and the abrupt turns make this a satisfying, some say classic telemark run, requiring a strong snowplow. Beginners are discouraged from descending this trail because falls ruin the snow for those who can ski this fine run.

(A good nearby day hike for casual walkers is the Round Bald hike up the AT from Carver's Gap, as described in the earlier entry on the AT on the Southern Balds.)

From the small AT parking lot, 1.25 miles above the lower gate, the

AT continues into the woods as a steep hiking trail. After climbing the next rise, the trail drops steeply off Roan to Hughes Gap, an unskiable descent that quickly leaves the deep-snow zone.

THE OLD BALSAM ROAD

The easiest-rated Old Balsam Road branches left from the summit road at a U.S. Forest Service gate, 0.85 mile above the gate at Carver's Gap. The road is on the sunny side of the mountain, so its open portions lose snow more quickly than other trails on Roan. Despite that, evergreens line the road and snow is usually fine when the summit road is skiable. The road undulates in an interesting way and terminates at the Eagle Cliff Natural Area, approximately 3.0 miles from the summit road. The road rises and falls, but stays generally at 5,800 feet, eventually offering unique views near its end that skiers don't see from the higher trails.

THE CLOUDLAND TRAIL

This trail begins in parking lot 1, 1.5 miles above the summit road gate at Carver's Gap. The summit road offers multiple access to the Cloudland Trail, as described in the earlier summit road section.

The Cloudland Trail ranges from easiest to most difficult, and can be broken into four identifiable sections. The total one-way length is 1.5 miles.

Section 1 leaves the elbow of the curve as the summit road enters parking lot 1. The trail winds into the thick spruce and fir forest, then turns right, climbing up and through a turn to the left, and levels where a side trail leads right to a rock observation deck. From this junction, the Cloudland Trail levels out, then descends and makes a sharp right as it exits the trees into an open meadow with a view of parking lot 2 and easy access to the summit road.

The trail follows the edge of the trees, then enters the woods again, winding past rhododendron. The summit road is accessible on the left. This stretch is rated more difficult, especially on the way back, where the turns above parking lot 1 make for a nice downhill run.

Section 2 leaves this point near the summit road and descends with a few turns through an open area, sometimes blown free of snow, and into the woods again for a gradual but straight downhill run. In this area, the summit road has veered left and is some distance through the trees from the trail. This downhill stretch runs directly out into parking lot 3, where skiers can join the summit road and other sections of the Cloud-

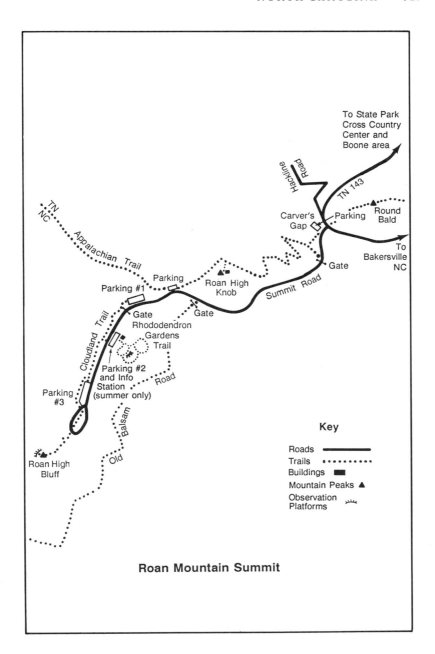

To State Park
Cross Country
Center and
Boone area

Hackline Road

TN 143

TN
NC

Appalachian Trail

Carver's Gap

Parking

Round Bald

To
Bakersville
NC

Parking

Gate

Roan High
Knob

Summit Road

Parking #1

Cloudland Trail

Gate
Rhododendron
Gardens
Trail

Gate

Parking #2
and Info
Station
(summer only)

Road

Parking
#3

Balsam

Old

Roan High
Bluff

Key

Roads ━━━━
Trails ••••••••
Buildings ▬
Mountain Peaks ▲
Observation
Platforms

Roan Mountain Summit

land Trail farther on. The downhill turns at the start make this first, 0.3-mile part of section 2 more difficult.

To stay on the Cloudland Trail, don't exit into the parking lot, but turn right 30 feet before the trail runs out into the open. In deep snow, the spur to the right can be hard to notice. The trail turns, crosses rustic wooden bridges, and stays level and rated easiest. The trail emerges into the summit road near the start of its end loop at the entrance to parking lot 3, 0.2 mile from its turn off the downhill grade. This total section is approximately 0.5 mile long.

Section 3 starts immediately across the summit road and bisects the road's end loop, rising to a high point and then descending to the end of the summit road loop. The snow at the road is often blown very shallow. This section is rated easiest and is approximately 0.2 mile long.

Section 4 leaves the end of the summit road loop as the Roan High Bluff Trail. After crossing an open area surrounded by picnic tables, the trail enters a beautiful spruce forest and begins a climb that takes many turns. At the top of the steepest section the trail levels out through rhododendron, then climbs gradually and reaches the wooden, observation platform on Roan High Bluff at approximately 0.5 mile from the summit road. High winds, blowing snow, and heavy feathers of rime ice often add to the spectacular view.

This section is rated most difficult and requires an uphill herringbone and accomplished snowplow, telemark, or parallel turning on the way down. This can be an exciting, fast return run.

Most people who ski the Cloudland Trail would agree with the U.S. Forest Service Recreation Opportunity Guide's assessment that it is "very close to ideal for cross-country skiing." In either direction, the skier can add interest to the trip by alternating between the summit road and the Cloudland Trail at any of the many connections.

RHODODENDRON GARDENS NATIONAL RECREATION TRAIL

This is a series of three loops, two of which descend through the 600-acre Rhododendron Gardens. On the uppermost loop, an observation platform overlooks the gardens and landmarks to the north like the Linville Gorge and Mount Mitchell.

Starting to the right of the visitor information cabin in parking lot 2, about 2.0 miles from Carver's Gap, the trail crosses the open area bordered by meadows. Loop 1 branches to the right amid the shrubs, but it can be hard to see if the snow is untracked. If you're the first one to ski the trail, keep straight, pass a more obvious branch to the left, and reach the view platform, also on the left. This approach, unlike the one to the deck on Roan High Bluff, can be skied.

Passing the deck, the trail reaches a junction, where a second trail branches left and, like the first leftward path before the deck, descends into the gardens. These lower garden loops afford access to the open meadows, where snow can be shallow due to wind. Whichever of the two garden access trails you take, exploration is the best way to enjoy these less-than-obvious meadow routes. Due to the descending access into the meadows, these trails are rated more difficult and can be lengthy if skiers choose longer routes in the open areas.

To the right at the second leftward trail junction, the first loop reenters the deep evergreens and winds back to the open area and the trail near the visitor contact cabin. This return route passes a place where a skier can enter a meadow through a small opening in the shrubs. At this point turn right, back into the forest. This section is often a fairyland of deep snow with branches so burdened that skiers must duck under boughs. This upper loop, a handicapped trail in summer, is rated easiest.

THE HACKLINE ROAD

The Hackline was built in the late 1800s as a road for stage coaches to reach the Cloudland Hotel atop Roan Mountain through Carver's Gap. Today, a 3.0-mile section of the road lies within Cherokee National Forest, still much as it was in the last century. The Hackline drops from the edge of Tenn. 143 just below Carver's Gap to the same road 2,000 vertical feet lower down.

The grade isn't steep, but an intermediate or more difficult rating is appropriate because the road is isolated and infrequently used and can be a fast trip in icy conditions. That the road drops to a much lower elevation requires deep snow to make it skiable. Usually, if there are 6 inches of snow at the 3,000-foot elevation of Roan Mountain State Park, the Hackline is skiable.

Just over 0.1 mile below the Tenn. 143/summit road junction at Carver's Gap, the Hackline starts steeply down on the left at the break in the guardrail. The road crests the prominent leading ridges of Roan on its switchbacking way down. The Hackline reaches Tenn. 143 at a small community of houses situated on a short road that leaves 143 to the right when driving up to Carver's Gap. This road is approximately 7.6 miles from the U.S. 19E/Tenn. 143 junction in the town of Roan Mountain.

To reach the lower start of the Hackline, walk up the side road 300 yards and go left on the obvious old road grade.

The Hackline is a spectacular one-way downhill run for better skiers with two cars. At times, though, the old road is an important alternative route to Roan when the main highway to Carver's Gap is closed by snow. When that happens, skiers usually park where the plows stop and ski up Tenn. 143 as far as they can. Strong skiers may want to avoid the main road and ski up the old Hackline, especially on weekends, when Tenn. 143 becomes the only way up for the many, less intrepid visitors. Under these circumstances, the Hackline offers more solitude and a far shorter route to the incredible snow depths and scenery of the nearly inaccessible summit of Roan. A descent via the AT and the Hackline represents an exciting downhill run of nearly 3,000 vertical feet.

For more information, contact

High South Nordic Guides, Roan Mountain State Park, Rte. 1, Roan Mountain, TN 37687. 615/772-4178.

Snow report: High Country Host organization, 800/222-7515 inside N.C. or 800/438-7500 from elsewhere in the eastern U.S.

Yellow Mountain Gap: Steep Terrain

Years before the American Revolution, a road crossed these high mountains at Yellow Mountain Gap. In 1781, a roughneck army of mountaineers used the road to cross the gap in a September snow storm to meet and defeat the British army. Its commander, Patrick Ferguson, had threatened to "lay waste" the isolated mountain settlements if they continued to support independence. Before Ferguson could attack, the mountaineers massed and marched to battle.

Although some terrain in the gap area is steep, intermediate and advanced skiers can still enjoy the old trace that carried the Revolutionaries, now the Overmountain Victory Trail, a National Historic Trail. A variety of other trails intersect the old road and access to nearby balds and high peaks is relatively easy. Most of the trails listed below are described as loops, but linking trails are mentioned where appropriate and can be used to create a variety of ski tours. Although they face the sun, meadows in this area often drift deeply with snow.

Trails in the gap are reached on Roaring Creek Road, SR 1132, which joins U.S. 19E 4 miles north of Plum Tree, N.C. After turning onto Roaring Creek Road, bear right at all road forks, climbing, with good views, to the sparsely settled head of a broad valley. Park at 4.7 miles at two U.S. Forest Service gates. In deep snow, the road may not be plowed all the way to gates, so keep track of your mileage from the junction and you'll know how far you must ski to the trailhead.

Cross-Country Trails

OVERMOUNTAIN VICTORY LOOP

This loop is a 1.5-mile circuit through forests and meadows. It is suitable for low intermediate skiers when skied in the direction described here.

At the parking area, the access road continues as a gated Forest Service road toward the distant gap. To the right, or east, a road-width trail is also gated. Take this road uphill to a fork in a flat. A gate blocks the right fork. Go left, and then swing right onto the Old Yellow Mountain Road (Overmountain Victory Trail) that climbs along a tree line to Yellow Mountain Gap. As the road levels at the gap, just before reaching the Appalachian Trail (AT), a side trail goes left, descending to a junction with the gated Forest Service road from the trailhead parking area. Go right there, not up, but nearly level across the open meadow on an old road grade that enters the woods. A timber road branches left, and the loop trail descends, turning right and dropping to the gate at the first fork above the trailhead. Turn left onto your previous ski tracks and descend to the car.

The road grade across the meadow can be hard to find in deep snow, so skiers can learn its location by going in the opposite direction, or right at the gated fork, following the timber road through the woods to where it emerges into the fields. This way, the quick descent from the gap on the Old Yellow Mountain Road rates the trip more difficult.

Another loop can be added to this route by using the gated gravel Forest Service Road at the trailhead. This road climbs gradually, roughly parallel to the Old Yellow Mountain Road (Overmountain Victory Trail), in 0.7 mile to a junction. Left, behind a gate, a Forest Service residence is 100 yards away and may soon be available as a hostel to overnight skiers and summer hikers. To the right at the junction, a blue-blazed, gated road climbs steeply 0.2 mile to join the Old Yellow

Mountain Road where it levels in the gap at the right turn to the timber road.

APPALACHIAN TRAIL AND TIMBER ROAD LOOP

A high loop can be created by adding the AT and a timber road to the Overmountain Victory Loop. Using any of the three routes above, ski into Yellow Mountain Gap and turn right up the bald before reaching the AT. The route is steep but can be traversed in switchbacks along the fence and tree line. Near the crest, both the AT and an old road grade bear right into beech trees. They join and level for 0.5 mile, and then the AT crosses a stile and goes left and a timber road comes in on the right. Go right for a rousing downhill of 0.3 mile to the timber road that forms one leg of the Overmountain Victory Loop. From there, go left down to the car or right to where the timber road enters the meadow and goes on to Yellow Mountain Gap.

Reversing this loop requires a steep climb up the timber road but affords a descent of the open bald in switchbacks. This is strong intermediate skiing.

BIG YELLOW MOUNTAIN

The adventurous can climb even higher from the first loops, eventually reaching the open meadows of Big Yellow Mountain.

Proceed as just described to the junction between the timber road and the AT where the AT crosses the stile. Skiing across the stile, the open summit of Little Hump Mountain is 0.5 mile ahead. Going straight along the fence line, the Big Yellow Mountain Trail climbs to the Nature Conservancy-owned balds of Big Yellow Mountain. This is an out-and-back trip. If you wish to ski to the farthest reaches of the bald, a permit is required from the Nature Conservancy.

Where the southeastern flank of the bald drops into the valley, deep drifts form and are visible from nearby towns like Newland, N.C. These drifts often last into May and can make an enjoyable last-minute skiing site if you're willing to walk to them.

For more information, contact

The Nature Conservancy, SE Regional Office, Box 270, Chapel Hill, NC 27514. 919/967-5493.

Whiteside Mountain: A Summit Post Office

It seems that in each region, at least two places vie for the title of greatest this or that. Proponents of North Carolina's Whiteside Mountain claim that this peak has the highest cliffs in eastern America. The 400- to 750-foot faces are impressive, but New Hampshire's Cannon Mountain in Franconia Notch may indeed take the "highest" honor.

Whiteside Mountain's history includes its being a privately owned tourist attraction, complete with a post office on the summit. The Forest Service received the land in 1974.

The 2.0-mile loop over the summit, with spectacular views, is a National Recreation Trail, one leg of which is a former road and could be skied by advanced Nordic skiers. The trail is reached from Highlands, N.C., a popular and quaint tourist town. From the U.S. 64/N.C. 28 junction in Highlands, go east on U.S. 64 for 5.4 miles, then turn right on SR 1600. Stay on main road for 1.0 mile and turn left into the parking area. The trail begins at the steps, and overnight camping is permitted.

For more information

Visit the Highlands Ranger District, on U.S. 64, east of Highlands,
    on the way to Whiteside Mountain, or write,
District Ranger, U.S. Forest Service, Rte. 2, Box 385, Highlands, NC
    28742. 704/526-3765, Mon.-Fri., 8:00 to 4:00.

The Black Mountains: Contain the East's Highest Peak

Mount Mitchell, the East's highest peak at 6,684 feet, is one of eighteen summits above 6,300 feet in the Black Mountains. The Blacks' massive, serrated range juts north from the Blue Ridge and dominates northwestern North Carolina's horizons as a dark blue or black crest, often seen above low-lying clouds.

The dark spruce and fraser fir forests of the crest account for the name of the range. Explorer Elisha Mitchell's death on the highest peak in 1857 created public sentiment for giving the peak his name. Both Reverend Mitchell and Thomas Clingman had claimed to have measured the summit first.

Mitchell's grave caps the mountaintop, along with a view tower, gift shop, picnic shelters, nature museum, and parking lot. This is the heart of 1,500-acre Mount Mitchell State Park, North Carolina's first. The peak is reached by a 5-mile spur road from milepost 355 on the Blue Ridge Parkway. Along the way, motorists pass a restaurant, small tent-camping area, and ranger and maintenance facilities. The park encompasses only the first and highest peak in the range, leaving the bulk of the Blacks free of development.

A variety of trails offers access to the Black's spectacular crest zone, reputed to be North Carolina's snowiest site. Gaping landslide gulleys give the range an alpine appearance, and amid the skeletal remains of a once healthy summit forest, fine views abound. Scientists have attributed the forest decline to a pest—the balsam woolly aphid—to acid rain, and most recently, to the accumulation of airborne heavy metals in the soil. However it has occurred, Mount Mitchell appears to be developing a tree line, quite likely a human-induced one.

The state park, long a focus of ski and snow enthusiasts, is difficult to reach in winter. Although the park road and Parkway are plowed to nearby N.C. 80, the policy benefits rangers more than the public. The road is open for public access to hiking and skiing sites only when it is very clear, most often when snow cover is on the wane. Still, deep snow at these heights can make a trip to Mitchell attractive for skiers and backpackers (see also the entry on Craggy Gardens earlier in this section).

The spectacular Black Mountain Crest Trail is an out-and-back ridge-top trail with heads on the summit of Mitchell and on SR 1109 near Burnsville, N.C., northwest of the mountain. Luckily, the Crest Trail can be included in two different circuit hikes from the east side of the range. The Pisgah National Forest trailheads for these circuits are accessible even in midwinter because they are below 3,000 feet. Although convenient, that situation creates an arduous climb of almost 4,000 feet. A day climb to the peak is possible with a very early start, but the most rewarding winter experiences in the Blacks probably belong to backpackers from valley trails and day hikers and skiers from Parkway starting points.

Assuming the hiker or backpacker wants a midwinter, deep-snow experience, the eastern flank trails will be the first choice. Three of the five begin at popular National Forest campground recreation areas, Carolina Hemlocks and Black Mountain. Both lie amid impressive evergreen forests. The Colbert Ridge and Maple Camp Bald trails begin at Carolina

Hemlocks and the Mount Mitchell Trail begins at Black Mountain Campground. When combined with the ridge-top Crest Trail and the lower Buncombe Horse Range Trail, loop hikes crest peaks and include two backpacking shelters.

Backpack camping is not permitted within the boundaries of Mount Mitchell State Park, so plan your overnight spots on trails outside the park.

Winter Hiking and Backpacking on Mount Mitchell

BALSAM TRAIL

A popular summer nature trail on the summit, this trail branches left at the nature museum on the graveled trail to Mount Mitchell's view tower. In 0.7 mile, the trail returns to the main parking lot.

BLACK MOUNTAIN CREST TRAIL

From the summit, this orange-blazed trail offers views befitting the highest hike in the East. However, it is almost blocked in spots with annual growth; these "briars" are the thornless blackberry.

The trail begins at the northern end of the main parking lot at a number of log picnic shelters. It descends to a gap and rises to open views in 1.1 miles at Mount Craig (6,645 feet). (The short, round-trip day hike to Mount Craig, just 39 feet lower than Mount Mitchell, offers an idea of what the East's highest summit would be like if undeveloped.)

From Craig, the rugged trail climbs and dips past fine views. There is 6,593-foot Big Tom at 1.5 miles, then Big Tom Gap at 1.6 miles, and a junction on the right with the Big Tom Gap Trail to the Buncombe Horse Trail and Carolina Hemlocks Recreation Area on N.C. 80. The 6,611-foot Balsam Cone is reached at 2.1 miles, 6,583-foot Cattail Peak at 2.4 miles, and Potato Hill at 3.0 miles. The trail drops to Deep Gap Shelter (5,800 feet) at 3.9 miles (the shelter has four plywood bunks, floor space for six, and water 300 yards down the steep trail in front). At 4.0 miles, the Colbert Ridge Trail comes in on the right, having risen 3.7 miles from the Carolina Hemlocks trailhead. (Using trails from Carolina Hemlocks, the Crest Trail section just described can be the upper part of a loop.)

The trail climbs out of Deep Gap, crosses 6,200-foot Winter Star Mountain at 4.5 miles, then slabs west of Gibbs Mountain and Horse Rock to 6,427-foot Celo Knob at 7.4 miles. Descend from Celo on an old grade to the ridge line. The trail passes a mine shaft at 9.5 miles—stay on the path when hiking the lower part of this trail. When you reach a gate and a junction at 10.3 miles, go left, descending to Bowlens Creek, at 11.0 miles, and a concrete bridge crossing. Then the trail reaches Bowlens Creek Road, SR 1109 (3,012 feet) at 12.0 miles from the Mitchell summit.

Bowlens Creek trailhead is reached by turning onto N.C. 197 from U.S. 19E in Burnsville, N.C. In 0.7 miles, turn left onto SR 1109 for 2.4 miles to a left turn on a dirt road in the hairpin turn. Park 250 feet up the road past a house and near a Pisgah National Forest sign.

COLBERT RIDGE TRAIL

This white-blazed, 3.7-mile trail links Carolina Hemlocks Recreation Area and Deep Gap Shelter on the Crest Trail. Turn onto N.C. 80 from U.S. 19E at Micaville, N.C., and go 10 miles. Then bear right on SR 1159, Colbert Creek Road, before a grocery, the Toe River Bridge, and Carolina Hemlocks. Go 0.5 mile to trailhead parking on the right. The trail starts just south on the road.

After a gradual start, the trail ascends steeply up prominent Colbert Ridge to Deep Gap in 3,000 vertical feet.

BUNCOMBE HORSE RANGE TRAIL/MAPLE CAMP BALD SECTION

This section of the white-blazed Buncombe Horse Range Trail climbs from the vicinity of Carolina Hemlocks to a junction with the Big Tom Gap Trail, from which hikers may gain the Crest Trail and form a loop with the Colbert Ridge Trail. At Big Tom Gap Trail, the second, upper section of the Horse Trail goes left and follows a level grade, connects to the Mount Mitchell Trail from Black Mountain Campground and enables yet another connection to the Crest Trail and a longer loop back to Carolina Hemlocks trails, this time over Mount Mitchell itself.

The Buncombe Horse Range Trail's lowest trailhead (2,900 feet) is reached as if one were going to the Colbert Ridge Trail. At that trailhead, continue on SR 1159 for 0.5 mile and turn right onto a dirt road at the junction. Go 0.33 mile to the trailhead on the left, just past a brick house.

The trail starts gradually on an old logging road for 2.0 miles. Then it steepens to ascend the ridge to Maple Camp Bald and good views. At 4.0 miles the trail reaches a prominent railroad grade and the blue-blazed Big Tom Gap Trail, which goes right and up to the Crest Trail.

BUNCOMBE HORSE RANGE TRAIL/UPPER SECTION

From the trail's emergence on the railroad grade, it heads south on a gradual grade passing above huge landslide areas, and in 2.9 miles (6.9 from the start), it reaches Camp Alice Shelter (see Mount Mitchell Trail below). At 7.0 miles, the Mount Mitchell Trail comes in on the left from Black Mountain Campground, bound for the Mitchell summit.

Passing a shelter, at 8.0 miles, another road grade exits right, up to Steppes Gap Ranger Station at the state park entrance and N.C. 128. The Horse Trail continues very level, and at 13.3 miles turns left off the railroad grade and descends an old logging road to Forest Service Road 472 in 4.2 miles, 17.6 from the start. This upper, dirt-road trailhead, at 3,560 feet, is rarely reachable in snowy weather.

Going straight instead of turning from the railroad grade at 13.3, the grade continues gradually for 0.3 mile to a junction with NC 128 about 0.5 mile above the N.C. 128/Parkway junction. From this junction and from the road from Steppes Gap, the Horse Trail is a popular cross-country route (see the next section on cross-country on Mount Mitchell).

MOUNT MITCHELL TRAIL

Take N.C. 80 12 miles from Micaville, N.C., and turn right onto FSR 472 near the Mount Mitchell Golf Course. In 3.5 miles, the road reaches Black Mountain Campground. Cross the bridge into the campground, where the blue-blazed newly rerouted trail is clearly marked on the left.

At about 1.5 miles, pass the Higgins Bald Ground Trail, a 1.5-mile trail that ascends gently to an old USFS cabin site, and then more steeply rejoins the Mount Mitchell Trail.

The Mount Mitchell Trail continues past the turnoff for the Higgins Bald Trail in a park like setting of virgin spruce and fir. The trail reaches the Buncombe Horse Range Trail at 3.9 miles. Go left and in 0.1 mile, the Mount Mitchell Trail turns right into some woods, with the Camp Alice Shelter 200 feet to the left. (The shelter is in poor repair and often littered. There are ten wire bunks, a fireplace, a picnic shelter, and a horse corral.)

From the Horse Trail, the Mount Mitchell Trail climbs steeply in 1.6 miles over many blowdowns to the Mitchell summit, 5.6 miles and 3,900 vertical feet from the start. This trail can be a 14.6-mile trip by creating a loop. Go right on the Horse Trail near the shelter, left up the Big Tom

Gap Trail, south on the Crest Trail to Mitchell, and down the Mount Mitchell Trail back to the shelter area.

Cross-Country Skiing on Mount Mitchell

When the National Park Service gates are open at N.C. 80, skiers and backpackers can easily reach Mount Mitchell State Park. Near the park access road, N.C. 128, at Parkway milepost 355, a gate blocks further travel on the Parkway, allowing skiers to tour south to the spectacular Craggy Gardens area (covered earlier in this section).

Entering the state park, skiers can choose from three skiing sites.

BUNCOMBE HORSE RANGE TRAIL

Half a mile from the N.C. 128/Parkway junction, on the right, an old railroad grade leads north, becoming the Buncombe Horse Range Trail. Except for a rocky area in the first few hundred yards, this gradual, wide trail is a fine ski tour. The forest is large and open with many evergreens and birches. The trail stays at about 5,700 feet in elevation throughout its skiable 7.1 miles to the Big Tom Gap Trail. The Camp Alice Shelter (just described under the Mount Mitchell Trail) is 4.1 miles from the trailhead.

STEPPES GAP ROAD

At Steppes Gap, the N.C. 128 boundary of Mount Mitchell State Park at 6,000 feet, a ranger station marks the start of another good ski tour. Park on the left and begin the trail at a gate on the right side of N.C. 128 and right of the ranger station. The trail descends gradually for 2.5 miles to a junction with the Buncombe Horse Range Trail, 5.6 miles from its N.C. 128 trailhead (see above), and 1.0 mile from the Camp Alice Shelter (described under Mount Mitchell Trail).

Like the Horse Trail itself, this access makes a fine overnight trip to the shelter, 3.5 miles one way. As a day tour, the Steppes Gap road allows easier access to the more distant reaches of the Horse Trail, and the return trip to N.C. 128 at Steppes Gap is gradual.

SUMMIT ROAD

At times, the road to Mount Mitchell's summit will be gated inside the park when unplowed, and even occasionally when plowed, allowing skiing on the road or road side to reach the peak. The park's use of a rotary plow often creates an undisturbed lip of deep snow that is skiable, although far less than ideal. Skiers would no doubt prefer the road to be left unplowed above the ranger residences, with management access by snowmobile, especially if the plowed road is blocked to traffic anyway. In the absence of a policy promoting cross-country skiing and winter sports, road side snowdrift skiing may be the only way for enthusiasts to enjoy this snowy southern summit.

Cross-country ski rentals closest to the Blacks are in Asheville, North Cove, and the high-country area. Mount Mitchell snow reports are available by calling the state park number below.

For more information, contact

Toecane Ranger District, PO Box 128, Burnsville, NC 28714. 704/682-6146.

The US Forest Service South Toe River Trail Map of the Black Mountains may be obtained by sending $1 to National Forests in NC, PO Box 2750, Asheville, NC 28802.

Mount Mitchell State Park, Rte. 5, Box 700, Burnsville, NC 28714. 704/675-4611.

Grandfather Mountain: One of the South's Most Rugged

Grandfather Mountain is certainly one of the most spectacular and rugged peaks in the South. Like those of Mount Mitchell, Clingman's Dome, and Roan Mountain, Grandfather's crest is reached by a road. But the road at Grandfather is privately owned and reaches the first and lowest peak of the mountain. Unlike the heights on the other, publicly owned peaks, Grandfather Mountain's highest summits are reached only by trail. Another difference is that fees are charged for wilderness hiking, as well as for driving to the popular tourist development on the first peak, billed as "Carolina's Top Scenic Attraction."

That advertising claim may be true. Grandfather's three highest peaks reach to nearly 6,000 feet, but they seem to be higher. In 1794, explorer Andre Michaux climbed the peak and thought he'd "climbed the highest peak in all North America." The mountain rises more than a vertical mile above the surrounding lowlands, a dramatic drop comparable to many peaks in the Rockies. Although a few other southern summits equal that rise, none do so as impressively.

The mountain's location and character make it an awesome winter destination for hikers and mountaineers. Its snowy environment has attracted half a dozen ski resorts to surrounding mountains. And its rugged appearance makes it a winter destination with alpine hiking rewards and challenges.

The mountain's trails center around the unmistakable ridge line: a jagged crest that rises nearly 1,000 feet from the Mile High Swinging Bridge and Visitor Center to open meadows and hand-over-hand rock scambling on rocky peaks scaled with the aid of wooden ladders. Most people find this hike challenging enough in spring, summer, and fall. A winter trip requires even more preparation.

Although trails do rise from surrounding valleys and the total network boasts nine trails and nearly 30 miles of hiking, few loop hiking opportunities exist, so backpackers usually base camp where valley trails gain the heights and day hike. One of these hikes is the Grandfather Trail along the ridge. Under full winter conditions, ice-climbing gear can be appropriate to scale the snow- and ice-choked gullies of the Grandfather Trail.

Winter hikers usually gain access to the mountain trails from nearby valleys. The summit road is often closed by snow and ice, so no overnight parking is permitted at the mile-high elevation. When the road is successfully plowed, it is open on "good weather" winter days, most often weekends, but hikers must be back to the summit parking lot by 4:00 P.M. or a search starts. The drive up is a popular attraction for the half-million skiers who visit nearby resorts. When natural snow is sparse, skiers even use the trails, often hiking to Calloway Peak and skiing from there. But in severe winter weather, the mountain is for serious winter campers, hikers, and mountaineers.

Day and overnight use requires a hiking permit, available at or near trailheads and other locations. Rates are $3.00 per day for adults, $1.50 for kids four to twelve. A season pass, good for year-long hiking and camping, is $15.00. Motorists who drive up pay double the hiking rates but no additional fee to hike. The trail fees fund preservation and maintenance of a spectacular and unique private wilderness preserve. Trails are well cared for, and new trails are being built to create loop hikes and accommodate the increase in use expected when the last unfinished part of the Blue Ridge Parkway opens around the mountain in 1987.

The permit requirement is also a safety registration system. Campers may use many designated sites—marked on the trail map and at the sites by teepee symbols, signs, and firepits—or new sites if they are out of sight of trails. Winter campers must use a gas stove and camp in a low-impact manner. No fires are permitted at Hi-Balsam backpacking shelter at any time of year. There is also a three-sided shelter under the highest peak, on the Daniel Boone Scout Trail, that sleeps six and in winter is covered by a canvas closure over the front. The trail map is available at no charge. Write to the address given at the end of this entry.

Winter Hiking

SHANTY SPRING TRAIL

This white-blazed 100-year-old trail starts at the junction of N.C. 105/184 near Banner Elk, where permits are available at Scotchman Store, and climbs 2.0 miles to the Shanty Spring, just below the mountain's crest. This trail will likely be rerouted soon so that it will start a mile closer to Boone on Rte. 105, offering better views and climbing more gradually than the current steep route. From the spring, the Calloway Trail leads 0.5 mile up a rocky, icy area to Calloway Gap, a popular winter base camp at the junction with Grandfather Trail.

In 1986, an alternative to the Shanty Spring Trail was opened. The as yet unnamed trail leaves N.C. 105 near Adam's Apple Racquet Club, just north of the Shanty Spring Trail. The easy, graded trail climbs the profile ridge with fine views of the Grandfather face.

GRANDFATHER TRAIL

From the Swinging Bridge and Visitor Center, this blue-blazed National Recreation Trail undulates northeast through a spruce and fir forest, then climbs through fissures and up ladders over cliffs to views of three states at MacRae Peak, a huge ridge-line boulder accessible by ladder. From the peak, the trail drops over an icy face into MacRae Gap at 1.5 miles. Then it climbs ladders up and through tunnels before ascending an icy, cliff-lined gully to Attic Window Peak, named for a cave through the face to the left, halfway up the gully. From Attic Window Peak, the trail dips to a ladder and a junction with the trail to Indian House Cave, a good winter camp and the site of ancient artifacts. The next mile to Calloway Gap (3.0 miles from the start) traverses an icy, whaleback cliff top, to an open meadow, then goes over the next rise and cliff tops to the last descent into Calloway Gap. This section of the trail can be very dangerous.

At the gap and the junction with the Calloway Trail from Shanty Spring, the Grandfather Trail climbs 0.5 mile over easier terrain to a junction with the Daniel Boone Scout Trail from the valley to the east of the mountain. To the west, Watauga View looks down on Banner Elk, the Shanty Spring trailhead, ski resorts, and related ridge-top development. Calloway Peak is 0.1 mile away on the Boone Scout Trail.

DANIEL BOONE SCOUT TRAIL

This National Recreation Trail leaves the west side of U.S. 221 1.5 miles south of the U.S. 221/Holloway Mountain Road junction where it then leads to the completed Blue Ridge Parkway north from U.S. 221, which is the alternate for the Blue Ridge Parkway section not yet completed around the mountain. The Country Store at the junction, 1.5 miles north of the trail, has permits. Across from the trail is a two-story red building.

The trail climbs to the left from the trailhead to and across the Parkway to a junction with the Park Service Tanawha Trail. The Tanawha trail to the left reaches a right turn onto the Daniel Boone Scout Trail in 0.2 mile. To the right, the Tanawha Trail reaches a left turn onto another Grandfather Mountain Trail in 0.1 mile (see below for Grandfather Trail extension). And the Tanawha Trail going straight continues to Price Park Campground on the Blue Ridge Parkway. When the Parkway opens, the Boone Trail will not cross the Parkway but will go right and under it at a bridge to a junction near the Parkway's Boone Fork parking overlook. With that rerouting, both Grandfather Mountain trails will be to the left on the Tanawha Trail.

The Boone Trail goes right from the Tanawha Trail and climbs with white blazes through a dry stream bed and rhododendron tunnel to a campsite and water source (first left at the flat) and a junction with the Cragway Trail (next right after the campsite). From there the trail climbs, steeply at times, into a spruce and fir forest and crosses large outcrops to Viaduct View, a fine panorama of the new Parkway, Linville Gorge, the dramatic drop to the piedmont, and a large, wild part of the Pisgah National Forest.

After the trail levels, a path branches left to the cliff-top location of Hi-Balsam Shelter. Past the shelter trail, a campsite appears on the left, just across the trail from some plane crash wreckage, and the trail ascends steeply to Calloway Peak, whose highest point is 5,964 feet, marked by a white X at about 4 miles.

GRANDFATHER TRAIL EXTENSION/CRAGWAY

These trails form a loop with the lower half of the Daniel Boone Scout Trail.

Leaving the Boone Scout Trail parking area, cross the Parkway and go right on the Tanawha Trail, then left on the Grandfather Trail Extension, following blue blazes along a scenic old road grade above rushing Boone Fork. This trail leads into an isolated, high, bowl-shaped mountain valley under Calloway Peak. This gouge is claimed by some geologists to be the southernmost example of a glacial cirque, a former resting place of a glacier.

The trail continues on an easy grade, passes a gushing trail-side water source at about 0.3 mile from the Tanawha Trail, and passes the Cragway Trail to the left at 0.6 mile. A campsite is 0.1 mile beyond the junction on the left, and then the trail crosses small streams, reaching the larger Boone Fork at 1.0 mile from the Tanawha Trail. After crossing Boone Fork, the trail reaches a dead end with a side trail left to a huge outcrop and fine views of the entire valley. The trail will eventually go past the view and over the ridge to the north to join the existing Grandfather Trail at Calloway Peak, thus forming a big loop.

At 0.6 mile, the Cragway leaves the Grandfather Trail Extension and joins the Boone Trail to form an easy, less-than-two-hour loop hike. Views at top of Cragway are easily accessible by campers using sites on the Boone Trail. The Cragway Trail climbs steeply from Grandfather Trail Extension, following orange blazes, over many outcrops with an alpine feel and expansive views. The trail is strenuous in places but forms only a 1.0-mile section of a moderate loop hike. Late September autumn color on this trail is brilliant.

BLACK ROCK CLIFFS CAVE TRAIL/ARCH ROCK TRAIL

From MacRae Gap on the Grandfather Trail, the Arch Rock Trail drops steeply east following red blazes, reaching Grandview Pinnacle in 0.6 mile with views up at peaks and down to the trail's eventual destination, a rugged outcrop on the eastern flank of the mountain above the Blue Ridge Parkway. The trail drops again, from the Pinnacle to a junction at 1.2 miles with the cave trail at overhanging Arch Rock.

Black Rock Cliffs Cave Trail starts on the Grandfather summit road just below the switchbacks to the peak. The trail is yellow blazed and level past Arch Rock, at 0.5 mile, to a campsite (1.0 mile) below a big boulder with fine views. The last 0.3 mile descends to a cave opening marked by a yellow arrow. Outcrops near the cave entrance offer fine views. The four-room cave requires a flashlight for safe exploration; however, it is closed in winter to protect a hibernating, endangered species of mammal.

UNDERWOOD TRAIL

This trail enables hikers to avoid the ladder ascent of MacRae Peak and still reach destinations on the Grandfather Trail. The Underwood Trail leaves the Grandfather Trail 0.6 mile from Swinging Bridge; climbs, yellow blazed, through wild, impressive rock formations; then slabs into MacRae Gap through a northern evergreen forest and dramatic views up to Attic Window Peak. This trail joins the Grandfather Trail and the top of the Arch Rock Trail. The total length is about 1.0 mile.

For more information, contact

Backcountry Manager, Box 128, Linville, NC, 28646. 704/733-2013, weekdays 9:00 to 4:00, or 704/733-4337, seven days a week, 8:00 to 4:00. Ask for free map.

Land of Waterfalls: Offers Scenic Winter Walks

The southwestern mountains of North Carolina, particularly the area around Highlands, Cashiers, Brevard, and Rosman, are known as the Land of Waterfalls. Many are accessible, scenic winter walks. Whitewater Falls, nearly 500 feet, is reputed to be the highest in the East.

U.S. 64 links the towns mentioned above into an enjoyable winter sightseeing tour. But "waterfall walkers," especially in winter, should never climb near the falls. Many fatalities occur this way in summer. In winter, these normally slippery areas are often frozen as well.

Three falls, Looking Glass Falls, Dry Falls, and Bridal Veil Falls, are among the most popular.

LOOKING GLASS FALLS

This 60-foot waterfall is one of the area's most visited. It's on U.S. 276, 5 miles toward the Blue Ridge Parkway from the junction of U.S. 64, U.S. 276, and N.C. 280, 3 miles from Brevard on U.S. 64.

DRY FALLS

A short walk leads hikers behind this thundering waterfall, located on U.S. 64, 3 miles northwest of Highlands. A fence prevents the possibility of a fall. Be prepared for spray.

BRIDAL VEIL FALLS

A pull-out from U.S. 64 allows motorists to drive behind this waterfall, which is between Highlands and Dry Falls.

To receive local travel information, including details on interesting inns and attractions, contact

Brevard Chamber of Commerce, Box 589, Brevard, NC 28712. 704/883-3700, Mon.-Fri. 9:00 to 5:00. The office is on Main Street. The chamber publishes a "Land of Waterfalls" map that can be had by mail for $1.50, or for $.75 at the office.

For more information on Beech Mountain, contact

Fred's General Mercantile, 100 Beech Mountain Parkway, Banner Elk, NC 28604. 704/387-4838.

Snow report: High Country Host organization. 800/222-7515 inside NC, or 800/438-7500 from elsewhere in the eastern U.S.

For more information on The Pink Beds, contact

District Ranger, Pisgah National Forest, Box 8, Pisgah Forest, NC 28768. 704/877-3265.

Tennessee

Great Smoky Mountains National Park: Eastern America's First

From a distance, it is obvious that the Great Smokies live up to their name. This, eastern America's mightiest mountain mass, is indeed a preserve so vast that high mountains seem even higher.

Bisected by the North Carolina/Tennessee state line, the Great Smokies became eastern America's first National Park and is today the most popular. The Smokies' more than 90 inches of annual rainfall, second in the United States only to rain in the Pacific Northwest, has created a lush forest of such impressive diversity that the park has been designated an international biosphere reserve. Virgin forests cover entire mountains. More than 800 miles of trails wander through the park's half-million acres.

Winter visitors see a special view of this often overcrowded park. Not only is traffic light on the otherwise busy transmountain highway, Newfound Gap Road (NGR), but black bears, so regularly encountered and sometimes troublesome in summer, are rarely seen. Even winter fishing is available.

Because NGR is a major transportation corridor through this great wall of the Southern Appalachians, the road is closed only temporarily after heavy snows. As soon as is practical, the road reopens, enabling skiers, winter hikers, and sightseers to reach the park's lofty interior. Although the road is plowed, rangers may require chains between Cherokee, N.C., and Gatlinburg, Tenn., when conditions are icy.

Winter trail opportunities range from mountaineering-style day climbs of road-side crags to easy waterfall hikes. The winter backpacker will find the awesome expanse of this wilderness relatively uncrowded. The park's eighty-three back-country campsites and eighteen shelters, usually packed in summer, often provide solitude in winter.

Overnight back-country camping permits are required year-round, but backpackers will have an easier time in winter arranging camping privileges at popular shelters and back-country campsites. Mid-November through February is the quietest time on park trails. Reservations for the free permits and back-country information are available by phone, 615/436-9564. Whether or not you make a phone reservation, permits must be picked up in person any time before twelve noon of the day your trip starts, and backpackers must use the sites they have been assigned. In winter, backpackers can apply for or pick up reserved permits daily until 4:30 at Sugarlands Visitor Center near Gatlinburg, Oconaluftee Visitor Center near Cherokee, and Cades Cove Visitor Center. These centers are a fine first stop for park visitors. Even in winter, they feature interesting displays and exhibits, extensive publications, and information booths.

A word of caution: The Smokies receive less snow than northwestern North Carolina and West Virginia, but it is not uncommon for 30 inches of snow to arrive in one storm on the ridge tops. Although rain may be falling in Gatlinburg, the more than 6,000-foot crest of the Smokies should be taken seriously. As with other high southern summits, consistent periods of deep snow make it possible to enjoy "full winter conditions" in this mammoth park. Be prepared.

Take the time to acquire and read the park's regulations. Trail users should be aware that dogs, even if leashed, are prohibited on all trails.

Three of the Smoky's seven developed campgrounds are open in winter: Smokemont near Cherokee, Elkmont near Gatlinburg, and Cades Cove, also in Tennessee. From May 1 to October 31, these campgrounds offer reserved sites at an additional fee at Ticketron outlets or by mail from Ticketron, PO Box 2715, San Francisco, CA 94126. The Smokies' other four campgrounds, Cosby, Look Rock, Deep Creek, and Balsam Mountain are open from April to October on a first-come, first-served basis only. Summer amenities include camp-fire programs and guided hikes.

Sledding, tobogganing, and the use of similar snow-sliding devices are popular and encouraged in the Smokies. However, park policy prohibits the motorized towing of any sled or other device, and sledders as well as skiers are prohibited from using any road that has not been closed to motor vehicles.

Rangers suggest a number of fine sledding sites. The first two listed below are notable for their high elevation and consistent snow.

OLD NEWFOUND GAP ROAD

From the south end of the Newfound Gap parking area, the Old Newfound Gap Road descends into North Carolina. The upper end just below the parking lot is popular with sledders.

INDIAN GAP

Indian Gap is just over a mile above Newfound Gap on the gated Clingman's Dome Road. Sledders can use the Gap road's lower section.

CHIMNEYS PICNIC AREA

The Chimneys picnic area is between Newfound Gap and Sugarlands Visitor Center. Sledders should use the upper end of the picnic area to stay as far as possible from vehicles.

CHEROKEE ORCHARD

This motor loop near Gatlinburg is reached by Airport Road. The loop is gated so sledders can walk up the road and slide back down toward their vehicles.

Whether you are downhill skiing at Ober Gatlinburg or Cataloochee, or just winter vacationing, sightseeing is a worthwhile reason to visit the Smokies. The transmountain trip on NGR is a spectacular drive. The barren peaks and tall evergreen timber are reminiscent of the Pacific Northwest. As you near the park, tune your AM radio to 1610, and the Park Service's weather and information broadcasts will come in loud and clear.

Even winter campers in popular summer areas should be prepared to avoid bears. Day hikers should avoid bears on the trail, especially a mother with cubs, as calmly as possible, without running from them. Backpackers should exercise even greater caution, since the Smokies' nearly 500 Black bears are most active at dusk when the aroma of food drifts from campsites. Rangers require that food be hung or stored in the park's mesh-gated shelters. Backpackers should store food in airtight containers, separate food-preparation and sleeping areas, and avoid greasy, odorous foods. Dehydrated meals seem to be least attractive to bears. Never, ever feed a bear or abandon your pack as a "sacrifice." Both of these actions will make the problem worse for someone else.

The descriptions that follow suggest a number of winter hikes and ski tours. The listings describe trails and recreation sites designated or popular for specific winter uses. But a park as big as the Smokies offers nearly limitless opportunities. This is a park where the spirit of exploration can thrive. The most complete listing of the Great Smokies' trail opportunities is the Sierra Club Totebook, *Hiker's Guide to the Smokies.* Together, *Southern Snow* and the exhaustive listings of the Totebook should fully introduce visitors to the park's winter activities.

Summer or winter, Smoky's visitors find the park surrounded by an awesome array of tourist attractions, restaurants, and overnight accommodations. Most winter enthusiasts would probably enjoy the skiing-oriented atmosphere of Gatlinburg, with its wide variety of inexpensive overnight accommodations. (See the entry on Ober Gatlinburg in Part 2 for more information and Chamber of Commerce contacts.)

For more information or back-country reservations, contact

Great Smoky Mountains National Park, Gatlinburg, TN, 37738. 615/436-9564.

LeConte Lodge, PO Box 350, Gatlinburg, TN 37738. 615/436-4473.

Cross-Country Trails

CLINGMAN'S DOME ROAD

Clingman's Dome is the highest peak in the Smokies and the Deep South's premier Nordic ski site. The "Dome Road" starts at Newfound Gap (5,040 feet), and climbs to a parking area just 400 feet below Clingman's Dome (6,642 feet). Despite the Smokies' southerly location, this high summit receives substantial snow. Access is another plus. NGR to and across Newfound Gap is plowed as soon as possible due to its importance to travelers. The Dome Road is thus quickly accessible to skiers, and there is little likelihood that vehicles will disturb the snowy 7 miles of scenic ski touring to the summit. Clingman's Dome Road is gated whenever weather conditions make travel hazardous. The road is in effect closed to vehicles at all times that skiers might want to use it.

Although the Dome Road isn't as snowy as Roan Mountain and has fewer side trails for skiers, it is double the length of Roan's summit road. Also unlike conditions on Roan, the road-side growth on Clingman's Dome is a mature, towering red spruce forest that better shades the snow from the sun. The scenery is spectacular, and Gatlinburg's Smoky Mountain Nordic Ski Patrol, the first Nordic Ski Patrol in the South, regularly patrols the road.

Skiers should park at Newfound Gap parking area and walk across NGR and past the gate. Sledders may be using the lower half-mile of the road, but skiers soon outdistance them.

Indian Gap is just over a mile from the gate. An old Indian trail, expanded into a road in the 1800s, crossed the gap at this point.

Just over 2.5 miles up the road, the Spruce-Fir Nature Trail begins on the left. The 0.75-mile trail is self-guiding: numbered posts match paragraphs in a brochure you found at a trailhead dispenser. The trail is level and bears left once in the woods before looping back around to the start. This loop makes a fine turn-around circuit for beginning skiers. The trail offers an alternative to the road and awesome scenes within the Canadian-zone forests. Round trip from Newfound Gap, including the nature trail, is 6.0 miles.

At 3.4 miles on the Dome Road, the Fork Ridge hiking trail enters on the left, and on the right, a connector trail leads to the Appalachian Trail (AT). This is the Mount Collins area. Advanced skiers will find the AT a good side trip at this point. To the left on the AT, the Sugarland Mountain Trail goes right in 0.3 mile, reaching the Mount Collins Shelter in 0.4 mile. The shelter sleeps twelve. At 0.1 mile past the Sugarland Mountain Trail, the AT reaches Mount Collins. To the right on the AT from the connector trail, the trail is skiable to near Indian Gap, about 2 miles. The Mount Collins Shelter would be the backpacker's best bet for ski camping on Clingman's Dome.

After climbing gradually from its start, the Dome Road descends between 3.75 and 4.6 miles from Newfound Gap. (Skiers bound for the summit should remember that this will be an uphill section on the way back.) At 5.35 miles, skiers pass a long road cut hung with icicles.

At 6.85 miles, the road enters the parking lot on Clingman's Dome, a quarter-mile loop with fine views and with portable privies at its western end. From the lot (6,312 feet), the Clingman's Dome summit is reached by a steep, paved, road-width footpath that climbs the last 330 feet in 0.5 mile. Only skiers with a powerful snowplow will find this path skiable downward. Even then, soft new snow will be needed. At the peak, a spiraling, concrete ramp leads above the trees for a view from the 6,642-foot summit of the Smokies.

OLD NEWFOUND GAP ROAD

Beginning at the south end of the Newfound Gap parking lot, this old road grade descends into North Carolina and reaches NGR at a parking area. Although sledders use the road's upper end, skiers can begin at either end and enjoy the gradual, 4.0-mile grade. The trail is easy either way, but particularly downhill using two cars. Most intermediate skiers with one vehicle will go up the road for the view and maybe lunch at Newfound Gap, then descend for an 8.0-mile round trip.

CHEROKEE ORCHARD LOOP ROAD/ROARING FORK MOTOR NATURE TRAIL

The Cherokee Orchard Loop, near Gatlinburg, is a low-elevation ski tour available when heavy snow closes the loop road to cars. It makes a good alternative when NGR is closed to higher ground. Take Airport Road from Gatlinburg just under 3 miles to the start of the loop at a gate. Just beyond the gate is the 0.75-mile Noah "Bud" Ogle Place Trail, a fine ski tour past an old log cabin and a mill. Like the Old Newfound Gap Road, the lowermost section of the Cherokee Orchard Loop is popular with sledders.

Taking the right fork of the loop at the Ogle Place Trail, the road leads to the parking area at Cherokee Orchard in 0.4 mile. The Rainbow Falls and Bullhead trails to Mount LeConte start at this parking lot. Skiers reach another fork at 0.7 mile on the loop road. To the left, Cherokee Orchard Loop returns to its starting point and the car. But energetic skiers can take the right fork and ski the Roaring Fork Motor Nature Trail that ends on Tenn. 321 east of Gatlinburg in 6.0 miles. The Roaring Fork Road exit gate is another skier access point for the Roaring Fork Motor Trail. Both of these tours range from 1,500 to 3,000 feet in elevation.

BRADLEY FORK TRAIL

Under heavy snow, the sunnier North Carolina side offers a lengthy ski tour under the Charlie's Bunion area. Start at the Bradley Fork trailhead by turning right off NGR, 3.2 miles north of the Oconaluftee Visitor Center. Cross the river, turn left, and park at the gate, just outside the Smokemont Campground. This is a gated forest road that passes through a variety of forest growth and offers good stream-side waterfall views in its 5.5 mile length. The trail starts low: at 2,200 feet. Luckily for skiers the road is very gradual as it crosses wide bridges over the stream and ends at 3,200 feet.

Winter Day Hiking

CHIMNEY TOPS

Motorists climbing to Newfound Gap on NGR in Tennessee can't miss The Chimney Tops, two jagged summits rising 1,400 feet above the road. The wide, well-maintained trail up is steep and strenuous, particularly in snow; but it is also short, just 2.2 miles. The peak's spectacular views of Mount LeConte make this a rewarding, although challenging, winter day hike. Round trip is 4.0 miles.

The trail starts at Chimney Tops parking area on NGR, 6.7 miles south of Sugarlands Visitor Center. Chimney Tops Trail and Road Prong Trail descend together from the lot to the East Prong of Little Pigeon River. The combined trails cross four bridges before the Road Prong Trail continues upstream and Chimney Tops Trail turns right and climbs steeply to the summits.

MOUNT LeCONTE

This most spectacular peak in the park is covered at length in the next section, on Smokies backpacking trips. LeConte can also be a day hike on the Alum Cave Trail, especially in warm, snowless weather. In midwinter, though, this trail is for the experienced, well-equipped mountaineer. Often, hand-held safety cables on rocky sections can be buried under deep snow and bulges of ice. Under such circumstances, this trail can be technically demanding and skill, rope, ice picks, and crampons are necessary to safely reach the summit. In summer, this trail is the shortest route to LeConte Lodge.

The Alum Cave Trail starts 9 miles south of the Sugarlands Visitor Center on the left side of NGR. The trail climbs, crossing Alum Creek a number of times, as it passes through a scenic forest of hemlocks and reaches Arch Rock at 1.5 miles. The trail then climbs some more, crossing a small bald at 2.0 miles and reaching the overhanging cliffs of Alum Cave at 2.4 miles. A view on the left past Alum Cave reveals the next spectacular rocky areas: huge landslide scars. The trail climbs through these open areas and cables are in place higher up under one of LeConte's three summits. At 5.0 miles the trail intersects the Rainbow Falls Trail and a side trail to the Cliff Top viewpoint. Then it reaches the summit development, LeConte Lodge, at 5.1 miles. The peak's other fine view, Myrtle Point, is 1.0 mile on the Boulevard Trail from the lodge.

RAMSAY CASCADE/GREENBRIER PINNACLE

This is an easy hike and a good cross-country ski tour when the road is gated due to deep snow. The trail starts on the Ramsay Prong Road 5.0 miles from Tenn. 321 at a Park Service gate. To reach the trailhead turn onto Greenbrier Road from Tenn. 321 about 6 miles from Gatlinburg. In 1.0 mile, the Greenbrier Ranger Station appears on the right (a gate nearby is closed in deep snow and hikers must park there). Take the left fork at the junction of Ramsay and Porter's roads at 3.0 miles, and you will reach the rock barriers 2.0 miles farther, 5.0 miles from Tenn. 321.

The trail follows the road behind the barriers for 1.5 miles, then, at a former trailhead parking area, becomes a foot trail that crosses the stream a number of times on log bridges, reaching 75-foot Ramsay Cascade at 3.5 miles.

Winter Backpacking

MOUNT LeCONTE

Although it is home to a shelter and a variety of lodge buildings and is at times crowded, Mount LeConte is a premier Smokies destination. Day hikers can attain the summit, but in winter, particularly in snow, LeConte and neighboring high peaks are best considered an overnight trip. For one night or three, the LeConte area represents the best and most alpine region of the Smokies crest. These ridges hold the bulk of the park's spruce-fir forest and receive the greatest snowfall. But even in winter, shelters can be full at times. The best bet for a snowy winter trip with some solitude is midweek, between mid-January and mid-February.

The best high-elevation access is from Newfound Gap on NGR. The AT runs east from the gap at a relatively gradual grade (under deep fresh snow, expert cross-country skiers can enjoy it). This end of the park contains the highest peaks on the AT and noteworthy stretches of open rock and fine views at Charlie's Bunion and the Sawteeth. Mount LeConte is an adjoining ridge, and looping side trails permit circuit hikes, involving ridge walks, from lower elevations.

LeCONTE OVERNIGHT, OPTION A

An out-and-back alternative in this area follows the AT past the Boulevard Trail, which leads to Mount LeConte at 2.7 miles, and goes on to Icewater Spring Shelter in another 0.3 mile (sleeps 12), a 3.0-mile first day. The second day can retrace the AT to the Boulevard Trail, taking that trail to Leconte, or can continue on the AT from the shelter across Charlie's Bunion at 0.1 mile and the Sawteeth at 1.5 miles. In deep snow or ice, the latter route may be the Smokies' most challenging mountaineering experience. Take the proper equipment! The second night can be spent at Peck's Corner Shelter (sleeps 12), 0.5 mile off the AT on the Hughes Ridge Trail, which joins the AT 7.3 miles from Icewater Springs Shelter, making a second day of 7.8 miles. The third day can retrace the AT to the Boulevard Trail, 8.1 miles from Peck's Corner Shelter, and can then go 5.0 miles from the junction to the LeConte Shelter for the third night, making the third day's hike just over 13 miles. The fourth day can retrace the Boulevard Trail back over the narrow ridge, with its fine views of the Boulevard, to the AT and Newfound Gap, for a fourth day of 7.7 miles.

Bear in mind that this area is heavily used. The most scrupulous preparation and proper equipment are required to minimize environmental impact. Use will be lightest, and the experience most challenging, during the most severe weather. In that situation, this area is no place for the inexperienced.

LeCONTE OVERNIGHT, OPTION B

Near Gatlinburg, two trails climb LeConte to form a fine single-night backpacking loop. The trailhead, on the Cherokee Orchard Loop Road in Tennessee, is 3.4 miles from Gatlinburg via Airport Road. In deep snow, the road will be gated near the start of the loop, 3.0 miles from town, requiring hikers to walk 0.4 mile on the snowy road to the trailhead.

The Rainbow Falls Trail climbs LeConte Creek to frequently frozen Rainbow Falls at 2.4 miles. Above the falls, the trail veers out to Rocky Spur and good views. After joining the Bullhead Trail at 5.8 miles and the Alum Cave Trail at 6.4 miles, the trail continues 0.1 mile to LeConte Lodge and the Trillium Gap Trail (there is water 100 yards down this trail). Take the Boulevard Trail from the lodge to the shelter at 6.7 miles. On the second day, retrace the route to the Bullhead Trail and descend it to the same trailhead on Cherokee Orchard Loop where you started, 6.4 miles from the junction.

CHARLIE'S BUNION AREA, OPTION A

From the North Carolina side, a climb to the Charlie's Bunion area offers exposure to the warming sun and a destination with all the scenery and potential for severe weather a winter backpacker could want. The two options described, both in North Carolina, often start snowless, reach wintry summits, and have the added advantage of solitude and back-country campsites.

Start at the Bradley Fork trailhead by turning right off NGR 3.2 miles north of the Oconaluftee Visitor Center. Cross the river, turn left, and park at the gate, just outside the Smokemont Campground. This gated forest road, called the Richland Mountain Trail, starts at 2,200 feet. At 1.2 miles, turn right on the Chasteen Creek Trail and proceed to the Lower Chasteen Creek back-country campsite at 1.3 miles, 0.1 mile from the start of the Creek Trail.

At 3.4 miles, the road reaches the Upper Chasteen Creek back-country campsite. These back-country sites offer first-night camps if you start late or want a night to acclimatize at a relatively low elevation.

At 4.0 miles, the forest road ends and becomes a trail. At 5.3 miles, the trail meets the Hughes Ridge Trail. Left on that trail, the hiker passes two side trails and reaches Peck's Corner Shelter at 10.0 miles, 6.5 miles from the Upper Chasteen Creek campsite.

From the shelter, the AT is 0.5 miles farther. A left on the AT crosses the Sawteeth and Charlie's Bunion and reaches Icewater Spring Shelter in 7.3 miles, 7.8 from the Peck's Corner Shelter and 17.8 miles from the car. The next morning, backtrack 1.4 miles to Dry Sluice Gap and descend to the right on the Richland Mountain Trail 4.3 miles to the Bradley Fork Trail. Follow that trail another 4.3 miles to the parking site for a last-day hike of 11.0 miles and a total of 28.8 miles.

CHARLIE'S BUNION AREA, OPTION B

A single-night backpacking trip over the snowy Bunion starts at the Kephart Prong Trail, 7.0 miles north of the Oconaluftee Visitor Center. The trail starts at 2,700 feet and follows a jeep maintenance road, often crossing Kephart Prong on foot logs while the road fords nearby. Old Civilian Conservation Corps and Park Service facilities can be seen in the 2.1 miles to Kephart Prong Shelter (3,560 feet). Spend the night to make this a two-night trip, or continue to the right up the Grassy Branch Trail to reach the Richland Mountain Trail at 4.4 miles. Go left to reach the AT at 5.8 miles. Go left again, and the AT crosses Charlie's Bunion and reaches Icewater Springs Shelter at 7.2 miles, or 5.1 miles from Kephart Prong Shelter for two-nighters. The next day, hike 1.3 miles toward Newfound Gap, and go left down the Sweat Heifer Trail to Kephart Prong Shelter at 4.9 miles from Ice Water Springs Shelter, and the parking lot at 7.0 miles. The total loop is 14.2 miles. Icewater Springs Shelter is virtually in the center of this loop, so let the weather determine whether you climb the Grassy Branch or Sweat Heifer Trails. Save the Bunion for the clearer day, and whichever way you go, remember that the Sawteeth are less than a mile east of the AT/Richland Mountain Trail junction.

OTHER BACKPACKING LOOPS

The Smokies are too full of extensive, even multiweek backpacking loops to describe them all. The overnight trips described above focus on the park's highest, snowiest circuits through very spectacular scenery. And they are suggested specifically for midweek winter use, preferably including the less impacted back-country campsites whenever possible. Shelter users, even in winter when use can be light, should improve these heavily used areas by packing out more litter than they carry in.

Other options have other attractions. There are four quadrants to this huge park, and each has its own offerings, including winter solitude in deep, isolated valleys, easy access to lofty peaks, and the eerie feel of frozen forests far from the sound of cars.

The park's southwestern corner towers over Fontana Lake, where roadless wilderness meets quiet fingers of water. Back-country campsites in this area are among the least used in the park, and there are fine views.

In the northeastern section of the park, the high peaks of the AT are Guyot, Old Black, and Cammerer; the latter possesses one of the best views in the park. All these summits, as well as off-AT peaks like Sterling and Balsam High Top, can be linked into lengthy circuit hikes offering a variety of shelters and back-country campsites. Using the Sterling Ridge Trail and then the Balsam Mountain Trail, even skiers can tour to the crest of the Smokies with shelter accommodations on the way. For backpackers, the Walnut Bottoms area is beautiful.

The same might be said for any of the lower valleys well off the Appalachian Trail. Only a small percentage of park trail use occurs in these more remote areas. In winter, with fewer horseback riders, use declines even further. Winter is certainly a time to climb the highest peaks to ice and snow. But the Smokies provide a very special setting for another winter experience, the long wandering backpacking trip where nature's most solemn season is matched by empty trails.

Index

WITHDRAWN